# CANADIAN FOREIGN POLICY
# OLD HABITS AND NEW DIRECTIONS

*Andrew F. Cooper*
*University of Waterloo*

PRENTICE HALL ALLYN AND BACON CANADA
SCARBOROUGH, ONTARIO

**Canadian Cataloguing in Publication Data**

Cooper, Andrew Fenton, 1950-
    Canadian foreign policy

Includes index.
ISBN    0-13-582652-7

1. Canada - Foreign relations - 1945-

FC602.C66  1997      327.71     C96-932515-0
F1034.2.C66  1997

© 1997  Prentice-Hall Canada Inc., Scarborough, Ontario
A Division of Simon & Schuster/A Viacom Company

Prentice-Hall, Inc., Upper Saddle River, New Jersey
Prentice-Hall International (UK) Limited, London
Prentice-Hall of Australia, Pty. Limited, Sydney
Prentice-Hall Hispanoamericana, S.A., Mexico City
Prentice-Hall of India Private Limited, New Delhi
Prentice-Hall of Japan, Inc., Tokyo
Simon & Schuster Southeast Asia Private Limited, Singapore
Editora Prentice-Hall do Brasil, Ltda., Rio de Janeiro

ISBN 0-13-582652-7

Vice-President, Editorial Director: Laura Pearson
Acquisitions Editor: Cliff Newman
Developmental Editor: Imogen Brian
Editorial Assistant: Carol Whynot
Copy Editor: John Sweet
Production Editor: Marjan Farahbaksh
Production Coordinator: Deborah Starks
Cover Design: Monica Kompter
Page Layout: Heidi Palfrey

1 2 3 4 5  RD   01 00 99 98 97

Printed and bound in the United States of America

Visit the Prentice Hall Canada Web site! Send us your comments, browse our catalogues, and
more. **www.phcanada.com** Or reach us through e-mail at **phabinfo_pubcanada@prenhall.com**

*To Sarah and Charles*

# TABLE OF CONTENTS

# PREFACE

It has never been more interesting, or more perplexing, to study Canadian foreign policy. Certainly, the scope of inquiry available to students of Canadian foreign policy has broadened considerably with the immense sweep of change found recently in both the domestic and international landscapes. Conceptually, this process of change offers an opportunity for—and necessitates—a re-evaluation of the established frameworks of analysis that have traditionally shaped both scholarship and practice. Empirically, the need is to widen the focus of attention to take account of not only traditional concerns about war and peace but the expanding economic and social agendas.

Any attempt to assess the form and impact of Canadian foreign policy at the edge of the next century raises the question of newness. The end of the bipolar competition between the United States and the Soviet Union and the apparent ideological triumph of the marketplace provide obvious points of departure. So do all the various (and often contradictory) challenges associated with: the growing intensity of both the transnationalization of societal forces and the domestication of foreign policy; the role of the United States as the one remaining superpower and a more diffuse structure of influence in the international system; competing notions about security; and the heightened competition over market share and the need for renewed models and sources of leadership and institutional response.

The question of decline also must enter the discussion. At the national level, serious questions have been raised about the evolving nature of Canadian behaviour in the world. Just when the opportunity for Canada to play an enhanced role in global affairs has opened up in a variety of ways, many observers contend that it has been held back by an erosion of international will (with a shift from international commitment to instrumental self-interest) and domestic capacity (due to both the ongoing constitutional imbroglio and the limitation of financial means). At the bureaucratic level, the main debate revolves around the issue of control over the formulation and application of foreign policy. Any accurate treatment of Canadian foreign policy requires some detail about these ongoing co-operative/competitive relationships among the Canadian foreign ministry and other governmental departments and agencies as well as the relationship between the governmental foreign policy 'managers' and civil society.

The search for, and discovery of, new directions in Canadian foreign policy provides a key rationale and guide for this book. Above all, the volume constitutes an effort to close the gap between the speed of contextual transformation and policy adaptation and our understanding of these dynamics. At the same time, however, the attraction of identifying new directions in Canadian foreign policy should not hide the degree to which older habits have remained entrenched in the ways of thinking and the practice of foreign policy. Many of the core operating principles and methods of Canadian foreign policy remain as relevant today as they have been throughout the post-1945 period.

This book is not divided into chapters on either a strict chronological or an institutional-specific fashion. Rather, the work identifies both the continuity and change located in Canadian foreign policy on a thematic basis. The key is to take into account both the ingredients that have helped give Canadian foreign policy a distinctive profile in the past, and the abundant pressures that are forcing the pace of transformation in the 1990s. What stands out are both the richness of the Canadian foreign policy tradition and the growing complexity of choice. Even as its policy orientation shifts, because of both expanded possibilities and limitations, Canada will continue to look at and address foreign policy problems in a manner different from other countries.

The volume starts by looking at the character of Canadian foreign policy through a number of distinct lenses. The introductory chapter considers which conceptual perspective provides the most appropriate starting-point for a reassessment of Canadian foreign policy. While acknowledging the benefits of taking into account emergent alternative views, it is also suggested that main-stream scholarship—especially the middle power perspective—should not be abruptly discarded. The subsequent two chapters highlight specific components of the Canadian foreign policy tradition, namely the degree of concern Canada has placed respectively on diplomatic skill and international reputation. As detailed through a number of historical and contemporary snapshots, these components provide a sense of the continuity in Canadian foreign policy, even as they reveal some of its flaws in practice.

In moving on to the multifaceted process of change, a number of specific case-studies have been selected for illustrative purposes. These case-studies have been chosen for their importance to the ongoing set of debates about Canadian foreign policy. The first of these centres on the redefinition of security in the wake of the Cold War. The question of what security is looms as large in the mindset of policymakers as it ever has. But increasingly, the 'official' definition is contested by 'unofficial' voices at the societal level. The difficulty of coming to terms with how security is to be understood is further complicated by the intrusion of a host of competing political interests, agendas, interpretations and obligations into the debate. The most dramatic evidence of this intrusion comes out in the case-study of the Canada–Spain 'fish war,' an episode that may be analysed either from a standpoint that privileges a resurgence of the Canadian 'national interest' or from the standpoint of Canada's ongoing sense of commitment to 'international governance,' or equally from the standpoint that empha-sizes either political opportunism or the salience of bureaucratic politics. Because of the complexity of (and the emotions raised by) this issue, it merits chapter-length treatment.

The two agenda items that have constituted the essence, or the central pillars, of Canadian foreign policy through the post-1945 period are discussed in Chapters 5 and 6. These are peacekeeping and international development assistance. Long entrenched as part of a national consensus on foreign policy, these two issues are at the heart of the debate about renewal or decline in the 1990s. While providing enormous opportunities for the promotion of international governance, as well as active participation by a wide variety of governmental and societal actors, these issues also show the risk of confusion and retreat in the face of changing external and domestic conditions and instruments.

The final case-study looks at Canada's search for neighbourhood. In a dualistic fashion, Canada has sought to relocate itself in the world. On the one hand, Canada has attempted to deal with its closeness to the United States through more defined 'management' techniques. On the other hand, Canada has sought to avoid complete enmeshment on a continental basis by frequently resorting to a diversification strategy. This dualism is accentuated by a number of factors of importance in the 1990s, including the loosening of alliance ties and the intensification of the search for national well-being in the international economic order. Case material is provided by an examination of Canada's major regional relationships, with special attention given to Canada's engagment in the Americas.

The essential impetus for the preparation of this book has been provided by my experience in the classroom. While there is an enormous body of literature dealing with Canadian foreign policy, this material has become increasingly fragmented and specialized. The ability to teach a course on Canadian foreign policy, especially at the third- or fourth-year levels, accordingly has become more difficult. My aim has been an integrative one: to blend into a single text suitable for use at the upper-year levels an appreciation of both broader analytical concepts and the details pertaining to relevant (albeit cross-cutting) issue-areas. I have tried to further capture the sense of continuity and change found in Canadian foreign policy by building in a conclusion, which attempts to draw together some of the important features of past, present and future Canadian foreign policy.

Although the manuscript took shape in the 1995–96 academic year, my longer-term preparation has evolved through a classic lapidary process. Much of the initial push that nudged me to take a more sustained interest in Canadian foreign policy was imparted by the enthusiasm and commitment shown by the late John Holmes and John English. John Holmes encouraged me to participate in the seminar series he helped to convene at the Centre for International Studies, University of Toronto. John English drew me into a number of interesting projects through the Centre on Foreign Policy and Federalism at the University of Waterloo. Both of these leading scholar-practitioners provided a degree of mentorship to which I owe a profound debt.

I would also like to acknowledge the varied contributions of the academic collaborators with whom I have worked over the years. Richard Higgott, Kim Nossal and Les Pal not only helped widen my intellectual boundaries but provided stimulating and fun company on a series of research projects. Kim Nossal's book, *The Politics of Canadian Foreign Policy*, also provided a valuable guide in textbook writing. While my book has taken on a very different form, I believe the two works complement each other.

Numerous other people have helped me to rethink my interpretation of Canadian foreign policy. Among the many students of Canadian foreign policy, I would like to thank in particular David Black, Brian Hocking, Gordon Mace, Evan Potter, Angie Sauer, Heather Smith, Denis Stairs, Jean-Philippe Thérien, Bob Wolfe and Bob Young. Among practitioners, I would like to thank especially the many officials at the Department of Foreign Affairs and International Trade whom I have had contact with during and subsequent to the time I acted as Léger Fellow in the Policy Staff in 1993–94. I should add, however, that any errors, as well as judgments, are entirely my own responsibility.

The people at Prentice Hall Canada provided a model of efficiency. I would particularly like to thank Marjan Farahbaksh who tightly stage-managed the production process. David Dewitt, of York University, and Donald Abelson, of the University of Western Ontario, in their role as reviewers not only provided valuable advice, but their expressions of enthusiasm for the project were most encouraging. John Sweet, in copy-editing the manuscript, considerably tightened the presentation of the book both stylistically and substantively.

I have benefited enormously from the financial support provided for my research program by the Social Sciences and Humanities Research Council of Canada. I have also relied on the resources of a number of other institutions, most notably the Canadian Institute of International Affairs. I would particularly like to thank Gayle Fraser and all the librarians.

Terry Downey, in his position as chair, has been instrumental in maintaining a congenial and professional atmosphere within the Department of Political Science at the University of Waterloo. A special mention is due to Joanne Voisin, in her capacity as secretary for graduate studies, for all her technical help and psychological support.

My most enduring thanks, however, must be given to Sarah Maddocks and Charles Cooper. Most intimately, they have been the witnesses to the varied emotions that researching and writing this book—like any effort of sustained scholarship—brought to the fore. While trying to modify some of my own ingrained habits to make the process more comfortable and efficient, they have continued to actively encourage me to pursue new directions of endeavour. For their continued sense of understanding I am deeply grateful.

# ABBREVIATIONS

| | |
|---|---|
| APEC | Asia-Pacific Economic Co-operation |
| AQOCI | l'Association québécoise des organismes de coopération internationale |
| ASEAN | Association of Southeast Asian Nations |
| AWPPA | Arctic Waters Pollution Prevention Act |
| BCNI | Business Council on National Issues |
| BQ | Bloc Québécois |
| CAP | Common Agricultural Policy |
| CCIC | Canadian Council for International Co-operation |
| CEDAW | Convention on the Elimination of All Forms of Discrimination against Women |
| CEE | Central and Eastern Europe |
| CEO | chief executive officer |
| CHOGM | Commonwealth Heads of Government Meeting |
| CIDA | Canadian International Development Agency |
| CIIPS | Canadian Institute for International Peace and Security |
| COCOM | Co-ordinating Committee on Multinational Export Controls |
| CPCU | Canadian Participatory Committee for UNCED |
| CUSO | Canadian University Service Overseas |
| DAC | Development Assistance Committee (of OECD) |
| DEA | Department of External Affairs; after 1989: EAITC; after 1993: DFAIT |
| DFAIT | Department of Foreign Affairs and International Trade; formerly DEA and EAITC |
| DND | Department of National Defence |
| EAITC | External Affairs and International Trade Canada; formerly DEA |
| EDC | Export Development Corporation |
| EEZ | Exclusive Economic Zone |
| EU | European Union; formerly the European Economic Community (EEC) and the European Community (EC) |
| FAO | Food and Agriculture Organization |
| FFAW | Fishermen, Food and Allied Workers |
| FIRA | Foreign Investment Review Agency |
| FOE | Friends of the Earth |
| FSU | Former Soviet Union |
| FTA | (Canada–US) Free Trade Agreement |
| G-7 | Group of Seven most industrialized countries |
| G-77 | Group of Seventy-seven less developed countries |
| GATT | General Agreement on Tariffs and Trade |
| GNP | gross national product |
| IBRD | International Bank for Reconstruction and Development (World Bank) |
| ICAO | International Civil Aviation Organization |
| ICC | International Control Commission |
| ICHRDD | International Centre for Human Rights and Democratic Development |

| | |
|---|---|
| IDA | International Development Agency |
| IDRC | International Development Research Centre |
| IMF | International Monetary Fund |
| ITAC | International Trade Advisory Committee |
| ITO | International Trade Organization |
| LOS | (United Nations Conference on the) Law of the Sea |
| MTN | multilateral trade negotiations |
| NAC | National Action Committee on the Status of Women |
| NAFO | Northwest Atlantic Fisheries Organization |
| NAFTA | North American Free Trade Agreement |
| NATO | North Atlantic Treaty Organization |
| NDP | New Democratic Party |
| NEP | National Energy Program |
| NGOs | non-governmental organizations |
| NIC | newly industrializing country |
| NIEO | New International Economic Order |
| NORAD | North American Aerospace Defence Command; formerly North American Air Defence Command |
| OAS | Organization of American States |
| ODA | official development assistance |
| OECD | Organization for Economic Co-operation and Development; formerly the Organization for European Economic Co-operation (OEEC) |
| ONUC | United Nations Operation in the Congo |
| OSCE | Organization for Security and Cooperation in Europe; formerly the Conference on Security and Cooperation in Europe (CSCE) |
| PAFTAD | Pacific Trade and Development Conference |
| PBEC | Pacific Basin Economic Conference |
| PCO | Privy Council Office |
| PECC | Pacific Economic Co-operation Conference |
| PMO | Prime Minister's Office |
| R & D | research and development |
| RCMP | Royal Canadian Mounted Police |
| SAGITs | Sectoral Advisory Groups on International Trade |
| TNO | Trade Negotiations Office |
| UNAMIR | United Nations Assistance Mission in Rwanda |
| UNAVEM | United Nations Angola Verification Mission |
| UNCED | United Nations Conference on Environment and Development |
| UNCHR | United Nations Commission on Human Rights |
| UNDP | United Nations Development Program |
| UNEF | United Nations Emergency Force (Sinai) |
| UNFICYP | United Nations Interim Force in Cyprus |
| UNHCR | United Nations High Commissioner for Refugees |
| UNICEF | United Nations International Children's Emergency Fund |
| UNIFEM | United Nations Development Fund for Women |
| UNIIMOG | United Nations Iran–Iraq Military Observer Group |
| UNOSOM | United Nations Operation in Somalia |
| UNPROFOR | United Nations Protection Force, in the former Yugoslavia |
| UNRRA | United Nations Relief and Rehabilitation Administration |
| UPA | l'Union des producteurs agricoles (Quebec) |
| WTO | World Trade Organization |

# CONTESTED IMAGES

## CANADIAN FOREIGN POLICY IN A CHANGING WORLD

The time is ripe for a fundamental re-examination of the nature of Canadian foreign policy. Debates that dominated the post-1945 period no longer seem as relevant with the demise of East–West tensions and the accelerated processes of globalization and regionalism. As we move towards the next millennium a new—and pressing—set of questions concerning how and where Canada fits into the international system have come to the fore. While it may be disingenuous to suggest that Canada will miss the Cold War,[1] the passing of the imposed disciplines of that era has undoubtedly produced a sense of ambiguity concerning the foreign policy agenda. Without the constraints of a tight pattern of bipolarity, and the pressures for ideological conformity, there may well be an expanded space for innovative forms of activity and association. Yet this increased room for manoeuvre in terms of content coexists with a context of greater open-endedness and volatility. Rather than the relative comfort extant during the Cold War years, Canadian foreign policy now has to operate under conditions of heightened complexity and uncertainty.

The diversity in flavour of Canadian opinion may be quickly rehearsed. One instinctive response was to embrace the dramatic events of the late 1980s and early 1990s with a marked enthusiasm. With some solid justification, the impact of the changes associated with 'a changing power constellation, a growing international commitment to common values, an increasingly global economy, and a world beyond borders' was cast in a positive light with respect to the opportunities for Canada to make a difference.[2] As long as the old order remained intact, the parameters *vis-à-vis* the creative exercise of Canadian diplomacy were severely confined. The freeing up of these imposing structural limitations, therefore, could be interpreted as contributing to the fuller expression of Canadian talents in international affairs. One scholar suggested that Canada's special qualities and connections would allow it 'to play an increasingly important role' in the 'new multilateralism and evolving security systems.'[3] Another assertively voiced the opinion that 'the post-Cold War period has enhanced Canada's global rank.'[4]

The alternative mode of assessment focussed on the constraints considered likely to hold the Canadian performance on the world stage in check. According to this evaluation, Canada possessed the attributes of a fading, not of a rising, star among the constellation of global actors. Far from playing a lead role, Canada faced being bypassed and marginalized by the circumstances brought on through the transformation in international affairs. Canada had no reason to be complacent because of the collapse of the Soviet empire. The editors of the 1990–91 Carleton University annual survey of Canadian foreign policy, for example, warned: 'Canadians are in danger of living in the past and making policies in the rear-view mirror instead of looking forward to new roles and challenges.'[5] This sober take on Canada's role became more pronounced as the emergent contours of global conditions took firmer hold. Leigh Sarty, in an ambitious attempt to predict the future for Canadian foreign policy, held out the prospect that the wave of rising expectations would be turned into dashed hopes. In his words: 'The assumption that contemporary international change is working to Canada's benefit is open to serious questions.'[6]

The underlying ambiguity in Canadian thinking cannot be understood without some reference to Canada's own internal political circumstances. As the sources of international opportunity swelled out, the foci of Canadian domestic politics became seriously circumscribed. The long-standing obsession of Canadian political life with national unity and the question of Quebec's constitutional status intensified with the failure of the Meech Lake and Charlottetown accords, the revival of the Quebec nationalist/sovereignty movement under Lucien Bouchard and the events surrounding the 30 October 1995 referendum. The repercussions on Canadian foreign policy emanating from this series of domestic crises have been enormous. In terms of psychology, the atmosphere has encouraged an introspective outlook (to the point of self-absorption) by the federal government. Foreign policy issues have been filtered through an extremely sensitive and defensive political scene by both the Mulroney and Chrétien governments. Although this pervasive scrutiny has not ruled out foreign policy innovation, neither has it encouraged a comprehensive dynamic of outward-looking involvement. In terms of operation, the subordination of foreign policy to domestic concerns comes out strongly in the choice of foreign policy ministers. Joe Clark was reassigned (albeit reluctantly) by Prime Minister Mulroney in April 1991 to become the government's minister responsible for constitutional affairs, notwithstanding a solid seven-year record of achievement on the foreign affairs dossier behind him. Clark's replacements (Barbara McDougall, 1991 to 1993, and Perrin Beatty, June to November 1993) found it difficult to establish themselves as foreign ministers because of the number of political/policy intrusions. A similar pattern has emerged with the accession of the Chrétien government. When it came to picking a foreign minister based on either policy facility or political expediency, the latter motivation won out. With attention fixed on national unity, the choice of André Ouellet to serve both as the political minister for Quebec and minister of foreign affairs served the immediate interests of the Chrétien government. Only with the narrow 'no' vote did the breathing-space for the government expand. As part of a wider Cabinet shuffle in January 1996, the position of foreign minister was given to Lloyd Axworthy, who held out the promise of being a more engaged voice for Canada in the world.

The overall effect of this domestic preoccupation has been to distract and deflect time and energy away from the construction of an innovative foreign policy agenda. To be sure, making a difference in the post-1945 era had never been easy due to the existence of sundry internal tensions; but these tensions had become accentuated when Canada could least afford them. As one astute observer has put it, 'we have lost our footing and our bearings' just as a solid grounding is needed most: 'the challenges posed by the broader context have become sharper, and the internal tensions within Canada have been heightened. We have become a litigious society in a world where the ground is in constant motion.'[7]

Nor can Canadian foreign policy be separated from the twin crises of governmental legitimacy and organizational capacity. Consistent with most other Western countries, Canada faces an erosion of confidence in institutional delivery. A rising sense of public disenchantment with traditional sources of authority has contributed to multiple demands for the remaking of the political rules of the game.[8] At the very least, governments have had to recognize the need to negotiate and bargain with their publics in a more open and inclusive fashion. More particular to Canada, pressures toward a more open and inclusive strategy from government have reflected the changing political culture (with a rights-based psychology) created through the politics of the Charter of Rights and Freedoms and the Meech Lake and Charlottetown referendum debates on the constitution.[9] Compounding these forces of change is the serious and widening gap between governmental responsibilities and resources. Burdened with a combined federal and provincial debt of around $830 billion, Canadian governments no longer have the ability (or the will) to act on the basis of expensive promises. Unlike during the 1970s, money cannot simply be thrown at issues of concern. The long shadow of fiscal constraint, as cast in Ottawa and in the vast majority of provinces, consequently spills over the problem of governance. As the federal government streamlines and shrinks, a number of ancillary controversies about the distribution of federal/provincial responsibilities come to the fore, including cost-sharing and the transfers of monies.

While it is necessary to highlight these domestic determinants, these features are not in themselves sufficient to explain the dynamics of Canadian foreign policy in the post-Cold War era. From an exogenous perspective, the dominant impression is that of Canada as a country thrown off balance by the sheer extent and intensity of change. To fully grasp this feeling of loss of control, the transitional nature of the international system as it has evolved in the 1990s must be taken into account. Rather than moving from the embedded pattern of the old post-1945 order to a new equilibrium in neat linear fashion, this transmutation has been messy and uneven. The language used to describe these developments reflects this in-between stage. The images conjured up have shifted from stylized descriptions of stability contained in the phrase 'new world order' to a depiction based on a multi-level, multi-dimensional series of puzzles. The best known of these phrases located in the academic literature focus on the contradictory nature or 'turbulence' found in international relations.[10] Czempiel talks of an 'asymmetric broken grid of interactions.'[11] Neak and her colleagues prefer the picture of a 'tectonic plate-like grinding' between different forces in the international system.[12]

## The Leadership Vacuum

Turning this lens more closely on Canada, this cluster of puzzles may be broken down into two thematic subcategories. The first of these categories relates to the nature of leadership. On first glance, the United States emerged as the undisputed victor of the Cold War. Yet despite this initial impression and the burst of nationalistic rhetoric that accompanied it,[13] the 'unipolar moment' has left little afterglow. Moreover, the mood of triumphalism has not propelled the US in a unidirectional course of action as the 'global cop.' As the Gulf War and the crisis in the former Yugoslavia have attested to, the US has sustained the capacity to act as the 'one remaining superpower.' Abundant doubts persist, however, about whether it has the disposition to perform a central (never mind a hegemonic) role on a sustained basis. The key issue about American leadership of the future rests, as both Susan Strange and Robert Gilpin suggest,[14] not so much on capabilities in quantitative terms as on will and effectiveness in qualitative terms. On this criteria, any judgment concerning US leadership on the edge of the millennium is fraught with ambiguity. American foreign policy has taken on an increasingly erratic look. Notwithstanding its dominant role in the ideological defeat of Communism, and its vast reservoir of 'soft' as well as 'hard' structural power,[15] the US has wavered between wanting to bear too much and too little of the international burden. Held back by the restrictions of its own political agenda, the US has sent out mixed signals about the degree of commitment it possesses to take on responsibilities in the evolving international context. If the US remains out in front on some policy issues, on many others it lags behind.

The inability of the major secondary powers to adequately compensate for this gap in leadership further complicates the international situation. The scenario of Germany and Japan moving to share some of the structural leadership with the US has been well rehearsed.[16] These two countries have the economic resources that can be translated into leverage. Indeed, in certain areas the appearance of a shift towards a form of condominium at the top has been confirmed, most notably through the appearance of a 'Big Three' dealing with global macroeconomic management via a number of exclusive forums. Germany and

Japan have also assumed the lead on an issue-specific basis, i.e. the reconstruction of Eastern Europe, aid to the South, and an enhanced role on environmental and humanitarian matters (Germany's major role on climate change and Japan's contribution to the United Nations High Commissioner for Refugees, for example). Despite these signs of activity, however, there remain serious reservations about the faculty of these second-tier powers to supply an abundant measure of vision in the international arena. The culture of constraint remains thoroughly ingrained in post-1945 Germany and Japan. These inhibitions have been reinforced in the case of Germany by the collective focus on the long and arduous task of integration directed towards the former East Germany.[17] In the case of Japan, the issue has been further complicated by the structure of the reactive state. Built up through the intricate web of patron–client relationships, the factional system within the Liberal Democratic Party (LDP), and the well-established iron triangles between business, bureaucrats and politicians, the absence of authoritative governmental structures in Japan has been exaggerated by the falling fortunes of the LDP as the dominant political party in the 1990s.[18]

## Transnationalism

The second puzzle relates to the tensions at the spatial dimension of international relations. In the 1990s the 'high' security issues concerned with war and peace no longer hold absolute sway. The rising concerns have been those having to do with economic well-being and/or the broad range of social issues. By its very nature, this extended policy agenda stretches the boundaries of both discourse and action. Although how this plays out in the form of a 'global civic culture' should not be overplayed, the move towards transnationalism has become a core concern of international affairs. At one end of this continuum may be found the various forms of global activity (including joint ventures and cross-border strategic alliances) embarked upon by firms. As Susan Strange has underscored, firms have become an increasingly significant ingredient in the complex interrelationship between states and markets. Without disputing the persistence of conflict between governments and firms, firms have become increasingly integrated in those strategies designed to find ways to maximize national welfare through the enhancement of market share and competitiveness.[19]

At the other end of the continuum may be placed the vast array of societal forces. Parallelling the transnationalization of business culture, a good deal of societal group activity has found expression in the world political system during the 1980s and 1990s. This outward-looking face adopted by societal forces generally—and non-governmental organizations (NGOs) more specifically—has taken on a universalistic tone. Although not entirely 'sovereignty free,' many of the more 'cosmopolitan' societal groups may be said to have a diminished territorial state of mind.[20] The adoption of this outward-looking viewpoint, in turn, has had a profound impact on the way these groups play a role in the political system (associating increasingly with citizens of other countries) and in their expression of loyalties (the identification more with personal attributes and less with 'lines on a map').

By placing so much onus on cross-border activity, these forces to some extent share a perspective on the limitations of the national state. Firms and NGOs also have a commonality in the sense that they take advantage of new technology. The push towards an 'international business civilization'[21] has been propelled to a considerable extent by the dramatic innovations in the field of communications. In a similar way, satellite television, Internet dialogues, faxes, video cameras and camcorders allow societal groups to tap into a broader audience. The difference between them is found in terms of values. Whereas firms place business efficiency at the apex, NGOs place a higher priority on global justice and equity.

Still, what commonly have been depicted as the forces of transnationalism, globalization and interdependence cannot accurately be examined in isolation. These forces must be looked at as part of a wider process that has intensified the pattern of interaction between the international and domestic in politics. The process of adjustment to international forces runs parallel to a counter response at the local level. Part and parcel with a number of other forms of system friction, much of the post-World War Two settlement (based jointly on economic growth and social welfarism) has become unstuck. Sensitivity to this disembedded bargain, not surprisingly, has been felt most acutely at the lowest level of state–societal relations. As depicted in the business administration literature, cases of successful adaptation can be found in individual communities.[22] Out of this process of adjustment may even emerge new efficiencies, as the practice of subsidiarity and decentralization are promoted. Evidence of the existence of selective 'winners,' though, should not minimize the recognition of abundant (and clustered) 'losers' in the swing towards the new political economy. Being squeezed at the local level breeds not only innovation but also potent forms of protest and resistance. As Rosabeth Moss Kanter acknowledged at the February 1996 Davos World Economic Forum: 'Unless businesses demonstrate their commitment to the work force and to the communities in which they operate, we could see a populist uprising.'[23]

## RE-EXAMINING THE FUNDAMENTALS

Coming to grips with this contextual transformation is not an easy task for an analytical reappraisal of Canadian foreign policy. As the arena of debate has stretched out beyond the familiar terrain, the intellectual status quo must face re-examination. Whatever the attractions of the familiar, we need to review whether or not the fundamental concepts associated with the older debates of Canadian foreign policy can continue to act as valuable guides. Serious questions have to be asked about whether these concepts, on display for a number of decades, remain fresh or whether their shelf life has been reached. This is not to say that the familiar ways of looking at Canadian foreign policy should be extemporaneously expunged from the discussion. Any exercise designed to further the course of rethinking must start with a systematic overview of the central tenets that have shaped our understanding of this subject area over the entire distance of the post-1945 era. Only via an exploration of the recognized themes, at the nub of the established methods of studying Canadian foreign policy, are we able to determine their relevance. Only by starting in a manner that gives the traditional frameworks of reference the judicious treatment they deserve can their relevance be appreciated and weighed against the newer points of departure.

In aggregate, the mainstream Canadian foreign policy literature has carved out a distinct path for itself. Unlike other areas of academic research, all of the competing concepts have an indigenous quality to them. These concepts are in turn associated with three frameworks: Canada as a foremost or principal power; Canada as a satellite or dependent country; and Canada as a middle power. Whatever the differences (and rivalry) between these concepts, each is deeply ingrained in its own, largely made-in-Canada interpretation of the Canadian experience.

The middle power framework has been built on the solid foundation laid down by the distinctive group of scholar-practitioners who towered over post-1945 Canadian foreign policy. While acknowledging the individual differences among the writings and experiences of John Holmes, A.F.W. Plumptre and the other individuals in this cohort, the principles and purpose exhibited in their collective work exhibit a striking consistency: Canada can make a difference, so long as skill and a consistency of purpose are applied. Moreover, these beliefs continue to resonate through the debate on Canadian foreign policy. Although never regaining the pre-eminence enjoyed in the immediate post-1945 era, the legacy of this formative cohort remains strong. After an interlude of relative disinterest and decline in the 1970s, the middle power framework has undergone a rediscovery and revival in the 1980s and 1990s. Leaving aside for the moment the direct influence on the study of international relations made by Canadian political scientists, a taste of the ability of this conceptual framework to inform the ongoing historical debate may be captured in John English's two-volume biography of Lester Pearson.[24] The satellite framework of Canadian foreign policy is thoroughly intertwined, if not completely integrated, into the larger political-economy historical project in Canada. A steady stream of scholarly production has not only continued to draw on the rich tradition of the pioneers of this school of thought (most notably Harold Innis and Hugh Keenleyside)[25] but has continued to link historical studies with political science analysis. One can point, for instance, to Melissa Clark-Jones's *A Staple State*[26] as a representative sample from this school of thought. The connection of the foremost, or principal power, framework to an established corpus of scholarly work has been more tenuous. The perspective did receive nourishment in the initial stages of its development from the group of academics who collaborated on the 1975 edited collection *Foremost Nation: Canadian Foreign Policy and a Changing World.*[27] This project was a multi-disciplinary endeavour, bringing together a number of historians (Norman Hillmer, Ian Drummond, Robert Bothwell, Stephen Randall) and political scientists (Garth Stevenson, Maureen Appel Molot, David Leyton-Brown, Steven Langdon). Interest in this research program, however, has since fallen off completely in these two disciplines. The main counter-trend to this form of intellectual neglect appears in the business administration literature concerned with the growth and performance of Canada's multinational corporations. Alan Rugman, for one, has picked up on this theme in his portrayal of the Canadian-owned 'megafirm.'[28]

A concentration on these three dominant frameworks does not mean that the so-called 'second tier' concepts in Canadian scholarship should be completely neglected.[29] The comparative lack of influence of these alternative concepts, nonetheless, is one of the striking features of Canadian foreign policy scholarship. Canadian academics have demonstrated a marked disinclination to be swept along with the tide appearing from the United States. Event data analysis, stimulus-response and cognitive analysis, the utilization of foreign policy metaphors, the structure and process of foreign policy crises, and other forms of behavioural tools have never gained a secure foothold as modes of examination for Canadian foreign policy. Notable exceptions may be found, but even these feature extensive revisions to reflect Canadian realities. Kim Nossal has adapted the bureaucratic politics approach to gain insights on the Canadian milieu.[30] The Carleton University project on 'asymmetrical dyads' has a distinctly Canadian imprint.[31] Overall, it would appear that Canadian students of foreign policy retain a suspicious attitude towards becoming captives of fadism. The 'second tier' conceptual approaches have inspired little in the way of a successor generation. Although 'scientific' modes of analysis have received some boost from the increasing spillover of public choice or game theory into political science,[32] Canadian foreign policy has as yet been comparatively immune to the application of these modelling techniques.

If the extent of this conformity gives rise to understandable fears about staleness, the predominance of so few conceptual frameworks provides some built-in elements of strength as well. This compression facilitates a good deal of interactive debate. Only the most insular of analysts would attempt to write about Canadian foreign policy without directly or indirectly addressing the rival literature. Because of this process of (necessary) interaction, the hope of working towards a synthesis remains a possibility. While examining Canadian foreign policy behaviour through very distinct sets of lenses, some sense of overlap does emerge between the different frameworks. All focus much of their attention on the set of questions surrounding the interplay between international order and national autonomy. Rubbing up closely against each other might be uncomfortable; nonetheless, the possibility of a creative tension exists.

## The Principal Power Framework

Moving towards a closer look at the three competing frameworks, each has some merit concerning its permanent ability and value in capturing the essence of Canadian foreign policy. Of the three, the foremost or principal power framework has the shortest pedigree. The original notion that Canada had shot up to the apex of the international hierarchy of nations was fired by James Eayrs in a short salvo of an article published in 1975 in *International Perspectives*. In this piece, Eayrs took issue with the commonplace assumption that Canada should (and could) only play a confined role in international relations. In Eayrs's view, Canada's ascendancy mirrored its abundant economic strengths: 'Canada has almost sinfully bestowed upon it the sources of power, both traditional and new.... The technology is there, or waiting.... The manpower is there, or waiting.... The resources are there, or waiting too.' This rich profile, Eayrs concluded, allowed Canada to be accurately recast as a 'foremost power...foremost in the dictionary sense of most notable or prominent.'[33]

A number of Canadian political scientists quickly sought to put empirical meat on Eayrs's impressionistic bones of analysis. Peyton Lyon and Brian Tomlin, encouraged by the proliferation of quantitative studies of national capabilities, attempted to isolate Canada's global position through a relative power assessment based on military, economic, resource and diplomatic capabilities. Examining Canada in comparative terms, they concluded that Canada ranked at the upper echelon of the international standings (6th to be precise), a position as a 'major power' that placed it ahead of Japan. Rather than being at the 'upper crust' of the middle rank of countries, Canada from this perspective was interpreted as being part of a small élite grouping at the pinnacle of the international hierarchy. Mixing their modified 'complex interdependence' framework with a number of detailed issue-specific case-studies, David Dewitt and John Kirton further reconfigured this robust notion of Canada's ranking. While stopping short of calling Canada a 'great power,' these two authors concluded that Canada could be termed a 'principal power.' According to Dewitt and Kirton, recognition of this standing rested on three criteria. In similar fashion to Lyon and Tomlin, Dewitt and Kirton saw Canada coming of age as a principal power first of all because of its differentiated position 'at the top' of the international ladder. In a more nuanced fashion, they paid particular heed to two other features. The first of these related to Canada's ability to act 'as a principal on its own international activities and associations' rather than as an agent or mediator. The second was the putative ability of Canada to play a 'principal role in establishing, specifying, and enforcing international order.'[34]

The degree of conceptual sophistication attached to the principal power framework is impressive. So too has been its accuracy, empirically, in forecasting an 'increasingly diffuse, non-hegemonic international system.' These strengths, though, have not imbued it with popularity. Despite vigorous attempts at proselytism by its initiators, the principal power approach has remained a distinctly minority calling during the 1970s and 1980s. The valuable survey by David Black and Heather Smith pointedly comments on the lack of converts attracted to this framework among Canadian students of political science. Few, if any, of the graduate theses on Canadian foreign policy produced in those years incorporated the principal power framework into their analysis. With reference to the avoidance of the terminology of national capabilities and 'complex interdependence,' this avoidance behaviour conforms with the general reluctance of Canadian political scientists to embrace behavioural techniques. There also may well be some sort of ongoing psychological block attached to the hesitation on the part of Canadian political scientists to embrace any national-assertive viewpoint (despite—or even because of—their awareness of Wilfrid Laurier's prophecy that the twentieth century would belong to Canada). Certainly, the lack of willingness to embrace the principal power framework by Canadians is not shared by academics outside of Canada. Notwithstanding the widely held appraisal of Canada as a secondary country, a strand of international scholarly writing does exist that gives credence to the 'graduation' theme built into the principal power approach. While visible in sources outside of the US, the work of Charles Doran at Johns Hopkins–SAIS stands out in this respect. Whatever the accuracy of this image, Canadian political scientists have remained collectively immune to the lure of this sort of thinking. Black and Smith hone in on this sceptical attitude as evidence of a deeply rooted subjective appraisal of Canada's position in the world: 'Perhaps this lack of [cumulated interest] stems from the many problems which exist in their approach, or perhaps it rests on the simple fact that few students of Canadian foreign policy perceive Canada to be a principal power.'[35]

Faced with the lack of popularity for the concept as a whole, the most active of the proponents of the principal power framework have adopted what constitutes a fall-back position. Rather than backing away completely, Kirton especially has chosen to pick up on Canada's institutional prowess. This has meant, in practice, focussing on Canada's elevation to the status of 'a major and fully engaged G-7 player' as evidence of its principal power credentials.[36] The rationale behind this fall-back position is obvious: unable to win the hearts and minds of students of Canadian foreign policy on the proposition that Canada is a principal power, on the criteria originally set out in the early 1980s, attention has been redirected towards the status imparted to Canada by its inclusion in a closed body with an extremely restrictive right of entry. This attempt to revitalize the concept comes at an opportune time, amidst the uncertainty and tensions of the immediate post-Cold War period. Few can disagree that membership in the Summit has its benefits in a world where the future of global leadership and influence over the emergent agenda is being played out in a more multilayered manner. As Robert Wolfe has concisely put it, Canada's position at the G-7 table gives it a good deal of leverage: 'We are able to play on more issues, at a higher level...because of our G7 connection.'[37]

This resort to a fall-back position invites controversy. For a start, there is considerable disagreement about how Canada's G-7 status has translated into results. A number of critics have taken the view that rather than expanding Canada's scope of action, Canada's place in the G-7 has actually reduced its ability to perform effectively in the international arena. Grasping for a higher position in the international league standings, this argument goes, is a chimera. Canada should not direct its actions through the narrow confines of an exclusive club. It should seek comfort among a wide range of like-minded countries. The danger of belonging to the G-7 lies in the hubris this membership imparts, where a desire to be at the centre of action rather than a commitment to activity on an issue-specific basis becomes the prime justification for belonging. As one journalist wrote in the mid-1980s, Canada should 'quit pretending we're one of the world's major economic powers and take over leadership of the group we really belong to, the countries affected by decisions of the Big Five' by forming 'our own G-15 or G-20, a gang of the larger "middle powers" with the collective clout to make itself heard.'[38]

Canadian foreign policy decision-makers are unlikely to buy into these negative arguments. Having moved into the G-7, the focal point of their attention is hanging on to that advantage. Yet the more astute of state officials have expressed their own concerns about the way the G-7 operates. While eager to acknowledge the benefits derived from Canada's membership in the G-7, some reference is made to the costs. Gaining entry to the G-7 provides Canada with abundant rights. The downside is that this sense of belonging also elicits parallel obligations, which can tie Canada to a group consensus involving a lowest common denominator.[39]

Just how open to dispute the application of the principal power framework is in practice comes out by reference to the 1991 Gulf War. In reviewing the Canadian role as an alliance partner, an argument may be made that Canada's behaviour during this crisis was entirely consistent with its G-7 status. Canada's 'ability to deliver...in the face of international uncertainty and domestic division, ultimately placed it, along with only the United States, Britain, France and Italy,' Kirton writes, 'in a very exclusive club of the world's principal powers.'[40] Despite the confidence with which it is promoted, this contention remains a highly idiosyncratic one. None of the other writers who have scrutinized the Gulf War episode from a Canadian perspective share in any way the contention that Canada's contribution confirms Canada's principal power status. Far from representing Canada as a joint leader of the coalition, analysts of the middle power persuasion cast Canada in a supporting or followership role with a limited profile in Desert Storm. With no land combat troops involved, a naval contingent based primarily on four frigates, and an air force confined to 'sweep and escort' activities, Canada's participation is interpreted not as a foremost country with the ability to influence the result through the exertion of its power capability projection with respect to the military campaign; Canada's effort, on the contrary, is interpreted as resting primarily on its ability to lend legitimacy and diplomatic support for the actions of the United Nations through persuasion and other forms of quiet diplomacy. From a dependency perspective, in turn, Canada is seen as going along with a US-led initiative. Faced with US enthusiasm to go to war with Saddam Hussein's Iraq, Canada had little choice but to say 'ready, aye, ready.'[41]

True, the Gulf War can be seen as a unique event with few lessons for the future of the post-Cold War era. From a broader angle, the direction of international relations does appear to lend some support to an optimistic assessment about Canada's performance befitting its G-7 status. The flattening of the nature of international leadership plays to the strengths that Canada possesses. So does the expansion of the international agenda away from the traditional 'high' policy concerns about war and peace. Any shift towards a fragmented international system solidifies the impression of a Canada in the upper ranks of the global hierarchy. The downplaying of military power resets attention away from an area where Canada has made little if any claim to preponderance, towards other issue-areas where a better claim for Canada's significance can be made. Unquestionably, Kirton is back on solid ground when he claims that 'the new [post-Cold War] era has reduced the relevance of those military assets where Canada is relatively weak, and enhanced those economic, environmental and human development capabilities where it is at or near the top of the pack.'[42]

The future of the principal power perspective appears to rest on two factors. Quantitatively, an optimistic forecast about Canada's position in the hierarchy of nations hinges on the issue of whether or not Canada deserves to retain its G-7 place. Given the public debate that has broken out on this subject, the assumption of the retention of the status quo cannot be taken for granted. Many observers see Canada tenaciously 'hanging on' to a position that it should give up to countries hitherto ranked below it in the international system.[43] Some argue the merits of this case on equity grounds, from the standpoint that the opening up of the G-7 to developing countries would allow more appropriate international decision-making structures based on consultation, flexible rules of the game, justice, and the democratization of institutions.[44] Others argue purely on the grounds of right of passage. The *Economist* magazine has made its position felt on this debate by informing its international audience that Canada not only lies in the middle of the pack of the OECD countries in terms of GDP and purchasing power parity, but that it has fallen behind six developing economies (China, India, Russia, Brazil, Mexico and Indonesia) on the same statistical criteria.[45] The notion that Canada will eventually make way for a number of countries now outside the G-7 club has been picked up as well by the domestic media, as part of a sustained critique of Canadian under-performance in the international economy. In that this argument is consistent with the idea that Canada has acted (and spent) beyond its means for the past two decades, this image of decline has specific appeal for the deficit 'hawks' clustered on the financial pages.[46] The image of a downwardly mobile Canada was also seized upon by some elements of the Quebec sovereignty movement. The Bloc Québécois could enthusiastically embrace the ideals of liberal internationalism on an issue-specific basis, sounding at times more Pearsonian than the Liberal government, but the movement was quick to exploit any weakening in the hold of Canada's G-7 membership. Any downgrading of Canada's status suited the BQ's partisan purposes by showing that Ottawa's reach exceeded its grasp. 'Isn't it unrealistic of Canada to belong to the G-7,' one BQ MP stated: '[i]n my view, it's a very expensive club. It leads us to take part in activities that I don't think we have the money to take part in.'[47]

Qualitatively, any robust forecast about Canada's role in the world rests on the issue of national will. The opinion that Canada should apply itself in a more self-confident manner has received some recent nurturing. In an attempt to give a fillip to her political position prior to the October 1993 election, Kim Campbell voiced an impatience about the way Canada was doing things on the international scene. To the delight of the leading proponent of the principal power perspective, in a speech delivered in Vancouver, Campbell explicitly rejected the 'mantra that Canada is merely a modest middle power destined to go along with the multilateral-consensus of the moment...[expressing] instead that Canada has emerged as a major power, able to put forward its own values in addressing the problems of the new age.'[48] With the subsequent free fall in Campbell's own political fortunes, however, any expectation of Canada propelling itself forward under her leadership in an out-in-front fashion crashed. Consistent with Prime Minister Chrétien's own comfort zone (the preference for the Chevrolet over the Cadillac), Canadian foreign policy has reverted to a much more cautious and compact style at both the declaratory and operational levels. Chrétien has been willing to launch specific initiatives to show off and sell Canada's economic and technological prowess throughout the world. His projection of Canada, nonetheless, has remained low-key and utilitarian: 'We are not a superpower...and we don't want to be. We are a bilingual, incredibly diverse nation. A G-7 nation that is also a middle power. These advantages will continue to give us the edge in the years to come.'[49]

## The Satellite or Dependency Framework

The second framework, the satellite or dependency conceptual framework, has a much longer (although bifurcated) pedigree. The satellite strand is identified with the current of strategic affairs literature that interprets Canadian behaviour as being fundamentally constrained because of its close and comprehensive defence/military relationship with the United States. From this perspective, the common description of Canada's role on military security issues has been that of a loyal junior partner, with Canada either eagerly (the Americans' 'chore boy') or opportunistically (free-riding) going along with the US. While some political discomfort with this subservient position may occasionally arise at the élite and/or the mass level, Canada's ability to free itself from this form of entrapment is severely limited. The institutional ties established through the US/Western alliance system via NATO, the continental commitments through NORAD, and the Defence Production Sharing Agreement are too confining.[50]

The dependency strand centres on Canada's position of weakness in the international economic system. From what has been termed as well the economic nationalist perspective,[51] Canada is relegated to a subordinate position in the commercial domain. Mirroring the satellite line of argument, this critical perspective makes the case that the Canadian political economy is largely determined by its structural dependency on the US. The concentration is on the weakness and vulnerability associated with this client status, namely the level of foreign direct investment, the 'branch plant' nature of the economy, the low level of research and development, and the linkage of monetary policy to the need to ensure access to sources of foreign capital.[52]

Any assessment of this second framework must determine the accuracy or predictive value of its mode of analysis. Whereas the principal power framework may be taken to task for being excessively enthusiastic about Canada's capability in shaping the international agenda, the satellite framework may be criticized for tilting the balance too far over to a pessimistic outlook. The call for a radical disengagement (expressed historically through calls for a 'Declaration of Neutralism') so common in the satellite literature has been predicated on the assumption that Canada held little or no ability for autonomous activity within the system as it existed. The stark image of Canada being confined to a close lock step with the US, however, is not entirely supported by the evidence. Even within the strict confines of bipolarity, and the tight alliance structure of the Cold War era, Canada was not completely constrained in terms of its military/defence behaviour. As a growing volume of revisionist studies have demonstrated, Canada had a good degree of space to resist important aspects of US policy. The responses of the various Canadian governments on Korea, the October 1962 Cuban missile crisis and the bombing of North Vietnam in December 1972 do not lend much support to the notion of Canada as a consistent pawn of the US in the security sphere. If Canada may be labelled with some validity as a first follower in the Western alliance, this role did not imply that Canada was content to defer to each and every American action.[53] A judicious, albeit cursory, glance at the later record of the Trudeau government on the defence questions adds to this impression. A heavy weight has been placed by the critics within the satellite school on the extension of Canadian compliance through this period, as displayed most clearly in the decision of the Trudeau government to allow cruise missile testing in Canada. Here again, this image of constraint or curtailment is tempered on more detailed scrutiny. When the focus of analysis is broadened to encompass a wider span of issues, Canada's ability to pursue its own policies stands out. The decision in 1982 to 'go along' on cruise testing has to be balanced with an appreciation of the willingness by Trudeau to risk launching a number of novel initiatives in the face of American opposition. These ventures comprised moves by Canada on the North–South relationship and the suffocation of nuclear arms at the same time.

The spectrum of debate about the space that is available for Canada to operate in has been stretched out considerably in the course of transition to the post-Cold

War era. The pessimistic perspective is taken up most vigorously in a recent book by Marci McDonald.[54] This book is a forceful polemic written by a Canadian journalist with extensive professional experience in the United States. In style, it serves as an update of James Minifie's *Peacemaker or Powdermonkey: Canada's Role in a Revolutionary World*.[55] In substance, it is a volume preoccupied with the dynamic of subordination generated by the US–Canada connection. Fixated on the multifaceted sources of constraint built into the relationship through the 1980s and early 1990s, McDonald predicts a future of continued contraction in Canada's international room for manoeuvre. This confinement, while extending right across the policy agenda, is seen as being most pervasive in the security arena. A case in point concerns Canada's entry into the Organization of American States (OAS). Looking at the OAS strictly as an instrument for pulling Canada closer into the US's orbit, McDonald showcases Canada's support for the US's invasion of Panama in December 1989.[56]

What is missing in this dissection is a balanced look at the OAS as a source of opportunity as well as abbreviation. Contrary to the assumptions of the satellite perspective, a good deal of the evidence relating to Canada's involvement in the OAS points to a greater, not lesser, differentiation between Canada and the US in terms of national interest and ways of doing things. One illustration of this process was Canada's response to the Haitian crisis. Unwilling to participate in a military intervention force under US command, Canada directed its attention to alternative activities (through OAS Observers Mission, the enforcement of sanctions, etc.). Another illustration centres on Canada's attempts to widen the institutional mandate and architecture within the OAS. These activities, it may be added, are entirely consistent with the ascendant view that the post-Cold War period offers the prospect of an expansive array of choice in terms of the Canadian defence/security agenda. This view is perhaps put best by Jockel and Sokolsky, who argue that any rethinking of Canada's approach must 'recognize explicitly that Canada is at liberty to choose its security commitments.'[57]

The political economy literature, which emphasizes Canada's structural deficiencies, suffers from a similar set of defects. Fundamentalist proponents of this line, as featured in a voluminous literature produced through the post-1945 era, saw Canada moving inexorably towards 'semi-industrialized underdevelopment' through the sheer force of circumstances. Canada's economic position could only be increasingly squeezed and subordinated as the web of continentalism tightened. Given the rigidity of this interpretation, revisionist trends inevitably emerged within the dependency school itself. In tandem with the emergence of the state autonomy school at the domestic level, a more sophisticated wave of literature appeared by the late 1960s. As opposed to the fundamentalist tradition, this new wave adopted a less deterministic approach to the making of Canadian foreign policy. In an ongoing push for Canada 'to take its destiny more firmly in its own hands,'[58] the availability of choice—or agency—was elevated in opposition to the confines of structure. The research program directed by

Stephen Clarkson, the best-known propagator of this new wave, bears out this conclusion. Rather than concentrating on the fixed symptoms, sources and products of entrapment (the cards Canada was dealt), more attention was accorded in this program to the requirement for will at the national level (how Canada played its cards). As spelled out in the concluding chapter of the collection of essays Clarkson edited in 1968, under the title *An Independent Foreign Policy for Canada?*, these changes need not be revolutionary in tone. Canada did 'not need the mountain-moving voluntarism of Mao Tse-Tung...[it] simply needs a leadership that can make it clear to the public—if not in a little Red Book at least in a White Paper—what role Canada can play and how its objectives are to be achieved.'[59]

The fortunes of this new wave of the dependency school went through a series of dramatic ebbs and flows from the late 1960s through to the present day. As one of the leading intellectual gadflies to the government, Clarkson scored some initial successes in his effort to goad the Trudeau Liberals to break with the settled patterns of the past and reconfigure Canadian foreign policy. On the one hand, the series of seminars that served as the basis for the *Independent Foreign Policy* volume provided much of the impetus for the foreign policy review started up by Trudeau after he took over from Pearson as Liberal leader and prime minister in April 1968.[60] On the other hand, the set of attitudes cultivated in this intellectual exercise helped condition a move towards a more diversified strategy of foreign economic relations, implemented through the so-called third option. Any thought that this exercise would prove to be a decisive turning-point, however, was short-lived. The limits of this design were, from the economic nationalist perspective, all too obvious. The true test of will centred on the ability of Canada to unilaterally reshape its own economic strategies. Rather than avoidance, through an outward-looking strategy of diversification, the central issue of the Canada–US connection turned on how to tackle this 'asymmetrical' relationship head-on through a decisive and coherent domestic-oriented approach.

The record of achievement by the Trudeau government in the early 1980s raised the possibility of an effective management strategy. While not entirely favourable in terms of results, the experience of statist intervention went some way towards confirming the salience of choice over structure. As witnessed by the implementation of the National Energy Program (NEP), the lesson for economic nationalists seemed to be that, so long as an initiative enjoyed 'a privileged position in the federal government,' the contextual constraints of Canada's position in the international political economy could be overcome even on the most controversial issue. Notwithstanding the impression of retreat in other components of the Trudeau government's program, Clarkson concluded that on a segmented basis the potential for autonomous activity remained high. Where there was a will and imagination, there was a way. As Clarkson surveyed the scene in 1982: 'Canada had established a powerful precedent [on the NEP] that, when it judged an industry to be of strategic importance, it could intervene to reorient its development to serve what it viewed to be the national interest. The U.S. had signalled by its acquiescence that, press though it would on behalf of its corporations, it would give way to a Canadian government determined to pursue what it believed to be a reasonable and necessary course of action. Canada had re-established the right to interfere in its own affairs.'[61]

Conversely, the intellectual (and psychological) discomfort of the economic nationalist school has been profound when conditions turned. By the later 1980s and 1990s, all but the most sanguine economic nationalists had sunk back into a fundamentalist form of structural determinism. Given the combination of political/ideological forces under way, this changed mood is understandable. If still displaying some elements of dynamism in the international arena, this type of Canadian leadership did not meet the rising expectations of the economic nationalists. By the end of his time in office, Trudeau had cast off most of the trappings of an economic interventionist strategy. This U-turn, in the eyes of the economic nationalists, contributed to the momentum of the Conservatives' agenda; it led to a policy vacuum, leaving 'Canadians susceptible to continentalism's siren call when it came in the form of Brian Mulroney's extravagant promises that free trade would bring better jobs, cheaper goods, and a rosy future.'[62]

Nor, in the aftermath of the Mulroney era, could this shadow easily be lifted. Certainly there was little in the way of a revival of optimism concerning Canada's prospects. Far from locating new opportunities for choice in Canadian foreign policy, economic nationalists have emphasized the way the boundaries of autonomy have been hemmed in through political and economic circumstances. Politically, economic nationalists point to the return to the cautious style of the past. Taking their cue from the evolution of mainstream debate, the Chrétien government is said to have shifted back towards a 'brokerage approach...straddling the centre of the political spectrum' more reminiscent of Mackenzie King than of Pierre Trudeau.[63] Economically, the positioning of debt and international competitiveness at the apex of the Liberal policy agenda is seen as being indicative of the way priorities have become distorted. Reinforced by a general sense of malaise concerning the future of sovereignty and the role of the nation state, it is argued that, by virtue of its concentration on this combination of issues, the Liberal government has limited its options for autonomous national action.[64]

Amid all this pessimism, questions must be asked about the future relevance of the economic nationalist perspective. Intellectually, the centrifugal orientation of this current of thinking is out of sync with the centripetal tendencies extant within Canada at large. In harmony with the Southern Ontario/Toronto base of most of its leading proponents, the centralist, statist orientation of the economic nationalist is explicit. The lack of regional distribution displayed in this school of thought contributes to a heightened speculation about whether this perspective can capture the vast breadth of the Canadian experience in the 1990s. No less than in other countries, enormous faultlines have been opened up in Canada because of the speed and variable impact with which economic and social adjustment has hit. Faced with a structural crisis clustered on the basis of industry and region, with its attendant problems of unemployment and a declining standard of living, one increasingly vocal form of political expression has been a self-consciously parochial one. Fighting in a defensive spirit, to address issues of dislocation, the locality has been made the prime site of struggle. In contradictory fashion, the nucleus of economic nationalist thinking may be seen to be out of step as well with the dynamics of transnationalization found within the high-profile elements of the non-state community. Rather than joining in a debate focussing largely on the limits of national autonomy, many of these non-state actors have moved to a very different prospect centred on the task of building coalitions across borders.

Questions may also be raised about how well the economic nationalist perspective captures the essence of Canada's position within the contemporary international political economy. The mixed signals concerning American commitment to the international system have provided some considerable impetus for Canada to draw closer in terms of its own relationship with the US over the last decade. Fearing the consequences from American passive/aggressive behaviour, this shift in response has meant closer attention to Canadian–US relations. A predictable environment is sought. Notwithstanding concerns that this trend constitutes by its very nature a tightening of the continentalist embrace, a heightened focus on Canada's core relationship is not in itself evidence of a loss of Canadian will. In terms of the 'complex interdependence' framework, for example, the opposite is true. A shift towards a concentrated bilateral approach is precisely what is needed to cope with the sheer complexity of the Canada–US connection. Rather than disengaging, it is argued, the 'asymmetrical' relationship is best dealt with through the implementation of more sustained and effective management techniques. Referring back to the academic work of Keohane and Nye in the 1970s, it must be mentioned that these scholars found that the inequities of outcome in the Canada–US relationship during the 1950s and 1960s were not as one-sided as the worst-case scenarios would assume due to the disproportionate time and energy Canada devoted to working this relationship.[65]

Finally, the economic nationalist framework tends to judge success or failure in quite restrictive terms, through a calibration of unilateral strategies. In doing so, the potential Canadian contribution in the expanded international agenda is missed. No longer are countries primarily interested in the protection of their security or economic integrity as judged by the degree of external penetration. Rather, their priorities are related more and more to doing something in terms of both national competitiveness, and the interconnected economic/social issues (poverty and human welfare, ecology and human rights), which are essentially global and interdependent in nature. This broad set of issues is not easily dealt with by a single nation state—even the most powerful one, the US.[66] As such, any attempted solution to these issues requires some form of skillful multilateral management, either through established institutions (the United Nations, regional organizations, etc.) or through ad hoc forms of coalition and confidence building[67]—in other words, precisely those areas where it is said that Canada has the most potential to carve out distinctive niches for itself in the post-Cold War world.

## The Middle Power Framework

The third perspective, the middle power framework, has had considerable durability as a guide for Canadian thinking and policymaking. Formulated in the context of World War II, this framework is indelibly identified with the so-called 'golden era' of Pearsonian internationalism, which stretched from the late 1940s through to the 1960s. In orientation, it was associated with the emergence of a distinctive world-view and set of practices. At its core, the concept of middle power diplomacy signified 'a certain type and a certain content of foreign policy' based on an attachment to multilateral institutions and a collaborative world order.[68] This mindset epitomizes the leitmotiv drawn by Keohane for this category of countries: 'a middle power is a state whose leaders consider that it cannot act alone effectively, but may be able to have a systematic impact in a small group or through an international institution.'[69]

The consensual acceptance of the symbolic and instrumental underpinnings of middle power diplomacy waned considerably during the late 1960s and 1970s. In keeping with Prime Minister Trudeau's own critical outlook on this orientation, the comprehensive review of Canadian foreign policy (published as *Foreign Policy for Canadians* in June 1970) argued that this established way of assessing Canada's place in the international arena needed to be replaced. Contesting the relevance of the status quo in Canadian foreign policy, the supposed inability of the middle power nation to deal with new complexities was targeted especially for disapprobation. On the basis of the review's harsh assessment, 'Canada's "traditional" middle-power role in the world seemed doomed to disappear.'[70]

Predictions about the death of the middle power perspective in Canadian foreign policy, however, have been highly exaggerated. Middle power statecraft has displayed remarkable resilience as the orthodox expression of Canadian foreign policy. At odds with his original distaste for the approach, Trudeau's declaratory language over time absorbed the expression. In the midst of his well-publicized initiative on disarmament and peace, for example, Trudeau proclaimed: 'Preventing the spread of nuclear weapons is in the interest of superpower, middle-power and micro-state alike.'[71]

A similar cycle was repeated in the 1980s. Keen to depart from the Liberal legacy, Mulroney's Progressive Conservative government embarked on a very different course in many key aspects of its foreign policy. This departure featured most prominently, as noted above with respect to the economic nationalist framework, a warmer attitude towards the United States and a continental economic relationship. This adjustment in tenor and direction, however, did not mean an end to the relevance of the middle power perspective for Canadian foreign policy. Whether to compensate for the FTA or not, the Mulroney government continued to define and interpret its actions in the international arena in accordance with the set tenets of middle power statecraft. As one respected Canadian think-tank summarized on the basis of the Conservatives' record in their first term of office: 'Canada's primary identification today is not that of a junior continental partner to a superpower, nor a second-tier actor in the Western Summit Seven or the North Atlantic Treaty Organization (NATO)...it is that of a vigorous, activist middle power.'[72]

The informative value of this fixed orientation rests on a number of factors. At a simplistic level, the middle power framework provides a balance absent amid the other contending perspectives. On the one hand, the notion of Canada as an 'in between' country offers a more modest assessment of Canada's capabilities than the overt sense of optimism and pessimism found within the contending frameworks. This fits, no doubt, with the stereotype of Canada (and Canadians) having a caution bred in the bone. Jokes abound about this inclination: 'Why do Canadians cross the road? To get to the middle.' Yet this cautious assessment may also be grounded in sound experience. Canada may indeed be most safe in the middle. Certainly the middle power framework has the attraction of being equivocal. While cognizant of the limitations on Canadian actions imposed by structural-level impediments, it also allows a certain degree of agency for Canada on a segmented, issue-specific basis. In other words, it assumes some ability on the part of Canada to make a difference through its own distinct approach in international affairs. What is needed to capitalize on these opportunities is an agile and flexible form of statecraft on top of a firm sense of international commitment.

Consequently, this approach meshes comfortably with Canada's self-perception. It allows Canadians to look back at the genealogy of this approach with a sense of pride. It conforms to a 'way of doing things' established in the international (and, traditionally at least, domestic) arena—usually referred to as a preference for accommodation, consensus and voluntarism. If this comfort level has admittedly worn thin over time, the middle power notion still appears to be a good representative fit. In the words of one NGO representative: 'whether we like it or not, Canada is not a major economic and military power. We are a middle power. Such prestige, voice, influence and clout as we have on the world stage—and we have a lot of it, far out of proportion to our relative strength as an economic power—is there because we have a history of altruism, compassion, fairness, and of doing things irrespective of our own national self-interest in economics or politics. We have been respected and we have a voice in the world not because the world perceives us to be powerful but because the world perceives us to be good.'[73]

It is one thing to suggest that Canada remains content to present itself as a middle power; it is quite another to say that this is the best—or most appropriate—

garb to wear. As with the other frameworks, questions must be posed about the sustained persuasive ability of the middle power concept.[74] One of the long-standing weaknesses of the middle power framework has been the strong normative tendency contained within it. Central to this tendency is the article of faith which says that middle powers act uniformly as good international citizens.[75] This strong sense of positive appreciation for middle powers stands out as a common bond between practitioners and critical commentators alike. Prime Minister Mulroney, in the aftermath of the Gulf War episode, echoed the sentiment that Canada had both the national will and the capability to act according to a sense of international obligations: 'As middle powers, we must ensure our interests will continue to be protected by the international legal system. We must use our strengths to support a revitalized United Nations system, to improve the position of those less well-equipped to help themselves.'[76] Although considerably harsher in his assessment of the operational application of these principles, Stephen Lewis, the former Canadian ambassador to the United Nations, has been just as effusive about the potential role of middle powers in the international system: 'I have always seen Canada and other middle powers serving as a voice to offset the major powers. I think Canada and some of the smaller members of the European Community, such as Holland, as well as Norway, Sweden, Finland, Australia, New Zealand—that whole grab bag of countries that verge collectively on angelic perfection—should act as an uncompromising voice when they think the major powers are going too far, rather than behave as uncritical allies. We need a group of countries that believe in internationalism, above all, and that can be counted on to support multilateral institutions and agencies.'[77]

Animated by a persistent fear of international anarchy and lawlessness prevalent in Canadian thinking, this kind of interpretation is not completely irrelevant. Still, the emphasis on morality and 'good works' (or the necessity to do more to be 'on the side of the angels') incorporated in these analyses has the tendency to blur as much as it clarifies. The notion of good international citizenship, by its normative nature, is highly prone to distortions, ambiguity and nostalgic mythology. Despite the implicit claim of moral superiority, Canada certainly does not have an unblemished record with respect to international issues. Canada's foreign policy performance has been censured on a number of occasions for its passivity and/or abdication of responsibility in responding to international crises. On Biafra and East Timor, to name just two illustrations, the gap between Canada's words and its deeds has led to charges of self-deception or hypocrisy. In a variety of other cases, the enthusiasm on the part of Canada for interventionism on the world stage has been a source of embarrassment. That is to say, the voluntaristic current in foreign policy has been construed not as helpful fixing but rather as indicative of self-righteous meddling or a 'busybody' disposition.[78]

The special context of the 1990s gives another twist to this problem. The stimuli for Canada to continue to display (and to be seen as displaying) a committed stance in international affairs remain strong. This instinct, though, may well contain a snare. In the context of agenda change, which places a higher priority on national competitiveness and 'getting one's own house in order,' the image of Canada as a selfless 'good international citizen' may be considered by opinion-leaders to be counter-productive in that it strikes the wrong chord and opens up a capability–commitment problem. Pressure for engagement remains; but so does a counter-pressure to distance (or downplay) Canada from 'excessive' forms of internationalism. The expression of the theme concerning the limits of Canadian activity comes out in the various attempts by André Ouellet to purge the notion of Canada as a guide or 'boy scout' from the play book of Canadian foreign policy. On one occasion, Ouellet stated that it was foolhardy for Canada 'to try to be a Boy Scout on your own, to impose your own rules on others when indeed nobody else is following it is absolutely counterproductive and does not lead to any successful future.'[79]

Another identifiable problem has been the number of analytical gaps found within the middle power framework. This perspective is expansive about the 'wriggle room' Canada has available to it in the global domain; it is less ample in its assessment of where and how statecraft may be applied. In scope, pride of place is given almost exclusively to the multilateral domain. In terms of form, the prime target is on the mobilization of international reform efforts—especially those requiring considerable co-operation and collaboration through joint or coalition-building activity. In intensity, the discussion does not stray too far from the application of the techniques of statecraft required to gain an international presence. The framework pays little heed to the dynamics of intergovernmental relations on the bilateral or regional front. Besides an ingrained faith in the practices of quiet diplomacy, the middle power concept has had little to say about either the evolution of the Canada–US connection or Canada's sense of neighbourhood. Nor, apart from its concentrated focus on the activities of the small group of decision-makers in the 'golden age,' has this perspective directed attention towards the process by which Canada's own policy has been made. The confined lens provided by the traditional middle power literature, for all these reasons, does not easily capture the growing complexity of Canadian foreign policy in the 1980s and 1990s.

## TESTING THE ESTABLISHED BOUNDARIES

After examining the major strengths and deficiencies of these contending frameworks on an individual basis, some assessment may be made of them collectively. What stands out, amid the differences between them, is the commonalities that bind them together. All of them pay some considerable heed to the definitional issue of where Canada sits within the international order, whether this is done on the basis of quantifiable or intuitive criteria. Indeed, this convergence serves as the starting-point for Maureen Appel Molot's influential review article, entitled 'Where Do We, Should We, or Can We Sit: A Review of

Canadian Foreign Policy Literature.'[80] From her detailed inspection of the conceptually oriented literature on Canadian foreign policy, Molot traces the themes of role, status and position running right across the spectrum.

Not only are the differences between the contending frameworks predicated largely on a divergence in their evaluation of how Canada is located in the global hierarchy, but the internal variations among the proponents of any one of the frameworks hinges on the same point. The subtle change in language between 'principal' and 'foremost' and 'major' power is informative in this respect. So is the variation on the theme of dependency played out between the economic nationalists and the followers of Immanuel Wallerstein and the adherents of the world system school. By placing Canada in the category of 'semi-peripheral' countries,[81] it may be asserted that the interpretation of the world system school moves nearer to the middle power framework. The extent of this proximity comes out even more clearly in the augmented work of Philip Resnick. Dissatisfied with the veracity of the expression 'semi-periphery,' Resnick tried to add 'further gradation' to the concept to take into account the changes that took place in Canada from the 1970s onwards. In doing so, he came to term Canada a country on 'the perimeter of the core,'[82] a redefinition that moves the emphasis further towards an 'in between' perspective. The variation between the different strands that comprise the orthodox middle power take on Canadian foreign policy is also significant. On the one side there are the established writings, which tend to single out Canada as the quintessential middle power. On the other side there are the modified writings, which champion the view that Canada may well have served as the model for middle power statecraft in the past, but that Canada may no longer be exceptional in terms of its attributes or abilities. This latter strand indicates the way that middle power diplomacy has evolved in a co-operative manner (through joint initiatives). It also points to the evidence of growing competition within this grouping.

The other element of commonality that exists is the salience each of the contending frameworks gives to the notion of national interest and national identity. Whatever the contrast in their perspective with respect to national needs and preferences, each assumes a collective vision of how the nation sees itself and acts in the international arena. Whether explicitly or implicitly, this vision is interconnected with a deeply ingrained depiction of Canadian society and its values. Each of the frameworks, in its own particularistic fashion, is state-centric, showcasing élite attitudes and top-down modes of decision-making.

Ongoing efforts have been made to modify these frameworks to take into account recent changes in the international system. The marked surge of interest in rethinking and redefining Canadian foreign policy through the middle power lens is especially noteworthy. Following Robert Cox's plea that the value of the middle power perspective needed to be constantly demonstrated, a number of recent studies have attempted to update and reinvigorate this concept. As Cox put it, 'the middle power role' should not be evaluated as 'a fixed universal' but as 'a process not a finality...something that has to be rethought continually in the context of the changing state of the international system.'[83] This process of re-evaluation has meant, in practice, a surge of interest in 'relocating' Canada's position in the wider constellation of middle powers, as well as a bid to make a better bridge between the international and the domestic in Canadian foreign policy. The first element has scrutinized Canada, in comparative terms, with mainly traditional like-minded countries (Australia and the smaller European countries being the usual candidates). The latter element has worked to extend the form of analysis to integrate Putnam's notion of 'two-level games.'[84]

These innovations have come in the face of an amplified debate about whether these familiar ways of looking at Canadian foreign policy any longer serve as a meaningful prism of analysis at the end of the 1990s. Two sets of voices may be discerned as particular sources of contestation. The first set includes the various strands of revisionists already mentioned. Supplemented by the discourse/action of public opinion leaders and journalists, this group (in all its abundant variation) has made a serious effort to challenge the accepted frameworks in order to close the gap in our understanding about where Canadian foreign policy has come and where it is going. A second set encompasses those critical theorists who have taken aim at the underlying assumptions and 'silent voices' in the traditional literature. The mien of this set of critical voices is directed towards a concerted interrogation of established concepts, decision-making personnel and modes of thinking. The conceptual sweep of much of this work takes it well beyond the purview of a focussed discussion on Canadian foreign policy.[85] Specific components of this literature, however, have a good deal to say about Canadian foreign policy, extending the debate about who and what is studied.

An ability to mix a critical assessment about the gaps or 'silences' in the traditional Canadian literature with an architectonic concern with the practice of Canadian foreign policy is well illustrated by reference to the writings of feminist scholars on the issue of gender and Canadian foreign policy. As Deborah Stienstra makes clear, '[g]ender relations analysis in the context of Canadian foreign policy draws on [the] notions of critical theory and interpretative method' in order to 'identify those assumptions about the unequal power relations of gender which have become embedded in the practices, ideas, and institutions of Canadian foreign policy' with an interest in 'the theoretical questions we ask or that we consider significant in Canadian foreign policy analysis.'[86] Serious treatment is given to both the reconceptualization of Canadian foreign policy and its operation through a 'gendered lens.' A willingness to blend critical analysis with a practical engagement towards the operation of Canadian foreign policy is sited in the work of Sandra Whitworth. While extremely critical of the lack of acknowledgment of the 'gendered nature' of Canadian foreign policy in the foreign policy review process, for example, Whitworth counsels against staying on the margins 'in despair of ever being heard.' Rather, the point is forcefully made that 'what the current foreign policy review process exemplifies is the need for continued consultation and confrontation with Canada's foreign policy elite.'[87]

## ORIENTATION AND STRUCTURE OF THIS VOLUME

This book favours the middle power framework. Notwithstanding all the dissent about its claims to authentically represent Canadian foreign policy behaviour, this framework remains the consensual champion among the competing conceptual frameworks. Displaying a considerable degree of resilience against criticism, the middle power framework has demonstrated an unremitting ability to remain at the epicentre of dialogue. It provides the pivotal frame of reference not only for the principal power and dependency/satellite perspectives but also for the new wave of critical thinkers, as demonstrated by a recent article by Mark Neufeld, on 'Hegemony and Foreign Policy Analysis: The Case of Canada as Middle Power.'[88] Still, if favoured because of its privileged (even 'hegemonic') position in thinking and action, the imprinted limitations of the middle power framework need to be acknowledged and addressed. One need not accept all the assumptions of the latest critical wave, concerning 'new ways of analysing' Canadian foreign policy and other aspects of international politics, to accept that many of their criticisms are valid. The middle power perspective needs to open up still further to the issues and actors missing in the traditional literature. From Neufeld's vista, it is precisely in this domain that the attempts to 're-locate' Canada through a revised middle power framework suffers 'important liabilities'; in that the focuses on the 'state bureaucracy' and the 'national interest' neglects 'the important role played by social forces and societal structures in determining state action' and obscures 'the degree to which state policy can serve some parts of the "nation" better than others.'[89]

The established frameworks and these newer critical voices are to a considerable extent binary. Put together in some form of creative (although still awkward) harness, the interplay between the familiar and the critical perspectives does much to complement and enrich our analysis of Canadian foreign policy. This duality interlays the central theme of this book, that the overall pattern of Canadian behaviour in foreign policy can only be understood against the background of the tensions between the old habits ingrained in the middle power perspective and the thread of the new directions woven into the transition towards altered ways of thinking and acting. Only by looking at the interactive process between the traditional character of Canadian foreign policy and the way in which these key mental images have been scrutinized and/or undercut can the conceptual and operational mapping of Canadian foreign policy be fully extended.

This interplay between old habits and new directions is played out through the assessment of a number of enduring attitudes and issues built into larger debates about the expression of Canadian foreign policy. The starting-point is a detailed discussion of the quintessential habits that did so much to shape the means and ends of Canadian post-1945 diplomatic activity. In terms of tools or instruments, the extended snapshot contained in Chapter 1 serves to underscore the priority that Canada placed in its so-called 'golden age' of diplomacy on the use of skill in terms of its statecraft. Considerable evidence may be mustered for the argument that these games of skill not only allowed Canada to deploy its limited room for manoeuvre in a creative fashion during the 1950s and 1960s but that these practices provided some residual benefits in allowing diplomatic flexibility and agility to be stored up to the present. By pointing towards an orderly and imaginative process of adjustment, however, this positive assessment presents only one side of the story. Over the past two decades Canada's established habits of diplomacy have faced multiple forms of contradiction and negation. Downplayed in the 1970s as part of Trudeau's reassessment exercise, these built-in skills have had to be reinvented and supplemented through the infusion of alternative sources of expertise in the 1980s and 1990s, as part of the momentum towards the politics of inclusion. Another significant dimension where the tension between older habit and newer directions is played out comes with the character factor: the way Canada plays its cards is important, but so is the motivation behind this style of play.

To balance the picture between means and ends, the reputational theme is addressed in Chapter 2. Looking backwards, the devotion paid by Canada in the postwar period to playing by the rules of the game comes to the fore. The focus by Canada on both the key economic institutions and the informal regimes gives some sustained credence to the notion of Canada as a first follower of the post-1945 international system. As with skill, though, much of the established consensus on Canada's character in international affairs has come unravelled. The span from the 1970s to the 1990s saw a variety of attacks on Canada's record as a 'good international citizen.' Coming from a number of different directions, at the heart of all these attacks was a challenge to Canada's image as a consistent supporter of the international economic order.

In terms of the substantive features of the changing agenda, from the Cold War to the post-Cold War era, the issue of security is designated for special attention in Chapter 3. Nowhere, arguably, is the tension between the old, accepted ways of thinking and the new and critical efforts to analyse the meaning and implications of change more obvious than on the issue of security. The attempt to redefine security in the post-Cold War period encompasses two intertwining debates. The first of these debates revolves around the evolution of the traditional or official military/security debate. Without a clearly defined enemy or 'other' to mobilize against, this debate revolves around the clash between the older habits, tied up with being an alliance partner, on the one hand and the impetus towards moving in a new direction, associated with preventative diplomacy and regional security, on the other. The alternative or unofficial debate has provided sustained impetus towards stretching the definitional and practical boundaries of security. With the heightened attention directed towards national competitiveness in the international arena and economic polarization in the domestic arena, the debate about security has spilled over into the economic arena in a very different way than in the past. At the same time, a massive fault-line has opened up about the meaning of security. Whereas the older habit looks at security in national, territorial and public terms, the alternative perspective views security in individualistic/group identity, universalistic and private terms.

In directing attention in Chapter 4 towards the specific case-study of the Canada–European (or more precisely, Canada–Spain) 'fish war,' this dualistic approach for exploring the intellectual and policymaking terrain is reversed. At face value, this conflict may be interpreted as an issue that reveals the conceptual and operational salience of environmental security in the 1990s. On closer examination, the issue becomes more multilayered. It is misleading to see Canadian foreign policy on the fish issue through an exclusively 'green' lens. National (and localistic) interests reinforced the idealist/globalist rationale for taking aggressive action. In particular, a power-based approach on the East Coast resource issue was explicitly linked to the issue of regional economic decline. Pulling Canada back from an extended tilt towards the new direction of 'gunboat' diplomacy was the staying power of constructive internationalism as a guide to a negotiated (as opposed to a coercive) solution to the crisis.

Chapters 5 and 6 address in some detail the two issue-areas that have been taken to form the twin pillars of Canadian post-1945 foreign policy, namely peacekeeping and international development assistance. Both issues reveal the contradictory impulses of post-Cold War Canadian foreign policy. With the collapse of bipolarity, expectations about Canada's capabilities in helping to extend these activities were raised higher, to the point where it was commonly assumed that Canada would provide some degree of leadership. Yet, despite a well-entrenched habit of commitment, both Canada's aspirations and its achievements *vis-à-vis* this sort of involvement have perceptually waned. In part, this reversal in fortunes has been propelled by the sheer enormity of the change in international conditions. In peacekeeping, this state of affairs has been influenced by the expansion of the complexity (and risks) of the mandate. In development assistance, it is compelled by the force of various cross-pressures (i.e., how, where, to whom should aid be allocated). In addition to the systemic pressure, domestic conditions have acted as a brake rather than as a motor for these forms of activity. The initial drive towards global commitment has been offset by the fear of domestic 'overstretch,' inspired by a relative decline in resources.

If these functional issue-areas exhibit a form of contraction, Canada's geographic concern has shown some signs of expansion. This changing sense of neighbourhood serves as the basis for the analysis in Chapter 7 on Canada and regionalism, with special reference to the transformed relationship between Canada and the Americas. While sharing space with this region, as components of the Western Hemisphere, the Americas has not in the past registered on Canada's mental map in any coherent way. Sharing little in the way of a common identity,

Canada preferred to look to Europe (and to a lesser extent the Asia-Pacific) for connections. The enthusiasm with which Canada has embraced a deepened North American Free Trade Agreement (NAFTA) and an expanded OAS is clearly a sign of a better appreciation of spatial realities. Any talk of Canada taking on a new 'vocation of the Americas' should not be taken too far, however. Old habits, with good reason, die hard. Canada's fear of 'excessive' regionalism remains. While willing to move closer to the Americas, Canada remains unwilling to lock itself into that region. As witnessed by approaches to Asia-Pacific Economic Co-operation (APEC) and its initiative on an institutional NAFTA–European Union (EU) link, Canada wants to keep its options open.

By structuring the book around the dual contours of old habits and new directions, the fundamental pattern of continuity and change in Canadian foreign policy is highlighted. The assumption is made that the conventional modes of examining Canadian foreign policy generally, and the middle power perspective more specifically, still have the capability to lend some considerable insight on the crucial issues before Canada. While the established concepts, and concerns, associated with the privileging of the older habits of Canadian foreign policy behaviour retain considerable value as signposts in navigating the driving dynamic of change, however, it is also conceded that this traditional mode of treatment is not enough. In the moment of transition at the end of the twentieth century, and at the closer intersection of the international and the domestic, the standard repertoire of analysis has to be embellished. To fully tease out the complex—and often contradictory—puzzles relating to Canadian foreign policy on the edge of the twenty-first century, a more diverse guide is required.

## NOTES

[1]   See Janice Gross Stein, 'Living with uncertainty: Canada and the architecture of the new world order,' *International Journal* XLVII, 3 (Summer 1992), 614–29. This theme has been made popular by the work of John J. Mearsheimer, 'Back to the future: instability in Europe after the Cold War,' *International Security* 15, 1 (Summer 1990), 5-56.

[2]   Department of External Affairs and International Trade, EAITC, *Foreign Policy Themes and Priorities*, 1991–92 Update (Ottawa: December 1991), 2.

[3]   David A. Welch, 'The new multilateralism and evolving security system,' in Fen Osler Hampson and Christopher J. Maule, eds., *Canada Among Nations 1992–93: A New World Order?* (Ottawa: Carleton University Press, 1992), 86.

[4]   John Kirton, 'Canada gets a chance to make its mark,' *Financial Post*, 6 July 1993, 6.

[5]   Fen Osler Hampson and Christopher J. Maule, 'After the Cold War,' in Hampson and Maule, eds., *Canada Among Nations 1990–91: After the Cold War* (Ottawa: Carleton University Press, 1991), 2.

[6]   Leigh Sarty, 'Sunset Boulevard revisited? Canadian internationalism after the Cold War,' *International Journal* XLVIII, 4 (Autumn 1993), 749.

7   See Giles Paquet, 'The Canadian malaise and its external impact,' in *Canada Among Nations 1990–91*, 37.

8   See, for example, Charles S. Maier, 'Democracy and its discontents,' *Foreign Affairs* 73, 4 (July–August 1994), 48–64; David Held, 'Democracy, the nation-state, and the global system,' in Held, ed., *Political Theory Today* (Stanford: Stanford University Press, 1991).

9   Alan C. Cairns, *Charter Versus Federalism: The Dilemmas of Constitutional Reform* (Montreal and Kingston: McGill–Queen's University Press, 1992).

10  J.N. Rosenau, *Turbulence in World Politics: A Theory of Change and Continuity* (Princeton, NJ: Princeton University Press, 1990).

11  Ernst-Otto Czempiel and J.N. Rosenau, eds., *Global Changes and Theoretical Challenges: Approaches to World Politics for the 1990s* (Lexington, MA: Heath, 1989), 118–21.

12  Laura Neak, Jeanne A.K. Hay and Patrick J. Haney, *Foreign Policy Analysis: Continuity and Change in Its Second Generation* (Englewood Cliffs, NJ: Prentice Hall, 1995), 10.

13  Charles Krauthammer, 'The unipolar moment,' *Foreign Affairs* 70, 1 (1991), 23–33.

14  Susan Strange, 'The future of the American Empire,' *Journal of International Affairs* 42, 1 (Fall 1988), 1–14; Robert Gilpin, *The Political Economy of International Relations* (Princeton, NJ: Princeton University Press, 1987), 345.

15  Joseph S. Nye, *Bound to Lead: The Changing Nature of American Power* (New York: Basic Books, 1990).

16  See, for example, Hans W. Maull, 'Germany and Japan: the new civilian powers,' *Foreign Affairs* 69, 5 (Winter 1990), 91-106.

17  See, for example, Josef Joffe, 'After bipolarity: German and European security,' *European Security after the Cold War*, Adelphi Paper 284 (London: January 1994), 37–46.

18  Kent E. Calder, 'Japanese foreign economic policy formation: explaining the reactive state,' *World Politics* XL, 4 (July 1988), 517-41.

19  Susan Strange, 'States, firms and diplomacy,' *International Affairs* 68, 1 (January 1992), 1–15.

20  See, for example, Andrew Linklater, *Beyond Realism and Marxism: Critical Theory and International Relations* (London: Macmillan, 1990).

21  Susan Strange and John Stopford, *Rival States, Rival Firms: Competition for World Market Shares* (Cambridge: Cambridge University Press, 1991); Robert W. Cox, 'Structural issues of global governance,' in Stephen Gill, ed., *Historical Materialism and International Relations* (Cambridge: Cambridge University Press, 1993).

22  Rosabeth Moss Kanter, 'Thriving locally in the global economy,' *Harvard Business Review* (September–October 1995), 151–60.

23  Quoted in Madelaine Drohan, 'Capitalism must develop a heart, executives told,' *Globe and Mail*, 2 February 1996. Kanter elaborates that 'If the class division of the industrial economy was between capital and labor, or between managers and workers, the class division of the emerging information economy could well be between cosmopolitans with global connections and locals who are stuck in one place.' 'Thriving locally,' 151.

24  John English, *Shadow of Heaven: The Life of Lester Pearson Volume One: 1897–1948* (Toronto: Lester & Orpen Dennys, 1989); *The Worldly Years: The Life of Lester Pearson Volume Two: 1949–1972* (Toronto: Alfred A. Knopf, 1992).

25  See, for example, Harold A. Innis, 'Great Britain, the United States and Canada,' in *Essays in Canadian Economic History* (Toronto: University of Toronto Press, 1956), 394–412; Hugh Keenleyside, 'The American economic penetration of Canada,' *Canadian Historical Review* VIII, 1 (March 1927), 31–40.

26  Melissa Clark-Jones, *A Staple State: Canadian Industrial Resources in Cold War* (Toronto: University of Toronto Press, 1987).

27  Norman Hillmer and Garth Stevenson, *Foremost Nation: Canadian Foreign Policy and a Changing World* (Toronto: McClelland and Stewart, 1975).

28  Alan M. Rugman and John McIlveen, *Mega Firms* (Toronto: Methuen, 1985).

29  Michael K. Hawes, *Principal Power, Middle Power, or Satellite? Competing Perspectives in the Study of Canadian Foreign Policy* (Toronto: York Research Programme in Strategic Studies, 1984).

30  On the study of bureaucratic politics as an 'unexplored' field in Canadian foreign policy, see Michael Tucker, *Canadian Foreign Policy: Contemporary Issues and Themes* (Toronto: McGraw-Hill Ryerson, 1980), 60. See also Kim Richard Nossal, 'Allison through the (Ottawa) looking glass: bureaucratic politics and foreign policy in a parliamentary system,' *Canadian Public Administration* 22, 4 (Winter 1979), 610-26.

31  See, for example, Brian W. Tomlin, Michael B. Dolan, Harald von Reikhoff and Maureen A. Molot, 'Foreign policies of subordinate states in asymmetrical dyads,' *The Jerusalem Journal of International Relations* 5, 4 (1981), 14–40.

32  See, for example, Patrick James and Anoop Prihar, 'Comparative foreign policy: an evaluation of stimulated bargaining among Canada, Japan and the United States,' *Journal of American and Canadian Studies* (Tokyo) 8 (Fall 1991), 73–104; and Patrick James, 'Energy politics in Canada, 1980–1981: threat power in a sequential game,' *Canadian Journal of Political Science* 26, 1 (March 1993), 31–68.

33  James Eayrs, 'Defining a new place for Canada in the hierarchy of world power,' *International Perspectives*, May/June 1975, 15–24.

34  David Dewitt and John Kirton, *Canada as a Principal Power* (Toronto: John Wiley, 1983), 38.

35  David R. Black and Heather A. Smith, 'Notable exceptions? New and arrested directions in Canadian foreign policy literature,' *Canadian Journal of Political Science* 26, 4 (December 1993), 760. See Charles Doran, *Economic Interdependence, Autonomy and Canadian/American Relations* (Montreal: Institute for Research on Public Policy, 1983).

36  Testimony by John Kirton to House of Commons Standing Committee on Foreign Affairs and International Trade, *Minutes of Proceedings and Evidence*, 21 February 1995, 16:12.

37  Robert Wolfe, 'Should Canada stay in the Group of Seven?' *Canadian Foreign Policy* III, 1 (Spring 1995), 52–3.

38  Don McGillivray, 'Canada's pretence exceeds its stature,' *Ottawa Citizen*, 7 May 1986.

39  Testimony by Gordon Smith to House of Commons Standing Committee on Foreign Affairs and International Trade, *Minutes of Proceedings and Evidence*, 22 February 1995, 16:45.

40    John Kirton, 'Liberating Kuwait: Canada and the Persian Gulf War, 1990–91,' in Don Munton and John Kirton, eds., *Canadian Foreign Policy: Selected Cases* (Scarborough: Prentice Hall, 1992), 382.

41    For these contrasting perspectives, see Bernard Wood, 'The Gulf Crisis and the future world order,' and Reg Whitaker, 'Prisoner of the American Dream: Canada, the Gulf and the new world order,' in Mark Charlton and Elizabeth Riddell-Dixon, eds., *International Relations in the Post Cold War Era* (Toronto: Nelson Canada, 1993).

42    Kirton, 'Canada gets a chance to make its mark.'

43    Testimony by Roy Culpeper, North–South Institute, to the House of Commons Standing Committee on Foreign Affairs and International Trade, *Minutes of Proceedings and Evidence*, 3 April 1995, 21:40.

44    See, for example, The Report on the Commission on Global Governance, *Our Global Neighbourhood* (Oxford: Oxford University Press, 1995), 146.

45    'War of the worlds: a survey of the global economy,' *Economist*, 1 October 1994, 36. See also 'Canada: seat at G-7 but wobbly,' *Economist*, 27 February–15 March 1993, reprinted in *Globe and Mail*, 1 March 1993.

46    See, for example, Peter Cook, 'A G7 in which Canada does not belong,' *Globe and Mail*, 11 October 1994; editorial, *Globe and Mail*, 11 October 1994.

47    Statement by Nic Leblanc, Longueuil, to the House of Commons Standing Committee on Foreign Affairs and International Trade, *Minutes of Proceedings and Evidence*, 23 February 1995, 17:14.

48    Kirton, 'Canada gets a chance to make its mark.'

49    Quoted in Rosemary Speirs, 'PM's Asian trip called a $6 billion success,' *Toronto Star*, 19 January 1996. See also Giles Gherson, 'Swapping Mulroney's Cadillac style for a Chevrolet foreign policy,' *Globe and Mail*, 18 May 1994.

50    A classic statement of this argument remains John Warnock, *Partner to Behemoth: The Military Policy of a Satellite Canada* (Toronto: New Press, 1970).

51    Hawes, *Principal Power, Middle Power, or Satellite?*

52    Classic statements of this argument remain: Kari Levitt, *Silent Surrender: The Multinational Corporation in Canada* (Toronto: Macmillan, 1970); Ian Lumsden ed., *Close the 49th Parallel* (Toronto: University of Toronto Press, 1970).

53    This revisionist literature includes, for example, Douglas A. Ross, *In the Interests of Peace: Canada and Vietnam, 1954–1973* (Toronto: University of Toronto Press, 1984); Jocelyn Ghent-Mallet and Don Munton, 'Confronting Kennedy and the missiles in Cuba, 1962,' in Don Munton and John Kirton, eds., *Canadian Foreign Policy: Selected Cases* (Scarborough: Prentice Hall, 1992), 78-100.

54    Marci McDonald, *Yankee Doodle Dandy: Brian Mulroney and the American Agenda* (Toronto: Stoddart, 1995).

55    (Toronto: McClelland and Stewart, 1965).

56    McDonald, *Yankee Doodle Dandy*, 334.

57    Joseph T. Jockel and Joel J. Sokolsky, 'Dandurand revisited: rethinking Canada's defence policy in an unstable world,' *International Journal* XLVIII, 2 (Spring 1993), 392.

58    Stephen Clarkson, *Canada and the Reagan Challenge* (Toronto: James Lorimer, 1982), 293. The range of choice open to Canada also informs the work of Glen Williams, as illustrated in *Not for Export*, 3rd edition (Toronto: McClelland and Stewart, 1994). Once a choice has been made, however, Williams emphasizes that future options are constrained by 'path dependencies.'

59    Stephen Clarkson ed., *An Independent Foreign Policy for Canada?* (Toronto: McClelland and Stewart, for the University League of Social Reform, 1968), 264.

60    Bruce Thordarson, *Trudeau and Foreign Policy: A Study of Decision-Making* (Toronto: Oxford University Press, 1972), 11–12.

61    Clarkson, *Reagan Challenge*, 82.

62    Christina McCall and Stephen Clarkson, *Trudeau and Our Times, Volume 2: The Heroic Delusion* (Toronto: McClelland and Stewart, 1994), 432-3.

63    *Ibid.*, 430.

64    *Ibid.*, 429. The ongoing search for 'made in Canada' solutions has been directed, for the most part, towards the social policy domain. See, for example, Andrew F. Johnson, Stephen McBride and Patrick J. Smith, eds., *Continuities and Discontinuities: The Political Economy of Social Welfare and Labour Market Policy in Canada* (Toronto: University of Toronto Press, 1994).

65    See also David Leyton-Brown, 'The multinational enterprise and conflict in Canadian–American relations,' *International Organization* 28, 4 (Autumn 1974), 733–54. A structural critique of this 'interdependent' position is provided by Wallace Clement in 'Continental political economy: an assessment of relations between Canada and the United States,' *The Canadian Review of American Studies* 10, 1 (Spring 1979), 77–87. Clement argues that it does not make sense to abstract specific issues in dispute from their historical context: 'Canada has been molded to the demands of the United States....many of the cases in which it appears that the Canadian state has "won" a victory over the will of the US state in fact serve to draw Canada further within the orbit of the United States and to make it ever more dependent,' 84.

66    Joseph S. Nye, Jr., 'What New World Order?' *Foreign Affairs* 71, 2 (Spring 1992), 83–96.

67    Robert O. Keohane, 'Multilateralism: an agenda for research,' *International Journal* XLV, 4 (Autumn 1990), 731–64; Miles Kahler, 'Multilateralism with small and large numbers,' *International Organization* 46, 3 (Summer 1992), 681–708; John Gerard Ruggie, *Multilateralism Matters: The Theory and Practice of an Institutional Form* (New York: Columbia University Press, 1993).

68    See Paul Painchaud, 'Middlepowermanship as an ideology,' in J. King Gordon ed., *Canada's Role as a Middle Power* (Toronto: Canadian Institute of International Affairs, 1966). See also John W. Holmes, *The Better Part of Valour: Essays on Canadian Diplomacy* (Toronto: McClelland and Stewart, 1970).

69    Robert O. Keohane, 'Lilliputians' dilemmas: small states in international politics,' *International Organization* 23, 2 (Spring 1969), 295.

70    Quoted in Thordarson, *Trudeau and Foreign Policy*, 69.

71    Parliament of Canada, House of Commons, *Debates*, 9 February 1984, 1212. See also Ivan Head and Pierre Trudeau, *The Canadian Way: Shaping Canada's Foreign Policy, 1968–1984* (Toronto: McClelland and Stewart, 1995), 7.

72 'The wider world: challenges for the second Mulroney mandate,' *Review '88 Outlook '89* (Ottawa: North–South Institute, 1989), 2. For a thorough analysis of the broader themes of change and continuity in Canadian foreign policy, see Kim Richard Nossal, *The Politics of Canadian Foreign Policy* (Toronto: Prentice Hall, 1989), 52.

73 Craig Copland, President of Feed the Children, Canadian Coalition for the Rights of Children, testimony to the Special Joint Committee of the Senate and of the House of Commons, Reviewing Canadian Foreign Policy, *Minutes of Proceedings and Evidence*, 8 June 1994, 32:13.

74 For a need to reassess this position, see the sophisticated examination by Denis Stairs, 'Will and circumstance and the postwar study of Canada's foreign policy,' *International Journal* L, 1 (Winter 1994–5), 14–17. See also Andrew F. Cooper, Richard A. Higgott and Kim Richard Nossal, *Relocating Middle Powers: Australia and Canada in a Changing World Order* (Vancouver: University of British Columbia Press, 1993).

75 See, for example, Bernard Wood, *The Middle Powers and the General Interest* (Ottawa: North–South Institute, 1988).

76 Notes for a toast by Prime Minister Brian Mulroney, at a dinner in honour of the Prime Minister of Sweden, Mr. Ingvar Carlsson, External Affairs and International Trade Canada, 25 June 1991.

77 Stephen Lewis, interviewed by Jim Wurst, 'The United Nations after the Gulf War: a promise betrayed,' *World Policy Journal* 8, 3 (Summer 1991), 547.

78 See, for example, Blair Fraser, 'Canada: mediator or busybody?' in J. King Gordon ed., *Canada's Role as a Middle Power* (Toronto: Canadian Institute of International Affairs, 1966); Peyton Lyon and Brian Tomlin, *Canada as an International Actor* (Toronto: Macmillan, 1979).

79 Quoted in Jeff Sallot, 'Ouellet rules out "Boy Scout" role in human rights,' *Globe and Mail*, 16 May 1995.

80 *International Journal of Canadian Studies* 1–2 (Spring–Fall 1990), 77–96.

81 See, for example, Immanuel Wallerstein, *The Capitalist World-Economy* (New York: Cambridge University Press, 1979).

82 'From semi-periphery to perimeter of the core: Canada in the capitalist world economy,' in *The Masks of Proteus: Canadian Reflections on The State* (Montreal and Kingston: McGill–Queen's University Press, 1990), 180. See also Glen Williams, 'On determining Canada's location in the international political economy,' *Studies in Political Economy* 25 (Spring 1988), 107–40.

83 See Robert Cox, 'Middlepowermanship, Japan, and the future world order,' *International Journal* XLIV, 3 (Autumn 1989), 826.

84 Robert D. Putnam, 'Diplomacy and domestic politics: the logic of two-level games,' *International Organization* 42, 3 (Summer 1988), 428–60.

85 See, for example, Ernie Keenes, 'Paradigms of international relations: bringing politics back in,' *International Journal* XLIV, 1 (Winter 1988–9), 41–67.

86 Deborah Stienstra, 'Can the silence be broken? Gender and Canadian foreign policy,' *International Journal* L, 1 (Winter 1994–5), 108.

87   Sandra Whitworth, 'Women, and gender, in the foreign policy review process,' in Maxwell A. Cameron and Maureen Appel Molot, eds., *Canada Among Nations 1995: Democracy and Foreign Policy* (Ottawa: Carleton University Press, 1995), 94.

88   *Studies in Political Economy* 48 (Autumn 1995), 7–29.

89   *Ibid.*, 10. See also Laura Macdonald, 'Canada in the new world order,' in Michael Whittington and Glen Williams, eds., *Canada Politics in the 1990s*, 4th edn. (Toronto: Nelson, 1995), 40–54. Macdonald writes that 'Despite the fact that Canadian foreign policy did not always conform to the ideals of "middlepowermanship," this self-image continued to shape the views of both supporters and critics of Canadian foreign policy throughout the Cold War period.' She goes on to say, though, that 'It is doubtful...whether the "middle power" self-image can survive intact the recent dramatic changes in the world,' 41.

# GAMES OF SKILL

## THE ESTABLISHED CHARACTER OF CANADIAN STATECRAFT

Much of the influence Canada has enjoyed in international affairs over the course of the post-1945 era rested on its diplomatic skills. The deft display of Canadian statecraft received a good deal of critical appreciation from prominent players on the international stage. John Kennedy praised the Canadian foreign service as 'probably unequalled by any other nation.'[1] Henry Kissinger, never one to hand out kudos gratuitously, extolled the high quality of Canada's diplomatic contribution: 'Canadian leaders had a narrow margin of manoeuvre that they utilized with extraordinary skills.'[2] Canada's diplomatic techniques, and record of achievement, have acted as a source of immense pride within the country as well. To understand Canada's role in the international arena, therefore, some detailed scrutiny is needed of the manner in which these 'games of skill' were played out during their ascendant phase.

The persistence of this mode of operation must also be appraised in the context of the number of challenges rendered to its supremacy. Encouraged by particularly fortuitous historical circumstances, the central character of Canadian diplomacy flowered during the so-called 'golden era' of Pearsonian foreign policy from the late 1940s to the early 1960s. Within the defined limitations set by the conditions of bipolarity, Canada showed its creativity in operating as a go-between and intermediary. As the external opportunity for displays of these particular sorts of talent diminished, a series of internal debates about the need for a basic overhaul of Canada's established range of skills ensued. From the late 1960s to the early 1980s, in keeping with the priorities of the Trudeau government, the debate focussed on the need for upgrading Canada's diplomatic skills to cope with constitutional and managerial change. In the 1980s and 1990s, with the Mulroney and Chrétien governments, the debate has shifted towards one of adding value to Canadian diplomacy through a greater integration of state and societal interests. All of these challenges and debates have been inspired by questions concerning the adequacy of the traditional skills to meet the tasks at hand.

## The Style of Canadian Diplomacy in the Post-1945 Period

Canadian statecraft in the immediate post-1945 era presented a modest but practical face. Canada did not pretend to have the enormous power capabilities of the great powers. Nor did it believe it had the capacity to launch solo initiatives out in front of other actors. A sound foreign policy for Canada meant that its 'reach ought not to exceed its grasp.'[3] Canada was content to be the industrious tailor of the international system, stitching together workable compromises out of rather patternless and (often) threadbare material. Canada compensated (sometimes to the point of overcompensation) for its lack of structural resources through dexterity and sound practices. If only rarely exciting, this type of endeavour constituted the sum of the parts of a vast amount of incremental and laborious work. Considerable onus was placed on the reactive ability, knowledge and collective discipline of the Canadian diplomats themselves in working within a broad and flexible game plan.

Along the continuum running from critic to problem-solver,[4] Canada placed itself squarely on the problem-solving side. Canada was content to let other, more assertive countries—most notably, other self-identified middle powers such as Sweden, Australia and India—take the lead in ambitious initiatives designed to reshape the international system. By way of contrast, Canada chose to direct the bulk of its activities towards the art of the possible;[5] i.e., attempts to deal with difficulties relating to the actual workings of the system as it stood. Instead of being categorized as a system reformer, Canada is best labelled as a system maintainer. On both the macro and micro scale of issues, Canada concentrated on making a difference in a tangible as opposed to an intellectual fashion. Ideas by themselves were deemed not to be enough. The key was in delivering results when and where it mattered, in times of crisis and deadlock.

In keeping with this confined approach, Canada placed great weight on selectivity. Functionalism served as the core organizing principle in Canada's patterned form of behaviour.[6] As emphasized by most students of Canadian foreign policy, this concept had as its foundation the notion that responsibility in selected areas of international organization should be commensurate with specialized interests and task-related experience. The benefits of adopting functionalism were in large part symbolic. Where standing with respect to specific forums of decision-making rested with the burdens assumed, Canada was lent enhanced status in the international system (often with tangible spillover benefits in terms of institutional positions) in the domains in which it held a high degree of resources and reputational qualifications. This differentiated status in turn distinguished the place of Canada in the international arena from the 'minor' actors. As described by one commentator, this sort of arrangement, in which responsibilities were delegated according to a country's capabilities, had a distinctly hierarchical flavour: 'In Canada's view, problems of international relations could be best managed by apportioning them according to functional concern to international institutions where experts would meet together, and questions could be dealt with on their merits. Political representation should take into account both the nature of the problem under discussion and the capacity of states to contribute to their resolution. In this fashion, Canada could be expected to play an important role.'[7]

Apart from status, functionalism offered instrumental value for Canada. Functionalism legitimized the application of issue-specific strengths and skills possessed by individual countries. On the basis of this criteria, Canada could marshal its time and energy in a compartmentalized way. Instead of pointing Canada in the direction of diffuseness, where Canada tried to 'do everything' and 'be everywhere,' functionalism underscored the logic of Canada defining its priorities, identifying its areas of comparative advantage, and calculating how best its resources could be applied to maximum advantage. As suggested, a prime theme that runs through the writings of the practitioners underpins 'the danger of overextending one's diplomatic resources.' To depart from this logic, it was argued, risked Canada's credibility, in that it would be pressed to make decisions and sacrifices it did not want to make, and play parts it did not want to play.[8]

By making choices, in terms of priorities, Canada placed itself in a better position to achieve the desired results on specific issues. This ability was in turn reinforced by a number of other attributes of Canadian diplomacy. The first of these relates to the associational activity favoured by Canada. The habit of consultation and collaboration were thoroughly inculcated. Without the structural power available to the great powers, Canada had to rely on coalition-building to mobilize support. This type of work, rather than emphasizing self-help, concentrated on working with others. As John Holmes, in one of his many valuable 'sermons' on diplomacy, spelled out: 'Diplomacy...is a game of skill in which countries without adequate weight to be decisive in world politics and economics play whatever hands they can muster. To do so they need more friends than enemies.' These friends were not just important 'to stop someone else's wars but to help us establish international rules to protect our own vital interests.'[9]

A second attribute was the institutional orientation of so much of Canada's statecraft. A classic joiner, Canada concentrated a good deal of its attention on working through established institutions such as the United Nations (UN) and its specialized agencies, the General Agreement on Tariffs and Trade (GATT), the Organization for Economic Co-operation and Development (OECD), the International Monetary Fund (IMF) and the World Bank, among others. A constant in terms of the application of operating procedure was that Canada could do little by standing on the sidelines. The only way that Canada could influence issues generally, and counterbalance the enormous influence of the greats specifically, was by constructive involvement at the centre of action. In the case of the UN, this active engagement revolved around a multitude of activities including 'getting together sponsors for compromise resolutions, lobbying to avoid dangerous conflicts, collaboration with the efforts of the Secretary General, and in a thousand ways seeking to reduce tension.'[10]

The third attribute centres on the tenacious style driving Canadian diplomacy. Canada might not aspire to the heroic approach entertained by the critics within the middle power constellation, exhibiting instead a pragmatism and preference for compromise. Nonetheless, an intensity of feeling fed and sustained Canadian diplomacy. Having embraced an issue, Canada sought its preferred outcome by 'applying pressures surgically.'[11] Quiet, Canadian diplomacy might have been; irresolute it was not. This type of engagement, with both an entrepreneurial and technical dimension, encompassed acting as a catalyst with respect to diplomatic efforts in the sense of triggering initiatives; the planning and convening of meetings, setting priorities, and drawing up and fleshing out proposals; as well as a wide range of more routine activity surrounding liaison efforts, shuttle diplomacy, the use of formal and informal forums, working the corridors, and other means to push a given process forward.

## The Contribution of Canadian Diplomacy in the Post-1945 Period

In moving to an examination of the results, as well as the means, of Canadian diplomacy, it is the higher-profile performances pertaining to Korea and the Suez crisis that stand out. Both of these episodes demonstrate the limitations as well as the extent of the virtuosity of Canadian statecraft. The willingness of Canada to act as a 'bridge' or 'linchpin' did not completely exclude mediatory activity across the two antagonistic blocs: Canada's initiatives towards the Soviet Union in October 1955 indicate its willingness and ability to move some way in this direction. For the most part, however, this type of inter-bloc diplomatic activity was left to non-aligned or neutral states. Canada concentrated on being a 'helpful fixer' in the intra-bloc context: attempting to defuse tensions among Western powers (during the 1956 Suez crisis) or urging restraint on the alliance leader (during the Korean War). In the language of the present-day critical analysts, the main thrust of Canadian activity was 'prompted by the desire to regulate...conflict between core states...within the [US] hegemonic sphere.'[12]

The skill with which Canada, or more precisely Canadian diplomats such as Lester Pearson and his contemporaries, applied the arts of negotiation and accommodation comes out in the classic accounts of these crisis situations. Denis Stairs, in his magisterial account of the Korean case, depicts the success of Canada's diplomacy of constraint directed towards the US. Designed to shape the nature of the American involvement in the war, Canada's statecraft was directed at multilateralizing the police action. As Stairs writes: 'Every attempt by the American authorities...to extend the objectives or the conduct of hostilities beyond the limits which defined the United Nations role in the crisis produced a conflict between Ottawa and Washington. For the Canadians most directly involved, the politics of the Korean War consisted largely in the attempt to make the collective, or United Nations, aspect the dominant one.'[13]

On the complicated Suez issue, Canada's skills not only enabled a brokered (and face-saving) settlement to be reached between the belligerents on the ground but allowed the acute differences behind the scenes between the US and Britain to be smoothed over. Reacting quickly to the crisis, Canada exhibited its ability to engage in mediation and conflict-resolution through the introduction of a concrete and multifaceted plan of action. Taking up the themes of an immediate cease-fire, the establishment of a United Nations Emergency Force (UNEF) to separate the antagonists, and the creation of the machinery through the UN General Assembly for a permanent political settlement in the Middle East, Canada sold this package through quick-footed lobbying and the use of its array of contacts among the parties involved. While in retrospect this plan may be criticized for the degree of optimism or even naïvety attached to it, the immediate impact of the achievement should not be devalued. As John English notes: 'The UNEF initiative strengthened the United Nations, moderated the tensions between Washington and London, and helped to maintain both the Commonwealth and NATO.'[14]

In many ways, Suez became the defining episode of post-1945 Canadian diplomacy. Canada revealed that on a key issue, which had enormous spillover implications on intra-bloc relations and institutions, it could have an impact on the international system by getting it right in terms of its games of skill. By responding to this crisis as swiftly and intelligently as possible, Canada need not be a passive bystander. By exploiting these skills, Canada also won recognition and kudos as exemplified by Pearson's winning the Nobel Peace Prize in 1957. In similar fashion, the Korea episode showed that Canada could have some decisive influence in reining in the US on selective issues.

Cases of this type, however, remained atypical. The firm impression one gets of Canadian diplomacy is not of spectacular but rather mundane activity. Indeed, the low-key, cautious quality of this type of activity laid the foundation for a gradual build-up of derision about the Canadian contribution among international opinion-leaders, an attitude that fed into later challenges on the domestic political front concerning this mode of statecraft's putative irrelevancy and outmoded nature. The familiar bred contempt. The *New York Times,* apocryphally or not, is commonly thought to have labelled 'Another Worthwhile Canadian Initiative' as the most boring newspaper headline it had ever issued.

Still, worthwhile was what a good deal of Canadian diplomacy proved to be. Reference to a number of the more routine type of Canadian initiatives, featuring the traditional Canadian concerns with institution-building and confidence-building, illustrates this point. A good example of Canada's capacity to break procedural deadlocks was manifested in 1955, when Canada engineered a package deal over the opposition of its major allies in which twenty-seven new members were admitted to the UN General Assembly. More systematically, Canada's determination to make a difference (albeit at the margins) on a controversial and highly technical issue came out in the proceedings of the UN

Disarmament Commission. Making use of its institutional access through its permanent seat on the Atomic Energy Commission, Canada continually offered a voice of moderation and a source of constructive proposals both in terms of process and substance. As Legault and Fortmann describe, with its 'moderation, prudence, mediation, search for a serious atmosphere of discussion, and modest contribution to debate,' much of the Canadian activity was directed towards just staying the course until the atmospherics for progress improved.[15]

## The Shifts in Diplomatic Style under Diefenbaker and Trudeau

In moving ahead, it is tempting to suggest that the ingrained character of Canadian diplomacy, as laid out in this somewhat stylized fashion, has been completely dislodged. In the wake of the series of challenges confronting the old ways of conducting statecraft, many observers looked back to the earlier era of Canadian diplomacy with a considerable amount of longing and nostalgia. An article by Sandra Gwyn, written in 1978, captures this sense of loss: 'Where did it all go?... What happened to the creative imagination that was the mainspring behind NATO, behind the UN Peacekeeping Force, behind the kind of Commonwealth that could be redesigned to live on beyond imperial glories.'[16]

Good
quote

The weight of this mood of upheaval is strengthened still further by the contrast in tenor between the diplomatic initiatives associated with Lester Pearson and the 'golden age' and those associated first of all with John Diefenbaker and later with Pierre Trudeau. As opposed to the trademark quiet diplomacy of Pearson, the temperament of Diefenbaker and of Trudeau inclined towards the application of a bolder form of statecraft. Instead of being content to labour away in the background as the industrious tailor (or to use another metaphor, the responsible deputy in a posse of countries), they preferred to appear as one of the lead architects of change (or as lone gunslingers). This personalistic approach surfaces in the Diefenbaker interlude especially with respect to the Commonwealth, most notably in his proposal for a 15 percent trade diversification away from the US; his campaign against British entry into the European Common Market; and his struggle against the South African apartheid regime. With Trudeau, the 'go it alone' initiatives that stand out include his endeavours on North–South relations (1981) and the Peace crusade (1982-3) at the end of his career as prime minister.

Despite this body of evidence, it is not wholly accurate to say that the imprint of Canada's long-entrenched habits in the use of diplomatic skill has ebbed. Such a portrait glosses over the fact that, even under very different external conditions, a strong residual element of the familiar techniques has persisted. As is visible throughout this volume, notwithstanding all the twists and turns through the Trudeau, Mulroney and Chrétien years, much of the entrenched character built up over the decades remains highly salient for the performance of

Canadian diplomacy. Far from being swept aside, the themes of 'constructive internationalism' and 'safety in numbers,' which so informed the earlier era, have continued to find resonance in contemporary statecraft.

Indeed, in some ways it may be said that the inconsistencies and uncertainties surrounding the forms of personal diplomacy engaged in by Diefenbaker and Trudeau had the unintended consequence of reinforcing the positive image of Canada's traditional 'behind the scenes' diplomacy. In style, Diefenbaker's brand of prairie populism and the incandescence of his leadership qualities made the development of a coherent team approach difficult, if not impossible. Most of the Conservative leader's initiatives were launched in a rash, heat-of-the-moment fashion by the prime minister and lacked backup with respect to departmental input. As Ian Drummond states, with regard to the proposal for a 15 percent trade diversion to Britain from the US, the announcement of this plan 'seems to have been made without premeditation, and with no prior staffwork whatever.'[17]

The same sort of flaws were evident in the Trudeau initiatives. Poorly thought-out and flawed in execution, these activities contributed to some cynicism about their motives. As one critic not known for his support of hidebound Canadian practices stated, however well-intentioned these bursts of enthusiasm were in conceptual terms, in practice they undermined the effectiveness of the overall thrust of Canadian foreign policy: 'When the prime minister was engaged in an issue it was the centrepiece of Canadian public policy. But when the prime minister lost interest in or was not engaged in an issue, it was no longer the centrepiece.'[18] Trudeau's own principal secretary adds, in a similar vein, that 'critics railed about' the peace initiative not so much because they disagreed with its purpose but because they felt uncomfortable about its style.[19]

## THE CHANGING FACE OF CANADIAN DIPLOMACY

### Situational and Institutional Challenges

The hallmark of the Pearson era of Canadian foreign policy was a coherent but relatively closed approach to policymaking. An extensive process of consultation with the Canadian public was not among the older habits associated with the Pearsonian era of Canadian foreign policy. A small group of politicians and officials acted with a great deal of autonomy from societal forces to pursue their concept of the national interest. Using their iron grip—even monopoly position—over foreign policy, this tightly knit cohort of state officials pushed 'to lead Canadian public opinion in the direction of new obligations' in terms of international affairs in the immediate postwar era.[20]

This milieu had a number of positive attractions. Conceptually, it allowed Canada to fit to a considerable extent the central premise or model of traditional realism, in that the Canadian state could be regarded as a unitary actor with a particular perspective on the national interest. Practically, it allowed the mobilization of the skills associated with this tradition of Canadian statecraft. This combination, in turn, depended on a number of other factors. One of these, as suggested by Peter Dobell, was that 'the national consensus in support of Canadian foreign policy which persisted until about the end of the 1950s resulted from the good fortune that policies which very directly promoted important national interests could be advocated and defended in terms which largely satisfied the altruistic instinct which has been so strongly ingrained in the Canadian approach to international politics.'[21] This consensus was reinforced, in turn, by the ingrained centrality of 'high' geo-security issues within public discourse.

The result of this set of circumstances was a long (and often treasured) moment of opportunity for the old Department of External Affairs. Between the time Mackenzie King left the political scene and the time Pierre Trudeau appeared, the 'External Type' reigned supreme. Held together by a uniformity of background, temperament and sense of purpose, the senior officials (or 'wise men') from External Affairs were instrumental in conditioning the style of Canadian diplomacy. Among the large caste of 'Ottawa Men,'[22] only the mandarins at the Department of Finance and the Bank of Canada could be said to be rivals as the Canadian equivalent of the best and brightest in the Anglo-American world. While some vigorous differences of view did exist among this foreign policy élite, their ability to work as an effective team was testimony to their common pattern of intellectual/policy socialization and inculcation of a formidable professional *esprit*.

### The Trudeau Challenge

The erosion of the External Types' position in the Trudeau period occurred because of a debilitating combination of situational and structural factors. Most significantly, when he became prime minister, Trudeau neither valued nor appreciated the established strengths of Canadian diplomats. The skills on which they built Canada's reputation abroad, and their own tight control over the foreign policy decision-making at home, were seen by Trudeau as no longer either appropriate or satisfactory. This negative perspective was, in part, influenced by the contemporary intellectual backlash against the profession of diplomacy itself. Inspired both by its failure to resolve the Vietnam crisis and its 'outmoded' character *vis-à-vis* technological/communications change, diplomacy was perceived by a wide variety of academics and media analysts as morally and practically bankrupt. In another of his many critical salvoes directed at established practices, James Eayrs led the critical charge. Parallelling his attack on the orthodox position of Canada's middle power role in the world, Eayrs questioned the corpus of accepted wisdom about the function of diplomacy in international affairs. Not content with charging diplomacy with 'moral turpitude' and 'inefficiency,' Eayrs described the practice of diplomacy as being in 'deliquescence' ('melting into nothingness, fading away into limbo') in a changing global environment.[23]

Whatever one thinks about the normative content (or longer-term accuracy) with respect to this disapprobation, this formidable critique played into Trudeau's own dissatisfaction about the performance of the Canadian foreign service. In short form, these complaints may be listed under three headings: the first of these was that the Canadian foreign service was poorly managed; the second was that the foreign service was unrepresentative; the third was that the foreign service was out of touch with reality, both in terms of its connection with the political/policy situation in Canada and in terms of its analysis of key events abroad.

On each of these counts, a jury evaluating the Canadian foreign service in the context of the late 1960s might have been tempted to deliver a verdict of guilty as charged. The traditional reliance by the DEA on a form of 'flying by the seat of your pants' behaviour stood as the complete opposite of the logical and predictable techniques Trudeau and his advisers (particularly Michael Pitfield) were determined to implement. The classic 'External' style was tactical, not strategical, geared to ensuring agility rather than to working to definitive guidelines on the rational management of foreign policy. The DEA had long prided itself on its ability to deal flexibly with external situations, due to the high quality and experience of its diplomatic personnel. As one key member of the 'Old External' cohort readily acknowledged, 'principle or theory' played little part in the success obtained by Canada as a mediator during the Pearson years. Pearson himself was said to have operated by getting 'into the middle of a mess or crisis and by some kind of intuition, [getting] himself out of it—and in the process, [helping] others out of the mess too.'[24]

Contributing further to this negative assessment by Trudeau was the relatively homogenous composition of the External establishment. Not only was the DEA disparaged by Trudeau for being 'outmoded' in terms of its administrative skills and techniques, it was held up as the quintessential anti-model of an organization out of touch with the diverse nature (and heightened politicization) of Canadian society. A bastion of 'English' (or more precisely, Anglo-Celt) unilingual élitism, the DEA had found room for only the most talented (and likeminded) individuals from other backgrounds. Not only did this narrow form hit a serious political nerve, given the place of bilingualism and biculturalism on Trudeau's immediate agenda, but it made the DEA the target for ongoing criticism concerning the need for sensitivity to multiculturalism, gender representation and other forms of diversity.

On top of this number of serious bureaucratic problems came a critical targeting of External's 'reactive rather than active concern with world events.'[25] DEA's traditional functional priorities ran counter to Trudeau's determination to alter the perception and salience of Canada's national interest. The role of the helpful fixer, in terms of 'high' issue areas, was seen as *passé* in a world where issues such as the defence of the environment and social justice were becoming increasingly prominent. These were areas that had occupied little of External's time and talent in the past. To some extent this neglect was by design. Many of these aforementioned 'low' issues were seen within DEA to 'be faintly grubby, not at all where the action was.' But this gap was widened by default in that 'All that energy expended on being Mr. International Nice Guy meant precious little over for being tough about emerging international problems that were beginning to affect Canadians directly.'[26]

### The Quebec Factor

Another significant challenge to the familiar ways of doing things underscored the closer intermeshing of domestic politics with foreign policy. This challenge came in the form of the intrusion by a wide array of internal institutional actors, the combined effect of which was to fragment the process of decision-making. The most dramatic—and pervasive—of these challenges was presented by the Canadian provinces. Propelled by the momentum of the Quiet Revolution and the outward-looking expression of Québécois nationalism, the struggle between Ottawa and Quebec became an intense site of conflict over legitimacy and power. Amid the wider dynamics of this struggle over legislative powers, 'domestic' issues spilled over into the 'international' arena. Quebec argued that in international relations, as in other areas of government, it should be able to proceed autonomously in matters falling within its own jurisdiction. Specifically, it claimed the power to negotiate and sign treaties within the limits of its constitutional rights.

Acting on the basis of these claims, Quebec actively pursued its own aims and interests in the global arena. As part of its wider project of state-building, Quebec built up an impressive set of institutional structures and administrative capacities to express its statecraft. Quebec established a delegation in Paris, which was not an embassy but which was given quasi-diplomatic status by the French authorities. Quebec obtained membership as a participating government in the Francophonie and L'Agence de Coopération culturelle et technique. Quebec built up a web of offices in the US and in other selected parts of the world. The staff of the Quebec Department of Intergovernmental Affairs rose to 450 by the early 1980s. Operating through this infrastructure, Quebec could conduct an extremely sophisticated and effective para-diplomacy, which included 'state' visits, extensive lobbying campaigns (most notably, the one directed at the British with respect to the patriation of the Canadian constitution),[27] as well as more routine endeavours involving culture, immigration and economic activity.

### The Challenge from the Provinces

Affixed to the Quebec factor was a more generalized provincial challenge. Fundamental differences existed between the federal government and a number of other provinces (apart from Quebec) over decision-making and the conduct of foreign economic policy. These differences led to a good deal of frustration and tension at the intergovernmental level. Prime Minister Trudeau, for example, could lecture the gathering at the February 1978 economic conference of first ministers on the constitutional limitations on provincial activity: 'We all surely agree that international trade is a federal responsibility.'[28] Notwithstanding the sense of rivalry, though, these federal–provincial differences must be distinguished from the struggle that persisted between Ottawa and Quebec. Rather than being concerned with the symbols of statehood, the other provinces' challenge was tied directly to the furtherance of material interests. The issues under debate on the broader intergovernmental plane did not concern the 'international independence' or even many of the nuances of the 'international personality' of these provinces; they centred on practical questions concerning effectiveness and equity and the regional distribution of benefits.

The Alberta government in particular put pressure on Ottawa to bolster its trade programs through improved market intelligence and analysis, more and better-trained commercial attachés and counsellors in Canadian missions abroad, and increased diversification in markets for its resources, agricultural products and petro-chemicals. Taking advantage of the room opened up by Quebec, Alberta tried to fill many of these gaps itself. Alberta's own administrative capacity was expanded. Internationally, Alberta pursued an autonomous (albeit selective) trade approach. Premier Peter Lougheed led well-publicized trade missions to Japan (1972), Europe (1975), the United States (1976), the Soviet Union and the Middle East (1977), and Hong Kong, China and Japan (1983). New offices abroad were created in Tokyo, Hong Kong, New York, Houston and Los Angeles. Concomitantly, Alberta demanded that the federal government open up the decision-making process to allow the provinces a more substantial say in the management of Canadian trade policy. During the Tokyo Round of GATT trade negotiations, which ran from September 1973 to April 1979, Alberta pushed to participate as a full and equal partner. When refused in this demand, Premier Lougheed externalized his campaign, visiting Geneva (where the negotiations were being conducted) and requesting and receiving briefings from the Canadian, US and European delegations.[29]

## The Externalization of 'Domestic' Government Departments

The second main source of institutional competition to the authority of the 'old' External Affairs came via the extension of bureaucratic politics. As an array of traditional 'domestic' departments moved into the international arena, turf battles over responsibility and influence predictably ensued. This type of behaviour was driven in large part by ambitious ministers eager to embellish their personal and departmental standing and power base. One case in point was Eugene Whelan at Agriculture Canada in the 1970s. Consistent with the wider dynamic of externalization, the focus of Agriculture Canada's activities took on an enhanced international dimension under Whelan. Whelan pushed for equal status with External Affairs at the 1974 Rome World Food Conference; surplus products, under the jurisdiction of marketing boards (particularly eggs and dairy products), were given a much higher profile in the Canadian aid package; and Agriculture Canada displayed a greater willingness to loan skilled personnel to agencies such as the International Development Research Centre (IDRC) for projects in developing countries. Whelan himself began to play a prominent role in the administrative activities of a number of international bodies, such as the World Food Program.

Another illustrative case may be seen in the heightened influence of the newly created (1970) Department of the Environment. Jack Davis, as the first of many activist ministers of the environment, took a number of high-profile initiatives at the United Nations Conference on the Human Environment of 1972, which clearly edged on to the DEA's turf. These initiatives included the proposal that the International Joint Commission, which the US and Canada used for the settlement of transboundary disputes (including environmental problems), be adopted as a model for dealing with environment disputes at the global level.

A third illustration emerged on energy matters, a policy domain where first Donald Macdonald (through the introduction of Petro-Canada) and later Marc Lalonde (through the promotion of the NEP) drove forward ambitious (and controversial) policies that left External in the dark.[30]

By the 1980s this pattern of intrusion into international matters by line departments, with all its competition and compartmentalization, was fully embedded. As one participant, who had been on the receiving end of these cross-pressures, stated: 'It is a problem. I can assure you that, when I was Minister of International Trade, there was constant poaching by other ministers into our jurisdiction.'[31]

### The DEA's Response to the Challenges

Under the accumulative weight of these various challenges, External Affairs was forced to go through an extensive period of rethinking and relearning. Although never triumphant in recapturing its privileged position over foreign policy, External has to be given credit for parlaying these challenges into opportunities to upgrade its skills and expand its interests into other fields. Jettisoning much of its familiar mode of operation, External through the 1970s and early 1980s bought into scientific management theory and the construct of a coherent context for Canadian foreign policy. While the DEA old guard could (with some solid justification) decry all of the paraphernalia or baggage that went along with the embrace of this technocratic model—with its expanded bureaucratic apparatus, its organizational charts, its mania for consultation and concern for cost–benefits evaluation—this administrative transformation allowed DEA to go on the offensive in terms of winning back its lost status and authority.

At the core of this strategy, as indicated by a senior official, was the extension of the DEA's 'co-ordinating and overview capacity' with respect to international trade.[32] That is to say, the aim was to redefine DEA's traditional 'lead' position over foreign policy. Tactically, the means chosen meant an ongoing process of reorganization in the machinery of government. An impetus towards consolidation in the trade issue-area under the authority of the DEA built up in the Trudeau period, culminating in the January 1982 reorganization that merged the Trade Commissioner Service and the trade promotion units of the Department of Industry, Trade and Commerce. This amalgamation of the 'old' DEA into a revised structure was designed to place 'a greater priority on trade objectives in the conduct of our international relations, give greater emphasis to the international marketing of resources and services, and strengthen Canada's ability to adapt to changing world economic conditions' and to 'integrate the department more effectively into the broader economic process in Ottawa.'[33]

The Quebec challenge cut two ways in terms of the foreign service's relearning process. In some ways, the advancing preoccupation with Quebec proved a distraction. From an immediate standpoint, much of Ottawa's counter-offensive against Quebec centred on questions of jurisdiction in international affairs. Another component was directed towards countering the Quebec claim that it represented 'le fait français' in Canada. These thrusts had some instrumental pay-offs on an equity basis, through the refocussing of development assistance to francophone countries. But they had a downside in terms of efficiency: the delivery of aid was often subordinated (as with the 1968 Gabon episode) to status issues, or to an ambitious (and costly) campaign to sell the image of Canada as a bilingual and bicultural country in the francophone world. Over the longer haul, the sensitive antenna developed by the federal government concerning constitutional proprieties acted as an inhibitor rather than as a source of creative statecraft. Ottawa, on matters of potential breakups in other federal states, defended the status quo. From the Biafra crisis in 1968–9 to the Baltic states and Ukraine in the late 1980s, the foreign service advised caution. Any move that could be interpreted as a positive signal, and hence validation to the nationalist aspirations of Quebec, was to be avoided.

In other ways, the Quebec challenge may be seen as contributing to an upgrade in Canada's diplomatic skills. The infusion of talented francophones into the DEA during the late 1960s and 1970s paid immediate dividends to the Canadian foreign service. Not only did this process prove beneficial in terms of improving the DEA's organizational image (and so opening the doors for a more inclusive process of recruitment generally), but this different cohort facilitated the shift towards dealing with issue-specific change in the global agenda. Previously neglected issues, including cultural diplomacy, received a higher priority. Over time, other pay-offs accumulated. As the external dimension of the Ottawa–Quebec struggle became defused by the 1980s, the way could be prepared for an attempt to move towards some more rational (and flexible) distribution of activities, such as immigration, on an issue-by-issue basis.

Political factors drove this process. The Mulroney government wanted to make a clear distinction between its expressed desire to be a reconciliator and the Trudeau hard-line image. This *rapprochement* was signalled by the effective end of controversy over representation at the francophone summit. This long-standing impasse was broken by allowing Quebec full membership at the summit. In the context of Canadian politics of the mid-1980s, a move along these lines represented an important gesture of depoliticization and goodwill. As one journalist suggested: 'Mulroney's political objective at the [francophone] conference was to demonstrate that he could get on with Quebec in a way that Pierre Trudeau, who always resisted the province's international aspirations, conspicuously could not do.'[34]

Instead of concentrating on the symbols of statehood, attention began turning towards the task of finding ways in which the rival sets of government could take care of a core set of responsibilities in a way that would still allow some degree of co-ordination between them. This tilt reflected the build-up of concern about an 'over-extension' of governmental activities. Although grounded in philosophical and ideological concerns about subsidiarity and the devolution of power down to local levels, the crux of these ideas/activities demonstrated the growing perception of fiscal realities.[35]

## The DEA's Response to the Changing World Scene

The third major set of challenges to the 'old' DEA emanated from the changing nature of the international agenda itself. The transition from Pearsonian to Trudeauvian statecraft did not constitute a complete break with the traditional Canadian priority on the 'high' policy agenda of war and peace. Considerable notice continued to be devoted (although with an altered orientation) to a host of military/security issues surrounding *inter alia* verification and the proliferation of chemical weapons and other armaments. But, in keeping with the redefinition of what constituted the national interest, the importance attached to economic and social policy rose appreciably. This alteration is evident in the lofty place Canada gave to the Law of the Sea (LOS). Low on the priority level in the 1950s, this dossier came to the fore of Canadian foreign policy in the 1970s. As the fine reserve of Canadian skill was redirected towards newer types of issues, some old wine was put in new bottles. As in the Pearson era, Canadian diplomacy chose to try to make progress by building coalitions and patiently tackling intricate technical (and increasingly, scientific and legal) issues. This blend of continuity and adaptation with regard to the practice of Canadian statecraft received fulsome paeans from the elder statesmen who were around to watch. In the words of John Holmes, Canada deserved cheers for its contribution: 'We've never done anything more effective or skilful than our contribution to the Law of the Sea. But it's not on television, so no one really knows about it.'[36]

In terms of the pattern of association, Canada set much store on working through the Group of 12 (also known as the 'good samaritans'), a loose assembly of like-minded countries including Austria, Denmark, Finland, Iceland, Ireland, the Netherlands, Norway, Sweden, Switzerland, Australia and New Zealand. At the same time, Canada tried to build bridges with the coastal states found among the developing countries.[37] As such, a foundation was laid for a different sort of mixed or cross-cutting coalition which went well beyond the informal contact with (mainly Commonwealth) countries such as India in the 1950s and 1960s. The amplification of Canada's technical skills was epitomized by the prominent role given to Allan Gotlieb, Alan Beesley and others within the LOS negotiations. Far from being the classic generalist favoured in the past by External Affairs, this new type of diplomat brought a good deal of specialized expertise to bear on the issue. Moreover, despite the custom of rotation within the foreign service, these experts were able to stay the course of the protracted negotiations. Beesley, for instance, was involved with the architecture of the 'global constitution of the oceans' through the LOS for over fourteen years.

The positive spillover effect of this activity on Canadian statecraft was enormous. The concerted diplomatic effort on the LOS contributed to a store of technical acumen, credibility and goodwill, and bureaucratic memory, which could be expended on analogous issues. When a Soviet satellite fell in the Northwest Territories in the late 1970s, Canada could quickly swing into action to apply its diplomatic skills in the specialized area of space law. Taking care of 'routine' issues meant that Canada was ready to take a leadership role when an unusual situation occurred. Once again, a clear line could be drawn between the older and newer expressions of Canadian constructive internationalism. To knowledgeable observers, initiatives along these lines 'are as important as any Canadian contribution to international organizations in the 1940s and 1950s.'[38]

The DEA buttressed its revised claims for bureaucratic leadership through a serious drive to raise its game in terms of economic expertise and capacity. As the role and visibility of the trade policy side of the 'new' DEA were elevated, so were the rewards provided to a core group of responsible officials. In some instances this shift in emphasis was accomplished by an infusion of talent with specialist skills from other areas of government. Robert Johnstone, who moved to become the under-secretary in charge of economics policy at DEA, after a varied career as executive director of the Anti-Inflation Board, an adviser to the Bank of Canada, and deputy minister of industry, trade and commerce, may be categorized as one of this new breed of state officials. So may Sylvia Ostry, a former head of the Economic Council of Canada and chief economist at the OECD, who was brought in as deputy minister for international trade and G-7 sherpa at the end of 1983. The commonplace practice, though, was to tap into these sorts of specialist skills within the ranks of the newly integrated DEA. Neither of these tendencies represented a substantial departure in itself. Industry, Trade and Commerce (together with other elements of the national bureaucracy) had long had a presence in overseas posts and in the exercise of power in decision-making.

What was different was the degree of visibility accorded to the trade side of DEA, and the extent of its influence. Through the integrated foreign service, an assertive cohort of state officials from this stream worked hard to make foreign policy and trade policy one and the same.

The benefits of this activity were obvious, both in providing DEA with greater resources and muscle in inter-bureaucratic terms, and in enhancing it with a greater sensitivity and capability for dealing with the issues that loomed so large on the international agenda. But the additional complexities placed on politics and policy were as obvious as the aforementioned benefits. As they contributed to the DEA's organizational capacity, this ascendant wave of trade hands posed a very different set of challenges to the established ways of doing things. To some extent, the resultant tensions were based on status and turf. Trade specialists not only held more influence in Ottawa, they increasingly held high-profile ambassadorial posts abroad (as witnessed most clearly by the position of Ken Taylor, made famous in the so-called 1980 'Iran caper' involving the rescue of American diplomatic personnel). These tensions, however, were intensified by an important policy dimension.[39]

## The Challenge of Politicization

Part and parcel with these ongoing situational and institutional challenges to the foreign-policy-making process, the established character of Canadian statecraft was modified by the forces of politicization in the 1970s and 1980s. The notion that foreign policy had existed in a completely depoliticized state should be quickly disposed of at the outset. One need only think of the smooth transition of Lester Pearson from diplomat and External mandarin to secretary of state for external affairs, or the effortless shift by Mitchell Sharp from senior trade bureaucrat into a variety of Cabinet positions, including external affairs minister from 1968 to 1974. Conservative politicians made no attempt to hide the fact that they saw the Canadian foreign service as a nest for Liberals.

This caveat, at the same time, should not detract from the fact that the scope and intensity of this pressure towards politicization swelled substantially during both the Trudeau and Mulroney periods. Not only was the DEA devalued and discredited for not having the right sort of skills throughout the 1970s and 1980s, but the ability of the foreign service to rebound from its reduced circumstances was compromised by the presence of alternative—and well-connected—sources of foreign policy advice.

### *The Rise of the PMO and PCO*

The first of these pressures was inextricably intertwined with the rise of a number of powerful central agencies, most notably the Prime Minister's Office (PMO) and the Privy Council Office (PCO). This system of central agencies posed a structural threat to the primacy of DEA over foreign policy, as the process of decision-making on key issues took on a concentrated flavour. Originally, this design coincided with Trudeau's search for rationality. This search translated into considerable clout for Michael Pitfield, the main architect of this model of policymaking, who served as the clerk of the Privy Council from 1975 to 1979 and again in the early 1980s. As it developed, though, other types of pay-offs kicked in. By building an apparatus on a politicized basis, the ability of the prime minister to conduct foreign policy on his own, without the necessity of any close reference to the DEA, was considerably enhanced. This was important to Trudeau in principle. Indeed, it contributed to his ability both to pursue specific initiatives or 'circuit diplomacy,' and to act generally as his own foreign minister (with a rapid rotation of secretaries of state for external affairs).[40] The incentive for Mulroney to maintain this approach was reinforced both by his long-standing rivalry with Joe Clark, who served as secretary of state for external affairs from 1984 to 1991, and by the controversial nature of several of the initiatives he wanted to advance while in office, in particular the Canada–US free trade deal.

A cluster of individuals who had grown impatient with the established ways of doing things within the DEA sought to put their stamp on foreign policy making. Ivan Head, a former law professor and DEA official, operated out of the PMO as the central conduit between DEA and the prime minister between 1970 and 1978. Publicly identified as a critic of the orthodox style of Canadian foreign policy, Head's hold on the position as Trudeau's personal adviser (Canada's Kissinger, as he was often referred to) helped maintain something akin to a siege mentality within DEA.

A partial truce was only possible with the arrival of Allan Gotlieb. A lawyer by training, Gotlieb had one foot on the same sort of ladder as Head had climbed. In similar fashion to Head, Gotlieb had been a member of the informal advisory group on constitutional questions (including the role of Quebec on international matters) that Trudeau had set up in 1966 when he was justice minister. Like Head, Gotlieb had become frustrated with the traditional mode of operation of the DEA. Indeed, in the 1970s he spent time diversifying his policy interests and managerial skills by moving over to the Department of Communications as deputy minister. Although never establishing quite the same close personal relationship with Trudeau, Gotlieb filled much of the vacuum vacated by Head as the prime minister's foreign policy counsellor and point man (serving, for example, as Trudeau's sherpa for the 1981 Montebello G-7 summit). Unlike Head, though, Gotlieb kept his other foot firmly entrenched in External Affairs. His main administrative objective, from the time he returned as under-secretary of state for external affairs, was to reshape DEA as a central agency in its own right. He was determined both to re-establish the overarching position of DEA in the foreign-policy-making process and to provide the department with both the rationale and the material wherewithal to achieve this goal.

The relative equipoise in this competitive process achieved at the end of the

Trudeau period was slanted once again in favour of the PMO/PCO during the Mulroney years. While allowing Clark's department considerable leeway in terms of routine matters, Mulroney 'intensified the institutionalization of a source of prime ministerial advice on foreign policy.'[41] If less by conscious design than Trudeau's search for rational management,[42] this move back towards a concentrated approach made a decided impact on the making of Canadian foreign policy. Individuals identified as advocates of a closer institutional relationship with the US were placed in core positions of responsibility. Of these, Derek Burney stands out as the pivotal figure. Following in the footsteps of Head and Gotlieb, Burney established himself securely as Mulroney's chief foreign policy adviser. Formalizing his position of power after his success (when associate under-secretary at DEA) in orchestrating the March 1985 Shamrock Summit between Mulroney and Reagan, and getting the FTA negotiations off the ground, Burney became the prime minister's chief of staff in the spring of 1987. Throughout this time span, the channelling of politically sensitive questions through the PMO/PCO further 'contributed to the distancing of the Prime Minister from the external affairs portfolio.'[43]

Given Mulroney's own 'mostly inchoate' perspective on foreign policy matters[44] and his preference for brokerage politics,[45] this concentrated system proved highly effective in providing a strategic core to policymaking. Consistent with his instincts as both a labour negotiator and a political deal-maker, the key question for Mulroney was not whether a policy was harmonious in terms of its various components but the extent to which a policy was feasible. He possessed charm and cunning, but little vision. While willing to take risks, he depended on others for creative thinking. Although many, of course, disagreed with how and why the FTA agreement was implemented, few could reserve respect for the vigour and determination with which this initiative was pushed forward.

The downside of this concentrated system came to the fore in the latter stages of Mulroney's government. Running out of steam, with respect to both policy ideas and popular credibility, the control of the foreign policy process by the PMO/PCO turned from a strategic strength to a management deficit. The combination of an erosion of skill level with a sharpened sense of distrust pervading this system surfaced most clearly in two episodes picked up by the media for tighter scrutiny.

The first of these episodes was the so-called al-Mashat affair, the rather bizarre case of the former Iraqi ambassador to the US *circa* the Gulf War who was accepted on a fast track as a landed immigrant to Canada. The significance of this episode for a discussion of politicization within the foreign-policy-making process is the heavy-handed manner in which the PCO handled it. In what amounted to a 'star chamber' environment, a number of senior DEA officials were publicly blamed for not alerting the minister of external affairs to the details of this case. The fact that one of these officials was a nephew of the then Liberal opposition leader—Raymond Chrétien, a career foreign service officer and associate undersecretary of state for external affairs, who was coerced to sign a 'confession'—not surprisingly added to the charged and fearful atmosphere concerning partisanship and scapegoating.[46]

A second episode, of the same type, surrounded the apparent interference of the PMO in the activities of Canada's representative to the European Bank for Reconstruction and Development—interference that eventually led to the representative's premature recall from the post. Adding heat to this story, Stevie Cameron's best-selling exposé *On The Take: Crime, Corruption and Greed in the Mulroney Years* devoted a chapter to this episode.[47]

### *The Increasing Influence of Outside Experts*

Another sign of politicization came out in the scope of penetration by outside experts in the foreign-policy-making process. The phenomenon of bringing in outside experts on specialized tasks was not unknown during the Pearson era. One can think of an individual such as John Humphrey, from the Faculty of Law at McGill University, who (as a member of the Canadian delegation at the 1945 San Francisco Conference) was instrumental in founding the UN Division of Human Rights. Yet, in this earlier period, the exhibition of Canadian talent on an individual basis was for the most part directed outwards towards the constellation of international organizations, rather than inwards, to the domestic process. This type of UN work has brought with it a considerable amount of recognition and credit for both the individuals involved and for Canada. This is true of the United Nations Relief and Rehabilitation Administration (UNRRA) and the Food and Agriculture Organization (FAO), where the preparatory endeavours of Lester Pearson and other Canadian diplomats were so crucial. It is also true of the World Health Organization, where a Canadian, Brock Chisholm, became the founding director-general. Through the 1950s and beyond, this profile continued in the form of a host of similar activities through the High Commissioner for Refugees (UNHCR), the United Nations Children's Emergency Fund (UNICEF) and other specialized agencies.[48]

Within both the DEA and other central agencies, a pattern of ins and outers took firm hold in the Trudeau period. As with the accelerated movement of state officials between governmental departments and agencies, much of the impetus for this phenomenon derived from the highly innovative (and competitive) dynamic within the foreign policy process at the time. As the parameters of policy debate expanded, opportunities opened up for talented and energetic individuals to make an impact. Arguably the best-known illustration of this phenomenon in operation has been the multidimensional career of Maurice Strong. Prior to his high-profile work as secretary general of the 1972 UN Conference on the Human Environment and the 1992 Conference on Environment and Development (UNCED), Strong had moved from a successful career in the private sector to become the first head of the Canadian

International Development Agency (CIDA). More representative, perhaps, of the career path of the ins and outers cohort is someone like Margaret Catley-Carlson, who has moved between UNICEF and heading up CIDA and the World Population Fund.

As with the overall construct of politicization, the involvement of this type of ins and outers in the expression of Canadian foreign policy reached a crescendo during the Mulroney period. In some cases, the opening up of the process to outsiders brought with it positive rewards. The appointment of Stephen Lewis (the former leader of the Ontario New Democratic Party) as Canada's permanent representative to the UN deserves mention in this respect, especially for his work on human rights and the Program for Action for African Economic Recovery and Development. So too does the work of a large cohort of individuals involved on the women's rights issue. At the UN Decade of Women's Conference in Nairobi in July 1985, this cohort of 'femocrats' played a crucial part in brokering a breakthrough in the procedural log-jam (between the Reagan administration in the US and the Soviet Union and its allies) in which the conference had become stuck. One astute observer of this episode, who had been a crucial insider in the Trudeau era, allowed that these efforts to secure a compromise solution were in the best tradition of Canadian statecraft: 'Lester Pearson would have been proud.'[49]

The downside was that, instead of facilitating a coherent context for foreign policy making, this reliance on insiders/outsiders had the potential of giving off an impression of clutter and confusion. The assignment of a special adviser may be good politics, in that it raises the profile of the selected issue and signals that the government is trying to do something about it. But administratively, the results were often counter-productive, in that the appointment often sparked an open turf war over personnel and jurisdiction. A prime illustration was the rivalry between Sylvia Ostry, the ambassador for multilateral trade negotiations and G-7 sherpa, and Pat Carney, the minister for international trade; a situation made worse in the context of the Canada–US free trade negotiations because of the additional tensions between Simon Reisman and Carney (whom Reisman technically reported to) and Reisman and Ostry (who, as ambassador for multi-lateral trade negotiations, was part of the Trade Negotiations Office team but reported to the minister for international trade). Another case, which brought out similar sorts of problems, centred on the appointment of Arthur Campeau as Prime Minister Mulroney's special representative for the Rio UN Conference on Environment and Development (or Earth Summit). Although clearly attractive as a signalling device in terms of public opinion,[50] this appointment added another ingredient to an already complicated situation, for in the run-up to the Rio Conference a wide array of other actors were trying to refine their roles. These actors included an EAITC UNCED unit task force; a special adviser on the environment to the secretary of state for external affairs; and the national secretariat for UNCED in Environment Canada.

The hybrid case that appeared via the establishment of the Trade Negotiations Office (TNO) reveals the positive and negative effects of this insider/outsider process. As played out against the wider spectrum of politics and policy, the experience of the TNO revealed the ability of the national bureaucracy to mobilize under select conditions. By having Simon Reisman head it up, the TNO was able to tap into a wealth of institutional and negotiating experience extending from the 'creation' of the post-1945 international economic institutional framework through to the 1965 Canada–US Auto Pact and beyond. By giving Reisman *carte blanche* to pick the best and brightest of the federal public servants, an élite team could be created. As Doern and Tomlin detail: 'The chief negotiator created TNO in his own image, choosing bright and aggressive people who were convinced of their ability to take on the Americans and beat them with superior organization and skills.'[51]

This array of talent and resources, together with a generously broad negotiating mandate, had its practical organizational benefits. With Reisman refusing to be answerable to anyone except the prime minister and the Cabinet,[52] the TNO could avoid much of the convoluted interdepartmental consultative process so pervasive in Ottawa. This relative autonomy, however, also had its pitfalls. By pushing other departments (including the Department of Finance) out of the process, the pressure to deliver results was put squarely on Reisman and his team. With its volatile combination of high stakes, the delay tactics used by the Americans and the unabashed desire by Reisman to get a big bold deal, this pressure proved in the end to be detrimental to a successful outcome. As the talks bogged down amidst a great deal of personal animosity between Reisman and his American counterpart, the TNO ultimately lost its tight hold on the process to the PMO (or more precisely, Derek Burney) and the ministers for international trade and finance. Put another way, the method of managing (or even rescuing!) the negotiations reverted from the unique to the ordinary.

## The Societal Challenge

A third set of challenges to traditional Canadian statecraft derives from the increasingly important role of societal forces in policymaking. Since the late 1960s, the model of a centralized DEA, with formidable policy capabilities due to its own set of skills and the intrinsic importance of its mandate, had become thoroughly eroded. The 'fortress was besieged,' to use Stairs's apt phrase,[53] not only because of the intrusion of the array of state actors into the foreign policy domain; non-state actors, in the form of societal forces generally and non-governmental organizations more specifically, also penetrated this sphere of activity in a variety of ways.[54]

The closed nature of Canadian foreign policy in the Pearson years was most apparent in geopolitical issues such as Canada's participation in NATO and the Korean War.[55] Similar tendencies were evident in 'low' issues as well. In the multilateral trade issue-area, for example, Canadian commercial diplomats remained relatively immune from pressure by domestic economic groups over the formative meetings *vis-à-vis* the GATT in the late 1940s and early 1950s.[56] Although the business community was briefed formally (over time, through the interdepartmental Canadian Trade and Tariffs Committee, the Canadian Business Group on Multilateral Trade Negotiations and the Canadian Business and Industry International Advisory Committee) and informally to allow them to 'get the drift' of the talks, an extensive veil of secrecy was wrapped around the details. Even at the final stages of the negotiations on specific issues such as the new customs valuation and procurement codes, industry associations and firms as well as the provincial governments were kept at the margins.[57]

By the 1980s and 1990s societal interests had become a more integral component of the foreign-policy-making process. In general terms, this tendency is reflected in recent parliamentary reports on foreign policy. The Hockin–Simard Report on Canadian foreign policy stated in the mid-1980s: 'On some issues it is our impression that the public has become a major source of information and even policy guidance.'[58] The recent report of the Special Joint Committee Reviewing Canadian Foreign Policy has gone even further in this direction, elaborating on the 'feature of...growing democratization' in Canadian foreign policy: 'The range of foreign policy actors has expanded...to include private sector organizations, academic and professional institutions and NGOs, and they are contributing increasingly to both policy development and program delivery.'[59]

It needs to be stressed here that the influence of Canadian society has not been felt to the same degree right across the board. The ability of societal groups to shape Canadian diplomacy appears to span a continuum based largely on the character of the individual issue-areas involved. The influence of societal group pressure lagged behind in the defence/security area in comparison with the economic or social agendas. Canadian activity on geo-security issues, right up to the end of the Cold War, remained almost the complete monopoly of the state, with the Canadian government willing and able to go against the claims of vocal domestic interests to maintain credibility with its NATO alliance partners. As the deputy minister for foreign policy in DEA bluntly put it in 1983 during the controversy over cruise missile testing: '[The] pragmatism of a middle power' and the 'realism of an Alliance member' dictated that there 'will be times when government exercises its leadership somewhat ahead of public opinion.'[60] During the Mulroney period, Canada voted at the UN against a nuclear freeze proposal notwithstanding an upsurge of popular sentiment in favour of such a freeze. Significantly, both Canada's disarmament ambassador, Douglas Roche, and Stephen Lewis, Mulroney's first choice of UN ambassador, were forceful advocates of a more 'open' approach to policymaking. Roche for instance argued forcefully that: 'Too often, the conduct of international relations is considered only in terms of relations between heads of state or between officials.... We rarely talk about the role of people in the conduct of international relations. People, after all, make up the body politic. While a government may articulate the collective expression of the public mood, there can and must be a role for individuals—the critical human dimension—on the international scene.'[61]

As will be examined in a subsequent chapter, this closed condition could not last. Prompted by the collapse of the Soviet Union and of the bipolarity system, a dualistic defence/security debate has opened up in Canada as in other parts of the world. Although the narrower defence debate has continued to lag (as a relatively closed affair), within this new and all-encompassing security debate a marked element of catch-up has been taking place with respect to the extent of societal group participation. Notwithstanding some formidable obstacles, this agenda presents abundant opportunities for a new form of multifaceted and multilayered activity on at least a segmented basis.[62]

### The Trade Agenda

To a much greater and consistent extent than with the security agenda, the pattern of opening up decision making to allow the substantive input of societal groups has emerged in the economic agenda generally and the trade agenda more specifically. This development was to a large extent externally driven. As Canada in the 1980s entered into a new and delicate phase of negotiations on both the multilateral and bilateral fronts, an infusion of legitimacy and credibility was required. A closer domestic state–societal relationship, in which business groups were allowed access to policymaking on an institutional basis, facilitated this approach. To bargain effectively in the international arena, as much agreement as possible on the substance of the domestic 'game plan' was necessary.

A number of subsidiary benefits also ensued from this integrated process. The push towards a formalized system of access was perceived as being instrumental in building a strong client base for the Mulroney government's trade initiatives. Politically, this process was helpful in two different ways. Symbolically, it helped ease the impression of the 'two solitudes' built up between government and the business community during the Trudeau years.[63] Instrumentally, it did much to counter the activities of those societal groups opposed to trade liberalization; by mobilizing the supporters of domestic adjustment, the resisters to reform could be overwhelmed.[64]

The move to establish a closer relationship with business groups on the bilateral trade issue started in the agenda-setting stage.[65] Sparked by the report in September 1985 of the Royal Commission on the Economic Union and Development Prospects for Canada (the Macdonald Commission), which called for a 'leap of faith' towards Canada–US free trade, a permanent advisory committee headed by the former chair of Northern Telecom, Walter Light, was set up. The appointees to this International Trade Advisory Committee (ITAC) were to report to the international trade minister, but were also expected to provide Reisman and the TNO with the views of the private sector. To give more specific advice, fifteen sectoral advisory groups on international trade (SAGITs) were also appointed. To an experienced negotiator like Reisman, the value of this system was offset by its clutter. Indeed, he is said to have expressed 'nostalgia' for the simplicity 'for the old days' in which 'the consultation process was very simple.' 'In the new era of negotiations,' Reisman stated that he was faced with 'many different groups' whose claims had to be given 'equal time.'[66]

This backward-looking attitude, nonetheless, should not detract from the significance of the integrated system. As one overview of the FTA negotiations depicts, the SAGITs not only gave the TNO 'some crucial insights into key business sectors, but also expressed the symbiotic relationship that had grown up between the free trade negotiators and Canadian business.'[67] If arguably the fullest expression of this relationship, the foundations of the relationship went much deeper than this form of privileged access and consultation. Key state officials moved to engage representatives at the apex of the Canadian business community. Most significantly, a task force in External Affairs under Derek Burney began its trade policy review in 1982 with a number of meetings with business leaders (and provincial governments). Key components of the Canadian business community, for their part, signalled their conversion to the free trade agenda. Out in front in terms of its firm belief that 'Canada must get the Canada–US relationship right' was the Business Council on National Issues, an organization made up of the major corporations operating in Canada, represented by their CEOs. Moving in the same direction came the long-standing opponent to this type of commitment, the Canadian Manufacturers' Association.[68]

A parallel system, designed to enhance access and consultation, developed on the multilateral trade agenda. In terms of state–societal interaction, the key elements of this integrated structure included the International Trade Advisory Committee (containing selected members of the business community) and an analogous set of SAGITs. The complexity of this system may be witnessed by reference to the agricultural domain, in which the mix of First Ministers Conferences, the agriculture ministers' meetings, the Continuing Committee on Trade Negotiations, MTN–Agriculture Trade (which held regular meetings on the Canada–US bilateral negotiations as well as the multilateral negotiations) and the Federal–Provincial Agriculture Trade Policy Committee allowed a continuous flow of policy input from the provinces.[69]

### The Social Agenda and the Role of NGOs

The contrast between the closed-off system found in the Pearsonian years and the opening up of the decision-making process in more recent years is also evident in the area of the social agenda, encompassing the areas of human rights, social justice and the environment. To a large extent this process has been limited to an agenda-setting role—with the focus on information exchange and an alternative form of discourse. In some cases a high-profile campaign by non-state actors, backed by intense media coverage, has been able to push an issue on to centre stage of the policy agenda. This type of societal influence may be illustrated by the mobilization of established NGOs, and an ad hoc grass roots movement, during the time of the food 'shocks' of the early 1970s. In particular, this push from non-state sources was credited with helping raise the level of Canada's food aid contribution at the 1974 UN/FAO Rome Food Conference.[70] In an even more dramatic fashion, the nature of the Canadian government's response to the Ethiopian famine crisis of 1984–5 was altered and magnified by the sheer level and intensity of the public response to that event. As Joe Clark explicitly acknowledged, the government moved from a position of relative passivity to one of accelerated activism on this issue less from a sense of Canada's national interest than from a sense of the will of the people: 'Our job, it seems to me, is to set in place some mechanism that will make effective the desire of individual Canadians to help the millions of starving people.'[71]

In other cases Canadian NGOs have become interactive and integrated in the policy process itself.[72] The episode that epitomizes this trend is the activity surrounding the 1992 Rio UNCED. In order to facilitate and co-ordinate the role of NGOs in the lead-up to the Rio Conference, the Canadian Participatory Committee for UNCED (CPCU) was formed in the fall of 1990. The creation of the CPCU presented new opportunities as well as new challenges for Canadian societal groups. The opportunities came with the heightened standing accorded to the CPCU's members as insiders in terms of the negotiations. Beginning with the writing of a national report, and continuing to and beyond the Preparatory Committees for Rio, the CPCU became an integral part of the Canadian delegation. Five representatives from NGOs contained under the CPCU umbrella served on the official Canadian delegation.[73]

Still, this integrative process did not incorporate the entire constellation of the NGO environmental community. The divisions that existed in the 'green' movement were vividly demonstrated in the response of specific groups to the establishment of the CPCU. A number of key environment groups, most notably Greenpeace, declined to directly participate in the CPCU at all. Suspicious of the embrace of national governments, and the representation given to the business community in the Canadian delegation (especially the representation of the Council of Forest Industries of BC, the Canadian Pulp and Paper Association and the Fisheries Council of Canada), these groups preferred to stay at arm's length from the negotiating process. Other environmental groups, such as the Friends of the Earth (FOE), adopted a more ambiguous approach. Initially a member of the CPCU, the FOE became increasingly disenchanted with the policy-making process and backed out. As at the 1972 Stockholm Conference, these critical voices found an institutional outlet at Rio in the form of the parallel NGO conference—termed the Global Forum.

Furthermore, the groups that did join the CPCU and took an active part were highly diverse in their organizational make-up and goals. On one side there were various components of the environmental movement, such as the Canadian Environmental Law Association, the Sierra Club, Pollution Probe and Cultural Survival Canada. On the other side there were the NGOs with broader mandates, including the Canadian Council for International Cooperation (a coalition of 130 development NGOs in Canada), the United Nations Association in Canada, indigenous organizations (most actively the Native Council of Canada and the Inuit Circumpolar Conference), youth groups (through the Canadian Youth Working Group on Environment and Development) and women's organizations (Women and Environmental Education and Development). The diversity of groups represented made it extremely difficult for the CPCU to formulate and implement a systematic programme.

Despite the existence of all these problems, the integration of this broad array of NGOs into Canadian environmental diplomacy had a real impact on the workings of Canadian statecraft. To a considerable extent this impact was of a symbolic nature. Prompted by the work of the NGOs in the CPCU, Canadian diplomacy paid special attention to the multitude of legal and institutional questions surrounding the drafting of the Earth Charter (later named the Rio Declaration) as a non-binding declaration of principles. In terms of a comprehensive action plan, a concerted push was made by NGOs (in dialogue with their communities) to strengthen the Canadian commitment to Agenda 21 as a 'visionary document.' In this way these activist societal groups succeeded in keeping some highly sensitive issues such as gender concerns and the rights of indigenous peoples visible on the negotiating agenda. Even opposition members of parliament, who had been almost entirely left out of the preparatory process, conceded that NGOs 'actually may have changed the minds of the government delegation.'[74]

The NGOs also supplemented Canadian official activities at the Rio Conference in a tangible fashion. The NGOs boosted the technical skills of the Canadian delegation in a variety of ways. Throughout the UNCED negotiations, the groups within the CPCU provided not only alternative sources of information but expertise in terms of language of texts. As the national co-ordinator of the CPCU told the Parliamentary Standing Committee on the Environment in May 1992: 'I think the point has been made over and over again to NGOs, both formally and informally, that there are various lacunae, various gaps, within the technical dialogue, and it is felt that the technical expertise within the NGO community can be extremely productive.'[75]

It is important to note, furthermore, that the integrative pattern achieved in the Rio Conference was important not only in issue-specific terms but also as a model for activities on a broader plane. From a functional viewpoint there is abundant evidence of a spillover effect from Rio on to other UN conferences. One excellent example of this spillover could be witnessed in the process developed for the 1993 Vienna World Conference on Human Rights. Another involved the 1994 International Conference on Population and Development held in Cairo. As in the case of the 1992 Rio Conference, co-ordinating instruments for NGO participation in these conferences were put into operation. In the case of the Vienna Conference, NGO activity was mobilized primarily through the Human Rights Centre situated at the University of Ottawa, while in the case of Cairo, NGO activity was channelled through the Canadian Advisory Council for the International Conference on Population and Development. Through these instruments Canadian NGO activity was focussed on the process of negotiation and debate that took place during the Preparatory Commissions and the Vienna and Cairo conferences themselves. Although the parallel forums continued to attract a high level of support at these conferences, the locus of attention of a wide number of societal groups shifted in degree towards the official conference. While educational/experiential activity and transnational networking remained valuable for the Canadian NGOs through these alternative venues, the opportunity to make a difference in terms of decision-making had an instrumental effect in reshaping the nature of their participation.

Societal pressure played a part in pushing this integrative process. As one editorial from a Canadian newspaper stated, after the release in 1986 of the Mulroney government's Green Paper on Canada's International Relations: 'Canadians are knocking on the door of this country's foreign policy with more than messages to deliver: they want in.'[76] But unlike the activity centred on agenda-setting, this type of pressure was not the major motivating force for opening up the process of policymaking. The government, for its own part, tried to pull non-state actors into a closer sort of relationship. As on the trade agenda, this dynamic is wrapped up with questions both of legitimacy and of technical skill;[77] for the Canadian government, like many other governments, recognized the need to negotiate and bargain with their publics (including the components of the so-called counter-consensus)[78] in a more direct and comprehensive fashion. On top of this, important technical and administrative reasons existed for trying to draw societal groups more deeply into the decision-making process. One common feature found among NGOs has been an expanded repertoire and focus on specialized skills. Some groups have worked to perfect their monitoring, witnessing and interlocutory skills (for example, Amnesty International, Asia Watch and other organizations in terms of the monitoring of human rights violations), while others have expanded the range and sophistication of their legal competence.

Giving added weight to these tendencies has been the strong bureaucratic impetus for integrating societal groups more closely into the policy-making process. As Stairs suggested in a seminal article on the domestication of Canadian foreign policy, competing bureaucratic actors 'exploit the opinions of their respective constituencies as a source of leverage in the policy process.'[79] An expanded and strengthened client base provides a useful tool in administrative 'turf' conflicts. This point had even greater relevance given the context of the ongoing, intense and multidimensional bureaucratic competition in which this adaptive approach took place.

### The 'Democratization' of Canadian Foreign Policy?

It was one thing, though, to move towards an integrative approach towards societal participation on a segmented basis. It was quite another to implant a comprehensive system based on the premise of the 'democratization' of Canadian foreign policy. Some considerable momentum was generated towards this latter goal by the publication of the Liberal 'Red Book'[80] and the *Liberal Foreign Policy Handbook*,[81] both of which raised this 'democratizing' notion to the status of organizing principle. Once established in office, moreover, the Liberal government tried to communicate its continuing commitment to this ambitious objective via the establishment of two special joint parliamentary committees (with wide-ranging mandates to hold public hearings) and the staging of a 'National Forum' on Canada's International Relations in March 1994.

The innovative design of these measures stands out. An extensive dialogue about Canadian foreign policy was conducted through the channel of the parliamentary hearings. The massed voices of Canadian NGOs were heard in all their diversity. A telling piece of evidence concerning the willingness of the Canadian government to listen to this activist (and often highly critical) component of civic society may be found in a comparison of the NGO presentations before the Standing Committee on External Affairs and National Defence in 1970–71, on Foreign Policy for Canadians, and the numbers that appeared before the Special Joint Committee of the Senate and of the House of Commons, Reviewing Canadian Foreign Policy, in 1994. Both were major overviews of Canadian foreign policy, but in 1970–71 only twenty-nine NGOs submitted briefs to the committee; in 1994, 277 did, representing over half of the total. Another sign of this same trend was the generous space given to NGO representatives at the 1994 National Forum.

However, the impact of these new features should not be exaggerated. In some ways the Liberals were willing to take a very different path in pursuit of a new direction in foreign policy making; in other ways the Chrétien government simply consolidated familiar habits from the past. While opening up machinery for consultation in an unprecedented fashion, the impact of these features in actual policy terms—or even in terms of more systemic procedural changes—has been uneven. The synoptical impression one gets is that of a government trying to recalibrate its foreign policy on the basis of its own evolving calculus of a hierarchy of interests and capabilities.

One sign of the resilience of ingrained habits comes out in a brief review of the more recent changes in the bureaucratic machinery of Canadian foreign policy. These changes include a further renaming of the Canadian foreign service in

November 1993, to the Department of Foreign Affairs and International Trade. The evolutionary structure of this organization is far from complete. Even within a framework of ongoing reform, though, questions remain about the effective management of this domain. These questions centre on co-ordination issues, both vertically (DFAIT has remained a highly centralized organization, with senior officials reporting directly to the deputy minister of foreign affairs and deputy minister for international trade) and horizontally (with the separate elements within the integrated structure—political and economic, and regional and issue-specific—working in parallel rather than in tandem). What has been transformed, as a result of all the challenges applied over the past two decades, has been the centrality given to the delivery of programs. This concern with its 'clientele' emerges most clearly in the emphasis given to business/trade development, the results of which have been felt directly (reducing direct costs, introducing more sophisticated accounting practices, etc.) and indirectly (in recruitment, with greater emphasis on 'practical' skills, including fluency in targeted languages) on the corporate culture and practices of the Canadian foreign service.

In a paradoxical way the position of DFAIT may actually be strengthened by the constricted fiscal climate. DFAIT is facing serious budgetary reductions, but many other government departments and agencies (including the Department of National Defence and CIDA) have been cut more deeply. The widening international agenda (and concern about their own organizational status) will continue to encourage DND and CIDA to be concerned about foreign affairs, but limited resources may force them to rely more on DFAIT as the 'lead' agency. This reinvigoration of the 'professional' foreign service may be reinforced as well by the continued preoccupation of the other central agencies within government (including the PMO and PCO) on the 'national unity' and 'fiscal constraint' dossiers.

Some of the familiar habits may be reinforced still further by evidence of a backlash against the extensive participation of NGOs in the foreign-policy-making process. 'Democratization,' as it has been implemented through the hearings of the Special Joint Committee and the 1994 National Forum, has not moved ahead in a smooth, unidirectional fashion. For one thing, the marked increase in participation from activist societal groups has been offset by an apparent decline in the willingness of business groups to engage in public consultation (with all the attendant risks of exposing their views to criticism). Relatively few members of the business community either appeared before the Joint Committee or attended the first National Forum.[82] For another thing, the representative nature of the participating NGOs has been called into question. Not only the Reform Party but a number of academics and journalists have asked whether these groups have credibility in 'speaking for ordinary Canadians.'[83] Finally, frustrations developed at the governmental level about the capacity of this 'open' system to deliver precise proposals. In terms of intensity, many NGOs continued to operate in an adversarial mode (viewing government as the problem rather than the solution). In terms of form, the degree of consensus between NGOs was curtailed both by philosophical differences and by organizational maintenance issues.[84] In terms of scope, the NGOs were not inclined to accept the premise that Canada should in any way limit its activities in international affairs.[85]

Against this background, it is not surprising that there are several signs of a recalibration of this pattern of consultation on Canada's international relations. By the time the second National Forum was held, in September 1995, representation tilted back towards non-NGOs, with a heavier emphasis on the inclusion of members of the business community and foreign policy experts from academia and other professions.[86] A contraction of the 'democratization' process was also signalled by a number of other institutional changes. Rather than putting into place the ambitious proposal of a new mechanism for 'foreign policy consultation, research and outreach that will bring together government practitioners, parliamentarians, experts and citizens' (as proposed in *Canada in The World*, the Chrétien government's February 1995 statement on foreign policy), a more concentrated 'advisory board' of foreign policy experts was created. Moreover, DFAIT worked to more fully integrate its own structural capacity for dealing with issues of central importance to the NGOs. Most significantly, a Bureau for Global Issues (subsequently renamed the Global and Human Issues Bureau) was established to encompass an Environment and Nuclear Division, a Human Rights Division, a Human Security Division and a Peace Building and Human Development Division.

A real test of the evolutionary character of Canadian statecraft, of course, can only take place by examining how the combination of change and continuity played out in issue-specific fashion. This will be done in the later chapters on security, the fishing 'war' with Spain, peacekeeping, development assistance and the search for regional 'neighbourhood.' In each of these issues, the array of established skills of Canadian diplomacy are revealed. As in the past, considerable salience has been attached to 'problem-solving.' At the same time, many of these same issues illustrate the debates and process of adaptation concerning Canadian foreign policy conducted through the 1970s and 1980s. These include tensions over the 'functional' limitations of Canadian activity, centred on the increasing pressure to make choices concerning priorities; the tension between DFAIT and other departments; tensions about the delivery role for NGOs to complement (and compensate for) changes (and reduction) in governmental responsibilities; and the pattern of association in terms of Canadian diplomacy.

Before moving on to these cases, however, the other dominant theme of postwar Canadian foreign policy must be explored at some length. If the tactical nature of Canadian statecraft has been conditioned by 'games of skill,' the strategic vision of Canadian foreign policy was predicated on a set of fixed assumptions about the maintenance of international order. As with the means of statecraft, tensions existed between older habits and new directions about this goal. Canada's established preference throughout the post-1945 era was to 'play by the rules' in terms of its international obligations. In a fashion analogous to the traditional diplomatic instruments or techniques used by Canada, the primacy of this end was challenged by a new set of forces through the 1970s and 1980s. More to the point, the priority given to international obligations clashed against more immediate political pressures to defend the national interest. To understand the fundamental character of Canadian behaviour in global affairs, therefore, a fuller discussion of the reputational aspect of Canadian foreign policy must be undertaken.

# NOTES

[1]  Quoted in James Eayrs, 'Sunny side up,' *Weekend Magazine*, 17 December 1977, 4.

[2]  *White House Years* (Boston: Little Brown, 1979), 383.

[3]  John W. Holmes, *The Better Part of Valour: Essays on Canadian Diplomacy* (Toronto: McClelland and Stewart, 1970), vii.

[4]  K.J. Holsti, 'National roles conceptions in the study of foreign policy,' *International Studies Quarterly* 14, 3 (September 1970), 233–309.

[5]  Tom F. Keating, *Canada and World Order: The Multilateralist Tradition in Canadian Foreign Policy* (Toronto: McClelland and Stewart, 1993), 27.

[6]  For discussions of the functional principle, see John W. Holmes, *The Shaping of Peace: Canada and the Search for World Order*, vol. 1 (Toronto: University of Toronto Press, 1979), 29–73; A.J. Miller, 'Functionalism and foreign policy: an analysis of Canadian voting behaviour in the case of the United Nations, 1946–66,' unpublished Ph.D. thesis, Department of Political Science, McGill University, 1970.

[7]  Duncan Cameron, 'Canada in the world economic order,' in Paul Painchaud ed., *From Mackenzie King to Pierre Trudeau: Forty Years of Canadian Diplomacy, 1945–1985* (Quebec: Les Presses de l'Université Laval, 1989), 147.

[8]  Arthur Andrew, *Defence By Other Means: Diplomacy For The Underdog* (Toronto: CIIA, 1970), 97. See also Kim Richard Nossal, *The Politics of Canadian Foreign Policy* (Scarborough: Prentice Hall, 1989), 76.

[9]  John W. Holmes, 'The changing role of the diplomatic function in the making of foreign policy,' Occasional Paper, Centre for Foreign Policy Studies, Department of Political Science, Dalhousie University, January 1975, 10.

[10]  John W. Holmes, *Canada: A Middle-Aged Power* (Toronto: McClelland and Stewart, 1976), 36.

[11]  John W. Holmes, 'Most safely in the middle,' *International Journal* XXXIX, 2 (Spring 1984), 383.

[12]  Mark Neufeld, 'Hegemony and foreign policy analysis: the case of Canada as middle power,' *Studies in Political Economy* 48 (Autumn 1995), 27.

[13]  Denis Stairs, *The Diplomacy of Constraint: Canada, the Korean War and the United States* (Toronto: University of Toronto Press, 1974), 47.

[14]  John English, *The Worldly Years: The Life of Lester Pearson Volume Two: 1948–1972* (Toronto: Alfred A. Knopf, 1992), 145.

15  Albert Legault and Michel Fortmann, *A Diplomacy of Hope: Canada and Disarmament 1945–1988* (Montreal and Kingston: McGill–Queen's University Press, 1992), 94.

16  Sandra Gwyn, 'Where are you, Mike Pearson, now that we need you? Decline and fall of Canada's foreign policy,' *Saturday Night,* April 1978, 29. This sense of looking back to the 'golden era,' especially during crises, has been continued. Much of the discussion about Canada's role in the Gulf War also centred on the question of what 'Mike' Pearson would have done in the situation. See, for example, Hugh Winsor, 'War's foes and friends claim Pearson's legacy,' *Globe and Mail,* 11 February 1991.

17  'Canadian–British trade relations and the economic background to Britain's application to the EEC,' in Josef Becker and Rainer-Olaf Schultze, eds., *Areas of Conflict within the North Atlantic Triangle: Canada's Foreign Policy since the Second World War* (Bochum: Dr. N. Brocmeyer, 1989), 263. See also J.L. Granatstein, *Canada 1957–1967: The Years of Uncertainty and Innovation* (Toronto: McClelland and Stewart, 1986), 45.

18  Stephen Lewis, 'Canada pressed to take bigger global role,' *Toronto Star,* 26 November 1987.

19  Thomas Axworthy, 'To stand not so high but always alone: the foreign policy of Pierre Elliot Trudeau,' in Thomas Axworthy and Pierre Trudeau, eds., *Towards A Just Society: The Trudeau Years* (Markham: Viking, 1990), 46.

20  Holmes, *The Shaping of Peace,* 110.

21  Peter Dobell, 'The management of a foreign policy for Canadians,' *International Journal* XXVI, 1 (Winter 1970–71), 218–19. On the wider intellectual climate, see G. John Ikenberry, 'A world economy restored: expert consensus and the Anglo-American postwar settlement,' *International Organization* 46, 1 (Winter 1992), 290–96; 'Rethinking the origins of American hegemony,' *Political Science Quarterly* 104, 3 (Fall 1989), 375–400.

22  J.L. Granatstein, *The Ottawa Men: The Civil Service Mandarins, 1935–1967* (Toronto: Oxford University Press, 1982).

23  'Farewell to diplomacy,' *Saturday Night,* December 1968, 21.

24  George Ignatieff, quoting Hume Wrong, in a review of Glenn H. Snyder and Paul Diesing, *Conflict Among Nations: Bargaining, Decision Making, and System Structure in International Crises, Queen's Quarterly* 85, 4 (Winter 1978/9), 714–15.

25  *Foreign Policy For Canadians* (Ottawa: Queen's Printer, 1970), 8.

26  Sandra Gwyn, 'Where are you, Mike Pearson,' 30.

27  Robert Sheppard and Michael Valpy, *The National Deal: The Fight for a Canadian Constitution* (Toronto: Fleet Books, 1982), 216.

28  Jeffrey Simpson, 'PM lectures provinces as meeting bogs down,' *Globe and Mail,* 15 February 1978, 1.

29  Prof. Peter Meekinson, testimony to the Special Joint Committee of the Senate and of the House of Commons, Reviewing Canadian Foreign Policy, *Minutes of Proceedings and Evidence,* 26 July 1994, 48:27.

30  See Glen Toner and G. Bruce Doern, *The Politics of Energy: The Development and Implementation of the NEP* (Toronto: Methuen, 1985). See also Stephen Clarkson, *Canada and the Reagan Challenge* (Toronto: James Lorimer, 1985), 213.

31   Senator Kelleher, Senate Committee on Foreign Affairs, *Minutes of Proceedings and Evidence*, 21 March 1995, 17:19.

32   Robert Johnstone, testimony to the Standing Committee on External Affairs and National Defence, *Minutes of Proceedings and Evidence*, 30 January 1981, 30:15.

33   Office of the Prime Minister, *Release*, 12 January 1982. Quoted in Andrew F. Cooper, Richard A. Higgott and Kim Richard Nossal, *Relocating Middle Powers: Australia and Canada in a Changing World Order* (Vancouver: University of British Columbia Press, 1993), 37.

34   Richard Gwyn, 'PM learns the diplomacy of symbolism,' *Toronto Star*, 19 February 1986.

35   Although overshadowed by the Quebec referendum, signs continue about evolving arrangements over 'delegated authority.' See, for example, Robert Mckenzie, 'Quebec may share embassies,' *Toronto Star*, 29 March 1996.

36   Holmes, quoted in Bryan Johnson, 'Glamour scrubbed for sales pitch,' *Globe and Mail*, 3 December 1983.

37   Clyde Sanger, *Ordering the Oceans* (Toronto: University of Toronto Press, 1987), 25. See also Elizabeth Riddell-Dixon, *Canada and the International Seabed: Domestic Determinants and External Constraints* (Kingston: McGill–Queen's University Press, 1989).

38   John Holmes, cited in Gwyn, 'Where are you, Mike Pearson,' 35.

39   Michael Hart differentiates between the advocates of a bilateral deal with the US and the defenders of the multilateral faith inside External Affairs. Michael Hart with Bill Dymond and Colin Robertson, *Decision at Midnight: Inside the Canada–US Free-Trade Negotiations* (Vancouver: University of British Columbia Press, 1994), 89–91.

40   Kim Richard Nossal, 'Dividing the territory: the prime minister and foreign minister in Canadian foreign policy: 1968–94,' *International Journal* L, 1 (Winter 1994–5), 195–6.

41   *Ibid.*, 203.

42   Peter Aucoin, 'Organizational change in the machinery of Canadian government: from rational management to brokerage politics,' *Canadian Journal of Political Science* 19, 1 (March 1986), 3–27.

43   Nossal, 'Dividing the territory,' 203. See also Linda Hosse, 'New generation sees aggressive role for Canada,' *Globe and Mail*, 18 October 1991.

44   Nossal, 'Dividing the territory,' 200.

45   The prime purpose of political leadership for Mulroney was 'about the accommodation of interests and not the interplay of ideas.' Donald J. Savoie, *The Politics of Public Spending in Canada* (Toronto: University of Toronto Press, 1990), 90.

46   S.L. Sutherland, 'The Al-Mashat affair: administrative responsibility in parliamentary institutions,' *Canadian Public Administration* 34, 4 (Winter 1991), 573–603.

47   (Toronto: Macfarlane Walter & Ross, 1994). See also Jeffrey Simpson, 'What they did to Mr. McCutchan for saying the emperor had no clothes,' *Globe and Mail*, 13 May 1993.

48   For background, see Clyde Sanger, *Canadians and the United Nations* (Ottawa: Supply and Services Canada, 1988).

49   Tom Axworthy, 'Canada can be proud of its role in Nairobi,' *Toronto Star*, 25 August 1985. In a similar vein, the often critical North–South Institute praised this episode as a model of 'effective middle-power diplomacy in the multilateral area.' The North–South Institute, *Review '85 Outlook '86* (Ottawa: 1986), 4. Maureen O'Neil, a

key actor in the resolution of the Nairobi Conference in her capacity as deputy chair of the Canadian delegation, moved on to become the deputy minister of citizenship in the Ontario government and the head of the North–South Institute.

50   On Canadian environmental diplomacy more generally, see Andrew Fenton Cooper and J. Stefan Fritz, 'Bringing the NGOs in: UNCED and Canada's international environmental policy,' *International Journal* XLVII, 4 (Autumn 1992), 796–817.

51   G. Bruce Doern and Brian W. Tomlin, *Faith and Fear: The Free Trade Story* (Toronto: Stoddart, 1991), 165. See also Harald von Riekhoff, 'The structure of foreign policy decision making and management,' in Brian W. Tomlin and Maureen Appel Molot, eds., *Canada Among Nations 1986: Talking Trade* (Toronto: James Lorimer, 1987), 22.

52   Doern and Tomlin, *Faith and Fear*, 8.

53   Denis Stairs, 'Publics and policy-makers: the domestic environment of Canada's foreign policy community,' *International Journal* XXVI, 1 (Winter 1970–71).

54   As Stairs has put it: 'the Canadian government during the immediate post-1945 period did not have to cope with "any significant sense of domestic confinement" in its alliance policy.' Denis Stairs, 'Public opinion and External Affairs: reflections on the domestication of Canadian foreign policy,' *International Journal* XXXIII, 1 (Winter 1977–8), 132. See also the stimulating piece by Robert Bothwell and John English, 'The view from inside out: Canadian diplomats and their public,' *International Journal* XXXIX, 1 (Winter 1983–4), 63–7.

55   For a critique of this approach, see Franklyn Griffiths, 'Opening up the policy process,' in Stephen Clarkson ed., *An Independent Foreign Policy for Canada?* (Toronto: McClelland and Stewart, for the University League of Social Reform, 1968).

56   For one interpretation, which pays exclusive attention to élite views, see Granatstein, *The Ottawa Men*. See also Bruce Muirhead, 'Perception and reality: the GATT's contribution to the development of a bilateral North American relationship, 1947–1951,' *American Review of Canadian Studies* 20, 3 (Autumn 1990), 279–301. As one Canadian official, interviewed by Gilbert Winham for his comprehensive work on the Tokyo Round, put it: 'we don't have the [equivalent of the US] Chamber of Commerce coming to Geneva to tell us how to run the negotiation.' Gilbert R. Winham, *International Trade and the Tokyo Round Negotiations* (Princeton, NJ: Princeton University Press, 1986), 340.

57   Amid a general feeling of satisfaction about the performance of the Canadian negotiating team, a sense of disquiet could be found concerning the level of consultation forged with industry. One partisan observer took the view that while liaison procedures with business had improved during the Tokyo Round, it was still 'pretty much a hit-and-miss method from the start.' 'Government people came to industries and told them what was intended. Quite often, input by industry came after the fact.' Jack Murtra, the Conservatives' trade critic, quoted in Wally Dennison, 'Canadian team wins top grades in trade talks,' *Winnipeg Free Press*, 20 April 1979.

58   The Special Joint Committee of the Senate and the House of Commons on Canada's International Relations, *Independence and Internationalism* (Ottawa: June 1986), 8.

59   Report Of The Special Joint Committee Reviewing Canadian Foreign Policy, *Canada's Foreign Policy: Principles and Priorities for the Future* (Ottawa: Parliamentary Publications Directorate, November 1994), 6.

60  de Montigny Marchand, 'Foreign policy and public interest,' *International Perspectives*, July/August 1983, 8–9.

61  Address given by Douglas Roche, Ambassador for Disarmament, 'Re-Building the Human Dimension in International Relations,' Leningrad, USSR, 13 December 1986, 1.

62  Andrew Moravcsik, 'Introduction: integrating international and domestic theories of international bargaining,' in Peter B. Evans, Harold K. Jacobson and Robert D. Putnam, eds., *International Bargaining and Domestic Politics: Double-Edged Diplomacy* (Berkeley: University of California Press, 1993), 16.

63  For example, see James Gillies, *Facing Reality: Consultation, Consensus and Making Economic Policy for the 21st Century* (Montreal: Institute for Research on Public Policy, 1986).

64  On this wider theme, see Alan M. Rugman and Andrew D.M. Anderson, *Administered Protection in America* (London: Croom Helm, 1987), ch. 5.

65  Doern and Tomlin, *Faith and Fear*.

66  Quoted in Lorna Marsden, 'Timing and presence: getting women's issues on the trade agenda,' *Working Paper Series: Gender, Science and Development Programme*, International Federation of Institutes for Advanced Study, Toronto, July 1992.

67  Robert M. Campbell and Leslie A. Pal, *The Real Worlds of Canadian Politics: Cases in Process and Policy* (Peterborough: Broadview Press, 1989), 328.

68  Brian W. Tomlin, 'The states of prenegotiation: the decision to negotiate North American free trade,' *International Journal* XLIV, 2 (Spring 1988), 265; David Langille, 'The Business Council on National Issues and the Canadian State,' *Studies in Political Economy* 24 (Autumn 1987), 41–85.

69  Gilbert R. Winham, *International Trade and the Tokyo Round Negotiations* (Princeton, NJ: Princeton University Press, 1986). There remained important limitations to this mobilization strategy. A good example of a case in which it was difficult to get the Canadian business community on side was the 1991 'Prosperity Initiative.' Notwithstanding the enthusiasm of the BCNI for this competitiveness strategy, the kick-start of the Porter Report, and the existence of a high-profile private sector steering committee co-chaired by the president of Xerox Canada and Marie-Josée Drouin, executive director of the Hudson Institute, the campaign fizzled. Michael Demers, 'Responding to the challenges of the political economy: the competitiveness agenda,' in Frances Abele ed., *How Ottawa Spends, 1992–93* (Ottawa: Carleton University Press, 1992), 151–90. See also Michael Porter, *Canada at the Crossroads* (Ottawa: Business Council on National Issues and the Government of Canada, 1991).

70  Kim Kileen, 'Interest groups in the Canadian foreign policy process: the case of the World Food Conference,' unpublished MA thesis, Dalhousie University, 1980, ch. 6.

71  Quoted in Charlotte Montgomery, 'Canada to increase its aid to Ethiopia,' *Globe and Mail*, 7 November 1984.

72  Kim Richard Nossal, *The Politics of Canadian Foreign Policy* (Scarborough: Prentice Hall, 1989), 107–17.

73  See, for example, J. Bernstein and D. McGraw, eds., *Report of the Proceeding of 'Countdown to Rio'* (Ottawa: CPCU, 21–22 February 1992), 7.

74  Lynn Hunter (New Democratic member for Saanich–Gulf Islands), House of Commons, *Debates*, 7 May 1992, 10339.

75   House of Commons Standing Committee on the Environment, *Minutes of Proceedings and Evidence*, 7 May 1992, 74:71.

76   *Montreal Gazette*, 10 December 1986. 'Coming of age,' *Toronto Star*, 13 December 1986.

77   See, for example, Tom Keating, 'The state, the public, and the making of Canadian foreign policy,' in Robert J. Jackson, Doreen Jackson and Nicolas Baxter-Moore, eds., *Contemporary Canadian Politics: Readings and Notes* (Scarborough: Prentice Hall, 1987), 363–4.

78   Cranford Pratt, 'Dominant class theory and Canadian foreign policy: the case of the counter-consensus,' *International Journal* XXXIX, 1 (Winter 1983–4).

79   Denis Stairs, 'Public opinion and External Affairs: reflections on the domestication of Canadian foreign policy,' *International Journal* XXXIII, 1 (Winter 1977–8), 144–5.

80   *Creating Opportunity: The Liberal Plan for Canada* (Ottawa: Liberal Party of Canada, 1993), 157.

81   Liberal Party of Canada, *Liberal Foreign Policy Handbook* (Ottawa, May 1993).

82   Denis Stairs, 'The public policy of the Canadian defence and foreign policy reviews,' *Canadian Foreign Policy* III, 1 (Spring 1995), 91–116.

83   Kim Richard Nossal, 'The democratization of Canadian foreign policy: the elusive ideal,' in Maxwell A. Cameron and Maureen Appel Molot, eds., *Canada Among Nations 1995: Democracy and Foreign Policy* (Ottawa: Carleton University Press, 1995), 29–43.

84   'Extraordinary diversity of advice,' *Financial Post*, 24 March 1994.

85   Neufeld, 'Hegemony and foreign policy analysis.'

86   Paul Knox, 'Canadians wrestle with global change,' *Globe and Mail*, 12 September 1995.

# MINDING THE RULES

## THE REPUTATIONAL IMPULSE

An examination of diplomatic style and technique is highly valuable in getting to the essence of Canadian statecraft. Skill provides an extremely useful criterion by which Canada's tactics in the international arena may be judged. This analysis of diplomatic means, however, must be complemented by a closer look at Canada's foreign policy goals. An exclusive focus on the manner in which Canada played its hand allows only a one-dimensional perspective on Canada's role in global affairs. For a more balanced picture, attention has to turn by necessity to the rules by which Canada has said it wanted to play the game—and an assessment of Canada's performance on the basis of those guidelines. The overriding point on which this evaluation rests centres on the question of whether or not Canada can be considered 'a good international citizen' generally and a committed multilateralist specifically. By examining Canadian foreign policy through this reputational lens, a good deal can be learned about the equipoise between national interest and international order.

Together with skill, reputation provided the foundation of Canada's post-1945 statecraft. In terms of Canadian attitudes and actions, a rules-based behaviour was defined as the key ingredient to establishing and maintaining international order. As a self-identified middle power, Canada was expected to take on special responsibilities for constructive, institutional-based activity. In summing up the values behind Canada's postwar foreign policy, John Holmes laid special emphasis on the view that 'Countries which qualified as middle powers had to be very, very responsible and being responsible meant paying one's dues and not being irresponsible in word or deed.'[1]

In seeking some better understanding of this reputational impulse, as pursued over the time-frame of the entire postwar period, both an inside-out and an outside-in examination must be adopted. Canada's role in the international system, as well as the domestic attributes that helped to shape this impulse, must be scrutinized.[2] Only by looking at Canada from without and within, taking into account both international and domestic motivations, may a comprehensive grasp of its behaviour be garnered.

The high regard placed on responsibility corresponded with the mindset of the practitioners responsible for establishing what were to become the ingrained habits of Canadian statecraft. It does not seem too much of a generalization to say that the Canadian impulse towards reputation and responsibility was initially fashioned by a Presbyterian view of the world. Some of the more prominent members of the Canadian (Anglo-Celt) foreign policy establishment were sons of the 'manse' and/or missionaries. Many were educated at Victoria College at the University of Toronto. Well-meaning, and enriched with a good deal of zeal about the benefits of good international citizenship, this cohort applied a sort of secular religiosity to the creation of both a new global order and a committed Canadian foreign policy. This mindset contributed much to the 'nice' image of Canada in international affairs—with Canada displaying a sort of 'boy scout' or 'choir boy' enthusiasm for doing good deeds in the international arena. The fact that so many of the leading practitioners of Canadian foreign policy—not only in the formative stages (Pearson and Holmes especially) but later on (including Conservatives such as Flora MacDonald and Joe Clark)—seemed to be so 'nice' simply put a personalized touch on this fixed image. But these formative influences also contributed to the serious, industrious side of Canadian functionalism—with ample consideration of 'discipline' and 'limits.' This sense of constraint, as Denis Stairs has put it in his well-known article on 'Political culture of Canadian foreign policy,' was predicated on the notion that 'general principles of political action, no matter how carefully reasoned and how perfectly aligned with conceptions, in the abstract, of what is right and just, are of no use if they advocate what power realities make unworkable.'[3]

Canada's impulse towards reputation and responsibility meshed, as well, with the domestic 'rules of the game' as they evolved in the immediate post-1945 era. Canadian norms, or the fundamental features of Canadian political life, have tended to be characterized as consensus-seeking and accommodation.[4] As the recent constitutional battles over the Meech Lake and Charlottetown accords have highlighted, the level of accommodation traditionally witnessed in the Canadian political culture has considerably eroded in the 1980s and 1990s. Certainly the type of élite accommodation that served as the bulwark of Canadian political practice, and arguably the survival of the Canadian entity, no longer seems viable in light of contemporary conditions. Nevertheless, from the late 1940s through to the 1960s—or even the 1970s—these principles and practices still held sway. Formally, the constitutional structure gave pride of place to 'Peace, Order, and Good Government.' Informally, Canadian politics tried to blur divisions through a system of arrangements and trade-offs designed to manage (if not solve) problems. These accepted values were in turn projected out into the international arena. As Thomas Hockin (himself a scholar/practitioner) set out in an influential article *circa* the late 1960s, the Canadian pattern of exhibiting flexibility and a spirit of 'patience and compromise' in its diplomatic style is also firmly rooted in its political culture.[5] Much of the continuous momentum behind Canada's *modus operandi* for acting as a diplomatic bridge-builder or helpful fixer has been propelled by the Canadian tradition of bargaining and negotiated compromise. These domestic habits also inculcated in Canada a faith in the workings of international institutions and rules-based behaviour, arguably to a much higher degree than in other countries. Organizational maintenance and enhancement remained a Canadian forte.[6]

Looking from the outside in, the related question of how Canada was situated in the international arena must be taken into account. Canada's reputational impulse fits well with the argument that middle powers have acted as supporters of the international system. According to Robert Cox, a trenchant critic of the middle power concept, it is this impulse towards the creation and maintenance of world order that stands at the heart of middle power behaviour, that is to say, 'a [state's] commitment to orderliness and security in interstate relations and to the facilitation of orderly change in the world system' consistent with 'an environment within which their own interests and those of their populations could be pursued.'[7]

From this systemic perspective, the position of Canada is highly significant because it represents what may be termed the archetypal system follower in the post-1945 global system. Followership, in this sense, meant that Canada not only 'went along' in supporting the architecture of that order but also shared to a considerable extent the larger vision or belief system advocated by the US (as leader or hegemon) to underpin the system. Going along, though, did not mean unthinking and uncritical bandwagoning. While Canada saw the positive benefits accruing from a far-sighted form of leadership, it did not take this role for granted. Unsure of the willingness and/or ability of the US to operate in a consistent, principled fashion, Canada took it upon itself to strengthen the system. This condition necessitated continual work to ensure 'some limits to the ambition and reach' of the powerful as well as the general compliance of other actors.[8]

Akin to skill, the expression of Canada's followership in the international system may be differentiated or compartmentalized along the lines of issue-areas. In the geo-security relationship, the room for manoeuvre has been far more restricted than in the economic or social areas. The US, as Britain before it, has been regarded as the guarantor of safety for Canada, a search for a protector that found formal expression in the NATO and NORAD alliances. As pointed out in the Introduction, this typecasting of Canada's followership in the security sphere should not be exaggerated to the point of caricature (viewing Canada exclusively as the US's 'chore boy'). Yet, at least in comparative terms, this alliance membership meant that Canada's freedom of action was more readily available on the non-strategic agenda. No portrait of Canadian foreign policy should overlook in particular the opportunities (as well as the constraints) open to and cultivated by Canada in the formation and maintenance of the institutional mechanisms of the postwar economic order—a creative and constructive involvement facilitated in turn by the adaptation by Canada of the organizing principle of functionalism.

To be sure, the declaratory language of moral imperative has to treated carefully. Nonetheless, in keeping with Keohane's point about the international system as a whole, it is remarkable how this type of language was used in the discussion of Canadian foreign relations.[9] Rather than the rules being treated as convenient devices made necessary by external actors or conditions, adherence to these rules was said to be based on principle and obligations. In the aftermath of depression and war, the Canadian foreign policy establishment was highly vocal in its support of constructive internationalism and what Cox depicts as 'an orderly and predictable world environment.'[10] 'We always ask ourselves,' wrote Lester Pearson, 'not only what kind of Canada do we want? but what kind of world do we want.'[11]

Without devaluing the altruistic element, which comes out forcefully on development assistance and other issues, a certain logic may be discerned in this approach. In common with a number of other secondary countries, reputation was 'deliberately sought' by Canada as 'an asset for use in international life.'[12] As with the 'games of skill,' the contribution made by Canada with respect to international institution-building and maintenance drew rewards in terms of status. By taking on selective responsibilities, Canada gained not only symbolic prestige (as the quintessential 'good international citizen') but also tangible benefits in terms of institutional 'special' privileges and posts. As an individual, Pearson was constantly under consideration for top positions in the UN, NATO and other institutions. As a nation, Canada gained access to many of the key decision-making forums. At another level, constructive internationalism allowed Canada greater room to shape (and sometimes bend) the institutional arrangements and rules to its own liking. Much of this activity was directed at reining in the hegemon through this system of multilateral instruments and commitments. By operating through methods of co-operation that did not rely solely on power, Canada could also target specific areas, which had the effect of allowing it to act in favour of the international order where it best suited its own material interests. While this blend often meant that Canada was generally viewed as a stalwart defender of the status quo, it meant that in specific cases it could move towards the forefront of reformist challenges.

In many ways, then, Canadian rules-based multilateralism was based on a 'hard-boiled calculation of the Canadian national interest.'[13] Canadian national well-being was perceived to be closely dependent on international stability. Indeed, a strong current running through Canadian thinking and practice on foreign policy showcases the instrumental value of rules for a non-great power such as Canada. Only by having Canada, and other middle power supporters of the international order, become major stakeholders in a set of rules-oriented institutional arrangements could the principles of 'general compromise and general compliance' rather than 'lawlessness, in which the prizes go to the powerful and the predatory,' be maintained.[14]

# BUILDING AND EXTENDING THE POST-1945 INSTITUTIONAL STRUCTURE

## Present at the Creation

A fundamental objective of Canadian statecraft in the post-1945 period has been to widen and deepen the architecture of the international order. The primary emphasis has been on the development of multiple layers of rules and institutions, which would facilitate stability. One way of achieving this goal has been through the creation of what scholars have since termed 'regimes'; namely 'principles, norms, rules, and decision-making procedures around which actors' expectations converge in a given issue-area.'[15] For the postwar Canadian foreign policy establishment, this meant some form of development and recognition of an agreed form of behaviour in a given issue-area.

This focus meshed well with the functional orientation of Canadian foreign policy. In other words, it encouraged specialization in selected issue-areas on the international stage. This targeting could be done in either a discrete (narrow) or diffuse (wider) fashion. By picking selected areas, where it had some comparative advantage or specialized interest, Canada could maximize its impact. Among these chosen areas were included international civil aviation, the resettlement of displaced peoples,[16] resource issues specifically and trade generally, and international financial questions. This focus also meshed well with the institutional orientation of Canadian foreign policy. The management of distinctive functional areas depended on the presence of a well-established and operational institutional structure.

### *The International Civil Aviation Organization*

A good illustration of the Canadian reputational impulse within a discrete functional issue-area can be found with reference to international civil aviation. How willing Canada was to take on responsibility ('pay its dues') in this issue-area was displayed by the prominent role it played at the 1944 Chicago aviation conference. Again, reputation-building activity went hand in hand with skill. As one of Canada's delegates to the Chicago meeting, Escott Reid, writes: 'Canada became one of the three leading powers at the conference because we were the only delegation...with a carefully worked out comprehensive draft convention.'[17] This document became the basis for the negotiations on air-transport regulation and structure of the proposed international aviation organization. Canada backed up this diplomatic dexterity with a considerable degree of technical expertise. Consistently, however, Canada channelled this skill 'to launch an idealistic proposal.' The 'regime' created for the aviation system provided a model for global management. The institution at the centre of this system was the International Civil Aviation Organization (ICAO), founded in 1947 and located in Montreal.[18]

## The General Agreement on Tariffs and Trade

In the diffuse functional issue-area of trade, Canada's reputational impulse comes out with respect to its original support for the establishment of the International Trade Organization (ITO). It must be mentioned that Canada had a number of reservations about how the ITO was to operate in practice, especially in connection with the ITO's directive powers to push for full employment. The dominant Canadian concern, nonetheless, was to secure a strong and viable ITO in the interests of multilateral co-operation and non-discrimination within the postwar international trading system. As Dana Wilgress, the chair of the Canadian delegation to the ITO preparatory committee in 1947, put it, the contracting parties should 'seek to accommodate the differing situations and the legitimate aspirations and needs of the various nations of the world,' but 'must not...resort to expedients and indulge in compatibilities which would destroy our general objective.'[19]

After the failure of the ITO to win ratification in the US, Canada concentrated much of its efforts on furthering an internationalist approach to world trade problems through less ambitious means. The centrepiece of this approach was the extension of the provisions of the General Agreement on Tariffs and Trade (GATT). As Frank Stone has detailed, the GATT was 'not merely an international treaty containing a set of rules for trade; it has also evolved to serve many of the institutional and other functions that would have been given to the ITO, if it had come into being.'[20] These included a permanent framework for international consultations on world trade policy developments and problems; a common framework for conditioning the trade policies and practices of individual member states, supplemented by a number of codes and agreements established through the existence of the GATT; a setting for negotiations for liberalizing trade via a series of 'Rounds'; agreed procedures for settling disputes; and the provision of facilities for collecting and disseminating information. In the standard work on Canada's involvement with the GATT, Stone gives special attention to the Canadian 'legalistic' bias, 'in the sense of emphasizing its functions as a body of trade law; favouring a minimum of exceptions, and emphasizing the need for conformity with GATT provisions.'[21] 'Among its members,' he added, 'few have been consistently more zealous than Canada in the general management of GATT activities.'[22]

Canada's behaviour in the GATT reveals the logic behind the overall Canadian strategy towards the international system. Consistent with the notion that Canada's high degree of participation was targeted towards not only symbolic prestige but also tangible benefits in terms of institutional 'special' privileges and posts, Canada won a form of 'insider' or 'core' status within the GATT. One measure of the success of Canada's performance at this form of politicking was the frequent selection of Canadian officials to key posts. Dana Wilgress, most notably, served as the first Chair of the Contracting Parties to the GATT in 1947.[23] This 'insider' presence, in turn, allowed Canada to have an influence 'above its weight.' Although Canada's stature as a commercial power should not be underestimated, it seems clear that the Canadian 'leading' role in trade diplomacy was out of proportion to its place in the international hierarchy and owed much to skill and reputational attributes.[24]

The instrumental management of Canada's trade policy was also well served via the GATT system. As on security issues, an important ingredient found in Canadian commercial statecraft featured the diplomacy of constraint. This was consistent with Canada's ingrained faith in quiet diplomacy. In order to consolidate its 'special relationship' with the US, this mode of statecraft had a strong bilateral component. Specifically, Canada used quiet diplomacy to attempt to modify the US's behaviour through a mix of ad hoc contact and the use of 'proper diplomatic channels.' Given the unequal nature of the Canada–US relationship, though, multilateral means held greater salience as a vehicle for constraining the US's policies and practices. On almost any issue, Canada could utilize its coalition-building skill to defend its interests with the help of likeminded countries. Because the GATT constituted an exchange of obligations and rights, the ability to hold the behaviour of the US (and the other major trading powers) in some check was enhanced in the multilateral setting. While this ability was far from absolute, its relative merits remained attractive.

## *International Agricultural Policies*

Where the GATT proved ineffective as a form of restraint or discipline on the 'bigs,' Canada looked to other ways to prop up the international trade regime. A good example of Canada's first followership, largely outside the GATT framework, may be seen in the international food system. First followership entailed a double burden of responsibility. On the one hand, these followers attempted to keep potential 'spoilers' in line. In particular, Canada worked hard to try to temper the restrictive practices of the EC's emergent Common Agricultural Policy (CAP) in terms of free access for agricultural goods. Much of this campaign was conducted in tandem with the US's own attempts to rein in the EC. At the time of the Treaty of Rome, Canada, with other middle powers, pushed for the formation of a special committee of the Organization for European Economic Co-operation (OEEC) to examine the problem. It also participated in a number of consultative meetings (June 1959, May 1960) between the EC and representatives of the major agricultural exporting nations for the purpose of discussing the implications of the CAP. To the same end, Canada joined with the US and other agricultural exporting nations to play an instrumental role in the move, through the Contracting Parties of the GATT, to establish a panel of distinguished economists (in 1958) to report on trends in agricultural trade with particular reference to the impact of protectionism on primary products.

On the other hand, Canada, as a first follower, placed considerable onus on trying to get the US to understand the responsibilities of its own leadership role. In doing so, it was prepared to place the US's international commercial transactions under surveillance and to publicize transgressions from the 'rules of the game' by the US. The original target of these criticisms was the US request, and receipt in 1955, of a waiver from GATT obligations so as to allow it to restrict the import of agricultural products under section 22 of its own Agricultural Adjustment Act (covering price-supported agricultural products). Canada recognized the extent to which this action weakened the structure and credibility of the agricultural trade system. As T.K. Warley makes clear: 'At a time when other exporters were highly agitated about agricultural trade restrictions, the architect of the trading system and the custodian of liberalism was giving primacy to national interests.'[25]

In the 1960s, the main source of friction between the leader and the first follower shifted towards the methods used by the Americans to dispose of their surplus wheat and dairy products. These methods, involving tied sales, barter, straight gifts and the sale of goods for soft local currency, were regarded by Canada as going far beyond the 'qualified' acceptance of extra-market channels for food distribution allowed for in the agricultural trade order. Consistently, Canada attempted to get the message through to the US that its real long-term interest outweighed its short-term domestic concerns. C.D. Howe, the long-serving Canadian trade minister, told the US secretary of agriculture directly that the American disposal techniques were 'unfair and unwholesome.'[26]

What Canada wanted was a consistent display of far-sighted leadership by the US. As in other areas of the international economic system, the US was encouraged to lead in the agricultural trade order by positive example. Although the actions of the EC and other actors were viewed as being potentially detrimental to maintaining stability, the deviations by the US were regarded as much more serious. Bluntly put, the order had to be saved from the actions of its own creator. In the words of a senior Canadian diplomat, signs of an erratic course on the part of the US left other actors 'confused and dismayed.'[27]

## The IMF and the World Bank

A variation on many of these same themes was played out on financial questions. Analogous to the international trading system, Canada strongly backed expanding the range and scope of the postwar international financial institutions. Canada provided a good deal of the backing for the creation of the International Monetary Fund and the World Bank. As in a variety of other areas, including international civil aviation, Canada positioned itself between the US and Britain. Canada's role as a mediator was particularly evident on the provision for some system of financial reserves, where the British (or more precisely, J.M. Keynes) were pushing for an International Clearing Union in support of those economies experiencing balance of payment difficulties, and the US favoured a far less ambitious form of stabilization fund. The detailed knowledge base of Canada's state officials contributed to the success of this 'bridging' exercise.[28]

## A (Stylized) Sketch of the Contemporary Record

In moving the discussion up to the present, what stands out is the continuity of so much of the reputational impulse emanating from Canada. A consistent theme, over the course of time, has been the promotion of a set of rules that are 'intended to be binding upon the big as well as the small.' In Cox's words, this search constitutes 'the realpolitik of the middle power.'[29] Somewhat of a timeless quality exists in Canadian declaratory expressions. Much of the language used to depict Canada's foreign economic concerns in the 1980s and 1990s echoes that of the immediate post-1945 era. Commanding the contemporary scene, as in the past, has been the Canadian concern for the establishment of as risk-free an environment as possible. Institutional means, concomitantly, remain the chosen route for building stability within the international economic system.

### *Foreign Policy in the Mulroney Years*

What is equally striking is the extent to which there has been a bipartisan consensus on this set of questions. Little in the way of the sharp division of opinion across party lines, so evident in spheres of domestic policy, may be found 'on basics' pertaining to the international economic system. The need for Canada to pursue international rules-keeping has been underscored by both Conservative and Liberal politicians. Joe Clark, the Conservative foreign minister under Mulroney, stated this view: 'We are not a great power. We cannot impose order or ignore it. We have no choice but to build it with others, co-operatively.'[30] During his extended stint as foreign minister, Clark may be said to have acted as the guardian of the multilateral tradition in Canadian foreign policy. Inculcated into Clark's world-view, to a degree well beyond any of the other ministers in the Mulroney cabinet, was the legacy of the Canadian habit of constructive internationalism. Indeed, Clark was as forceful in his advocacy of order and stability in the international arena as any of his Liberal predecessors. As he put it at the Punta del Este meeting, which launched the Uruguay Round of GATT negotiations, the need for a new agreement determining the rules of governance in international commerce was as vital in the 1980s as it was in the aftermath of World War II: 'In the 40 years since that creative burst of confidence, we have put those achievements at risk by taking them for granted. Countries which 40 years ago put the world ahead of narrow interests now apply protective trade measures outside GATT disciplines. The rules point one way, and governments go another.'[31]

In common with the world-view of Pearson and the foreign policy establishment from the 1950s and 1960s, Clark's idealism was tempered by a hard-headed calculation of Canada's—and his own—political interests. At a personal level, Clark wanted to differentiate in some distinctive ways his foreign policy from that of Prime Minister Mulroney. The inspiration behind this attitude was obvious. Not only was Mulroney the man who (in an atmosphere of considerable animosity) had ousted Clark from the leadership of the party in June 1983, but the political philosophies of the two Conservative politicians sharply diverged. Clark's tinge of 'red toryism,' most visible in social and economic policy, remained at odds with Mulroney's business-oriented conservatism.

Still, it would be misleading to suggest that Clark's views were exceptional among the Conservative hierarchy. If his 'boy scoutism' was often more pronounced than that of his ministerial colleagues, the underlying principles on which Clark's views rested were little different from mainstream opinion. As the nature of the international system was transformed in the 1970s, 1980s and 1990s, the Canadian response was put to a new and intense type of test. The diminution in the American will and/or capacity to manage the international economic system in a benign or creative fashion, in combination with the ascendancy of countries with far less allegiance to the post-1945 order, increased Canada's feelings of vulnerability and uncertainty. As such, the defence of order reflected a sensible conservatism based on the fear of mounting dangers. As John Crosbie, from his vantage point as trade minister in 1989, warned, Canada risked being 'smashed' if a new set of rules was not established: 'Canada is a middle power and the [international trade negotiations] are of tremendous importance to Canada.... We need the rule of law in trade affairs.'[32]

### Foreign Policy under Chrétien

With the Liberals' return to office, Canada's commitment to the orthodoxy of a rules-based multilateralism was vigorously renewed. The *Liberal Foreign Policy Handbook*, released prior to the 1993 election, declared: 'A regime of international law and order must be expanded to compete with—and eventually replace—the old reliance on power relations and coercion.'[33] The review of foreign policy carried out by the Chrétien government reiterated Canada's reliance on international institutions and regimes to formulate the rules of global economic integration: 'A rules-based multilateral system remains the best protection for Canada being side-swiped by the "big boys on the block."'[34]

As with the Conservatives, particular Liberal ministers were prepared to champion the rules-building cause. Of these individuals, Roy MacLaren stands out. While Ouellet's contribution as foreign minister cannot be discounted completely, it was MacLaren who provided the intellectual spark to the Chrétien government's approach to international trade. A former diplomat, who built a prominent business career in the publishing world, MacLaren had remained part of a distinct minority among Liberals, who had opposed the economic nationalist tilt by the Trudeau government. Handed the portfolio of minister of international trade, MacLaren was therefore ready to stand up for what he believed in (and what he had prepared for during the Mulroney years in office). Consistently, MacLaren hammered home the same theme: 'I believe that the conduct of Canada's trade relations should rest on the quest for greater international security for Canadian exporters through agreed rule-making and enforcement.'[35]

In operational terms, Canada's role of system supporter has undergone some evolution. As the performance of the United States as the manager over the international trade system has mutated, Canada's functions in shaping the wider discourse and process have evolved in parallel fashion. The gap in leadership at the apex of the international hierarchy allowed some extension in Canada's relative freedom of action. Canada was prepared, in a number of ways, to use this expanded space of operation. Canada took the high road in a number of areas during the Uruguay Round of GATT negotiations. Canada's proposal for a new International Trade Organization (ITO), a formulation that translated subsequently into the World Trade Organization (WTO), looms large as an illustration of this type of positive action. Canada also was out in front in the attempt to work out an internationally agreed definition of subsidies and improved disciplines on the use of countervail duties.[36]

## Opposition to US Unilateralism

While the creative side of Canadian rules-based activity has found a number of outlets in the 1980s and 1990s, the defensive side remains a dominant feature as well. As much as in the past, contemporary Canadian behaviour has been conditioned by a concern to constrain the US's unilateral and protectionist impulses. This concern is evident in Canada's consistent efforts to channel American actions *vis-à-vis* trade remedies towards a multilateral and/or institutional dispute resolution context rather than resort to unilateral or bilateral tools. One illustration of this type of thrust has been seen in Canada's continuing opposition to the imposition of extraterritorial doctrine by the US. The main change over time has been that this type of controversy no longer surfaces on Canada–US bilateral questions, where the US attempted to use this doctrine as a lever to curb Canadian (economic nationalist) policy. Instead, it has come to the fore almost exclusively in cases where the US has attempted to apply the extraterritorial doctrine through sanctions on third parties such as Cuba. This latter type of case has pitted the desire of the US government to have a 'global reach' over multinational corporations against the Canadian government's desire to subject subsidiaries or 'branch plants' of American firms to 'the jurisdiction and direction of its own laws and policies.'[37]

Another illustration of Canada's continued opposition to American unilateralism on trade issues emerged in the 1980s with respect to the Super 301, legislation designed to target specific 'unfair traders.' Indeed, Canada's response to specific measures of this sort demonstrated the extent to which the bipartisan consensus has held up. Prime Minister Mulroney cautioned the US on the pitfalls of a return to 'the law of the jungle.'[38] On the Super 301, as in other cases involving US action directed at specific sectors, Canada came down firmly on the side of constructive forms of dispute resolution rather than coercive action. As MacLaren expressed it, Canada disapproved of the US's use of 'a unilateral device to remedy...unfair trading practices.... We are confirmed multilateralists in Canada. We seek our trade remedies in a multilateral context rather than primarily using bilateral tools of the type of Super 301.'[39]

### Continuing Support for International Institutions

Rather than giving up on the post-1945 institutions as they came under a new set of formidable challenges in the 1980s and 1990s, renewed attention was paid by Canada to showing the continuing value of these institutions in a changing world. This meant doing a better job of examining the evolving nature of middle power statecraft through an appreciation of the dynamic of the historical process linked to the development of international organizations. Because a middle power's response to this dynamic is part of 'a process not a finality,' to repeat Robert Cox's words, it should not be evaluated as 'a fixed universal' but as 'something that has to be rethought continually in the context of the changing state of the international system.'[40]

This ingrained faith in institutional solutions comes out as strongly on international financial questions. From an official Canadian perspective, the main issue in this sphere of activity focussed on rethinking the role and mandate of the major multilateral institutions, especially those identified with the Bretton Woods agreement. These institutions were required to adapt to the changing environment of the global economy of the twenty-first century in general, and to better deal with shocks (ranging from the debt crisis of the early 1980s to the issue—featured in the recent Mexican crisis—of national default in the 1990s) more specifically. As the director of DFAIT's Division on Economic Relations with Developing Countries stated before the parliamentary review committee: 'the management of financial shocks is the bedrock for our Canadian interests.'[41] What is clear is that Canada did not want to remain on the sidelines and allow the postwar institutions to decline in relevance. As another Canadian state official testified: 'we're not too content to sit back and monitor what they're doing. We have...[to continue to be] an agent for change and improvement and strengthening of these institutions.'[42]

The time and energy Canada has devoted to international financial matters has risen in profile during the time of the Chrétien government. Many of the intricate details surrounding this response lie well outside the boundaries of this study; nonetheless, the broad outlines can be sketched out. First of all, Canada has worked to try to promote coherence and efficiency in the activities of the myriad institutions with responsibilities on financial matters (including not only the IMF and the World Bank, but the OECD and the WTO). Secondly, Canada thought seriously about ways (including studying proposals for the introduction of some form of an intervention tax, such as the so-called Tobin tax, on financial transactions by the IMF) of providing stability in exchange markets and ensuring immediate assistance to countries that have serious balance of payments problems. Thirdly, Canada has given priority to examining and improving current surveillance measures, as well as to updating financial support mechanisms, through international institutions. By getting more adequate information about potential crisis situations through constant vigilance, it was hoped that the element of surprise would be taken away.

## ASSESSING CANADA'S REPUTATIONAL CLAIMS

### Status Seeking

Having built up the impression that Canada's reputation as a 'good international citizen' rests on a solid declaratory/operational foundation, which has persisted from the immediate post-1945 period up to the present, it is necessary to test the Canadian performance in a more rigorous and comprehensive fashion. Notwithstanding the claim that Canada has faithfully embraced the established multilateral order, this image of Canada's character has not been universally accepted. On the contrary, a number of counter-claims have been made that contest—and devalue—the notion of a wholehearted Canadian commitment and sense of responsibility to this set of international/multilateral rules of the game as a dominant feature in Canadian foreign policy.

The first critique targets Canada's motivation for adopting a high-profile stance on the international stage in the first place. Rather than being propelled primarily by a sense of responsibility towards the creation of an international order, the Canadian impulse to support international institutions and conventions is said to be stimulated by what may be termed 'status seeking.'[43] From this point of view, the high degree of salience given over to functionalism in Canadian behaviour had less to do with questions of resources and comparative advantage and more to do with stature. The benefits of adopting functionalism were, from this critical perspective, twofold. Symbolically, a 'good international citizen' approach provided a country such as Canada with enhanced status in the international system, allowing it to be distinguished from both the great powers and the minor players. Instrumentally, the approach offered tangible spillover benefits in terms of institutional positions on both a national and personal basis.

Historians who have adopted this view of Canada's behaviour have paid considerable attention to the drive of the cohort of 'Ottawa Men' surrounding Lester Pearson at External Affairs. A flavour of the type of debate may be gained by reference to an early flurry of controversy about the nature of the motivation behind Canadian diplomacy in the immediate post-World War II period. In an article informed by the wider revisionist current of the time, and published not in a 'professional' journal but in the 'popular' *Canadian Forum*, Jack Granatstein and Robert Cuff took on what they considered the 'accepted version of Canadian foreign policy after 1945.'[44] While appreciative of the diplomatic skills of the Pearsonians, Granatstein and Cuff cautioned against a portrait of Canadian behaviour that contrasted the impulse towards a virtuous international 'involvement' pushed by these individuals with the 'old isolationism' favoured by the strain of Canadian politicians—notably Mackenzie King—who thought 'the best policy for Canada was to be left alone and to leave alone.'[45] Building on the notion of status seeking, namely, that with the assumption of responsibility came representation and influence, Granatstein and Cuff demonstrate that functionalism not only allowed Canada to 'get a share in decision-making';[46] this model also allowed the 'ambition and talent' of the Pearsonian cohort to be more fully appreciated. As the two authors detail: 'In the prewar era...the policies of Mackenzie King held sway.... The war and its quantum jump in Canadian power had seemingly altered all that, and the Department [of External Affairs] attracted some of the ablest men in Canada. If Canada retreated to prewar somnolence once again, the people would either leave External or wither. It is no slur to Pearson [and the others in this cohort, who] wanted Canada to play a role that fitted their talents. The largest possible role in the world for Canada meant the largest possible role for them, a role they believed themselves completely capable of carrying out.'[47]

· The twist that Granatstein and Cuff put on their assessment concerns the role of Mackenzie King. Rather than interpreting King's role as that of an 'obstructionist,' holding back the wave of Canadian commitment to a new international order, they see his caution as an anchor that imposed the necessary 'disciplines' and 'limitations' on Canadian activity. The danger for King was that any bold form of commitment served as a licence for overstretch, which would lose, not add, political points at home. As Granatstein and Cuff squarely put it: 'Involvement meant trouble, and trouble meant strain on the fabric of national unity.'[48]

As John English contended in his quick rebuttal to the Granatstein and Cuff article, there were some difficulties with this line of argument if taken too far.[49] The contrast in the relative amount of influence possessed by the 'professionals' over Canadian foreign policy in the two historical periods should not be exaggerated. After all, many of the most committed of the Canadian internationalists, including Pearson himself, rose through the ranks of External Affairs in the 1930s. Nor can it be said that the 'Ottawa Men' represented a monolithic and united entity. In terms of his attitude towards 'involvement,' Pearson occupied a middle position within External, between the idealists represented by Escott Reid on one side and the pragmatists such as Hume Wrong and Norman

Robertson on the other. Still, as English himself acknowledges, 'pride' as well as 'principle' played a part in determining Canadian behaviour.[50] Being there allowed a greater world role for Canada. While wanting to help build up a habit of co-operation internationally, especially over disputes and crises, Canada also was interested in staking out its own position as a responsible and influential player. This search for influence in the decision-making process paid off when Canada was 'listened to with great attention, not only by the big powers but also by the smaller countries.'[51]

## Order over Justice

Another critique that attempts to re-evaluate Canadian foreign policy motivations focusses on the normative bounds of Canada's commitment as a 'good international citizen.' Looking at Canada not from an inside-out but from an outside-in perspective, a wide number of scholar-activists have taken Canada to task for concentrating its activities on system maintenance rather than on system reform and transformation. One rich source of criticism from this current of discourse/action may be found in the work of Cranford Pratt. Pratt finds Canadian behaviour to be wanting on a variety of counts. Temporally, Canada is treated as a country in retreat from its tradition of 'humane internationalism.'[52] Despite the continued presence of abundant strength for cosmopolitan values within Canadian society at the mass level, the erosion of support for this set of ideas at the élite (or 'dominant class') level is said to explain this marked divergence. Substantively, special attention is paid to the 'defensive' and 'negative' attitude adopted by Canada towards the creation of a New International Economic Order (NIEO) as laid out by the Group of 77 in the 1970s.[53] When challenged by a set of innovative proposals which would benefit developing countries but might prove costly to Canada, Pratt concludes that Canada has wrongly put its own national interests before the interests of the international community.

As with the 'status seeking' critique, the argument about a Canadian retreat from 'humane internationalism' should not be overdone. Throughout the post-1945 era, Canada has subordinated the concepts of 'redistributive justice' and 'equity' to the concepts of 'stability' and 'order' in international affairs. Canada has tended to take a safety-first approach on the issue of international economic reform. As shown by its willingness to support a number of selected commodity stabilization schemes, Canada favoured a degree of flexibility with regard to the shape and application of the international system. By opposing any fundamental transformation of the international order, however, Canada defined the limits of its reach.

The confined nature of the Canadian approach was borne out on a variety of other issues, for example on the granting of 'special rights' to developing countries under the GATT. Far from being convinced of the advantages gained by the developing countries through the establishment of any 'new discriminatory measures in the form of preferences,' during the Pearson years Canada remained convinced that it was precisely this group of countries which posed a threat to the international system by 'undermining the GATT principle of non-discrimination.'[54] As Mitchell Sharp, an individual symbol of the extent of continuity in Canadian public life, elaborated in 1965: 'On the question of whether as a middle power we should be more helpful, there may be something to this.... I would suggest, however, that one of the reasons...why we don't always agree with the aims of the underdeveloped countries at the United Nations, was that we were very doubtful about some of the policies that were proposed. We were very doubtful, for example, about the desirability of having preferences in trade in favour of the underdeveloped countries. We felt this was undesirable, and we urged them to press forward in getting rid of the discriminations that exist rather than go forward into a system of preferences.'[55]

By placing the Canadian position in a proper historical context, the dramatic shift played up in Pratt's analysis is moderated. Far from a unidirectional move away from 'humane internationalism' in the 1980s and 1990s, a more erratic and uneven pattern may be found. On some issues, Pratt's pessimistic view of Canadian foreign policy is borne out to a considerable extent. On other issues, alternatively, this view may be seriously challenged. If Canada may be cast as being in retreat on development assistance, as will be discussed later in this volume, it may also be cast as a country advancing on some other increasingly salient social agenda items (including women's rights), which were ignored during the Pearsonian era. On this type of social issue, the progress was due in large part to the mobilization of a wave of activist social groups in the 1960s and 1970s, which as Pratt noted in 1983 had taken up a position 'in serious opposition to many components of the present consensus which underlies Canadian foreign policy.'[56] This 'counter-consensus,' while still held back in terms of their influence on foreign decision making, was significant in that it previewed many of the concerns that were to figure prominently in the redefinitions of security and rights in the next decade of foreign policy debate. The key belief of these non-state actors was that ethical obligations should not be constrained by territorial boundaries, but form a set of universal standards that must apply to all human beings in a common global community.

In any case, Canada should not be singled out in an idealistic fashion as an 'exceptional' country. This question of exceptionalism relates to two other problems found in Pratt's analysis of Canada as a middle power with a 'humane internationalist' tradition. The first of these problems stems from the exclusionary nature of this categorization. During the era of East–West conflict, as suggested in the previous chapter, Canada's preference was to work closely with a number of other countries that sought to lead through persuasion rather than through reliance on sheer weight or strength. Such countries as the Netherlands and the Scandinavian countries spring to mind. There was some considerable logic to comparing the policies of Canada to these 'like-minded' countries in the way that Pratt does. At a time of global transition, in the 1980s and 1990s, the position of these core countries has been supplemented by the enhanced role taken on by a broader set of countries. Many of the countries hitherto identified with the G-77 have shown themselves more willing to engage in mixed or cross-cutting forms of joint activity with industrialized countries, where there is a common interest in managing shared challenges. Rather than being seen mainly as potential economic (or diplomatic) competitors, therefore, these countries have been recognized as potentially useful coalition partners on at least a segmented basis.

Another problem with the normative approach taken by Pratt relates to the demanding standards set for Canadian statecraft, which are difficult to meet even for the like-minded countries that have been the long-standing opinion-leaders on North–South and development issues. The result, it may be suggested, reinforces the pessimism so evident in Pratt's analysis. Instead of pointing towards the opportunities with respect to a 'new life' for Canada as a middle power, in the way that other academics (Black and Smith, to name just two) and practitioners (the 1992 Citizens' Inquiry into Peace and Security, for example) have done, Pratt almost exclusively highlights the constraints.

## Canada as a Multilateral 'Chisler'

Another critical treatment of Canada's foreign policy record looks in more detail at the inconsistencies in Canada's multilateral behaviour throughout the post-1945 era. Most bluntly, a recent article by Ernie Keenes contends that Canada's claim to be a wholehearted supporter of the multilateral system is little more than an elaborate myth.[57] Despite an attempt to push forward a radical form of revisionism, the main significance of Keenes's work may be that it serves as an antidote to the idealism emanating not so much from practitioners but from the scholars and activists within the counter-consensus strain.

While Pratt emphasizes the direction Canadian foreign policy should have taken in accordance with the values of 'humane internationalism,' Keenes conducts an intense 'internal critique' of the factors that are said to have undermined Canada's commitment to the multilateral 'article of faith.'[58] A close reading of Keenes's work brings out the coincidence between his perspective and the orthodox perspective favoured by the older cohort of 'Ottawa Men.' For all their abundant differences over values, such as the merits of state autonomy and politicization/depoliticization of foreign policy, these perspectives agree at least to the extent that they point to the 'pursuit of bilateralism through multilateral means,' *vis-à-vis* the Canada–US relationship, and the subordination of the altruistic to the instrumental. There is less difference than one would have thought between John Holmes's emphasis on the 'hard-boiled calculation of national interest' and Keenes's appreciation of the 'consciously self-interested' approach adopted by the Canadian state élite.[59]

Nor is Keenes's voice a lone one when it comes to directing attention to the 'gaps' in Canada's adherence to multilateral norms and values. Keenes's voice may well be the most robust, but it must be seen as part of a larger chorus that has taken up the same song. Academically, the fullest expression of this revisionist drive is captured in the edited collection by Claire Cutler and Mark Zacher, entitled *Canadian Foreign Policy and International Economic Regimes*.[60] The central concern of this volume is the tracing of the discrepancies between the enthusiastic declaratory statements of Canadian state officials and the uneven practice concerning multilateralism and economic liberalization. In its comprehensive analysis, a picture emerges of Canada as a more 'ordinary' as opposed to an 'exceptional' country. In contrast to the widely held portrait of Canada as a country that tried its best to firmly adhere to the rules of the game, and so enhance its reputation as a system maintainer, Canada is seen as a calculating operator. As the two editors conclude: 'The picture of Canadian policies towards international economic regimes portrayed in many of the chapters is not that of a country that is particularly unique or irresponsible. Rather it is a picture of a country that is quite pragmatic and, hence, inconsistent in its adoption of certain policies.... On various issues Canada has supported and opposed [the principles of multilateralism and economic liberalism] in varying degrees at different times. Canada has been a very normal country that has not been above the fray of international politics.'[61]

Building on this framework, with its emphasis on the lack of 'absolute support' for multilateralism and non-discrimination by Canada, the contributors to the Cutler and Zacher collection elaborate on this type of behaviour in a variety of issue-areas. Michael Webb points out in considerable detail, for example, how from the time of the creation of Bretton Woods financial institutions Canada was prepared to violate the 'norms, rules, and decision-making procedures,' on international monetary issues, 'just as did overseas countries.'[62] Webb details how, as early as 1950, Canada allowed its dollar to float despite the fact that this move was at odds with the IMF rule of fixed parity. Webb's conclusion, therefore, is that Canada gave only 'qualified support' to this nascent regime.[63]

### Challenges to Trade Liberalization

As with Keenes's appraisal, nonetheless, the bulk of the attention in this edited collection is given over to Canada's mixed record in the trade arena. In the 1960s, one action held up as a prime illustration of this sort of behaviour was Canada's imposition of an import surcharge on a targeted set of goods.[64] Another case pointed to in the same negative fashion was Canada's reluctance to go along with the proposal during the Kennedy Round of GATT negotiations (1963–7) for 'linear tariff reductions' or equal percentage cuts in tariff instead of the traditional product-by-product bilateral negotiations. As Finlayson and Bertasi highlight, Canada argued for an 'exception' on the basis of Canada's particularistic economy, for under this revised scheme Canada's resource-based economy would have benefited less than other economies with a greater manufacturing profile.[65]

In the 1970s and early 1980s, pride of place is given to the new face (or more accurately, faces) put on Canadian policy. Admittedly, the events of the early 1970s completely changed the bilateral context in which the overall Canadian foreign economic policy was made. In traumatic fashion, the so-called 'Nixon shocks' of 15 August 1971 signalled a rupture in the traditional pattern of management of the US–Canada relationship through the techniques of quiet diplomacy and access. Canada saw these shocks, featuring both the suspension of the convertibility of US dollars into gold and the placement of a 10 percent surcharge on manufacturing goods entering the US, as an indication of the unwillingness and/or incapacity of the US to adhere to the major tenets of the postwar economic order. The fact that the US did not exempt Canada from the import surcharge marked a hiatus in the much-proclaimed special relationship between Canada and the US. After all, as John Connolly, the US secretary of the treasury, bluntly told the Canadians, these measures were designed 'to shake the world. And that, brother, includes you.'[66] The sense of transition was reinforced when President Nixon addressed a joint session of the Canadian parliament in April 1972. The US president used this opportunity to make explicit the implications of the so-called 'Nixon doctrine' for Canada, namely that each country had to define its own interests, ensure its own security and take responsibility for its own progress.

These events helped to shape, for a brief period of time at least, a more self-help-oriented Canadian approach. In functional terms, as borne out by the strengthening of the Foreign Investment Review Agency (FIRA), the establishment of Petro-Canada and the Canada Development Corporation, and the introduction of the National Energy Program (NEP), priority was given to the strengthening of the Canadian economy by both the 'judicious use of Canadian sovereignty'[67] and the co-ordinated development of Canadian resources. As Charles Pentland convincingly argues, a dominant underlying theme in Canadian economic strategy was the push towards (and the later pull-back from) 'the adoption, in a mild form, of the sort of neomercantilism fashionable in many states' responses to the global economic crisis of the 1970s...represent[ing]...a logical extension of the mild form of statism we have seen on the domestic scene.'[68]

In geographical terms, as will be examined more extensively in the later chapter on neighbourhood, the main thrust of the Canadian approach was a search for counterweights to reduce the vulnerability with regard to the US. This so-called 'Third Option' of bilateral diversification had many facets. Nevertheless, centrality was given to the pursuit of a new constructive relationship with the European Community, epitomized by the signing of a Framework Agreement on Commercial and Economic Cooperation in July 1976. As Keenes describes this 'internationalist' version of bilateralism: 'Canada pursued closer relations with the EEC through the Framework Agreement (the so-called 'Contractual Link'), with Japan, and with a range of NICs [Newly Industrializing

Countries]....multilateral rules and institutions were not irrelevant or contradictory to this process, but the focus was more self-consciously selective, state-centric, and self-interested.' It had become clear that in the 1970s the international political economy was 'less multilateralist and more competitive, indeed even predatory, and that Canada could not afford not to respond in kind.'[69]

The other face of the new Canadian trade approach was a more defensive one, as exhibited by Canadian behaviour during the time of the Tokyo Round of GATT trade negotiations (1973–9) on the issue of developing-country imports. To pick up on Krasner's terminology, the use of selective instruments in the form of non-tariff barriers was attractive to Canada given the 'particularistic' nature of the design of these instruments.[70] Selectivity offered the attraction of allowing Canada to cater to what may be called its 'juxtaposition of strength and weakness,'[71] pressing for more stable and secure access in its competitive sectors at the same time as it retained a substantial element of manoeuvrability in terms of safeguards for its own import-sensitive producers. Consistent with an image of a calculating operator, Canada embraced many of the subtle methods of the new protectionism on a case by case basis.

One does not have to swallow this revisionist tonic straight up to allow that this type of endeavour offers a valuable service for the study of Canadian foreign policy. In terms of substance, the debate about Canada's historical performance as a supporter of multilateralism and trade liberalization will in all likelihood continue. Whereas Cutler and Zacher see Canada's multilateral glass as being at least half empty, other scholars still see Canada's glass as at least half full. A solid defence of Canada's record has, in particular, been proffered by Tom Keating in his book *Canada and World Order*. While acknowledging the various 'limits' and 'compromises' in Canada's multilateral faith,[72] Keating is judicious in locating this behaviour in the wider international context. These include the self-help measures deployed by the major actors in the international political economy (including not only the European Community and Japan, but also the US); the widespread use of the 'gaps' and 'loopholes' allowed by the international trading system;[73] and the support provided for some of Canada's 'exceptions' by likeminded countries (Australia and New Zealand, for instance, also opposed the proposal for 'linear tariff reductions').

In terms of process, the reappraisal by Cutler and Zacher is compelling in that it showcases the intermeshing of domestic politics and foreign policy. With formerly 'low' issues increasingly in command, internal societal forces have been more involved in 'domestic' issues having international ramifications and in those 'international' issues that spill over into the national arena—ineluctably, as Putnam would have it, a two-level game.

What stands out about the Canadian approach to international trade is that this dynamic reflected the bisected nature of the Canadian economy. Where Canada has some competitive edge, sectoral forces have pushed for a greater degree of multilateralism and trade liberalization. During the Tokyo Round, the pulp and paper, aluminum and steel, and chemical sectors put continuous pressure on the Trudeau government to aggressively tackle the problem of barriers against processed material. In many other cases, this heightened form of internal pressure has imposed a strong element of constraint, pulling Canada away from acting on these principles because of concern that this type of activity might cause pain to uncompetitive sectors, making them more vulnerable to the exigencies of the changing international economic system. While the Trudeau government placed a high priority on global economic development, it was also sensitive to the needs and interests of Canadian manufacturing, largely concentrated in Ontario and Quebec. As such, it was willing to do things such as reimposing global quotas on footwear imports from low-cost sources[74] and tightening customs inspections of imported automobiles when the going got tough for the local industries concerned.

In placing greater attention on the theme of internal–foreign policy interplay, with consideration given to the 'important influence of Canadian domestic factors' as a force both of constraint and of support for liberal multilateral regimes,[75] the revisionist thrust offered by Cutler and Zacher also links up a number of disparate strands of Canadian scholarship. Although viewing this dynamic in less symmetrical terms, Pratt has also highlighted the impact of domestic actors as both active stimuli and inhibiting forces with respect to international commitment. So too has the ongoing research program of the North–South Institute. Writing in 1982 in his capacity as executive director of the institute, Bernard Wood pointed to the two extremes of this duality. On the one hand, Wood recognized that the heightened 'narrowness and reticence' in the Canadian position in the Tokyo GATT Round was brought about because of the rearrangement of domestic interests at home. On the other hand, Wood allowed that the bias towards self-interest over altruism was being further tilted forward by the process of change in trade relationships. In gauging the impact of the backlash (in language which emphasized the 'fatigue' factor) in Canada, Wood noted that this defensive response was inspired by a 'prevalent Canadian assumption that [it] has been playing by the "rules of the game" and carrying more than its share of the "burden" of low-cost imports—Canadian critics refer to "boy-scoutism" and "naivete."'[76]

The discrepancy between image and performance in the Canadian approach to foreign economic matters also informs much of the work by Michael Hart. Although not a scholar in the classical sense (his analytical production began when he was an 'insider' to the policy process), what is striking about Hart's revisionist tendencies is how much they parallel Keenes's. Although these tendencies are certainly not in tandem (the intellectual conversation between them is certainly restricted), their views on the Canadian record share many characteristics. Both privilege Canada's bilateral tendencies over multilateralism. Both highlight the inconsistencies, opportunistic impulses and 'myths' in Canada's performance. Both focus on the (relatively autonomous) role of the Canadian state élite.[77] This parallel in their points of view comes out most strongly on the issue of the nature of Canada's original support for the ITO in the immediate postwar era. The consensus view remains that the 'Canadian government... strongly supported the ITO.'[78] In making this case, Keating quotes an External Affairs document to the effect that, notwithstanding 'all of its weaknesses, the ITO project is an inspiring internationalist approach to world-trade problems, and the Charter represents perhaps the most ambitious project of international legislation yet attempted.'[79] When the ITO project was abandoned, Keating adds, Canadian officials continued 'to work for the strengthening of the GATT' rather than embarking on a 'full-scale retreat from multilateralism.'[80] Keenes and Hart break sharply away from this consensus. Keenes writes that 'in order to protect their autonomy, Canadian officials welcomed the replacement of the ITO with GATT.'[81] Hart, albeit in a more nuanced fashion, reaches the same conclusion.[82]

Extending this mode of analysis temporally, Hart has continued his critique on Canada's credentials as 'a good multilateral citizen.' He has been especially scathing of Canada's record on a number of issues, arguing that Canada has 'gained a reputation for being a nation of artful chisels.'[83] There is, unquestionably, something in this critique. One illustration of Canada's 'chisling' behaviour that Hart points to is on the question of agricultural trade within the GATT context. Notwithstanding Canada's traditional standing as a pillar of the agricultural trade system, Canada's performance during the latter stages of the Uruguay Round of GATT trade negotiations appeared to befit a country acting on the basis of an explicit 'self-help' approach as opposed to the pursuit of liberal, multilateral reform. This defensive type of statecraft was particularly evident in Canada's resistance to changes in GATT's Article XI and its internal system of supply management. Rather than being portrayed as principled, Canada's performance during the Uruguay Round was viewed by a variety of close observers as ambiguous to the point of hypocrisy.[84]

### Offsets and Countertrade

Another aspect of trade policy in which Canada has exhibited this type of opportunistic behaviour, it is suggested, is in the area of barter or countertrade. In declaratory language, Canada has been a long-standing critic of any form of compensation trade. In the immediate post-1945 era, Canada labelled this type of practice as an inefficient and regressive approach. In 1949, C.D. Howe, the minister of trade and commerce, laid out the position that has dominated official Canadian thinking ever since: 'The Canadian government is not favourably disposed towards barter agreements between governments. It believes in multilateral trade and is opposed to any system of trade which tends to interfere with multilateral trade.'[85]

Despite this claim, Canadian behaviour on countertrade has not been entirely consistent. As Hart notes, 'Canada's chisling encompassed [d]iscriminatory government procurement contracts...encrusted with offsets and other perform-ance requirements.'[86] Canada's motivation for institutionalizing the practice of mandated offsets, with particular reference to the purchase of military equip-ment, has been shaped by a perception of Canadian self-interest. At one level, the demand for offsets on major capital projects such as aircraft, helicopters, sub-marines and ships has allowed Canada a number of advantages in the way of research and development and technology transfer. The compensation basket added on a deal, whether through an industrial benefits package or a form of co-production, has allowed Canada to develop technological skills otherwise unavailable to it. A classic case of this sort was the contract for the supply of six Halifax frigates, shore facilities and related support, signed in July 1983 (expanded to twelve ships in 1987). Among the major benefits negotiated under this long-term program was the creation of a design, development and construc-tion capability at Saint John Shipbuilding and a Canadian electronics integration system at Paramax Electronics in Montreal. As the Department of National Defence put it, the contract called for 'the establishment of a continuous and autonomous Canadian capability in warship and warship systems production, including combat systems design, integration and testing, and...the integration of two or more major electronic subsystems, including the software, to be carried out by one or more Canadian-controlled companies.'[87]

Offsets have also been considered as expedient means for developing better market access for Canadian goods. Usually this motivation has featured some form of marketing assistance provided by the sellers of major weapons systems. This pattern is best illustrated by reference to the 1980 deal with the McDonnell Douglas Corporation for $2.4 billion worth of F-18 aircraft and associated pro-jects. McDonnell Douglas won the order largely on the basis that it agreed to provide Canada with $2.9 billion worth of benefits. Although it was not oblig-ated to buy other products and services, McDonnell Douglas did agree to help find customers for a variety of Canadian goods and services. These items ranged from purchases of Canadian-made parts and equipment by McDonnell Douglas to 'socio-economic' benefits including co-production agreements, export devel-opment assistance, joint ventures and even tourism projects.

Other projected purchases by Canada's armed forces, including the (nuclear) Canadian Submarine Acquisition Project, were based on similar calculations. The main reason for looking offshore for submarines was simply that Canada didn't have the design expertise for vessels with the necessary under-ice capabilities. The industrial benefits package offered under the project, however, opened up the possibility of establishing this type of capacity in submarine building, with the provision of a worldwide product mandate. As the project manager for DND put it, 'One of the primary objectives of the project [is] maximizing Canadian industrial participation.'[88] Likewise, one of the major justifications for the pur-chase of the EH-101 helicopters was said to be its benefits in research and devel-opment and export sales. As Paul Manson, the former chief of staff at the

Department of National Defence and president of Paramax, stated: 'This [deal] will provide sustainable, high-technology industry and enormous job creation for Canada.'[89]

What further motivates these Canadian activities, of course, has been the regional dimension in its offset policies. A key rationale for all the large capital projects acted upon or considered in this manner has been the distribution of the industrial benefits across Canada. All of the projects mentioned above were explicitly broken down according to commitment imposed on contractors, *vis-à-vis* industrial benefits, along regional lines. For example, in the case of the frigate project (with the last ship due to be delivered at the end of 1996), the contract specified that $4.4 billion (1987–8 dollars) in industrial benefits were to be achieved between 1983 and 1997. This total included regional commitments to the Atlantic provinces of $1,584 million, to Quebec of $1,338 million, to Ontario of $662 million and to the western provinces of $106 million.[90]

Few, if any, observers would disagree with the assessment that these types of activities have an opportunistic or convenient flavour to them. Still, the Canadian experience even on these controversial issues is far from being cut and dried. When placed in a wider context, the nuances stand out. For a start, the barrage of criticism generated within Canada by these practices needs to be taken into account. Because procurement practices become political 'footballs,' issues of efficiency and regional equity surface in an intense way.[91] This was particularly evident in episodes such as the struggle between the Manitoba and Quebec governments over the contracts for the maintenance and service of the Canadian F-18s. Against this background, some major players openly questioned the entire *modus operandi* of the federal government's military procurement system. In early 1993, for instance, the president of Bombardier's North American aerospace group publicly stated that Ottawa should rethink its policy of breaking up its major defence projects into dozens of pieces across the country. This scattergun style, it was claimed, contributed to a weakening of 'the existing centres of excellence' and to the existence of overcapacity in the sector.[92]

This negative reaction, it should be added, is further encouraged by the recent change in situational and structural factors. Cynicism about the abuses of the political system with respect to lobbying practices and inside political deals reached a crescendo in the latter stages of the Mulroney government. The blocking of the extravagant contract for EH-101 helicopters fit snugly with the Chrétien government's desire (and success) in playing up the Chevy–Cadillac stylistic dichotomy with its predecessor. From an external angle, the transformation of the security environment brought about by the demise of the Soviet Union and the end of the Cold War weakened appreciably the military/industrial argument concerning the need for major capital projects (with resultant opportunities for offset). Although the notion of a peace dividend could be disputed, both government decision-makers and societal groups challenged the efficacy of major defence-spending projects (especially for 'redundant' items designed for anti-submarine warfare) when social programs faced tight financial constraints and deep cuts.

In any case, it must be allowed that Canada's compensation practices were restricted to a narrow range of activities. The open way in which Canada operated in the military-related offsets—Prime Minister Trudeau stated that 'not only do we not object to...[this] more sophisticated form of countertrade...we practice it'[93]—may be contrasted with the sensitivity with which Canada responded to any charges that it was involved in the conduct of civil offsets. This sensitivity was especially evident in the case of procurement of civil aviation (a code over which activity was the subject of long and hard negotiation beyond the timeframe of the Uruguay GATT negotiations). Although overshadowed later by all the attention given to Mulroney's personal involvement during the episode, the issue of offsets was the original source of controversy when Air Canada entered into a contract to purchase the European Airbus A-330 and A-340 aircraft at the same time as Canadair was awarded a contract to build components for the Airbus. Canada was accused by the American government and by companies such as Boeing of engaging in the practice of civil offsets. As one US trade official charged: 'We think the US firms can compete in terms of price and so on, but that some offset arrangements have entered into the deal, contrary to the aircraft code of the GATT.'[94] Indeed, helped by the spotlight shone on it by the Canadian media (particularly by a number of 'exposé' stories on the *Fifth Estate* television program), this issue continued to reverberate through the FTA negotiations. Despite public accusations of underhanded dealings, however, Canada continued to claim that its practices were above board. And while there was some smoke, there was no concrete evidence of a fire around the episode.

Nor, it needs to be mentioned, did Canada enter into the 'external' dimension of countertrade in any strategic or state-led activist fashion. Unlike a wide number of other countries, Canada has not used countertrade as a diversified and systematic means for dealing with the problem of market access. Rather, the Canadian government's response has remained tactical and ad hoc in nature. If countertrade was entered into, it was done as a solution of last resort.

This is not to suggest that there were no temptations to break from orthodoxy. In the 1970s and early 1980s, countertrade became a factor in cases where Canadian interests had tapped into an important emerging market and then were confronted by some form of 'mandated' countertrade. A prime example of this type of experience was the giant Bukit Asam mine project on South Sumatra Island in Indonesia. In other cases, countertrade was introduced at a late and sensitive stage of trade negotiations. The best known of this type of case is Atomic Energy of Canada selling Candu-type reactors and technology to Romania. Both of these deals caused a great deal of embarrassment for the Trudeau government. In the Indonesian case, Canada's Export Development Corporation (EDC) and the Canadian International Development Agency (CIDA) had put together a $180 million 'parallel financing' package to help win

Canadian firms contracts relating to the mine project, a package that was placed in limbo by the Indonesian countertrade demands. In the Romanian deal, as the EDC made clear, countertrade introduced in this ad hoc fashion constituted 'a costly and cumbersome way to do business.'[95] Stung by the image of Canada being repaid with Romanian goods such as buses, cars and rolled steel (albeit not strawberries, as often suggested), Jean Chrétien (then the minister of energy) tried to distance his department and himself as much as possible from the deal.[96]

These temptations were accentuated during the initial stages of the Mulroney government. Soon after his first election victory, Prime Minister Mulroney stated that 'Canadian companies have to get out and find new markets—and that means exploring different ways of doing business...including countertrade.'[97] A number of reasons may be put forward to explain this thinking. The first of these was Mulroney's own experience in the mining industry, as president of the Iron Ore Company of Canada. Faced with the reality that countertrade was a 'fact of life' in the mining sector, Mulroney had visited Romania in the fall of 1980 to meet with officials at the Romanian Ministry of Foreign Affairs about the possibility of some form of compensation deal.[98] A second reason is tied to the brief burst of enthusiasm for countertrade (which died away with the launch of the FTA negotiations) in media and policy circles. Mulroney's first senior policy adviser (Charles McMillan) had long been a persuasive advocate that Canada had to meet the 'dynamic influences in international trade' with greater flexibility and awareness.[99] A spate of newspaper articles, including one by Diane Francis entitled 'Exotic trading ideas may help our economy,' argued that Canada's lack of creativity in trading techniques had stymied the country's adaptation to an increasingly competitive environment. This attention was in turn part of a wider intellectual appreciation of the benefits of 'unorthodox' trading techniques as part of a new mode of governmental/firm diplomacy.[100]

Amid all this process of rethinking and reorientation by other departments and provinces (Saskatchewan and Manitoba, for example, were drawn into compensation deals on resources such as potash), External Affairs kept the faith. Although bending to the realities of unorthodox trading practices to the extent of upgrading information gathering and information dissemination for its 'clientele,' External drew the line at a facilitative approach. One senior DEA official stated prior to the 1984 election that Canada 'opposes the policy of countertrade and views it as a regressive trade practice.'[101] In the departmental reply to the recommendations laid out by the Special Joint Committee of the Senate and the House of Commons that a greater proportion of Canada's trade with developing countries should be conducted on a countertrade basis, the DEA reiterated that 'this type of trade arrangement can distort multilateral trade flows and needlessly complicate trading practices, often to the detriment of the importing country itself. As a general practice it is not...in the best interest of an international and payments system.' In maintaining its stance that the best way forward was not to defect from but to affirm the principles of the postwar international trading system, the Department signalled that 'Canada will seek, together with other like-minded countries in the forthcoming Multilateral Trade Negotiations and elsewhere, to achieve agreement on appropriate disciplines on the use of counter-trade practices.'[102]

## Multilateralism versus Bilateralism

The firmest ground on which criticism of Canada's foreign policy record stands may well be the argument that the dominant influence on Canadian behaviour has been bilateralism, not multilateralism. According to many observers, the elevation of multilateralism to the status of first-best option gives a misleading and distorted impression of Canada's performance. Strategically, this alternative line of argument gives preference to Canada's search for some form of special relationship with the US, whether through the convention of quiet diplomacy or by some form of institutionalized arrangement. Tactically, from a similar angle, considerable weight is placed on the way in which Canada tried to use the multilateral route to reinforce its own bilateral relationship with the US. Consistent with a desire to gain immediate economic advantage, Canada is said to have concentrated its attention at the GATT talks on the specific task of getting better access to the American market rather than on the diffuse task of expanding its trade in other markets.[103] Rather than viewing multilateralism as the prevailing principle that has governed Canadian foreign policy, with bilateralism occasionally intruding as a 'high risk' exception, the lens should be reversed.[104]

Much evidence can be mobilized to support the claim that it has been multilateralism and not bilateralism that has been 'exceptional' in the Canadian approach. It goes without saying that Canada has concentrated a great deal of its diplomatic effort on its major, contiguous economic partner in North America. This relationship not only consolidated the development of a more diversified and regularized form of diplomatic contact; it also provided Canada with some choice of options. One choice was a move towards a formal trade treaty along the lines of the abortive 1947–8 free trade negotiations.[105] Another was an extension of the type of sectoral deal established in the Defence Sharing Production Act and built on through the 1965 Canada–US Auto Pact.

At the level of both discourse and action, the choice of route for Canada to take was never a foregone conclusion. Throughout the post-1945 era, as Keenes has concisely put it, the Canadian 'state elite engaged in considered debates about the merits of bilateralist and multilateralist alternatives and the extent of protectionism and liberalization entailed by these alternatives.'[106] A strong (albeit minority) opinion long pressed that Canada should not put all its eggs in the multilateralist basket, not because it was wrong in principle to do so but rather because this approach did not ensure the safety of Canadian interests. Frustrated with the inability of the GATT negotiations to get the desired results in the early 1950s, the more impatient members of the state élite called for defection. Simon Reisman, for example, then a young official at the Finance Department, said he wanted the opportunity 'to work a big deal' with the Americans as an alternative to the multilateral trade path.[107]

For a period of approximately thirty-five years, this wish remained unfulfilled. Notwithstanding all of the frustration with the incomplete nature of the multilateral structure, the orthodox Ottawa consensus held up. Only in the early 1980s did sufficient disenchantment with multilateralism build up to bring this debate out in a more sustained and open fashion. The conceptual attractions of multilateralism remained obvious, both in terms of allowing Canada to enhance its status at the centre of the international trade negotiations and in channelling the Canada–US relationship into the multilateral arena. In practice, however, this approach no longer translated readily into tangible gains for Canada in the 1980s. A number of trade experts, most notably Rodney de Grey, openly questioned the appropriateness of Canada devoting so much energy on the 'rules of the game' when the nature of the international trade game itself was changing so quickly and substantively.[108] Far from indicating strength, it was suggested that this approach merely hid Canada's declining leverage with respect to the rearrangement of the international hierarchy of production, regionalism and emergent centres of economic power.[109]

This sense of disenchantment was exacerbated by change in the nature of the bilateral 'rules of the game' in the early 1980s. Whatever its usefulness for addressing 'yesterday's experience,' the focus of multilateralism on points of procedure, dispute resolution and disciplines appeared increasingly outmoded as a means of managing Canada–US relations generally and securing secure access to the US market more specifically.[110] As evident by the volume and intensity of the application of US trade remedies and countervail action towards Canada, which amounted to a form of 'contingency' action—directed 'when and where you need it'[111]—this traditional approach no longer served as an effective means of defusing the tide of American protectionism. Bilateralism, on the basis of this logic, could no longer be pursued largely through multilateral means; bilateralism had to be firmly embraced on its own merits as a basis for a reconstituted set of rules.

### The Canada–US Free Trade Agreement

Operating on these assumptions, Derek Burney and the ascendant cohort in DEA successfully wielded together a new official consensus in Ottawa. Reversing the priorities of the past, the goals of 'order' and 'stability' were to be pursued through bilateral means, which could then be directed into the multilateral arena. This group took hold of the agenda-setting mechanism in the pre-negotiating stage of the FTA. In September 1984, Burney took over the leadership and reorganized the DEA task force on Canada–US free trade, established in the fall of 1983 following release of the federal government's trade policy review. By the time of the report of the Royal Commission on the Economic Union and Development Prospects for Canada—with its call for a 'leap of faith' towards bilateral free trade—this task force had two years of experience and was ready to go public with its own report.[112]

The main question that must be asked relates not to the overall rejigging of preferences concerning multilateralism and bilateralism, but whether these two approaches are mutually inconsistent and incompatible. For the opponents of bilateral free trade, the answer is clear: the FTA constitutes a fork in the road,[113] which once taken allows no return to the multilateral faith. By taking the bilateral direction, this argument went, Canada diminished its own range of options at the national level. The immediate problem associated with this process of institutionalization stemmed from its exclusivity. A narrower North American focus raised the spectre of Canada being locked into a 'North American fortress.' At one level, this shift raised serious questions about Canada's image in the world, in that 'it carried the risk that third parties might perceive Canada as having reduced its political intent by virtue of establishing closer economic relations with the United States.'[114] At another level, this shift was said to have the potential of limiting the effectiveness of Canada's own bilateral diplomacy. Given Canada's asymmetrical position *vis-à-vis* the US, opponents of the bilateral deal contended that the isolation of Canada within a more confined space or neighbourhood reduced its zone of comfort with respect to its ability to temper American behaviour on issues of immediate concern. There were also problems associated with this move from a wider perspective. If continentalism succeeded in crowding out Canada's other connections, Canada's room for manoeuvrability in the international arena might become more limited.[115] More indirectly, any diminution (or vote of non-confidence) in Canada's commitment to multilateralism raised the possibility of a demonstration effect, which might 'jeopardize or undermine the stability of the GATT system'; even the Macdonald Royal Commission considered this 'a steep price for Canadians to pay.'[116]

The proponents of the FTA deal had a very different outlook on these questions. Far from undermining the international trading system, this form of bilateralism was said to compose a mechanism to buttress and revitalize multilateralism. In the words of two prominent liberal economists, 'multilateral and bilateral free trade are part of the same package.'[117] The shift undertaken by the Mulroney government, according to this logic, served less as a decisive break than as a form of measured adjustment to the (problematic) status quo. Instead of being regarded as stark alternatives, bilateralism and multilateralism have been presented as complementary elements of a 'two-track' path. While choosing to enter into a closer economic relationship with the US, Canada could also remain true to its traditional supportive role in the international order. As the External Affairs task force stated, 'the choice for Canada is not between multilateral or bilateral approaches to trade but how both avenues can be pursued in a mutually reinforcing manner.'[118]

Operationally, this mix of multilateralism and bilateralism allowed Canada some greater manoeuvrability. During the actual process of bilateral negotiations, the 'two-track' approach provided Canadian policymakers with space enough to take the heat out of the most controversial issues. Concrete decisions on agricultural marketing and a number of other sensitive questions were deferred to the GATT. Once implemented, this fall-back—or insurance—approach allowed a means by which Canada could weather the storms of American protectionism in the absence of an operationally effective system of multilateral rules and regulations; as such, it could be considered a 'smart, not sinister' move.[119] More ambitiously, it was hoped that the new set of legally binding arrangements (intended to secure and remove barriers to mutual trade) worked out in the bilateral Canada–US context could be extended over time to the multilateral sphere in the form of the creation of tighter disciplines. Targeted especially in this fashion were the areas of dispute settlement, which, with the creation of the Canada–US trade commission involving panels and arbitration, went beyond the dispute-resolution provisions contained in the GATT; and the agreement on the definition of subsidies, which went well beyond the multilateral codes established in the Tokyo Round.[120]

Some advocates of the FTA agreement took this line of argument even further. Far from being restrictive or limiting, they contended that the FTA worked to regenerate the overall constructive multilateral element in Canadian foreign policy. At the very least, it was felt that any Canadian government (and especially Mulroney's Conservative government) negotiating this type of bilateral arrangement would have some considerable incentive to show that an institutionalized special deal with the Americans would not impair Canada's capacity to look after its own interests in the international arena. Indeed, as John Whalley has suggested, Canada may well have a tendency to overcompensate for the FTA, in the sense that free trade with the US might increase 'the pressure on Canada to elevate its middle-power diplomatic role. The need is to demonstrate that Canada's sovereignty has not been impaired by the agreement, that Canada is a separate country that takes foreign policy positions independent from the United States.'[121] In a more instrumental vein, Peter Morici adds: 'Multilateral progress continues to be an important goal for Canada as a means both for further broadening market opportunities and for balancing its growing commercial cooperation with the United States with expanded economic interests abroad.'[122]

## Commitment and Convenience

From this evaluation it seems obvious that the extent of Canada's self-assessment of its commitment to the 'rules of the game' has been overdrawn. Canada's operational record has not lived up to the declaratory language concerning its desire and capacity to be a good international/multilateral citizen. One is left with a less rarefied—or unique—impression about Canada's performance.

Canadian governments have traditionally subordinated 'reform' and 'equity' to 'order' and 'stability' in the international system. Moreover, when the multilateral route has been found wanting, Canada showed itself willing and able to entertain the alternative, bilateral route.

Canada's selective forms of retreat have to a large extent been prompted by changes within the international economic system that were beyond its control. As the pattern and quality of American leadership over the international system was transformed in the 1970s, 1980s and 1990s, Canadian first followership was severely tested. The diminution in the American will and/or capacity to provide a benign or creative form of leadership increased Canada's feelings about a declining comfort zone. These feelings were accentuated further by the ascendancy of a multitude of actors and practices far less compatible with the rules of the post-1945 system. Domestically, the political stakes involved in upholding the rules have risen with the heightened pressures for adjustment.

What loss of credibility has taken place because of these convenient tendencies has been in some measure as well an unintended consequence of Canada taking such pride (to the point of hubris) in its reputation as a system supporter. Having won enormous symbolic (through a privileged seat at the table) and instrumental (by way of leverage) kudos from this image over the span of the post-1945 era, Canada was reluctant to let go even when a less lofty approach might have served Canada better. From this angle, Canada faced a tremendous self-imposed moral hazard, in the sense that Canada's actions were held hostage to the internalized experience—and raised expectations—of the past.

Canada's role as a system supporter should not be completely devalued in terms of either motivation or outcome. Canadian state officials continued to be obsessed with rule-making in the international system. And the language they deployed (Joe Clark went so far as to pronounce that 'In their way, these GATT rules are as important to us as our own constitution')[123] in making this claim certainly may be criticized for being out of proportion with Canada's willingness to advance an agenda in the 1980s and 1990s of 'progressive liberalization internationally' without the allowance and even facilitation of 'governmental intervention in the domestic economy.'[124] But, to be fair, this obsession reflected the embedded Canadian realities. Conceptually, informed by a prevalent concern about its position in a free-for-all in the international economy, Canada perceived a secure and orderly system as being the best architecture for defending its national interests.

In practice, Canada's pragmatic instincts militated against a full-scale retreat from internationalism. Canada's bilateral deviation was itself inspired by a search for effective rules of the game in another form. Furthermore, while eager to win a special deal with the Americans because of the high level of integration of Canada's economy with the US, even the Mulroney government knew the pitfalls of lending credence to the scenario of Canada being left alone with the US on the North American continent. The maintenance of Canada's reputation for a supportive international role remained crucial in keeping this distinction.

Canada's commitment to institutional development, as the foundation of a rules-based order, remained as strong in the post-Cold War era as it was in the post-World War II period.

It may be added that Canada recognized the boundaries of its deviatory behaviour. If quite prepared (albeit with some feelings of guilt) to skilfully bend the rules, by exploiting the 'gaps' and 'loopholes' in the system, Canada did not completely break with orthodoxy. While willing to engage in some segmented forms of self-help, managed or neo-mercantilist behaviour on a tactical basis, Canada did not seriously entertain the notion—never mind the practice—of a more ambitious and generalized form of strategic trade policy. Whatever the attractions of this model, the reputational risks on top of the organizational constraints were too formidable.[125]

Canada's behaviour, then, can be said to be as much convenient as committed.[126] When facing outward, with a focus on other actors' behaviour, Canada's commitment to the rules of the game has been fully engaged. When this commitment has meant taking action that would hit sensitive nerves at home, however, Canada has shown some decided reluctance to give unconditional support for this type of collective action at the international level. Casting aside the deep-set habits associated with its established reputational impulse, Canada changed the nature of its calculus and operated in a more ordinary and constricted fashion.

# NOTES

[1]  John W. Holmes, *The Shaping of Peace: Canada and the Search for World Order*, vol. 1 (Toronto: University of Toronto Press, 1979), 237.

[2]  John W. Holmes, 'The United Nations in perspective,' *Behind the Headlines* 44, 1 (Toronto: Canadian Institute of International Affairs, 1986).

[3]  Denis Stairs, 'The political culture of Canadian foreign policy,' *Canadian Journal of Political Science* 15, 4 (December 1982), 675.

[4]  Carolyn J. Tuohy, *Policy and Politics in Canada: Institutionalized Ambivalence* (Philadelphia: Temple University Press, 1992).

[5]  Thomas Hockin, 'Federalist style in internationalist politics,' in Stephen Clarkson ed., *An Independent Foreign Policy for Canada?* 119–30. See also Stairs, 'The political culture of Canadian foreign policy,' 667–90.

[6]  Hockin, 'Federalist style,' 121.

[7]  Robert Cox, 'Middlepowermanship, Japan and the future world order,' *International Journal* 44, 4 (Autumn 1989), 824–5.

[8]  Cox, 'Middlepowermanship,' 824. See also Andrew Fenton Cooper, Richard A. Higgott and Kim Richard Nossal, 'Bound to follow? Leadership and followership in the Gulf conflict,' *Political Science Quarterly* 106, 3 (Fall 1991), 391–410.

[9]  Robert Keohane, *After Hegemony: Cooperation and Discord in the World Political Economy* (Princeton, NJ: Princeton University Press, 1984), 126.

[10]  Cox, 'Middlepowermanship,' 824.

11  Quoted in John A. Monroe and Alex I. Inglis, eds., *Mike, the Memoirs of the Right Honourable Lester B. Pearson, Vol. 2: 1948–1957* (Toronto: University of Toronto Press, 1973), 33.

12  Arthur Andrew, *Defence By Other Means: Diplomacy For The Underdog* (Toronto: CIIA, 1970), 18.

13  John W. Holmes, *Canada: A Middle-Aged Power* (Toronto: McClelland and Stewart, 1976), 6.

14  A.F.W. Plumptre, 'Changes in the international environment,' in *Canada's approach to the next round of GATT negotiations,* (Toronto: Canadian Export Association, 21 February 1973), 3.

15  Stephen Krasner ed., *International Regimes* (Ithaca, NY: Cornell University Press, 1983), 2.

16  Susan Armstrong-Reid, 'Canada's role in the United Nations, Relief and Rehabilitation Administration,' unpublished Ph.D. thesis, Department of History, University of Toronto, 1981.

17  Escott Reid, *Radical Mandarin: The Memoirs of Escott Reid* (Toronto: University of Toronto Press, 1989), 175.

18  Craig Murphy, *International Organization and Industrial Change: Global Governance Since 1850* (New York: Oxford University Press, 1994). Murphy states that the Montreal location for the ICAO 'recognized the Canadian role in arbitrating the British–American dispute...and encouraged Canada to continue to act as the agency's main benefactor as well as fulfilling the American intention to move the centre of world governance across the Atlantic,' 194.

19  Address of Hon. L.D. Wilgress at final plenary meeting of the ITO preparatory committee, 22 August 1947. Quoted in B.W. Muirhead, *The Development of Postwar Canadian Trade Policy: The Failure of the Anglo-European Option* (Montreal and Kingston: McGill–Queen's University Press, 1992), 50. See also Frank Stone, *Canada, the GATT and the World Trading System* (Ottawa: Institute for Research on Public Policy, 1984).

20  Frank Stone, *Canada, the GATT and the World Trading System* (Ottawa: Institute for Research on Public Policy, 1984), 32.

21  *Ibid.,* 40.

22  *Ibid.,* 41.

23  A.F.W. Plumptre, *Three Decades of Decision, Canada and the World Monetary System, 1944–75* (Toronto: McClelland and Stewart, 1977), 13.

24  During the meetings on the ITO, Canada was referred to by the other contracting parties as one of the 'Big 3.' B.W. Muirhead, *The Development of Postwar Canadian Trade Policy: The Failure of the Anglo-European Option* (Montreal and Kingston: McGill–Queen's University Press, 1992), 50.

25  'Western trade in agricultural products,' in Andrew Shonfield ed., *International Economic Relations of the Western World 1959–1971, Vol. 1 Politics and Trade* (London: Oxford University Press for the Royal Institute of International Affairs, 1976), 347. See also Theodore H. Cohn, 'Canada and the ongoing impasse over agricultural protectionism,' in A. Claire Cutler and Mark W. Zacher, eds., *Canadian Foreign Policy and International Economic Regimes* (Vancouver: UBC Press, 1992), 63–5.

26 'Benson listens to Canada in key decisions on wheat,' *Financial Post*, 21 January 1956, 7.

27 'U.S. role in GATT termed crucial,' *Financial Post*, 6 December 1955.

28 A.F.W. Plumptre, *Three Decades of Decision*, 141. Canada was also able to interject some valuable ideas of its own. See Tom F. Keating, *Canada and World Order: The Multilateralist Tradition in Canadian Foreign Policy* (Toronto: McClelland and Stewart, 1993), 54.

29 Robert Cox, 'Globalization, multilateralism and democracy,' The John W. Holmes Lecture, *ACUNS Reports and Papers 1991–2*, 1.

30 Quoted in Leigh Sarty, 'Sunset Boulevard revisited? Canadian internationalism after the Cold War,' *International Journal* XLVIII, 4 (Autumn 1993), 753.

31 Quoted in 'Trade rules needed to halt world decline, Clark says,' *Winnipeg Free Press*, 16 September 1986, 14. See also his address to the Grains Council, 'Farm and foreign policy are tied tightly together,' Winnipeg, 7 April 1987.

32 Quoted in Darryl Gibson, 'Crosbie fears GATT failure will "badly smash" Canada,' *Winnipeg Free Press*, 14 November 1989.

33 Liberal Party of Canada, *Foreign Policy Handbook*, May 1993.

34 Report of the Special Joint Committee Reviewing Canadian Foreign Policy, *Canada's Foreign Policy: Principles and Priorities for the Future* (Ottawa: Parliamentary Publications Directorate, November 1994), 33.

35 Testimony to House of Commons Standing Committee on Foreign Affairs and International Trade, *Minutes of Proceedings and Evidence*, 8 March 1994, 2:7.

36 See John M. Curtis and Robert Wolfe, 'Nothing is agreed until everything is agreed: first thoughts on the implications of the Uruguay Round,' in Maureen Appel Molot and Harald von Riekhoff, eds., *Canada Among Nations 1994: A Part of the Peace* (Ottawa: Carleton University Press, 1994), 110.

37 David Leyton-Brown, 'Extraterritoriality in United States trade sanctions,' in Leyton-Brown ed., *The Utility of International Economic Sanctions* (London: Croom Helm, 1987).

38 Quoted in Linda Diebel, 'Mulroney supports Japan in trade battle with U.S.,' *Globe and Mail*, 14 July 1989.

39 Testimony to House of Commons Standing Committee on Foreign Affairs and International Trade, *Minutes of Proceedings and Evidence*, 8 March 1994, 2:7.

40 See Robert Cox, 'Middlepowermanship,' 826. See also 'Multilateralism and world order,' *Review of International Studies* 18, 2 (April 1992), 161–80; and 'The United Nations organizations and hegemonic decline,' draft manuscript, 1987.

41 Testimony to House of Commons Standing Committee on Foreign Affairs and International Trade, *Minutes of Proceedings and Evidence*, 22 February 1995, 18:8.

42 Louise Fréchette, associate deputy minister, Department of Finance, testimony to House of Commons Standing Committee on Foreign Affairs and International Trade, *Minutes of Proceedings and Evidence*, 22 February 1995, 16:56.

43 Bernard Wood, *Middle Powers and the General Interest* (Ottawa: North–South Institute, 1988).

44  J.L. Granatstein and R.D. Cuff, 'Looking back at the cold war: 1945–54,' *Canadian Forum*, July–August 1972, 8.

45  *Ibid.*, 10.

46  *Ibid.*, 10.

47  *Ibid.*, 10.

48  *Ibid.*, 10.

49  'Revisionism revisited: a response,' *Canadian Forum*, December 1972, 16–19.

50  *Ibid.*, 17.

51  Raminsky Papers, File PWCP, to T.A. Stone, 7 August 1944. Quoted in J.L. Granatstein, *The Ottawa Men: The Civil Service Mandarins 1935–1967* (Toronto: Oxford University Press, 1982), 306 (footnote 70).

52  Cranford Pratt, 'Canada: an eroding and limited internationalism,' in Pratt, *Internationalism Under Strain: The North–South Policies of Canada, the Netherlands, Norway, and Sweden* (Toronto: University of Toronto Press, 1989).

53  *Ibid.*, 29.

54  Quoted in Grant L. Reuber, *Canada's Interest in the Trade Problems of Less-Developed Countries* (Montreal: Private Planning Association of Canada, 1964), 6.

55  Mitchell Sharp, Minister of Trade and Commerce, quoted in Gordon Hawkins ed., *Middle Power in the Market Place: A Discussion of Canadian Trade Policies* (Toronto: Canadian Institute of International Affairs/University of Toronto Press, 1965).

56  Cranford Pratt, 'Dominant class theory and Canadian foreign policy: the case of the counter-consensus,' *International Journal* XXXIX, 1 (Winter 1983–4), 100.

57  Ernie Keenes, 'The myth of multilateralism: exception, and bilateralism in Canadian international economic relations,' *International Journal* L, 4 (Autumn 1995), 755-78.

58  *Ibid.*, 758.

59  *Ibid.*, 759.

60  A. Claire Cutler and Mark W. Zacher, eds., *Canadian Foreign Policy and International Economic Regimes* (Vancouver: UBC Press, 1992).

61  *Ibid.*, 15.

62  Michael C. Webb, 'Canada and the international money regime,' in *ibid.*, 158.

63  *Ibid.*, 160.

64  Tom F. Keating, *Canada and World Order: The Multilateralist Tradition in Canadian Foreign Policy* (Toronto: McClelland and Stewart, 1993), 139.

65  Jock A. Finlayson with Stefano Bertasi, 'Evolution of Canadian postwar international trade policy,' in Cutler and Zacher, *Canadian Foreign Policy and International Economic Regimes*, 24.

66  Quoted in Kim Richard Nossal, *The Politics of Canadian Foreign Policy* (Scarborough: Prentice Hall, 1989), 72. See also Raymond Heard, 'Who said anything about a special relationship,' *Montreal Star*, 6 October 1971.

67  C.C. Pentland, 'Domestic and external dimensions of economic policy: Canada's Third Option,' in Wolfram F. Hanrieder ed., *Economic Issues and The Atlantic Community* (New York: Praeger in Cooperation with the Committee on Atlantic Studies, 1982), 141.

68   *Ibid.*, 150. See also Ernie Keenes, 'Rearranging the deck chairs: a political economy approach to foreign policy management in Canada,' *Canadian Public Administration* 35, 3 (Autumn 1992), 381–401.

69   Keenes, 'The myth of multilateralism,' 772.

70   Stephen Krasner, 'The Tokyo Round: particularistic interests and prospects for stability in the global trading system,' *International Studies Quarterly* 23, 4 (December 1979), 491–531.

71   Charles Lipson, 'The transformation of trade: the sources and effects of regime change,' *International Organization* 36, 2 (Spring 1982).

72   Keating, *Canada and World Order*, 121.

73   For a comprehensive discussion of these features, see Jock A. Finlayson and Mark W. Zacher, 'The Gatt and the regulation of trade barriers: regime dynamics and functions,' *International Organization* 35, 4 (Autumn 1981), 561–602.

74   Margaret Biggs, *The Challenge: Adjust or Protect* (Ottawa: North–South Institute, 1980).

75   Cutler and Zacher, *Canadian Foreign Policy and International Economic Regimes*, 5–6.

76   Bernard Wood, 'Canada and Third World development: testing mutual interests,' in Robert Cassen et al., eds., *Rich Country Interests and Third World Development* (London: Croom Helm, 1982), 117.

77   Alan M. Rugman, in quite a scathing review of *Decision at Midnight*, criticizes Hart's 'one-dimensional' account for being 'too self-centred and self-serving.' Hart, Rugman suggests, is too traditional in his view of the role of the provinces and the private sector: 'He sees these as groups to be managed and fed information in briefing sessions, but whose views make no impact on the negotiations.' Review of Hart, *Decision at Midnight*, in *Canadian Foreign Policy* II, 3 (Winter 1994), 124–8.

78   Keating, *Canada and World Order*, 63.

79   *Ibid.*, 63.

80   *Ibid.*, 63.

81   Keenes, 'The myth of multilateralism,' 763.

82   Michael Hart, *Also Present at the Creation: Dana Wilgress and the United Nations Conference on Trade and Employment at Havana* (Ottawa: Centre for Trade Policy and Law, 1995). Hart quotes from DEA's Annual Report for 1948, to the effect that 'The Charter [for the proposed ITO] is not a perfect document…. There was a consensus of opinion…that the compromise reached was the best that could be achieved in view of the inherent difficulties of the task and the fact that the charter entered into fields of international economic relations which had hitherto remained unexplored,' 50.

83   Michael Hart, *Mercantilist Bargaining and the Crisis in the Multilateral Trade System: Finding Balance between Domestic and Foreign Trade Policy*, Working Paper, Centre for Trade Policy and Law, Carleton University and the University of Ottawa, 1989.

84   Jeffrey Simpson, 'A two-headed agricultural policy,' *Globe and Mail*, 17 November 1989; Hyman Solomon, 'Canada's contortions on supply management,' *Financial Post*, 15 March 1990; Barry Wilson, 'Canada takes on two roles at the same time,' *Western Producer*, 14 December 1990. See also Richard A. Higgott and Andrew Fenton Cooper, 'Middle power leadership and coalition building: Australia, the Cairns Group, and the Uruguay Round of trade negotiations,' *International Organization* 44, 4 (Autumn 1990), 589–632.

85   House of Commons, *Debates*, 9 February 1949, 393.

86   Hart, *Mercantilist Bargaining*, 21.

87   Department of National Defence, *1994–95 Estimates*, Part 111, National Defence (Ottawa: Minister of Supply and Services, 1994), 126. Within the larger industrial benefits commitment, $457 million worth of R & D benefits were to be paid to Canadian industry.

88   'Nuclear submarine dilemma: to buy or not to buy,' *Financial Post*, 1 December 1986.

89   Testimony to the House of Commons Standing Committee on External Affairs and National Defence. Quoted in Tim Harper, 'Why big money keeps nurturing helicopter deal,' *Toronto Star*, 30 June 1993.

90   *1994–95 Estimates*, Part 111, 125–6.

91   See Robert M. Campbell and Leslie A. Pal, *The Real Worlds of Canadian Politics: Cases in Process and Policy* (Peterborough: Broadview Press, 1989), 19–52.

92   'System hurts firms, says aerospace chief,' *Ottawa Citizen*, 28 January 1993.

93   Quoted in 'Trudeau tries to save huge Indonesian deal,' *Toronto Star*, 12 January 1983.

94   Giles Gherson, '"Buying from Airbus would be unfair," U.S. tells Crosbie,' *Financial Post*, 23 April 1988.

95   Quoted in David Stewart-Patterson, 'Ottawa tries to ease countertrade issues,' *Globe and Mail*, 23 April 1984.

96   Margaret Munro, 'Barter arrangement for reactor comes as news to energy minister,' *Vancouver Sun*, 11 August 1983.

97   Address to the First Ministers Conference, Regina, 1985. Quoted in Giles Gherson, 'Rising tide of countertrade changes rules for Canadian exporters,' *Financial Post*, 20 April 1985.

98   Deodra Clayton, 'Barter deals must not clash with domestic trade rules,' *Financial Post*, 12 September 1981; 'Iron ore mining: it's export or die,' *Financial Post*, 13 June 1981.

99   Charles J. McMillan, 'The pros and cons of a National Export Trading House,' in K.C. Dhawan et al., *International Business: A Canadian Perspective* (Don Mills: Addison-Wesley, 1981), 243.

100  For a spirited intellectual defence of these practices in the wider IPE literature, see Susan Strange, 'Protectionism and world politics,' *International Organization* 39, 2 (Spring 1985), 233–59.

101  Quoted in Mark Lukasiewicz, 'Countertraders travel a two way street,' *Globe and Mail*, 11 June 1983.

102  External Affairs Canada, *Canada's International Relations: Response for the Government of Canada to the Special Joint Committee in the Senate and the House of Commons* (Ottawa: 1985), 3.

103  See B.W. Muirhead, *The Development of Postwar Canadian Trade Policy: The Failure of the Anglo-European Order* (Montreal and Kingston: McGill–Queen's University Press, 1992).

104  G. Bruce Doern and Brian W. Tomlin, *Faith and Fear: The Free Trade Story* (Toronto: Stoddart, 1991), 45–6.

105   See Robert Cuff and J.L. Granatstein, 'The rise and fall of Canadian–American free trade, 1947–8,' *Canadian Historical Review* LVIII, 4 (December 1977), 459, 482; Michael Hart, 'Almost but not quite: the 1947–8 bilateral Canada–U.S. relations,' *American Journal of Canadian Studies* 19, 1 (Spring 1989), 25–58.

106   Keenes, 'The myth of multilateralism,' 756.

107   Muirhead, *Development of Postwar Canadian Trade Policy*, 67.

108   See Ronald Anderson, 'Freer world trade trend unlikely to be resumed,' *Globe and Mail*, 28 September 1978; 'Lack of Canadian clout reflects trade realities,' *Globe and Mail*, 31 August 1979. See also Rodney de Grey, *Trade Policy in the 1980s: An Agenda for Canadian–U.S. Relations* (Montreal: C.D. Howe Institute, 1981); R. de Grey, *United States Trade Policy Legislation: A Canadian View* (Montreal: Institute for Research on Public Policy, 1982).

109   Hart, *Mercantilist Bargaining*.

110   Doern and Tomlin, *Faith and Fear*, 285.

111   Gilbert R. Winham, *Trading with Canada: The Canada–U.S. Free Trade Agreement* (New York: Priority Press, A Twentieth Century Fund Paper, 1988), 37.

112   Government of Canada, *How To Secure and Enhance Access to Export Markets* (Ottawa: Department of External Affairs, 1985).

113   Donald Creighton, *The Forked Road: Canada, 1939–57* (Toronto: McClelland and Stewart, 1976).

114   Winham, *Trading with Canada*, 21.

115   See, for example, Jim Turk, *Free Trade With the United States: The Implications for Canada* (Ottawa: Canadian Centre for Policy Alternatives, 1985).

116   *Report of the Royal Commission on the Economic Union and Development Prospects for Canada*, vol. 1 (Ottawa: Minister of Supply and Services Canada, 1985), 303.

117   Richard G. Lipsey and Murray G. Smith, *Taking the Initiative: Canada's Trade Policy Options in a Turbulent World* (Toronto: C.D. Howe Institute, 1985). See also Murray G. Smith, 'A Canadian perspective,' in Robert M. Stern, Philip H. Trezise and John Whalley, eds., *Perspectives on a U.S.–Canadian Free Trade Agreement* (Ottawa/Washington, DC: IRPP/The Brookings Institution, 1987), 54–9.

118   Government of Canada, *How to Secure and Enhance Canadian Access to Export Markets* (Ottawa: Department of External Affairs, 1985), 3. For Pearson's own search for balance between multilateralism and bilateralism, see Monroe and Inglis, eds., *Mike, Vol. 2*, 32.

119   Comment by J. David Richardson on paper by Margaret Biggs, 'An international perspective,' in Robert M. Stern, Philip H. Trezise and John Whalley, eds., *Perspectives on a U.S.–Canadian Free Trade Agreement* (Ottawa/Washington, DC: IRPP/The Brookings Institution, 1987), 15.

120   Testimony by Gilbert Winham to House of Commons Standing Committee on Foreign Affairs and International Trade, *Minutes of Proceedings and Evidence*, 16 November 1994, 12:14. See also Gilbert R. Winham, 'NAFTA and the trade policy revolution of the 1980s: a Canadian perspective,' *International Journal* XLIX, 3 (Summer 1994), 472–508.

[121] John Whalley, 'Comments' on Jeffrey J. Schott, 'Implications for the Uruguay Round,' in Jeffrey J. Schott and Murray G. Smith, eds., *The Canada–United States Free Trade Agreement: The Global Impact* (Washington, DC: Institute for International Economics, 1988), 176.

[122] Peter Morici ed., *Making Free Trade Work: The Canada–U.S. Agreement* (New York: Council On Foreign Relations, 1988).

[123] Paul Knox, 'Clark urges GATT members to start talks,' *Globe and Mail*, 16 September 1986.

[124] John Gerard Ruggie, 'Unravelling trade: institutional change and the Pacific economy,' in Richard Higgott, Richard Leaver and John Ravenhill, eds., *Pacific Economic Relations in the 1990s: Cooperation or Conflict?* (St. Leonards, NSW: Allen and Unwin, 1993), 36–7.

[125] Roy MacLaren made a point of explicitly rejecting strategic trade theory. Roy MacLaren, 'The road from Marrakech: the quest for economic internationalism in an age of ambivalence,' *Canadian Foreign Policy* II, 1 (Spring 1994), 3. On the possibility of implementing strategic trade and industrial policies in Canada, see Richard G. Harris, *Trade, Industrial Policy and International Competition, Royal Commission on the Economic Union and the Development Prospects for Canada, Research Study No. 13* (Toronto: University of Toronto Press, 1985).

[126] For an excellent discussion of the committed and convenient concepts, see Robert L. Paarlberg, 'Ecodiplomacy: U.S. environmental policy goes abroad,' in Kenneth A. Oye, Robert J. Lieber and Donald Rothchild, *Eagle in a New World: American Grand Strategy in the Post-Cold War Era* (New York: Harper Collins, 1992), 207–32.

# STRETCHING THE BOUNDARIES OF SECURITY

## DEBATING THE MEANING OF SECURITY

The tension between old habits and new directions in Canadian foreign policy is most marked in the evolving debate about security. Driven by the sea change in circumstances created by the end of the Cold War, the 'essentially contested' nature of the concept of security has surfaced in a provocative and comprehensive fashion.[1] During the post-1945 era, there existed a commonplace understanding about what the essence of security implied. In terms of both thinking and policy practice, the concept was applied to state security, and the security of states was predicated on the existence of some physical threat to territorial sovereignty. The question of whom security was directed towards was equally straightforward, in that the target of concern or the distinctive 'other' was almost uniformly the Soviet Union and the Warsaw Pact countries. With the enormous changes in international politics precipitated by the collapse of the Soviet Union in 1991 and the disappearance of the bipolar rivalry between the United States and the Soviet Union, this uniformity of opinion ended. In Canada no less than elsewhere, right at the top of the list of vital questions that needed to be addressed in the new environment was the issue of what was meant—or just as significantly, not meant—by security. Key assumptions, formerly accepted with little or no discussion, faced a serious, sustained and diversified challenge.[2]

At the immediate policy level, the process of reorientation sparked a renewed 'defence debate' centred on the adaptation of national defence policies to the implications of what are invariably characterized as the 'challenges of the changing world order,' the 'transformation of the international system' and the 'new security architecture' of the post-Cold War era. Central to the budgetary component of this defence debate was a re-examination of what government spent on defence and, more importantly, why. Such governmental reconsiderations were driven to a considerable extent, particularly in Canada, by the relentless concern with cost-cutting and deficit reduction, and a belief that a handsome 'peace dividend' could be realized from the shifting international environment. But the desire to reformulate security also stemmed from a widespread belief among policymakers that the international system had changed so radically since the 1980s that policies and programs designed for Cold War conditions simply no longer were appropriate. Overtaken by the inexorable force of events, much of the underlying rationale behind Canada's strategic thinking appeared outdated.

At the level of ideas, the transformed context stimulated an expanded debate about the form and focus of security. Underneath, at the edges, and sometimes alongside the official debate about security there developed another vigorous (albeit uneven and often fragmented), unofficial type of discourse/activity about security. From this vantage point, Canadian security can only be examined through a very different lens. The official Canadian debate about security, notwithstanding all the attempts at updating and reinvigoratating contained within it, continues to locate security in statist terms. From this orthodox perspective, security is analysed in 'vertical' terms via the conduct and resolution of conflicts between states.[3] The locus of attention is concentrated on issues relating to military production and arms transfer, as well as force posture, strategy and tactics—all of which have to be managed on an interstate or intergovernmental basis. Critics of the official view alternatively define security more broadly, focussing not on the geopolitical context but on universal categories such as the fundamental values encompassing the economic, legal and environmental spheres. Rather than analysing security as the safety of states from attack and territorial intrusion, the primary concern is directed towards what has been termed 'human security.'[4]

Moving beyond the 'vertical,' security is accorded a 'horizontal' dimension as well, which takes into account the pattern of governance and provision of justice inside as well as outside a national domain. Extending the boundaries of concern beyond the familiar dimensions of war and peace and externally precipitated organized violence, salience is given to economic and social issue-areas.[5]

In many respects, of course, these two basic ways of conceptualizing security exist as two solitudes with a deep faultline between them. The official view gives primacy to the notion that governments should and must act as guardians of a 'national' interest.[6] The unofficial conception of security is informed by the desire to elevate societal needs and interests to the apex of the security agenda. Rather than the defence of the integrity of the nation state, the highest priority is given to the protection of the essential rights of individuals and groups. Where the official view lays emphasis on public performance, via the pursuit of international order and stability, the unofficial view highlights particularistic issues of justice and the private safety of people's lives on an individual and collective basis. One critic of the official view, appearing before the 1994 Parliamentary Review, stated that: 'By now it's clear that the threats to the security or well-being of people in much of the world have not diminished with the end of the Cold War....the structural violence of unjust social systems remains. The failure of many societies to meet basic human needs continues, as does the widespread denial of human rights and democracy.'[7]

The distance between the two perspectives, however, should not be exaggerated.

If a good deal of tension and rivalry may be found between them, in many ways this space has been narrowed both by their intellectual coexistence and by the way the two debates have overlapped with each other in policy terms. A persuasive call for a creative dialogue to further bridge this gap has been made by a number of well-known scholars. Barry Buzan has observed that a 'simple-minded' view of security, which constitutes a substantial barrier to progress, should be rejected in favour of a 'more fully developed and broadly based concept.'[8] Fred Halliday, in a wide-ranging article on the state–societal relationship, has added in a similar vein that the traditional compartmentalization of security prevents a more nuanced, accurate and conceptually challenging approach to understanding the transformation in international relations.[9] A parallel integrative dynamic may be found in terms of outcome, as the multifarious influence of the unofficial debate has permeated into the official vocabulary and activity. Ample recognition has been given to the existence of non-military sources of instability in the economic, social, humanitarian and ecological fields. The top priority of Canadian foreign policy, according to one of the co-chairs of the Special Joint Committee Reviewing Canadian Foreign Policy, is 'human security,' which he defined as 'human rights, economic prosperity and environmentally sustainable development.'[10]

This chapter tries to lay out some of the trends towards both fragmentation and integration found in the narrative and operational debate about security. It starts with a review of the evolving 'official' debate about the future of security and 'national defence' at the governmental level. An attempt is then made to trace some of the elements of the 'unofficial' debate emanating from societal interests. Given the extensive range of these issues, a complete map is not drawn up; rather, the duality of these debates, with particular reference to the fact that security is no longer exclusively regarded as being 'external' or 'internal' in nature, is provided through illustrative sketches. On the one hand, the manner in which these debates rub up against each other in a conflictual fashion is detailed. On the other hand, the evolving pattern of diplomacy, which allows for a new form of accommodation or even partnership in at least a segmented fashion, is touched upon.

## THE OFFICIAL DEBATE

### The Debate over the 'Peace Dividend'

The official debate turns on the question concerning the extent of the transformation in the security domain. From the broadest possible point of view, the post-Cold War era began with a marked increase in security. With the demise of the 'other,' the clearly identified presence of which lay at the heart of the entire rationale for the military/defence strategy of the West, the traditional sense of danger passed. True, during the Cold War era Canada had always remained somewhat removed from the likely theatres of battle in the scenarios of past East–West conflict; but there was a general recognition that in the era of intercontinental ballistic missiles and nuclear weapons, the country did not enjoy the status (to use the expression of the leader of the government in the Canadian Senate in 1924, Raoul Dandurand) of a 'fire-proof house, far from inflammable materials.'[11] By the end of the Cold War, the Canadian government's overriding security concern, reflected in the White Papers of 1971 and 1987, was over the impact of a central nuclear exchange between the United States and the Soviet Union, a fear which drove much of its policy towards the North Atlantic Treaty Organization (NATO) and the European region; for a scenario of this sort would very possibly happen over Canadian airspace, and so involve mass destruction and loss of life within Canada.

Serious differences of interpretation could nonetheless be found over the extent to which the diminution of the sense of danger from direct physical threats had given way to a concern with 'threats without enemies.'[12] For the foreign policy constituency, Canada's sense of liberation from the long-standing risks (and one may add commitments, in terms of contributing to a forward defence) associated with the defence of the West against the Soviets has been dramatic and complete. The opportunity in terms of the freedom of manoeuvre this condition gave to Canada was signalled by André Ouellet. Given that 'we do not have enemies anywhere,' Canada's foreign minister stated that the focus could now be redirected towards dealing with 'practical issues that affect their everyday lives.'[13]

The view that 'the Cold War is no more'[14] did not signify that Canadian foreign opinion leaders were sanguine about the nature of the transformation. If no longer facing the possibility of attack or invasion by the armed forces of another state, or the engulfing destruction of systemic nuclear war, Canada was widely perceived as facing a number of diverse threats, which are in many ways less predictable and less easy to plan for than the traditional dangers. One policy analyst, who has straddled the line between foreign policy insider and outsider, went so far as to say at the beginning of 1992 that 'the end of the Cold War, while stopping the global confrontation of the two superpowers, has opened up more instability, [and] more challenges to security, and more dangers of armed conflict in the world.'[15] Another, from her vantage point as secretary of state (Latin America and Africa) in the Liberal government, echoed this pessimistic note: 'In the post-Cold War era, I think we do see that there is not indeed the peace dividend we had hoped to see…[rather] we see conflagrations multiplying, it appears, everywhere in the world.'[16] Attention was duly paid less to the prospects for the putative 'new international order' and more to the identification of the different sorts of disorders freed up by the release of the controls imposed by bipolarity. These disorders included the eruption of a number of unresolved conflicts pent up from the past, together with a rush of different challenges relating to the emergent context of globalization and interdependence. In the former category were issues relating to specific ethnic and/or territorial tensions; in the latter category fell demographic, economic and environmental stresses relating to questions of migration, resource scarcity and disease.

The defence constituency saw a greater degree of continuity of conditions. The 1994 Defence White Paper did recognize that there was a 'significantly reduced threat of nuclear annihilation' in the post-Cold War years, and that the 'fundamental realignment in the global balance of power' allowed 'progress toward a safer world.'[17] Where the defence constituency's outlook differed was in the greater weight it gave to the direct dangers faced by Canada from inter-state sources. Although acknowledging the impact of the indirect manifestations from intrastate and/or transnational issues on Canada's security and well-being, it continued to locate danger primarily in statist terms: that is to say, on threats to state security arising from the belligerent actions of other states (such as arms racing, weapons proliferation or intrusions on to the territory of other states) or from governmental breakdown or disorder. For example, officials will point to the dangers posed by North Korea's nuclear weapons program; a possible con-frontation between India and Pakistan; hyper-nationalism in Russia; regional tensions in southeast Asia and the Middle East; the potential fallout from regional conflict and disintegration in China and other countries; and the rise of 'rogue' states (with the trafficking of nuclear weapons etc.). While the Department of National Defence was vague in laying out definitive scenarios of this sort,[18] advocates of this view from outside of government tended to look backwards in search of the future. As a representative of the Conference of Defence Associations stated: 'We must remember that history has not really ended. After a decade or so, when the current instability has been replaced by new alignments, the traditional forces and geopolitics will exert themselves once again. We would then need to be prepared for serious problems emerging over the competition between new powers and new groups of powers.'[19]

## The Debate over Military Expenditure

One way in which this debate was played out hinged on resources. As in the past, a good deal of the ongoing struggle inside governmental circles related to the question of what type of military equipment best served Canada's interests generally and eased the so-called commitment–capability gap more specifi-cally.[20] From a foreign policy perspective, Canada had a desire to continually retool so as to counter its widely held image as a cheap or even free rider in terms of NATO. The purchase of sophisticated equipment was one form of con-tribution (or ticket) to gain access to the table (or, put another way, entry into the 'tent') of alliance deliberations.[21] Access was also important from a defence perspective. But this political/diplomatic motivation, in terms of having a pres-ence, was supplemented by a technical/strategic motivation. The driving force here had to do with the dynamic of high technology: once Canada fell behind or lost the capabilities to perform particular military functions, by declining to spend money on capital equipment and on new weapons, it was considered to be very difficult if not impossible to get these capabilities back.

What was different about this component of the debate were the high stakes involved. What support the defence constituency had traditionally enjoyed within Canada was eroded in the aftermath of the collapse of the Soviet Union. Unlike the 'greats' in the NATO alliance, Canada had no pretence to be a military power in the first place.[22] As Edgar and Haglund comment, this psychology contributed to 'the lingering suspicion held by many Canadians that there is something inherently dubious about military expenditures in a country that, in their eyes, has no interests that could effectively and ethically be safeguarded by the use of force.'[23] Given this situation, Canada had a predisposition to eagerly grasp the prospect of a 'peace dividend.' This impetus was reinforced by the circumstances of fiscal constraint that Canada found itself in. Because Canada's image of itself was not wrapped up with military prowess, Canadians had little problem with retrenchment of its armed forces. When faced with the choice of where to tighten the belt, defence could be squeezed with little outcry.

In addition to this unfavourable climate at the level of the mass public, the defence constituency faced a serious challenge to its position (and credibility) at the élite level. This came in the form of the Canada 21 Council, a blue-ribbon group that had coalesced in the last months of the Mulroney government to form a private 'royal commission' on the future of Canada's international relations. Its conclusions, released in March 1994, hit the defence constituency where it was already exposed.[24] Given that 'the prospect of an attack by the armed forces of another state or upon Canada's allies is now so unlikely that the case for maintaining [Canada's present] policy is no longer convincing,'[25] the report recommended a radical upheaval of the status quo. Targeted definitively, in this robust manner, were the established priorities and practices in terms of equipment. Calling for an end to spending designed for general-purpose combat capabilities, the report stated that Canada should concentrate its attention on securing the equipment necessary for peacekeeping activity. Instead of heavy artillery, air-to-ground fighter support and anti-submarine warfare, Canada should focus on the procurement of small patrol ships, transport and armoured personnel carriers for infantry.

In the face of this first challenge, the defence constituency hit back with considerable force. Criticizing the Canada 21 report for defining Canadian activity in too restricted a fashion, the supporters of this perspective argued that the flexibility built into the traditional approach must remain the cornerstone of Canada's defence policy. Only by maintaining a general or multi-purpose combat-ready armed forces, capable of activity across a wide spectrum, could Canada meet the various challenges before it. By this logic Canada did not need to (and should not) make hard choices about resources. If the Canadian military needed to do with less, this process of scaling down could be achieved by other means (the use of contingency forces) than by concentration on the argument put forward by Canada 21 that 'Canada cannot be everywhere and do everything.'[26]

This argument about instruments extended inevitably to one about principles. Under the weight of circumstances, and given the lack of sympathy within domestic popular opinion, the defence constituency was prepared to go along with a number of bold reforms in terms of the deployment of Canadian military personnel. Despite the loss of credibility these moves engendered among Canada's allies, there was no sign of public disagreement from DND on either the decision in September 1991 to withdraw all but 1200 troops from the Central Front in Germany or the decision to close completely the Canadian Forces bases at Lahr and Baden-Soellingen. On the contrary, both of these decisions were deemed to be justified by the transformation in the strategic context[27] and were readily incorporated into a revised plan of operations concerning Canada's contribution to NATO. Rather than being interpreted as a reversal in Canada's commitment, with Canada no longer willing or able to pull its weight, this change in posture was said to be a necessary adjustment to changing circumstances. The charge that Canada had somehow 'turned its back' on European security, according to this perspective, 'betrays a fundamental misreading of how to measure Canada's commitment to Europe. It also suggests a fear of change.... Canada has always been prepared to do the things that matter in European security...the question is not whether we are committed to the security of the Euro-Atlantic region—it is a question of how we can best make a real contribution to Euro-Atlantic security, one that meets the challenges of today and tomorrow, not those of the past.'[28]

## The Debate over NATO and the Role of OSCE

Where the defence constituency held the line on the Canadian commitment to the Western alliance was on the concept of collective security: the means could be modified somewhat, as part of a revision exercise, but this concept *per se* was held sacrosanct. The need for this firm foundation rested, as the 1994 Defence White Paper laid out, on a combination of factors, relating mainly to the set of values held in common with the Western alliance, the practical advantages derived from using standardized equipment and military procedures, and most vitally, the supposed inability of reconstructing a collapsed foundation in a time of future crisis.[29]

The foreign policy constituency took quite a divergent tack. Playing down the mission of collective security,[30] this perspective raised the profile of the alternative concept of common security. Once again, the Canada 21 report was in the vanguard of this movement. Indeed, the enthusiasm with which it pursued these themes—in 'preference to active alliance participation'—allowed this élite commission to be equated in the mind of at least one critical observer with the populist proposals of the vocal (but marginal) Report of the Citizens' Inquiry into Peace and Security.[31] The DND commentary on the Canada 21 report, for its part, questioned the international acceptance of the concept of common security.[32]

Given the radical nature of some of its proposals, the Canada 21 report was not digested whole by DFAIT. Some parts were totally unpalatable, in that they might preclude concerted action between Canada and its allies.[33] These elements included the suggestions that Canada completely avoid peace enforcement that involved 'high intensity combat.'[34] On many other issues, though, the Canada 21 proposals were complementary to the general tenor of thinking within official Ottawa about the direction of Canadian foreign policy. Above all, the Canada 21 proposals underscored DFAIT's own preference for the projection of Canada's interests via innovative diplomacy as opposed to the exertion of military resources.

The flexible attitude with respect to foreign policy innovation is captured in a variety of ways within the Euro-Atlantic context. For one thing, the foreign policy constituency has been keener than the defence constituency to extend the membership of NATO eastward. While acknowledging the need to 'allay current Russian concerns over NATO expansion,' DFAIT's 1995 statement *Canada in the World* lent open support for 'an evolution in NATO's vocation and membership.'[35] By contrast, DND hedged its bets on the expansion issue; while approving in principle the enlargement of NATO in an easterly direction, the opportunities are still subordinated to the constraints engendered with this option.

The foreign policy constituency has also expressed far greater enthusiasm for diversified forms of activity beyond NATO. A prime illustration of this attitude can be found via the Conference/Organization for Security and Co-operation in Europe (CSCE/OSCE), a forum in which Canada has taken on an extended role. In large part, the attraction of this forum derived from its ability to fill gaps left open by NATO. Designed as a vehicle for the collective security of the West, NATO has had a difficult time in redefining its role in the post-Cold War years. The maintenance of peace and stability, both without and within the borders of its member states, is very different from its historical task of deterring external aggression. With these difficulties in mind, the OSCE serves an important complementary function. As a body encompassing former members of the Warsaw Pact as well as NATO and non-NATO Western countries, the OSCE acts as a handy bridge-building device for dialogue and security co-operation. At the same time, the comprehensive nature of the OSCE process gives it some additional advantages over NATO as a vehicle for transformation. With the ability to address 'the economic, political, and social facets of security, rather than focussing on military matters,' as one Canadian scholar put it in 1994, 'this forum already possesses the raw material for coping with the non-traditional sources of tension in today's Europe.'[36]

More specifically, the OSCE has had a variety of attractions for the Canadian foreign policy constituency. Symbolically, an influential role in this forum was perceived as a useful way in which Canada could signal the persistence of its Euro-Atlantic 'vocation.' Widely perceived to be losing its European credentials, political and diplomatic collaboration along these lines provided an offsetting impression or optic about Canada. Instrumentally, the OSCE's agenda honed in on areas where Canada enjoyed some specialized interest and/or comparative advantage. Most notably, Canada has been at the cutting edge of the push for a deepening of the 'human dimension' of the OSCE (with a stronger human rights regime), along with the development of a mandate for preventative diplomacy, conflict management and dispute resolution. In light of these dynamics, the main (and far from easy) challenge that remains is for Canada to 'take the lead in helping to design and formulate ways [the OSCE] could translate its broad principle of keeping the peace into practical measures.'[37]

## THE UNOFFICIAL DEBATE

The unofficial debate extends the concept of security to a much wider range of issues. Under this wider lens, security threats are more pervasive than traditional rivalries and confrontations between states. 'Real' security, it is argued, must encompass a much wider spectrum, relating to the questions of the reference points for security.[38] Removing the privileged status of the nation states, alliance structures and concerns over external aggression from other states, the definition of security is refined and expanded to cover the holistic concerns of private citizens.[39] The essence of security, or safety, from this standpoint rests on negative as well as positive criteria, namely the lack of insecurity on the part of individuals and groups. As another critic of the official Canadian security agenda stated before the parliamentary review: 'The ending of the Cold War has created a new and much broader security agenda. Canada's survival is no longer tied to the outcome of a potentially apocalyptic struggle over which Canadians have little influence. No longer are international power and influence measured largely in the military currency that Canada could never aspire to possess in large amounts. In the new era of globalization and growing interdependence, the distinction between domestic and foreign policy...has little meaning.'[40]

By opening up the concept of security in this manner, the debate becomes not only more complex but also somewhat more blurred and even amorphous in nature. The meaning of security in traditional military and territorial terms is fairly clear. What is meant by security when the term is used to denote the economic well-being of individuals, the social protection of groups, harmonious communal relations and the safeguarding of basic human rights is less obvious.[41] If more fragmented, however, the debate has become richer in flavour. Without the restrictions and relative discipline of the official debate, the unofficial debate has unlimited space in which to be provocative. Going beyond the sightlines of the familiar, the critical discourse of the unfamiliar is insightful in many ways. It not only picks up much of what was left out of the older debate; it also directs attention to both the sources of state–societal tension and co-operation on attempts to address emergent issues.

# The Security–Economics Nexus

## The Official Debate

One way in which the unofficial debate cuts very differently from the official debate is on the question of a security–international economics nexus.[42] The official debate visualized a tangible, but confined, connection between the two agendas. A firm connection was made between Canada's burden-sharing in the Western alliance and its stature as a 'resource storehouse.'[43] In keeping with its functional orientation, Canada took on a considerable degree of responsibility for the provision of scarce supplies. Much of this activity was narrowly directed at defence purposes (uranium, non-fuel minerals). Some attempt, however, was made to broaden this mandate. For example, in the early 1960s, Prime Minister Diefenbaker proposed the idea of setting up a NATO food bank for the distribution of surplus food to developing countries. By playing this role, Canada not only reinforced its claim to a seat at the table on functional grounds, but it was also able to extract some tangible benefits in the way of access to technology.

By the 1970s this type of nexus had come completely unstuck. Any belief that the notion of an Atlantic Community rested squarely (and comfortably) on the pillar of co-operative security in resources was rendered invalid by the subordination of collective to national interests. Although the notion of some form of NATO pact to ensure resources security was mooted during the time of the oil/commodity shocks of the 1970s, Canada and its alliance partners went their separate ways on policy outcomes. From a Canadian perspective, this set of circumstances encouraged not new forms of co-operative behaviour but a shift to a Canada-first approach. Indeed, they played into the notion of Canada as a principal power. In Eayrs's eyes, and those of a good many practitioners (most notably, Allan Gotlieb), the resource shocks of the early 1970s confirmed the upward movement in terms of Canada's place in the world. Unlike the majority of Western powers, which had a good deal of pain inflicted on them by these shocks, the heightened salience of resources as an instrument of leverage presented Canada with an ideal opportunity to positively reassess its 'capabilities in a world where the substance, and hence the distribution of power has undergone swift and radical change.'[44]

All of this being said, firm limits have remained in place on how far Canada has deemed it feasible to go in explicitly linking security and international economics. In particular, Canada has displayed a steady scepticism about the efficacy of coercive diplomacy. At the international level, this scepticism reflected Canada's continuing desire to channel activity through multilateral means. Even at the pinnacle of the Cold War, when it seemed clear who the enemy was, Canada steered a middle path between participating in collective action and resisting the imposition of unilateral measures. Canada was willing to go along with a collective effort on the part of the Western alliance intended to deny the passage of strategic goods to the Soviet bloc (mainly via the export control provisions of the Co-ordinating Committee on Multinational Export Controls (COCOM)). It was unwilling to wholly conform to the restrictive terms of the US's own Trading with the Enemy Act.

As the lines of East–West confrontation became less well demarcated through the 1970s and 1980s, Canada's search for a balance between the perception of its multilateral obligations and its own national interest became more convoluted. Canada's behaviour with respect to the Afghanistan/Korean Airlines flight 007 episodes can only be described as awkward (with punitive actions being for the most part limited to symbolic gestures). At the domestic level, paralleling the declining fortunes of the advocates of the principal power perspective, the trend has been to downgrade Canada's own capabilities to engage in solo variations of coercive diplomacy. A recent DFAIT study states that, in cases where another country's actions may be judged to be unacceptable by the international community, Canada would need to encourage 'multiple state participation' by way of an effective response.[45] Concern was also expressed, it must be noted, about the damage inflicted upon the commercial reputation of Canadian firms as reliable suppliers if sanctions were not imposed 'pursuant to a broadly supported international consensus.'[46]

In the place of these older, focussed types of debates, a number of jagged but intersecting debates have risen up in the 1980s and 1990s. The first of these debates relates to the themes of Canadian competitiveness and efficiency in the international economy. From the official perspective, this element of the security debate is wrapped up with the integrity and influence of the country. The dangers of relative loss of economic competitiveness are twofold: internationally, there are a multitude of symbolic and tangible problems associated with the loss of competitiveness; internally, there are serious dangers attached to the loss of national capacity in the way of loss of governmental legitimacy and effectiveness. As Stopford and Strange have bluntly put it: 'wealth is needed to preserve the state more from internal rather than external threats to its cohesion and survival. Without wealth or the prospect of future sources of wealth, even if there is no external security threat, the state falls apart.'[47]

These concerns have shaped the discourse and the policy direction of the Mulroney and Chrétien governments. Both governments have tied the stability and material well-being of the country into a process of adjustment towards economic rationalization and efficiency. The thinking of the Mulroney government was initially laid out in the 1985 foreign policy document *Competitiveness and Security*: 'Our dependence on trade means that we are economically secure only if we are internationally competitive.'[48] The core ingredient of its operational economic program was to lend momentum towards economic integration with the US. This agenda, it was argued, presented opportunities for an improved standard of living, not threats to be avoided.

In its attempt to get the economy right, the Chrétien government has followed roughly the same course.[49] While far more sensitive about the costs inherent in the pursuit of international efficiency and competitiveness—in particular, the problems of 'jobless growth' and the increasing inability of government to 'effect socially desirable outcomes' in an interdependent world[50]—the Liberal government has operated on the assumption that there is no turning back from the competitiveness/efficiency agenda. The costs of a U-turn are simply seen as being too high. These costs include, *inter alia*, the erosion of international business confidence; the loss of national prestige (as manifested by such things as increased pressure on G-7 membership) and bargaining leverage in trade negotiations; the dependence on external sources for lending elicited by the accumulation of external debt; and the inability to perform adequately in other areas of foreign policy because of diminishing resources. As witnessed by the onus placed on the trade 'Team Canada' approach, the Chrétien government has gone to great lengths to give the impression of Canada as a country competing as a single entity in the international arena. To give this notion a further fillip, the Chrétien government made a concerted effort after it came into office to raise productivity issues (labour markets, retraining, infrastructure) to the apex of the political/economic debate.

### The Unofficial Debate

The unofficial debate pays greater heed to the costs of efficiency and competitiveness in terms of their impact on generating insecurity among individuals. Under the load of forced adjustments in the 1980s and 1990s, individuals and groups who have traditionally looked to the federal government for help in terms of insulation and cushioning against change no longer feel safe.[51] A basic corollary to the globalizing economic system impinging on their economic well-being has been a reduced capacity of government to manage change, and with it a sharper delineation between winners and losers under conditions of uncertainty and risk.

The political expression of protest, arising out of this sense of insecurity, emerged most forcefully over the negotiations on the FTA and the GATT. As part of a larger dynamic, the liberalizing agenda galvanized a tremendous amount of resistance as well as support. One persistent face of this resistance movement has been defensive and inward-looking, with activist societal groups spearheading a territorially bounded campaign against what they see as the state of communal insecurity produced through the implementation of the FTA and the GATT. As part of this campaign, the language of security has been incorporated to represent these threats. The pull of continentalism was described as 'the subversion of the national economy' and an 'economic occupation.'[52] An official from the Quebec farmers' organization, Union des producteurs agricoles (UPA), defended the resistance to the imposition of a GATT deal in similar terms: 'all national groups tend to consider food self-sufficiency to be an attribute of national political sovereignty and an essential factor in collective stability and security.'[53]

The other face of this resistance has been transnational and outward-looking, with non-state groups attempting to build coalitions across borders. A precursor to this sort of activity may be illustrated by a reference back to the case of agriculture. As part of their resistance to liberalization, a considerable number of Canadian farm groups (including the UPA, the Dairy Farmers of Canada, the Canadian Chicken Marketing Agency and the Canadian Egg Marketing Agency, often in conjunction with the International Federation of Agricultural Producers) conducted their own transnational lobbying efforts prior to the conclusion of the Uruguay GATT Round of negotiations in December 1993.

## Human Rights

### *The Official Debate*

The way in which the unofficial debate cuts very differently from the official debate also comes out on the human rights agenda. The Canadian government has both led and lagged in terms of the human rights agenda over the last decade. On a number of issues, the Canadian government has displayed international leadership on human rights. Prime Minister Mulroney's overt and public calls for a linkage between human rights and development assistance, made at both the Commonwealth and francophone summits in 1991, provides an interesting illustration of this thrust. So too does the Canadian response to the coup in Haiti in September 1991, which ousted President Jean-Bertrand Aristide. Moreover, in his address at Stanford University, Mulroney made at least passing reference to the association between international human rights and domestic violence: 'invocations of the principle of national sovereignty are as out of date and offensive to me as police declining to stop family violence simply because a man's home is supposed to be his castle.'[54]

In terms of discourse, it is clear that the evolution of policy thinking by the Chrétien government has been towards a new synthesis that highlights the importance of human rights within a broader concept of security. *Canada in the World*, the government's 1995 foreign policy framework, made an explicit link between human rights and the fostering of a stable international environment: 'The Government regards respect for human rights not only as a fundamental value, but also as a crucial element in the development of stable, democratic and prosperous societies at peace with each other.'[55]

Declaratory policy aside, the dominant theme in the operational side of Canada's human rights diplomacy continues to be the search for balance between human rights and security of access for Canadian goods. Unlike activist societal groups, it was argued, the Canadian government could not afford to take a unidimensional approach to bilateral relations. As one state official analysed the difference, 'NGOs bring a particular focus to an issue and that's not the whole story....when government is taking a policy dimension on an issue, it's not only looking at the human rights dimension of that relationship; it has to look at a lot of other issues.'[56] From an official perspective, therefore, the emphasis has been on conducting human rights policy on a country by country basis rather than by attempting to embrace a uniform strategy applicable to all situations. Where there was evidence of human rights abuse, the Canadian government was willing to take some forms of responsive action; but this action was not done in a way that would jeopardize trade and commercial links. The economic security of Canadians had priority over the human rights of foreigners.

This search for balance is evident in Canada's policy towards China. In the aftermath of the June 1989 Tiananmen Square massacre, Canada was prepared to take a number of limited (and mostly symbolic) punitive actions.[57] Canada, however, quickly pulled back from even this modest form of protest, with a resumption of 'normal' relations with China. The lure of the vast commercial benefits to be found in China was too compelling. As early as August 1989 the Mulroney government moved to facilitate (through an Export Development Corporation loan) a deal in which Northern Telecom was to supply telecommunications equipment to China. Moreover, the emphasis on China as a 'priority market' was continued by the Chrétien government. Chrétien's targeting of China in a concerted fashion was said to be 'strongly motivated by trade and investment concerns' and his 'particularly bullish [view] on the potential of the huge and fast-growing Chinese market.'[58] Acting on these assumptions, Chrétien mobilized an impressive 'Team Canada' delegation (including nine provincial premiers) to go to China in November 1994. On this tour, human rights issues were downplayed.[59] The Liberal government was simply not willing to sacrifice its prospects of building 'an economic partnership with China that will create jobs and prosperity in Canada' on the altar of human rights.[60]

A similar set of circumstances (and constraints) existed in Canada's relationship with a number of newly developing economies. A prime example was Indonesia, a country that Canada had targeted since the 1970s for an expansion of investment and trade. Because of Indonesia's brutal occupation of East Timor, serious human rights trade-offs were placed in the way of Canada exploiting these commercial opportunities. These trade-offs became more sensitive with the political and media fallout from the Dili episode, the November 1991 massacre of unarmed demonstrators in the capital of East Timor. The Canadian government was willing to address the East Timor/Dili issues through classic quiet diplomatic means: acting with other like-minded countries through the UN Commission on Human Rights; pushing the Indonesian government to bring to trial and punish those responsible for the Dili incident; working for the implementation of the recommendations of the special rapporteur on torture; and ensuring access to East Timor for additional humanitarian organizations and human rights groups, such as the International Committee of the Red Cross. What the Canadian government was not willing to do was to completely cut off diplomatic discourse and/or commercial relations with Indonesia: the risks attached to either approach were judged to be too high. The only concession made in the way of punitive action was a suspension of a $30-million component in the aid program.

### The Unofficial Debate

This downplaying of human rights in the official agenda was strongly contested by activist societal groups with a focussed concern and expertise in this issue-area. In terms of substantive policy, these groups contrasted their own value-driven approach with the pragmatism displayed by government. The promotion of human rights and democracy, according to these groups, should come before the advancement of trade. Consistent with this view, these social groups have vigorously advocated a universal set of human rights standards, viewing any commercial–human rights trade-off as unacceptable. In terms of style, at odds with the quiet diplomacy favoured by the Canadian government, activist societal groups such as East Timor Alert Network adopted a publicity-oriented approach. Any means necessary were used to keep human rights issues in the glare of the media/public spotlight. This strategy was helped immensely, of course, by new technology in the field of telecommunications. Satellite television, computer networks and faxes cut down the tyranny of distance, while video cameras, camcorders and forms of electronic media allowed these groups to get their message through to a wider audience.

## The Security–Identity Nexus

### Women's Rights

A third way in which the unofficial debate cuts very differently from the official debate emerges on the security–identity nexus. One important area in which the competing priorities of the Canadian government and societal activists have clashed has been in women's rights. One expression of mobilization in this issue-area has been defensive in nature. Women's groups, together with allies in labour organizations, religious organizations and anti-poverty associations, resisted the FTA on the basis that jobs for women (especially those clustered in the textile and other low-paying sectors) would be among the first victims of economic integration.[61] Parallelling the trends in the environmental and human rights issue-areas, the other expression of mobilization has been in an outward direction. As the effort to redesign the political agenda accelerated, serious attempts were made to build new types of transnational links. Under the impetus of a common defence against the forces of harmonization and ratcheting down of standards, a variety of Canadian societal groups expanded their links and communication networks in the United States (and eventually, with the implementation of NAFTA, to Mexico through the Common Frontiers project and other initiatives).

In keeping with this outward-looking approach, international coalition-building has become a significant component of the repertoire of Canadian women's rights activists. Most notably, women's organizations have shown a considerable degree of solidarity on human rights and equality of women issues. In the 1980s the main target of activity was the passage and implementation of the Convention on the Elimination of All Forms of Discrimination against Women (CEDAW). In the 1990s attention turned more directly on the issue of recognition of women's rights as a fundamental component of the human rights agenda. As Kathleen Mahoney has argued, 'Where human rights were once considered matters of purely domestic concerns narrowly construed, global forces now mandate that they take on broader international dimensions, transcend borders, and command ever widening participation in their definition and implementation.'[62]

At a general level, women's rights groups worked successfully to have such questions as gender discrimination and violence against women included directly at the June 1993 World Human Rights Conference. The extent of the international women's network was highlighted by the fact that over 130,000 women in 100 countries signed a petition demanding that women's rights be treated as a specific thematic item on the agenda, and that gender issues were included as an integral part of all discussions.[63] More specifically, prompted by the horrific accounts of mass rape in the ethnic fighting in Bosnia and Herzegovina, both well-established and ad hoc women's groups combined in a campaign to put pressure on the international system to stop such assaults and to prosecute those responsible as war criminals.

While not entirely 'sovereignty free,' these outward-looking groups may be said to have a diminished territorial state of mind. This had a profound influence on the way they played a role in the political system (associating increasingly with citizens of other countries) and in their expression of loyalties (the identification more with personal attributes and less with 'lines on the map'). Seen in the 1960s and 1970s as part of the solution, national government has come in for a more critical assessment in the 1980s and 1990s. The emphasis of the women's movement on individual and group rights is entirely divergent from a concern with the exclusivity of national jurisdiction and territorially defined legal frameworks. As the petition addressing the issue of women's rights at the 1993 Human Rights Conference clearly shows, gender violence is viewed as 'a universal phenomenon.'[64]

By challenging these boundaries, women's groups manifested the extent of the faultlines between state and societal perspectives. These differences came to the fore on the question of gender persecution with respect to refugee claims in

Canada. As the president of the National Action Committee on the Status of Women argued, 'There's a whole area where there's being very little done and Canada could play a lead role.'[65] If the Canadian government could make value judgments against countries such as the Republic of South Africa for its state policies of apartheid, women's groups argued, why could it not take action in cases where countries such as the Kingdom of Saudi Arabia maintained state-sanctioned gender discrimination?

Yet despite intense pressure from societal activists, state officials initially resisted the claims of women's groups to privilege a new set of individual or group rights of non-citizens. As the minister of immigration in the Progressive Conservative government put it, 'I don't think Canada should unilaterally try to impose its values on the rest of the world. Canada cannot go it alone, we just can't.'[66] Each case, he added, would be decided on its individual merits. Although the government eventually relented, it may be added that another sort of proposal for Canadian international leadership on women's rights issues received little support. This was the call for Canada to impose sanctions or threaten to withdraw assistance from countries 'for the express reason that it systematically practices violence against women in gender-specific ways.'[67]

### Indigenous Peoples' Rights

Another area of state–societal tension has been on indigenous rights. To a considerable extent, this tension centres on traditional security related to issues of territorial integrity. There is an added dimension, however, in the form of the politics of identity and loyalty. At the core of many of the recent disputes on indigenous issues has been the question of who belongs to a community and who doesn't. Although outside the boundaries of the official or mainstream security debates in Canada, these controversies bear out the fact that Canada has not been entirely free from the politics of ethnic division within a country.

Throughout the post-1945 period, the Canadian government and indigenous groups have sharply differed over the use of land. Claims based on a view of the national interest achieved primacy over aboriginal rights. This divergence came to the fore on the issue of the establishment of military bases and the testing of weapons. To the Canadian government and to the advocates of the official defence perspective, this issue stands as a test of the strength of Canada's loyalty to the Western alliance. Conversely, to the indigenous people and their supporters, this issue demonstrates the need for the application of the principles of an unofficial security agenda to achieve 'real' security for individuals and groups.

A prime example of this type of tension came with the establishment of the NATO base for tactical low-level flying at Goose Bay, Labrador. This contribution had considerable value for the other member states of NATO, especially Germany, the Netherlands and Britain. It also had a number of ancillary benefits for Canada. As in the case of the Shiloh and Suffield bases, Canada's NATO allies paid for the use of the extensive training facilities at Goose Bay. The commercial pay-off for the local townspeople in Goose Bay and Happy Valley had also to be factored in.[68] On top of these types of direct economic advantages, moreover, this contribution was seen from a symbolic point of view as going 'very far toward meeting the very modest expenses of NATO membership.'[69] Critics, for their part, have questioned the validity of this alliance contribution argument. The view of the indigenous and non-state groups has been that the Canadian government has taken advantage 'of an international situation in order to pursue what it has identified as a domestic political priority...regional economic development.'[70]

Although the federal government conducted an assessment of the environmental impact of this activity, the local indigenous people—and their supporters in the Assembly of First Nations, NGOs such as Oxfam Canada and Project Ploughshares, and the Catholic and United churches—protested that this study addressed neither their land claims nor the question of personal safety. One well-known advocate for indigenous rights states that, in the decision to invite NATO countries to use an area belonging to native people for the training of jet fighter pilots, 'The Innu and the Inuit are completely disregarded.'[71] Another said that 'the conduct of military aircraft over-flights...are a violation of the Innu nation's sovereignty and self-determination.'[72]

The full extent of the faultline between the official and unofficial security agendas on this issue was revealed with the publication of the report of the parliamentary joint committee on defence policy. In general terms, the defence committee demonstrated some flexibility in arguing that 'military security is but one element of a broader concept of national security that must reflect political, economic, social, environmental and even cultural factors.' But on specific questions, the committee showed a disinclination to favour comprehensive and integrated policy solutions. In unequivocal fashion, the defence committee signalled its view that 'Canada's contribution to NATO is made in part through the provision of military flight training at Goose Bay, Labrador.' From the standpoint of the proponents of an unofficial security agenda, this stance showed the gap between assertions in favour of a broader concept of security and 'transcending the old military approach to security' in practice. In the words of the *Ploughshares Monitor*: 'the committee's cavalier treatment of the issue of low-level flight training...is a telling example of the moral emptiness and lack of vision' within mainstream security thinking.[73]

Acting to make this form of 'us' and 'them' conflict even more contentious is the wide-ranging clash of values and interests between Quebec and indigenous peoples. In common with other smaller national entities, the sense of perceived threat with respect to cultural and linguistic well-being has remained strong in Quebec. Both the projection of the Quebec personality in the international arena and the pursuit of economic development and the defence of French language rights at home are predicated on the need for and the value of its self-identity, and on its search for more policy space and autonomy. Quebecers are accustomed to mobilizing collectively on policy issues.

The full extent of the polarization between the Quebec government and the indigenous peoples in Quebec has been revealed on the Great Whale/James Bay hydroelectricity project. From the perspective of the Quebec state, this type of mega-project served as the pathway to economic security.[74] From the perspective of the Grand Council of the Cree of Quebec (the voice of the approximately 12,000 Cree who live in the region), alternatively, the project represented a direct threat to their territory and security as a people.

In tactical terms, the resistance of the Cree to the project was conducted largely through a transnational campaign. Replicating the means deployed by other societal groups, the Cree used a potent combination of skillful public relations and sophisticated lobbying techniques. While it must be noted that the Cree were supported in their campaign by a number of Quebec-based 'green' groups, including the Union Québécois pour la Conservation de la Nature, they took their message beyond the Quebec borders to the United States, where they concentrated on building a coalition of key individuals and environmental groups, including the New England Coalition for Efficiency and the Environment, the Audubon Society, the Natural Resources Defense Council and the James Bay Defense Coalition. The Cree were able by these means to target and influence the review of power contracts at the local state or city/municipality level.

Strategically, the Cree wanted to locate their struggle in the context of the struggle of indigenous peoples. Using its official status as an NGO in the United Nations system, the Cree directed considerable attention to building a sense of solidarity on the basis of a collective identity. Symbolically, the Cree pushed for the establishment of an International Year of Indigenous Rights. More substantially, they pressed the United Nations Commission on Human Rights to examine the question of Quebec sovereignty from the perspective of the minority rights of indigenous peoples.

An additional flashpoint centred on the Kahnawake and Akwesasne reserves in the aftermath of the Oka crisis of 1990. From the perspective of the Mohawks who live on these reserves, the central issue is their need to struggle to defend themselves against intrusions from the outside, whether by state officials in the form of the police (especially the Sûreté du Québec) or by private developers and local townspeople. By contrast, the majority of Québécois were prone to see the issue in a simple law-and-order context: that is, the actions of the Mohawks—both the shooting at the police and the blockading of roads—as little more than criminal actions. National safety, as well as national integrity and national state-building, had to be preserved.

The combination of a spillover from other issues (mainly smuggling, as the reserves straddle the United States border) and the changed constellation in Canadian politics (the accession of the Bloc Québécois, paradoxically, as the official opposition party in federal politics) helped fuel this particular situation. Effectively using the leverage of its position in Ottawa, the BQ has highlighted the need to restore legal authority over the indigenous communities. Arguing that organized crime was using the reserves as protected zones for their illegal activities, at least one BQ politician has called for 'a well-muscled intervention by the police and if necessary, the Armed Forces to rectify the situation.'[75] Although careful to make a distinction between a small number of criminals and the wider native community, Lucien Bouchard, as the leader of the BQ, suggested that joint Canada–United States action might be necessary as 'systematic violation of the law [is] totally unacceptable.'[76]

Structurally, predictions about an escalation in conflict have been further encouraged by the legacy of the involvement of the military in Canadian civic life. As Desmond Morton reminds us: 'Since the Korean war, the biggest military operations by the Canadian Forces have been carried out at home.'[77] This internal dimension of security is showcased by reference to the 10,000 soldiers mobilized (mainly in Quebec) for the October Crisis in 1970, and the deployment of a mechanized brigade group of the Canadian armed forces during the Oka crisis of 1990. The possibility of further involvement by the Canadian military in internal disputes, moreover, cannot be ruled out. Scenarios mooted along these lines, in the context of the volatility surrounding the October 1995 sovereignty referendum, can be broken down into two categories. The first of these hinged on widespread violence between an independent Quebec state and an indigenous population unwilling to accept the legitimacy of this claim.[78] The second relates to the division of the Canadian military, between those elements willing to become part of an armed forces for the new Quebec and those elements remaining allegiant to Canada.[79] While Morton warns against the temptation to seek solutions through any form of military intervention, he views the future with some trepidation: 'with the elimination of Canada's NATO bases in Europe and the scaling down of the army's war-fighting capacity, a venerable and controversial role returns.... Canada's land forces may be drawn into an historic but potentially self-destructive constabulary role.'[80]

## INTEGRATION AND FRAGMENTATION

### Criticism of the Unofficial Debate

It is tempting to devalue the unofficial security debate. Conceptually, this debate is extremely diffuse. By virtue of stretching the definition of security beyond the traditional concerns about territorial integrity, this debate may have considerable merit; but the cost of this loosening up of the conceptual boundaries is a lack of precision about the nature of security. Even sympathetic commentators of the unofficial debate observe that the intellectual 'turmoil' created through the process of 'reconceptualizing security' has bedevilled intellectual rigour. While important in allowing an escape from the rigidities of the official state-centred, national interest perspective, the unofficial debate has 'often come to resemble a grab-bag of different issue-areas, lacking a cohesive framework for analysing the complementary and contradictory themes at work.'[81] Instead of illuminating, the boundaries of the security debate have been stretched so far as to make the meaning of security amorphous and unoperational.

From a policy perspective, scepticism has been expressed about the applicability of denoting the bulk of the issues—especially those relating to the economic agenda arena—as 'security' issues. These issues, which are contentious given the forces of globalization and interdependence, it is argued, may be considered 'problems'; but they are not issues that should be categorized as 'threats.' To consider economic issues, such as structural adjustment, in terms of the 'security' agenda, from this sceptical point of view, is quite misleading. Rather than concentrating on the risks, the focus should be on dealing with these problems through a proper policy mix.[82]

This mode of thinking has been extended to the social rights agenda. Advocates of liberal-oriented policies hold that the 'triumph of the marketplace' will not only lift the degree to which economic well-being is encouraged and accommodated but that it will ultimately address many of the human rights 'problems' as well. From this outlook, an increasing respect for human rights on Western/Canadian terms can only come about with the momentum of economic growth. Canadian policy, therefore, should be geared towards enhancing its reputation as a reliable economic partner for internationally oriented reform policies. Put another way, security in human rights matters must follow the advance of economic security. Temporally, this approach was said to require a long-term perspective: Canada should seek to point out to countries with problematic records that desired economic outcomes would not only be obtained by observing human rights but would surely be damaged by disregarding them. The process of building a human rights regime on this basis was a complex one, requiring a good deal of patience and subtlety, with a heavy emphasis being given to gradually drawing the problematic countries more fully into the international system.

## Integration of the Unofficial and the Official

Nevertheless, if the unofficial debate has many disadvantages because of its inchoate nature, there is no question that the end of the bipolar military struggle marks a turning-point in thinking and activity on security matters. The distraction of the controversy over the 'end of history'[83] should not overshadow the fact that the 'old' thinking about security was found wanting in terms of its analysis of the end of the Cold War. By looking at policy issues almost exclusively in interstate rather than intrastate terms, it missed much of the key dynamics behind systemic change. The official debate, therefore, has had to enter a process of learning and adaptation to catch up to the reality that (whether one embraces the unofficial security discourse or not) security has become more complex and multilayered.

This process of learning and adaptation has generated a considerable amount of 'insider' debate—brought to the surface by the publication of the Canada 21 report and Canada's 'pull-out' from Europe—about what should be changed in Canadian defence policy. This debate pitted those concerned with entertaining new (albeit in some cases more limited and disciplined) ways of thinking and applying Canadian resources versus those who believe that little if anything has changed in the way of the fundamental pattern of international co-operation and conflict. Although this debate remains an ongoing one, the opening up of security policy in this fashion has allowed at least some degree of integration between the official and unofficial agendas.

This integrative process has come out in a number of forms. One way in which this process has been built up has come via the entry of non-traditional concepts into the official security debate. For example, the foreign policy establishment has embraced elements not only of common security but comprehensive and co-operative security (the three c's). This has meant, in practice, a heightened profile for 'reassurance' measures and 'security with other states rather than against them';[84] a broadening out of the ambit of security to include material well-being and quality of life; and the extension of the 'habit of dialogue' in a multifaceted way both in terms of forums and actors. One projection of this approach may be witnessed in the CSCE/OSCE. Another expression may be seen in the Canadian initiative on the North Pacific Co-operative Security Dialogue.

While running into many of the same definitional and operational problems associated with the unofficial discourse writ large, the attractions of this approach for Canadian foreign policy makers are obvious. At a general level, these security concepts allow Canada to develop many of its traditional areas of comparative advantage. The onus is on diplomatic skill, the use of multilateral channels, non-coercive solutions, incrementalism, the creative use of informal as well as formal means of communication, and a wide variety of confidence-building instruments. At a more specific level, these concepts open the way for non-state actors (either in an individual or group capacity) to play a significant role. Within the CSCE/OSCE, Canada took the lead in the campaign that led to the creation of the office of High Commissioner for National Minorities. In the North Pacific Co-operative Security Dialogue, Canada devoted considerable time and energy to so-called second track diplomacy: in addition to the official or government track, there was also an 'NGO (non-governmental organization) track of the Canadian initiative...designed...to explore issues and prospects for dialogue and to focus knowledge and awareness on the North Pacific.'[85] This second track has also featured a strong connection between select academics and the Department of Foreign Affairs, designed to further promote the 'three c' concepts.[86]

Another way in which this integrative process has been built up comes via the establishment of dual state-led and society-led institutions in specific security-related policy areas. An illustrative case in point is Arctic policy. As security concerns in the Arctic have shifted away from military/defence issues (including questions relating to Canadian sovereignty, submarines under the polar ice flows, and the defence early warning system) towards a more holistic agenda, the space for innovation has expanded. Both the Mulroney and Chrétien governments have been eager to display a degree of entrepreneurial and technical leadership in this area. Both governments have—over the opposition of the US—tried hard to establish an international Arctic Council. This proposal, however, was parallelled by an evolving form of societal mobilization. Outpacing the government's attempt to forge new co-operative links among northern polar countries, the Inuit have seized the opportunity created by the unfreezing of the Cold War debates to put their imprint on both the changing domestic and international policy agendas. The core forum here has been the Inuit Circumpolar Conference, a body representing indigenous peoples in Canada, Greenland and Alaska. This conference has moved towards a new stage of transnationalism, in forging a comprehensive Arctic policy in the circumpolar region as a whole, and in promoting (through the conference's NGO status in the UN) a universal declaration of indigenous rights.

The Canadian government's response has been to try to work in tandem with this form of transnational societal mobilization. The Mulroney government went out of its way to facilitate the participation of a Russian/Siberian delegation to the circumpolar summit held in Canada.[87] The Chrétien government has further legitimized the participation of the Inuit in a variety of ways. For one thing, it has allowed representation from the Inuit Circumpolar Conference at the Arctic Council; for another, it has appointed Mary Simon, the former head of the Inuit Circumpolar Conference, to serve as Canada's circumpolar ambassador.[88]

## Resistance to the Unofficial Agenda

The limits of this integrative thrust, nonetheless, are strictly marked. As noted, prior to all the international upheavals that transpired in the late 1980s, the security agenda remained far more impervious to societal pressure than did the economic or social agendas. Canadian strategy relating to policy in this 'high' issue domain remained almost exclusively the preserve of the state, with the Canadian government willing and able to go against the claims of vocal domestic interests to maintain credibility with its alliance partners.

Governments since the end of the Cold War have been willing to bend but not to break completely with this state-led approach. In substantive terms, both the Mulroney and Chrétien governments have treated the broadened definition of security with some caution, viewing a shift away from military/defence conceptions of security as necessary, although not at the same time decisively moving towards a comprehensive embrace of a non-military approach. An élite consensus has prevailed that Canada should remain an active member of NATO (although redefining its collective security role); that Canada should continue to belong to

NORAD; and that priority should be given to the purchase of at least some equipment to allow the Canadian armed forces to be operationally effective (although what exactly constitutes the hierarchy of priority continues to be debated).

The process of opening up the decision making also remains somewhat restricted in the security sphere. While the sensitivity among politicians and officials concerning the need for some degree of societal consultation and participation has increased appreciably, a number of security-related initiatives emanating from Canada have clearly been state led. This was true of the Mulroney government's initiatives on issues such as the establishment of a UN register for international arms sales, and it is equally true for a number of initiatives pressed by the Chrétien government, including the effort to establish a treaty that would ban anti-personnel land mines.

Societal groups have had their own reservations about the extent to which they should co-operate with government. Despite a closer relationship on specific creative exercises, in recognition that 'the end of superpower enmity provides Canada with an unprecedented opportunity to work for the development of global security structures,'[89] nothing approaching a complete partnership has been forged between the Canadian government and the non-state groups active on security issues. While societal forces have been ready and willing to use the expanded room offered them by government to participate in the policy process, there remains a deep-seated wariness about the actual embrace of government. At one level this attitude stems from frustrations about the actual mechanisms of consultation. Much of the effectiveness of the societal groups involved in the unofficial security discourse is based on their ability to get their message across in an immediate and effective manner through instant modes of communication. Any impediment via confidentiality rules (and other informal constraints) therefore raises difficult organizational questions. This type of dilemma also reflects ongoing suspicions about being managed (or co-opted) by government.

At another level, these same societal groups are interested in doing what is 'right' according to their own value system, rather than what is 'necessary.' If interested in resolving issues, in a variety of specialized areas of activity, the proponents of the unofficial security discourse are not classic 'problem solvers' found elsewhere in the policy arena. In terms of the framework developed by Robert Cox, they cannot be said to be taking 'the world as [they] find it, with the prevailing social and power relationships and the institutions into which they are organized, as the given framework for action.' Rather, they constitute the archetypal critical theorists and practitioners, standing 'apart from the prevailing order of the world' and directing their attention 'toward an appraisal of the very framework of action, or problematic' that defines the parameters for the problem solvers.[90]

This critical outlook has served as the foundation for the challenge in the unofficial discourse to the dominant assumptions about the meaning of security. Motivated and legitimized by this framework, the concept of 'common' security has both been widened and deepened through this discourse. As the salience of particularistic identities within global society have been recognized in a new and compelling way, the 'parochial definitions of Canadian interest'[91] are perceived as a constraining element rather than as a source of innovation. The high priority given by government to the enhancement of Canada's security through an expansion of the 'national weal' is perceived, with some degree of accuracy, as subordinating concerns for international social justice and safety on an individual and collective basis to the desire to make Canada an efficient trading country. This form of trade-off, from the perspective of the unofficial discourse, allows authoritarian governments to consolidate their own internal security at the expense of components of their own population.

The unidirectional, outward-looking approach to security adopted by the Canadian government has also attracted ongoing criticism. To obtain 'common' security, not only does the performance of foreign states need to be monitored and modified: Canada's own domestic standards with respect to the provision of private and public security for all of its citizens, whatever their position or status in society, have to be scrutinized as well. Canada must be consistent in applying the same principles within its 'own borders' as it applies to other countries.[92]

A good illustration of how Canada's involvement at the international level can become compromised by its own domestic image remains the issue of security for children. Pushed by growing public interest in the issue, Brian Mulroney took the opportunity to play a personal and prominent role (as co-chair) at the September 1990 New York World Summit for Children. In keeping with the traditional Canadian diplomatic approach, the prime minister emphasized the usefulness of this gathering as a catalyst, claiming that 'the summit has the potential to put children's issues on the top of [the] international agenda' in the same way that the UN Conference on the Human Environment in Stockholm in 1972 put environmental problems on the agenda. The summit was also seen as a facilitator for further technical/specialist work by public officials. As Mulroney stated: 'Summits do what nothing else can do. Put leaders face to face with each other and raise public awareness of issues. There is nothing like [that] for galvanizing a bureaucracy.'[93] But Canadian activity at this summit was, in the end, overshadowed by criticism (and charges of hypocrisy) at the domestic level. A common argument was that Canada was hardly well positioned to press for children's welfare at the global level given the condition of children in Canada. As an editorial in the *Globe and Mail* bluntly put it, Ottawa should lead by example: 'Brian Mulroney can show leadership at the summit by pledging money to fight disease and hunger at home, a shameful item of unfinished business that Canadian activists who have travelled to New York for the meeting will not let him (or the other delegates) forget.'[94]

International activism acted, therefore, as a two-edged sword. While it might well serve the international reputation of Canada and, by extension, its leaders, it also served to intensify the process of domestic scrutiny. Echoes of this sensitivity have continued to reverberate on this issue. Like the Mulroney government, the Chrétien government has come under attack for not taking children's rights seriously enough. Most notably, the January 1996 Team Canada trade mission to India was partially derailed by the media attention given to the crusade against child labour practices. This embarrassment was compounded by the refusal of the best-known child activist to take up an offer to serve as a Canadian delegate to the meetings of the UN Commission on Human Rights (UNCHR).[95]

## CONCLUSION

This chapter has attempted to sketch out the widened boundaries of the Canadian debate (or more precisely, debates) about the nature and meaning of security in the post-Cold War era. With the transition in the international agenda, the disappearance of a defined enemy and the erosion of some aspects of the traditional state-centred orthodoxy, the understanding of what security is and who the concept covers has undergone considerable alteration.

However, the policy impact of the unofficial discourse should not be overly exaggerated. The emergence of a societal challenge, from the bottom up, still exists within the shadow of the official security debate. Not everything about Canadian decision making on the security agenda is in flux, in that many of the core values and policy manifestations of traditional Canadian behaviour have remained intact. The Canadian government still has a wide repertoire of tools—and a good deal of autonomy—with which to pursue its concept of the national interest in terms of territorial integrity, economic efficiency and global order. In this context, the contribution of activist societal groups will be largely limited to providing a critical voice in mapping out an alternative security agenda. Although some elements of the concepts of common or human security have become embedded in a widened security debate, tensions will continue along an extensive and deep faultline in terms of both the definition and the application of those concepts.

Conversely, though, the impact of the unofficial discourse should not be minimized. By offering alternative ways of thinking, it has helped not only to stimulate the process of learning but also to encourage 'new possibilities for creative statecraft' by which the Canadian government interacts in more imaginative ways with domestic policy communities.[96] While the shape of this process remains quite hazy, Canada stands out as a country that has tried seriously to adapt to this aspect of transition. The scope and shape of the Canadian security debates showcase the elements of both persistence and imagination found in the move towards a new architecture in the international system.

## NOTES

[1]  Barry Buzan, *People, States and Fear: An Agenda for International Security Studies in the Post-Cold War Era* (Hemel Hempstead: Harvester, 1991).

[2]  See, for example, Keith Krause, 'Redefining international peace and security? The discourse and practices of multilateral security activity,' *YCISS Working Paper Number 13*, March 1994.

[3]  See, for example, Fred Halliday, *Rethinking International Relations* (Vancouver/London: University of British Columbia Press/Macmillan, 1994), 143.

[4]  For a good exploration of this concept, see S. Neil MacFarlane and Thomas G. Weiss, 'The United Nations, regional organizations, and human security: building theory in Central America,' in the Academic Council on the United Nations System, *Regional Responsibilities and the United Nations System* (Providence, RI: 1994), 15–47.

[5]  See, for example, Ronnie D. Lipschutz ed., *On Security* (New York: Columbia University Press, 1995).

[6]  Hedley Bull, *The Anarchical Society* (London: Macmillan, 1977).

[7]  Ernest Regehr, Research Coordinator, Project Ploughshares, testimony to the Special Joint Committee of the Senate and of the House of Commons, Reviewing Canadian Foreign Policy, *Minutes of Proceedings and Evidence*, 5 May 1994, 8:10.

[8]  Barry Buzan, *People, States and Fear*, 3–4.

[9]  Fred Halliday, 'State and society in international relations: a second agenda,' *Millennium* 16, 2 (Fall 1987), 219.

[10]  Report Of The Special Joint Committee Reviewing Canadian Foreign Policy, *Canada's Foreign Policy: Principles and Priorities for the Future* (Ottawa: Parliamentary Publications Directorate, November 1994), 11.

[11]  This view, which underwrote much of Canada's isolationism in the interwar years, is discussed in Kim Richard Nossal, *The Politics of Canadian Foreign Policy*, 2nd edn. (Scarborough: Prentice Hall, 1989), 139–43. For a reconsideration of the isolationist argument, see Joseph T. Jockel and Joel J. Sokolsky, 'Dandurand revisited: rethinking Canada's defence policy in an unstable world,' *International Journal* XLVIII, 2 (Spring 1993), 380–401.

[12]  Gary Smith and St. John Kettle, *Threats Without Enemies: Rethinking Australia's Security* (Leichhardt, NSW: Pluto Press, 1992).

[13]  André Ouellet, testimony to House of Commons Standing Committee on Foreign Affairs and International Trade, *Minutes of Proceedings and Evidence*, 16 February 1994, 1:42.

[14]  Jean-Jacques Blais, a former minister of national defence, in an address to the Canadian Defence Producers' Association in December 1993, said, 'Canada need not fear for its territorial integrity. The Cold War is no more.' See also Canada 21 Council, *Canada 21: Canada and Common Security in the Twenty-First Century* (Toronto: Centre for International Studies, University of Toronto, 1994), 62.

[15]  Bernard Wood, 'A time of hope and fear: a new world order and a new Canada,' *Peace and Security, 1991–2* (Ottawa: Canadian Institute for International Peace and Security, January 1992), 9.

[16]    Christine Stewart, testimony to House of Commons Standing Committee on Foreign Affairs and International Trade, *Minutes of Proceedings and Evidence*, 23 March 1995, 20:20.

[17]    Canada, Department of National Defence, *1994 Defence White Paper* (Ottawa: Ministry of Supply and Services, 1994), 3.

[18]    *Ibid.*, 4–5.

[19]    Sean Henry, testimony to the Special Joint Committee of the Senate and of the House of Commons, Reviewing Canadian Foreign Policy, *Minutes of Proceedings and Evidence*, 5 May 1994, 8:15.

[20]    Rod Byers, 'Canadian defence and defence procurement: implications for economic policy,' in Denis Stairs and Gilbert Winham, eds., *Selected Problems in Formulating Foreign Economic Policy* (Toronto: University of Toronto Press, 1985).

[21]    For a good overview, see Tom F. Keating, *Canada and World Order: The Multilateralist Tradition in Canadian Foreign Policy* (Toronto: McClelland and Stewart, 1993), ch. 6.

[22]    See, for comparative purposes, Michael Clarke and Philip Sabin, eds., *British Defence Choices for the Twenty-First Century* (London: Brassey's, 1993).

[23]    Alastair D. Edgar and David G. Haglund, *The Canadian Defence Industry in the New Global Environment* (Montreal and Kingston: McGill–Queen's University Press, 1995), xiii.

[24]    Canada 21 Council, *Canada 21: Canada and Common Security in the Twenty-First Century* (Toronto: Centre for International Studies, University of Toronto, 1994). See also Special Joint Committee of the Senate and of the House of Commons on Canada's Defence Policy, *Minutes of Proceedings and Evidence*, 20 April 1994, 3 May 1994 and 2 September 1994.

[25]    Canada 21 Council, *Canada 21*, 62.

[26]    Janice Gross Stein, 'Canada 21: a moment and a model,' *Canadian Foreign Policy* II, 1 (Spring 1994), 11.

[27]    Testimony by Robert Fowler to House of Commons Standing Committee on Foreign Affairs and International Trade, *Minutes of Proceedings and Evidence*, 21 March 1995, 19:29. See also John Hay, 'Masse's plan takes aim at defence, but who are Canada's enemies,' *Ottawa Citizen*, 18 September 1991.

[28]    Kenneth J. Calder, 'Doing the things that matter: Canada and Euro-Atlantic security,' *International Journal* L, 4 (Autumn 1995), 701–20. See also Paul Buteux, 'Commitment and or retreat: redefining the Canadian role in the alliance,' *Canadian Defence Quarterly* 23 (December 1993), 12–16.

[29]    Canada, DND, *1994 Defence White Paper*.

[30]    Canada, DFAIT, *Canada in the World: Government Statement* (Canada: Canada Communications Group, 1995), 30.

[31]    Douglas Alan Ross, 'From a cheap ride to a free ride to no ride at all?' *International Journal* L, 4 (Autumn 1995), 724. *Transformation Moment: A Canadian Vision of Common Security* (Project Ploughshares and the Canadian Peace Alliance, March 1992).

[32]    See Special Joint Committee of the Senate and of the House of Commons on Canada's Defence Policy, *Minutes of Proceedings and Evidence*, 21 September 1994, 29:13.

[33]    Ross, 'From a cheap ride,' 724–5.

34   Canada, DND, *1994 Defence White Paper*, 57.

35   Canada, DFAIT, *Canada in the World*, 30. See also Allen G. Sens, 'Saying yes to expansion: the future of NATO and Canadian interests in a changing alliance,' *International Journal* L, 4 (Autumn 1995), 697.

36   Jennifer M. Welsh, 'Canada in NATO and the CSCE: an "Atlantic" vocation?' *Policy Options*, June 1994, 16.

37   Lloyd Axworthy, 'Forging the forces into peace police,' *Globe and Mail*, 27 July 1992. See also John Cruickshank, 'Keeping a foot in Europe,' *Globe and Mail*, 16 February 1990.

38   See, for example, Richard H. Ullman, 'Redefining security,' *International Security* 8, 1 (Summer 1983), 129–53.

39   See, for example, Charles Tilley, 'Prisoners of the state,' *International Social Science Journal* 44, 3 (1992), 329–43.

40   Tariq Rauf, Senior Research Assistant, Canadian Centre for Global Security, testimony to the Special Joint Committee of the Senate and of the House of Commons, Reviewing Canadian Foreign Policy, *Minutes of Proceedings and Evidence*, 5 May 1994, 8:19.

41   Keith Krause, 'Redefining international peace and security? The discourse and practices of multilateral security activity,' *YCISS Working Paper Number 13*, March 1994, 15.

42   For an excellent overview, see Vincent Cable, 'What is international economic security?' *International Affairs* 71, 2 (April 1995), 305–24.

43   See Melissa Clark-Jones, *A Staple State: Canadian Industrial Resources in Cold War* (Toronto: University of Toronto Press, 1987).

44   James Eayrs, 'Defining a new place for Canada in the hierarchy of world power,' *International Perspectives*, May/June 1975, 15. For Gotlieb's views, see 'The Western Economic Summits,' a speech by Mr. A.E. Gotlieb, Under-Secretary of State for External Affairs, to the Canadian Institute of International Affairs, Winnipeg, 9 April 1981.

45   Robert T. Shanks, 'Economic sanctions: foreign policy foil or folly?' *Policy Staff Commentary No. 4*, DFAIT, May 1994, 6. By itself 'unilateral action by Canada' would, it was considered, 'not likely...be successful in any but the rarest of cases'; in that the 'Canadian economy is not large enough to apply enough leverage to alter the behaviour of a target country.' *Ibid.*, 6. On Canadian foreign policy and sanctions more generally, see Kim Richard Nossal, *Rain Dancing: Sanctions in Canadian and Australian Foreign Policy* (Toronto: University of Toronto Press, 1994).

46   Shanks, 'Economic sanctions,' 5.

47   Susan Strange and John Stopford, *Rival States, Rival Firms: Competition for World Market Shares* (Cambridge: Cambridge University Press, 1991), 209.

48   Department of External Affairs, *Competitiveness and Security: Directions for Canada's International Relations* (Ottawa: Supply and Services, 1985),18.

49   For a critical perspective, see Maude Barlow, *Straight Through the Heart: How the Liberals Abandoned the Just Society* (Toronto: Harper Collins, 1995).

50   *Canada's Foreign Policy: Principles and Priorities for the Future* (Ottawa: Publications Service, Parliamentary Publications Directorate, 1994), 28.

51 On the wider changes in Canadian policy goals, see Lorraine Eden and Maureen Appel Molot, 'Canada's national policies: reflections on 125 years,' *Canadian Public Policy* 19, 3 (September 1993), 232–59.

52 See, for example, Maude Barlow, *Parcel of Rogues: How Free Trade is Failing Canada* (Toronto: Key Porter, 1990); *Take Back the Nation* (Toronto: Key Porter, 1991).

53 Jean-Yves Couillard, Second Vice-President, UPA, testimony to the Special Joint Committee of the Senate and of the House of Commons on Canada's International Relations, *Minutes of Proceedings and Evidence*, 22 July 1985, 7:25.

54 Notes for an address by Prime Minister Brian Mulroney, Stanford University, 29 September 1991, Office of the Prime Minister 1991.

55 Canada, DFAIT, *Canada in the World*, 34.

56 Testimony by John Noble, Director General, International Organizations Bureau, DFAIT, to the House of Commons Sub-Committee on Development and Human Rights of the Standing Committee on External Affairs and International Trade, *Minutes of Proceedings and Evidence*, 24 February 1992, 12:30.

57 Paul Gecelovsky and T.A. Keenleyside, 'Canada's international human rights policy in practice: Tiananmen Square,' *International Journal* L, 3 (Summer 1995), 564–93.

58 Edward Greenspon, 'Canada can't sway China on rights, PM says,' *Globe and Mail*, 19 March 1994.

59 André Ouellet, the minister of foreign affairs, claimed that the Liberal government would refrain from making open criticisms of Chinese human rights abuses. *Toronto Star*, 17 March 1994. Chrétien himself said that there is little point in Canada 'acting like a big shot' over China's human rights record because it lacks the capacity to hurt China economically. *Globe and Mail*, 19 March 1994.

60 Ouellet, DFAIT, Statement 94/25, 31 May 1994, 3. Quoted in Gecelovsky and Keenleyside, 'Canada's international human rights policy in practice.' See also Charles Trueheart, 'Canada, eying Chinese market, de-emphasizes rights issues,' *Washington Post*, 29 March 1994.

61 See, for example, Marjorie Griffin Cohen, *Free Trade and the Future of Women's Work: Manufacturing and Service Industries* (Toronto: Garamond, 1987).

62 Kathleen E. Mahoney, 'Human rights and Canadian foreign policy,' *International Journal* XLVII, 3 (Summer 1992), 557.

63 See, for example, Linda Hossie, 'Women want concerns raised at UN rights conference,' *Globe and Mail*, 7 November 1992.

64 See 'Making women's rights part of the global human rights agenda,' *Libertas: Newsletter of the International Centre for Human Rights and Democratic Development*, June 1992.

65 Stephanie Innes, 'Canada proposed as international refuge for abused women,' *Globe and Mail*, 30 November 1992.

66 Allan Thompson, 'Canada spells out stance on refugees,' *Toronto Star*, 15 January 1993.

67 Mahoney, 'Human rights and Canada's foreign policy,' 576.

68 Kevin Cox, 'Federal study of low-level flying ignores social costs, groups claim,' *Globe and Mail*, 13 February 1990.

69   Prof. Robert Spencer, testimony to the Special Joint Committee of the Senate and of the House of Commons, *Minutes of Proceedings and Evidence*, 4 June 1994, 27:11.

70   Harold Pickering, 'Foreign policy as an extra-territorial extension of public policy: the development of the "Military Training Industry" at Goose Bay, Labrador,' paper presented at the CPSA Meeting, 3 June 1991, Queen's University, 2.

71   Cox, 'Federal study.' For critical commentary from Innu sources, see Debora Lockyer, 'Low-level flying review and PR exercise,' *Windspeaker*, 9 May 1994; 'Innu find 130 deficiencies in government environment study,' *Windspeaker*, 15 August 1994.

72   Darrell Rankin, Canadian Peace Alliance, testimony to the Special Joint Committee of the Senate and of the House of Commons, Reviewing Canadian Foreign Policy, *Minutes of Proceedings and Evidence*, 5 May 1994, 8:19.

73   Bill Robinson, 'Old ideas in new packages,' *Ploughshares Monitor* XV, 4 (December 1994), 3, 6.

74   See Robert Bourassa, *Power from the North* (Scarborough: Prentice Hall, 1985).

75   'Bloc accused of stirring tensions on reserves,' *Ottawa Citizen*, 19 February 1994.

76   'Bouchard predicts U.S. intervention,' *Montreal Gazette*, 19 February 1994.

77   Desmond Morton, 'Peacekeeping begins at home in ominous proposal,' *Toronto Star*, 24 April 1994.

78   On these tensions, see Sonia Arrison and Elizabeth Keller, 'First Nations and the Québécois: clashes and compromises in Québec,' paper presented at the Canadian Political Science Association, Université du Québec à Montréal, 4 June 1995.

79   See, for example, the discussion in Alex Morrison ed., 'Divided we fall: the national security implications of Canadian constitutional issues,' *The Canadian Strategic Forecast 1992* (Toronto: Canadian Institute of Strategic Studies, 1991).

80   Desmond Morton, 'No more disagreeable or onerous duty: Canadians and military aid of the civic power, past, present, future,' in David B. Dewitt and David Leyton-Brown, eds., *Canada's International Security Policy* (Scarborough: Prentice Hall, 1995), 144.

81   Keith Krause and Michael C. Williams, 'From strategy to security: foundations of critical security studies,' paper presented at the annual conference, International Studies Association, Chicago, February 1995, 4.

82   Robert Dorff, 'A commentary on security studies for the 1990s as a model core curriculum,' *International Studies Notes* 19, 3 (Fall 1994), 27.

83   Francis Fukuyama, *The End of History and the Last Man* (New York: Free Press, 1992).

84   See David Dewitt, 'Common, comprehensive, and cooperative security,' *Pacific Review* 7 (Spring 1994).

85   Letter by Claude Boucher, from Policy Planning at the Department of Foreign Affairs, to the editor of *Peace and Security* (CIIPS), Autumn 1991, 23.

86   For a critical review, see Kim Richard Nossal, 'Seeing things? The adornment of "security" in Australia and Canada,' *Australian Journal of International Affairs* 49 (May 1995), 33–47.

87   Miro Cernetig, 'Arctic star rising,' *Globe and Mail*, 24 July 1992; 'Hands across the polar ice pack,' *Globe and Mail*, 10 October 1992.

88  Canada, DFAIT, *Canada in the World*, 29. See also Heather A. Smith, 'A northern foreign policy for Canada,' paper presented at ISA, San Diego, April 1996.

89  *Transformation Moment: A Canadian Vision of Common Security* (Project Ploughshares and the Canadian Peace Alliance, March 1992), 6.

90  Robert W. Cox, 'Social forces, states and world orders,' in Robert Keohane ed., *Neorealism and Its Critics* (New York: Columbia University Press, 1986), 208.

91  Kim Richard Nossal, 'Cabin'd, cribb'd, confin'd?: Canada's interest in human rights,' in Robert O. Matthews and Cranford Pratt, eds., *Human Rights in Canadian Foreign Policy* (Kingston and Montreal: McGill–Queen's University Press, 1988), 57.

92  Darrell Rankin, Canadian Peace Alliance, testimony to the Special Joint Committee of the Senate and of the House of Commons, Reviewing Canadian Foreign Policy, *Minutes of Proceedings and Evidence*, 5 May 1994, 8:17.

93  Quoted in Paul Lewis, 'World's leaders gather for summit meeting on children,' *New York Times*, 30 September 1990.

94  'A better start for the world's children,' *Globe and Mail*, 29 September 1990.

95  Lloyd Axworthy has tried to counter this image of neglect by signalling his intention to do something on a range of issues in this dossier. Indeed, at the UNCHR in Geneva, he announced that Canada intended to make the protection of children the 'central focus of our foreign policy.' Quoted in Jeff Sallot, 'Canada targets overseas child sex,' *Globe and Mail*, 4 April 1996. This theme was reinforced by the targeting of the international issue of commercial sexual exploitation of children. Notes for an address by the Honourable Lloyd Axworthy, Minister of Foreign Affairs, at the World Congress Against the Commercial Sexual Exploitation of Children, Stockholm, Sweden, 27 August 1996, DFAIT News Release, no. 93/35. Once again, however, the value of this activity has been questioned. See, for example, Alan Freeman, 'Laws on sex tourism a "toothless tiger,"' *Globe and Mail*, 24 August 1996; 'From peacekeeper to vice cop: Ottawa's international sex-tourism crack-down probably won't work,' *Alberta Report*, 29 April 1996, 7.

96  Andrew Moravcsik, 'Integrating international and domestic theories of international bargaining,' in Peter B. Evans, Harold K. Jacobson and Robert D. Putnam, eds., *International Bargaining and Domestic Politics: Double-Edged Diplomacy* (Berkeley: University of California Press, 1993), 16.

# THE POLITICS OF ENVIRONMENTAL SECURITY: THE CASE OF THE CANADA–SPAIN 'FISH WAR'

A detailed exploration of the Canada–Spain 'fish war' teases out many of the contradictions in Canadian foreign policy in the post-Cold War era. From one perspective, Canada's willingness to take direct action against Spanish fishing ships represented a new and controversial phase in Canadian foreign policy—a phase in which Canada's national interest assumed primacy over good international citizenship in a most explicit and unapologetic fashion. As Andrew Cohen has advanced this argument: 'Whatever the risk to its bilateral relations with Spain or with Europe, whatever the consequences to international law, Canada turned to gunboat diplomacy.... Here was the national interest at its crudest.'[1]

From another perspective, Canada's 'belligerence' on the high seas was represented as a change in diplomatic technique. Presented with a difficult problem that had evaded solution by negotiation and compromise, Canada sought to raise the stakes in order to settle the question of high seas fishing off the Grand Banks of Newfoundland once and for all. Canada's resort to the use of unilateral tactics, however, should not be taken prima facie to mean that Canada was moving away from its commitment to multilateral norms and principles. An alternative case could be put forward, that it was precisely because Canada placed so much value on 'global governance' that it was prepared to use any means possible to bring about an agreement based on order and universally accepted rules. In countenancing the practices of boarding and making arrests of vessels 'illegally' fishing in international waters adjacent to the Canadian 200-mile economic zone, according to this interpretation, Canada was not taking on the role of a 'pirate' but that of a responsible 'guardian' through an 'act of international leadership.'[2]

Intersecting with this debate about national interest versus international obligations is a set of questions concerning the implications of the Canada–Spain 'fish war' episode for the study and practice of environmental security. One of the subsidiary components of the wider security discourse in the 1990s has been the view that environmental issues should be studied as a prime cause of international conflict. Robert Kaplan, in a widely read 1994 article in *Atlantic Monthly*, highlighted the import of environmental degradation in what he termed the 'coming anarchy.'[3] Although Kaplan's piece directed its attention mainly to the crisis situation within Sub-Saharan Africa, other writers have attempted to locate this concern as a source of danger to the industrial countries of the North. Jessica Tuchman Mathews, for one, has argued that the connection between the environment and national values at the centre of the international system (including the US) is so tight that any threat to the global environment constitutes a threat to national security.[4] In making this claim, Mathews builds on the earlier work by Richard Ullman, which refers to a 'threat to national security' as 'an action or sequence of events that (1) threatens drastically and over a relatively brief period of time to degrade the quality of life for the inhabitants of a state, or (2) threatens significantly to narrow the range of policy choices available to a state or to private, non-governmental entities (persons, groups, corporations) within the state.'[5]

Elevating this focus (and sense of pessimism) about the interplay of the environment and conflict to a higher intellectual plane has been the work of the Canadian academic Thomas Homer-Dixon. Departing from the qualitative (often anecdotal) style of the analysts mentioned above, Homer-Dixon has embarked on a more scientific research program to understand the links between environmental degradation and violent conflict. The policy relevance of this research program is underscored by its aim of identifying 'key intervention points where policy makers might be able to alter the causal processes linking human activity, environmental degradation, and conflict.'[6] The central thrust of Homer-Dixon's work transcends the parochialism of a US-based approach by examining the impact of these links from a global framework, with special reference to the developing countries. Homer-Dixon's inclusion into the Canada 21 investigations, nonetheless, has allowed a ripple effect to take place between this larger research program and the particularistic Canadian context.

How does the Canada–Spain 'fish war' fit into this type of analysis? On the surface, the fit seems an extremely comfortable one. The concept of environmental security gained considerable impetus in Canada, as in other advanced industrial countries of the North, during the 1980s and 1990s with the ascendancy of issues such as ozone depletion and global warming on the political/policy agenda. The difficulty in making this connection was that these types of environmental issues (even on the basis of the worst-case scenarios that were proffered) could only be considered as having a detrimental effect on security in an indirect and incremental way. As another Canadian researcher has allowed: 'the issues of environmental change and security intersect not so much because of the actual degradation of the environment, though clearly this is of central importance and concern, but because of the perception and response of peoples and states to the degradation of the environment and to the effect such environmental disruption may have on human society.'[7]

The 'fish war' episode put a very different spin on environmental security. Instead of having an indirect effect on security, in the way in which the ozone depletion and global warming issues had, this episode revealed the immediate impact of a resource crisis on both thinking and practice. In terms of security studies, the crisis was seized upon as validation for refining the definition of security threats to guide policy choices. While many other components of the unofficial security discourse could be dismissed as being nebulous in nature, the fish issue confirmed that resource issues could become the real stuff of security. As Janice Stein noted in her presentation of the Canada 21 report: 'to understand the urgency of making hard choices, we need only to look at the threat to the security of our maritime population that has arisen from the depletion of fish stocks,' an issue in which 'the environment, the economy, and security are inextricably linked.'[8]

From a different angle, the link between the environment and security was not so simple. The mainstream security community tended to see security in national terms, privileging those issues that have a direct impact on the territorial integrity and material well-being of the nation state rather than those affecting humankind as a whole. In keeping with this point of view, security intruded on environmental issues most evidently when and where a foreigner (or 'other') was involved. This was true in the past on selective issues that had risen to the forefront, such as nuclear safety. It was certainly true in the case of the fish episode. The unofficial security discourse, by way of contrast, saw security in a more holistic fashion. This alternative approach to security studies and practice emphasized the link between environmental security and such broader issues as consumerism, democracy and militarism. The concern of the proponents of this revised (and widened) agenda was not so much with national sovereignty and territorial integrity, but rather with environmentalism as a fundamental value designed for the common good in societal relations. As still another Canadian scholar, in advancing the cause of the unofficial agenda, stated: 'Given the extant threats nations collectively face, especially with regard to planetary environmental degradation, it is clear that decision makers must think as globally as possible....nations cannot deal with environmental issues in isolation.'[9]

This official–unofficial divide reinforced the contradictory impressions about Canadian foreign policy. On the one hand, with its higher profile, the Canadian government's approach to the fish dispute could be lauded by the advocates of the unofficial security discourse because the link between environmental degradation and international tensions was finally being taken seriously. Given the emotional intensity that this conflict generated, the environmental dimension of the widened security agenda could no longer be dismissed completely as a fad. On the other hand, because of the Canadian government's own poor record of management, the advocates of a widened security agenda had significant misgivings about the way in which Canada handled the entire episode. Rather than choosing to learn a lesson about the need to integrate environmental and social considerations into economic decision making, the Canadian government was considered to have distorted its own part in the 'desecuritization' of the fish industry and to have hijacked the fish issue to serve its own perception of the national interests.

The Canada–Spain 'fish war' episode presents, then, a multilayered case-study of contemporary Canadian foreign policy. Empirically, it presents an interesting test concerning the resilience of Canada's older habits pertaining to diplomatic skill and the centrality of reputation. Without the 'disciplines' of the Cold War era, Canada has more potential to defect from its traditional way of doing things in terms of problems. If the parameters are expanding, though, there remain limits to how far Canada is prepared to go in the way of self-help measures. While embracing unilateral action in an unfamiliar way, Canada continued to justify this behaviour in terms of the health of the international order as well as the national interest.

Conceptually, the case presents a palpable issue-specific test of how far the 'new' security agenda could be stretched. The 'fish war' episode endorsed the need for conducting an altered sort of intellectual conversation (and, by implication, an altered policymaking process) on security issues. The crossover of this type of environmental issue into the official security concerns, however, also confirmed the essential incompatibility between the two agendas. The more they interacted, the more the two rubbed against each other in an uncomfortable way.

Procedurally, much of the dynamic of Canadian behaviour in the 'fish war' may be captured by examining the case through a very different lens. Indeed, the 'fish war' provides a classic demonstration of the usefulness of the notion of 'two level games' in exploring the simultaneous 'interactions between domestic and international politics.'[10] What stands out in the Canadian government's approach to the fish crisis is its 'Janus-faced' approach, whereby it tried to balance both its international and domestic concerns in a process of 'double-edged' diplomacy. The twist in the case of the 'fish war' was that, at the same time as a powerful coalition of domestic forces exerted pressure on the Canadian government to 'do something' on the issue, many of these same domestic forces had some considerable incentive to try to externalize the crisis: by placing the blame for the situation in the fisheries on 'foreigners,' the onus of responsibility in terms of causation could be redirected outside of Canada.

Other factors played into this application of the politics of external deflection. Some commentators wrapped the fish issue up with the national unity issue. Others saw a connection between the enthusiastic jingoism, or sense of national solidarity, stirred up by the 'fish war' and the sense of malaise endemic in so many Canadians because of government cutbacks and fiscal constraints. Whichever way one sliced it, however, this externalization strategy was at odds with the established character of Canadian statecraft. Driving this effort for direct action was the charismatic Minister of Fisheries and Oceans, Brian Tobin. DFAIT, unprepared to give ground to another bureaucratic challenger, took up the position of attempting to defend the traditional mode of conflict-resolution through negotiation. While largely overshadowed by the international dimension of the episode, the fish crisis also provided a site of struggle between those state officials eager and able to take Canadian statecraft in new directions, on the one hand, and the guardians of Canada's established diplomatic habits on the other.

## COMPETING INTERPRETATIONS

### Defending the National Interest

To suggest that Canada gave primacy to its national interest during the 'fish war' episode cuts against the grain of Canadian foreign policy behaviour. As revealed throughout this volume, the familiar view of Canada in the world has been that of a constructive internationalist. Canada's instinctive approach, based on the combination of philosophical *Weltanschauung* and its established forte with respect to practical statecraft, has been to seek compromise and consensus (most often through multilateral forums). With this tendency in mind, the sharp edge exhibited in some of the Canadian behaviour during the 'fish war' comes as a surprise. The whole episode jars, with an un-Canadian resound. Instead of persisting with an effort to delicately stickhandle through the convoluted issue, Canada feinted towards what might be described as 'rock 'em, sock 'em' tactics (more commonly associated with Don Cherry's robust brand of hockey videos than with the tradition of quiet and skillful Canadian diplomacy). At odds with its long-standing reputation as a helpful fixer, Canada gradually escalated the deployment of coercive tactics against the Spanish fishing fleet. These tactics, after a protracted build-up over the course of several months, reached a peak in March 1995 when Canadian authorities chased a Spanish trawler (the *Estai*) outside of Canada's 200-mile exclusive economic zone, fired a number of warning shots to force it to eventually stop, escorted it back into the port of St. John's, Newfoundland, and charged its captain with illegal fishing. Although the extent of force deployed by Canada in this action should not be exaggerated, at the very least these tactics signalled that Canada was no longer content to be confined by the strictures of its image as the 'boy scout' of international politics.

A number of other contextual features added to the sense of discordance and disjunction associated with this episode. The first of these features relates to the outpouring of approval arising from this tough stance. Given the level of discomfort Canadian opinion-leaders have had in the past with the use of coercive threats backed up by organized violence, never mind physical force, as techniques of statecraft, it might have been expected that Canada's shift to direct action would become the instant target of disapproval. Certainly, Canada's belligerence became the subject of some scorn and ridicule among the more sophisticated of Canada's journalists. William Johnson portrayed Canada's use of force as more farce than drama, in that the 'threat of boarding ships on the high seas, arresting their crews or cutting their nets seemed like a comic opera played in 17th century costumes, rather than international relations between Canada and the EU in 1995.'[11] Andrew Cohen likewise portrayed the episode in comic opera terms, staged on a set in which Canada was cast as a 'pirate' and the fisheries minister, Brian Tobin, 'paced the bridge like a puffed-up admiral.'[12] Cohen acknowledged, however, that if the spectacle was incongruous with Canada's standard stage role, 'Canadians cheered the high seas opera bouffe.'

A number of commentators went so far as to equate Canada's tough stance with a heightened maturity in world affairs. The mark of this maturity was a deepened appreciation of 'hard' realist tenets. One of these fundamental tenets was a subordination of international co-operation to self-help. Canada should exercise state power to protect 'part of this country's heritage.'[13] To do otherwise, in the absence of an enforceable regime for the 'straddling stocks' of fish, i.e. those species that went between Canadian and international waters, represented an abdication of self-interest.

The exercise of self-help in turn encouraged the application of self-defence measures. A mindset took hold among some public opinion leaders that the fish issue could best be dealt with through the use of state power. Doing much to inform this view was the traditional set of security assumptions concerning a vertically structured state system. The state constituted the defining boundary about the meaning of security, with security on the 'inside' and 'anarchy' on the outside. If found in a new guise, the fish issue represented a direct security issue involving territoriality and national integrity. As a *Toronto Sun* article by columnist Peter Worthington, entitled 'At Last Canada Stiffens Its Spine,' interpreted the situation: 'Our greatest post-Cold War threat comes from marauding foreigners overfishing. Protecting the resources of the Grand Banks and our territorial waters should be a non-debatable priority.'[14]

At first glance, of course, the targeting of Spain as the specific 'enemy' in the fish episode seems improbable on conceptual grounds. The well-known argument laid out by Bruce Russett suggests that democracies are unlikely to engage in militarized disputes with each other. When involved in a dispute, according to this claim, democracies are less likely to let it escalate in this fashion.[15] Although it needs to be emphasized that the 'fish war' did not go so far as to include actual military conflict, a low level of armed violence was utilized by Canada as part of its direct action. Moreover, both Canada and Spain engaged in a good degree of threatening behaviour in terms of gunboat diplomacy. A 'fish war' between two members of NATO, it also must be pointed out, runs up against the notion of alliance solidarity. True, NATO has not been exempted from internal conflict: Greece and Turkey, throughout the time of their membership within an Atlantic community, continued to engage in threats and bellicose activity towards each other. But this case could be excused as an extension of a century-old tradition of intense historical enmity, which the Canada–Spain pair did not possess.

To understand how Canada could shift its attitude to such an extent that it was willing to contemplate taking on Spain in an open conflict, some supplementary contextual material is required. In national terms, it is important to mention that Spain's democratic/alliance credentials were of a recent vintage. From before World War II through to the 1970s, Spain was ruled by the dictatorial Franco regime. Spain's historical status as an awkward member of the Atlantic community contributed to a tendency among some elements of the Canadian public (although not Canadian state officials) to stigmatize the 'other' during the 'fish war.' Despite its clear success in moving through the transition from dictatorship to democracy, Spain's image as a like-minded country was devalued. The major way of doing this was through frequent backward-looking references to Spain's non-democratic record. Generally speaking, the Canadian media described Spain in negative terms, with some commentators going so far as to depict it as either a country of the Armada in search of conquest or a country that had given succour to Hitler's Third Reich during the initial phase of the Franco era.[16]

By way of contrast, the firmness of Canada's 'familial' ties with Britain (through references to past episodes of fighting side by side, the Commonwealth linkage, etc.) was played up. This connection was useful in a concrete way, as part of a campaign intended to erode the EU's common front in support of the Spanish position on the fishing issue. The connection also had considerable value in image-building, signalling that Canada's tough approach found favour with another country that was also embroiled in an ongoing dispute with Spain over fish. Indeed, Canadian state officials made a number of highly publicized visits to the British front lines in Cornwall (the Cornish fishing fleet having had a number of run-ins of their own with the Spanish fishing fleet over tuna and other species), where they shared battle stories. As a result of this campaign (abetted by the efforts of the Canadian media), Cornish ports began to fly the Canadian flag in sympathy with Canadian actions on the high seas.

This push to proclaim the differences between Canada and Spain was encouraged as well by the confluence of the 'fish war' with the fiftieth anniversary celebrations of D-Day. Much was made during these celebrations of Canada's constructive contribution to the international system in the post-1945 era, a contribution centred on the pillars of mediation, peacekeeping and participation in international organizations. A significant sub-theme, underpinning this whole emotional outburst, was the manner in which these activities had been forged on the anvil of war. Only through its massive effort in the Second World War, the argument went, had Canada been able to graduate to win a major role (and voice) on the international stage.

An extension of this line of reasoning took the form that Canada's tough stand against Spain on the 'fish war' constituted a further stage in the same evolutionary process. The problem, some observers seemed to be saying, was that Canada had confined its international expression to that of saying 'ready, aye, ready' to forms of initiative integral to the global interest. This 'good international citizenship' encouraged an image of Canada as making enough of a contribution to keep up its credentials as a player; but it also contributed to an impression of Canada sinking slowly into a kind of lethargy, in which it had become a captive of its long-standing habits of behaviour. If seen as 'nice,' Canada was no longer seen as possessing the youthful vigour it had displayed in the past. Process had taken priority over results.

In tune with this same sort of logic, the best way for Canada's image as a vigorous actor to be revived was through some display of a more daring form of activity, directed at helping the national interest rather than propping up the international order. At this very crude level of psychological analysis, Canada's 'fish war' represented a type of collective mid-life crisis for Canada (with an abundance of insecurity and 'crankiness'). While reluctant to discard everything about its old style in foreign policy, Canadians as a collectivity were quite ready to indulge themselves in a different sort of adventure. One of Canada's leading pollsters attempted to sum up this attitude by saying that Canadians had moved from 'the boy scout, Johnny Canuck stage' through to 'the adult phase of our development.'[17]

In system-specific terms, the proposition can be made that the targeting by Canada of any fellow member of the Atlantic alliance in a 'belligerent' manner was facilitated by the loosening up of the discipline of the Western alliance in the post-Cold War era. The room for the NATO partners to disagree on a wide number of issues was extended as the common enemy disappeared. Yet even with a good deal of choice, Spain was a relatively predictable target. One factor worth considering relates to the lack of cognitive awareness between Canada and Spain, due to a lack of cultural insight. After all, Canada has had a number of disputes over fish with other countries (including the US and France); but none of these disputes escalated the way the fish conflict with Spain did. The other factor that cannot be underestimated is that Spain lacks the military muscle which the major powers possess.

In issue-specific terms, the rationale for targeting Spain was readily comprehensible. Canada's experience of attempting to achieve an agreement, or even some basic set of parameters for rule-making, with Spain on the fish issue had been acutely frustrating. Canada's relationships with the US and France might well have been marred as well by conflict over fish. However, the context was dissimilar. In relationship to these other countries, there existed at least the possibility of settlement (as witnessed by the lengthy negotiations over the East Coast fisheries with the US, or the equally long-drawn-out negotiations conducted between Canada and the EC/EU); with Spain, the prospect of a negotiated settlement never appeared to be on the cards. When discussing the fisheries issue, Spain repeatedly affirmed its historic rights (going back four centuries to the time of John Cabot) to unimpeded access to the fishing stocks of the Grand Banks. The issue of stock conservation, in bilateral terms, was non-negotiable: since 1977, when the measure was implemented, Spain had resisted recognizing Canada's 200-mile offshore zone.

On a number of occasions in the 1980s, Canadian authorities had taken up 'hot pursuit' activity directed at the Spanish fleet. In a precursor to the *Estai* incident, two Spanish vessels were chased across the Atlantic in 1986 by Canadian patrol vessels (with fisheries inspectors and armed RCMP officers on board). After eventually being apprehended, the vessels were forced to return to St. John's and the captains were charged.[18] The difference between the two cases was that the 1986 incident started after the Spanish vessels ventured into Canadian territorial waters. Indeed, Canada's justification for its use of this behaviour was premised on this assumption. The subject of controversy between Canada and Spain rested on the definition of territorial waters. For Canada, this meant the 200-mile economic zone; for Spain, alternatively, it meant the old 12-mile territorial limit.[19]

Provoked by this 1986 incident, Canada moved in a number of ways to institute a tougher surveillance and enforcement regime. These new measures included the use of more aircraft, the arming of fishery patrol officers, an increase in fines against violators, and the use of upgraded patrol boats equipped with light armaments.

Instead of abatement, however, the fish issue intensified in the late 1980s and early 1990s. In large part this situation resulted from the entry of Spain and Portugal into the EC in 1986. The process of accession gave Spanish fishing practices a further cloak of legitimacy—and added clout—in bilateral negotiations. The other EC countries with coastal waters of their own had little incentive to tone down Spain's activities on the high seas, as the externalization of its new partner's practices had the effect of reducing their own domestic sensitivities on fishing issues. A further complicating factor pertained to the technological advances made within the fishing industry. Whereas a decade earlier 'rogue' practices could be absorbed by the still abundant supplies of fish, the deployment by the Spanish and other fleets of increasingly sophisticated equipment (sonar tracking) and unscrupulous methods (including the kind of small-mesh nets found on the *Estai*) meant that resources were increasingly depleted. The once rich supplies of northern cod had been exhausted under the weight of over-fishing. Other less well known species, including the turbot/Greenland halibut, were in danger of extinction.

## The Promotion of Global Governance

To give primacy to the promotion of global governance suggests that Canada was justified in raising the stakes in terms of the fish dispute. Canada's unilateral actions may have transgressed accepted norms of international behaviour; that is to say, Canada's application of armed force in the protection of straddling stocks could be deemed to be 'illegal' in customary form. Canada's rationale for its actions, though, was not based on a formalized reading of international laws. From this perspective, Canada defended its move to take its campaign against over-fishing beyond the boundaries of its territorial limits as both necessary and right with respect to its global sense of responsibility. Far from denoting a sharp departure—going in an uncharted and potentially risky direction—this behaviour was said to be in close conformity with Canada's established habit of gearing its statecraft towards support for the international order. Instead of being shaped by hard-headed realist assumptions based on self-interest, Canada's unilateralism was shaped by a concern for institution-building and regulation, based on a desire to advance universalistic notions of well-being.

With respect to declaratory statements, Canadian state officials emphasized the particular set of circumstances that forced them to act as the 'guardian' or 'steward' over the domain of straddling stocks off the Grand Banks. To effectively manage the 'global common,' the narrow definition of sovereignty had to be discarded. Simplistically put, fish swim. Off the Grand Banks, many of the fish species swam between Canadian and international waters (often clustering in the so-called 'nose' and 'tail' areas, areas that were part of the important Grand Banks ecosystem but which were technically outside Canada's 200-mile zone). As a consequence, the type of renewable resource involved in the 'fish war' must be differentiated from those scarce resources that were located in a specific territory. Instead of a firm and tight delimitation on the basis of fixed boundaries, the boundaries had to be treated as being by their very nature porous. In a similar vein to many other forms of environmental threat, including acid rain and atmospheric pollution, the issue of fish depletion was complicated by the fact that these species 'don't respect borders.'[20] To deal adequately with the problem, therefore, the fish issue could not be addressed by a simple delimitation between an 'inside' and an 'outside' domain, or the protection of 'our citizens' versus the protection of the citizens of the 'other': it had to be dealt with in a comprehensive manner, for the good of all. As Brian Tobin stated with his characteristic verve: 'This issue is not about who gets what share of the fish pie that's out there.... What's at stake here is whether the fish pie itself is going to be sustained. Whether or not there's going to be any fish for anybody in the future... This wanton destruction of a protein resource that belongs to the world is every bit as irresponsible as the destruction of the rainforest. This is a crime against humanity.'[21]

With respect to problem-solving, these same state officials emphasized the need for Canada to take precipitous action because of the lack of an effective regime on high seas fishing. Unilateralism did not imply self-help, mercantilism or protectionism, intended to exclusively advance the material benefits of Canadians at the expense of others. Unilateralism was simply a tool to nudge Spain, and the rest of the EC/EU, to recognize their shared interest with Canada and other countries on the issue of conservation and management of living resources on the high seas. The action was not driven by a desire for conflict, but as a stepping-stone for international co-operation via the establishment of new international mechanisms to deal with the type of problem encountered off the coast of Newfoundland. The reference point was universal norms, not state power.[22]

This influence can be traced back to the current of Canadian thinking and practice that guided Trudeau's statecraft on a number of controversial environmental/resource flashpoints in the early 1970s. The most significant of these questions related to Canada's unilateral action on marine pollution.[23] Prompted by the voyage of the converted supertanker *S.S. Manhattan* through the northwest passage, and by American proposals to transport crude oil from Alaska through Arctic waters, the Trudeau government in 1970 unilaterally passed legislation through the Arctic Waters Pollution Prevention Act (AWPPA) declaring a 100-mile control zone around the islands north of the 60th parallel and banning the discharge of waste.[24]

In common with the actions during the Spanish 'fish war,' the formal legal justification for this earlier piece of unilateral legislation was shaky. The main thrust of Canada's argument, however, was not based on accepted practice. Moving beyond the status quo, Canada took the position that the framework of international law had to be extended in an evolutionary manner to encompass conservation measures (including seizure and arrest of vessels) beyond the limits of its (then) 12-mile territorial waters. As Alan Beesley, Canada's chief negotiator on the Law of the Sea Convention, explained, though Canada was 'well aware of the controversial nature of these measures,' it was 'aware also that international law is developed by state practice, that is, by unilateral measures gradually acquiesced in and followed by other states.'[25]

In terms of principle, this precedent provided Canada with a valuable tool to utilize on the issue of straddling stocks. Unilateral action in 1970 allowed Canada to establish control zones beyond the 12-mile limit to protect the environment in 'ice-covered areas' of the Arctic. Analogously, on the fish issue, Canadian action to effect control over the 'nose' and 'tail' of the Grand Banks was justified on the grounds that this move effected a form of stewardship (although not sovereignty) over an area, beyond Canada's 200-mile zone, in which an effective international regime was non-existent. In the build-up to the 'fish war,' Canadian state officials made frequent references to the validation that the AWPPA gave it in its campaign to take responsibility for the protection of the fish in the 'nose' and 'tail' of the Grand Banks. When addressing the issue in February 1994, before a vocal Newfoundland audience, Prime Minister Chrétien made an explicit linkage between the two cases: 'When...I was Minister of Indian and Northern Affairs, we had a problem in the North, danger of pollution of the northern waters. And even if the international community claimed that we have not the right, we passed a law, the Arctic Pollution Act.... Some countries did not recognize it, but it was applauded internationally because it was for a good reason. It was our responsibility to protect those waters for environmental reasons.... And we passed the law.' In the same way, he went on to add: 'I will not be afraid to confront the international situation [on the fish crisis]...because everybody who believes in conservation will be on the side of the people who will...protect the fishery.'[26]

In terms of practice, Canada's unilateral action on the AWPPA can be said to have worked in extending the framework of international law. As alluded to by Prime Minister Chrétien, a number of actors refused to accept the legality of Canada's actions. The most important of these was the United States. Yet over the course of time, Canada was able to gain the upper hand over these opponents by getting a general endorsement of its actions at the international level. The cause of 'environmental integrity,' even if it was pursued on the basis of a country such as Canada acting first and seeking ratification later, gained impetus over the subsequent decades. Canada's move to extend its control over both expanded territorial seas and the continental shelf, through the proclamation of a 200-mile economic zone in January 1977, gradually took on the status of an established consensus with respect to the sovereign rights of coastal states over the living resources within their 200-mile zone. A turning-point here was the third UN Law of the Sea conference, in which joint notions of 'optimum utilization' of the resources found within the 200-mile zone and the sharing of any 'surplus' with other countries concerned were advanced.

Regionally, Canada worked hard between 1972 and 1979 to complete the transformation of the Canadian-sponsored International Commission for the Northwest Atlantic Fisheries. Taking form as the Northwest Atlantic Fisheries Organization (NAFO), this forum provided the institutional structure on which the bulk of the Canadian hopes—and dashed expectations—were centred during the 'fish war.'

## The Politics of External Deflection

To give primacy to the politics of external deflection suggests that Canada tried to 'internationalize' the fish crisis so as to redirect attention away from internal problems. Two factors in particular were mooted as reasons for projecting the Canadian approach in this direction; one of these was directly related to the fish crisis, the other only indirectly.

Some considerable salience was given to the 'fish war' as an approach designed indirectly to build national solidarity and identity at a time of uncertainty and internal troubles. From this perspective, a good deal of attention was given to the way in which the 'fish war' instilled a sense of pride in Canadians when so many of the givens of their existence had been wrenched away. This focus on uncertainty returns the discussion to the idea of transition introduced at the outset of this volume. Confronted by the contradictory forces of globalization and localism, cross-cutting identities, and the combination of both new space for initiatives and a sobering sense of constraint, the 'fish war' served as a useful (though short-lived) distraction from everyday realities. As an article in the *Toronto Star* honed in on this theme: '[the fish war] has united Canadians in a common purpose just when they needed it most.... We were tired of constitutional wrangling, bored with O.J. and confused with the budget.... Now we have our own little Persian Gulf war to cheer us up. No other spectacle could unite...this country in such a heartfelt chorus of indignation.'[27]

Some Quebec commentators put a very different spin on this campaign. Rather than viewing the 'fish war' as a relatively benign form of distraction (getting Canadians to switch over from CNN's coverage of the O.J. trial to take in the latest bulletin from the Grand Banks), the fish episode conjured up memories of Anglo-Canadian jingoism from earlier in the century as exhibited on the naval and conscription questions. Although taking a very different form, contemporary campaigns of this kind were interpreted as being designed to obstruct Quebec's pursuit of national self-determination; the temporal connection between the fish war and the upcoming Quebec referendum should therefore come as no surprise. The external threat posed by the Spanish fleet was inextricably joined to the internal threat posed by the scenarios of separation and the dismantling of Canada. As Lysiane Gagnon has forcefully put it: 'Isn't it a remarkable coincidence that at a time when the country seems to be unravelling at the seams, the Canadian government suddenly discovers an external threat. It wouldn't be the first time in history that the rulers of a divided kingdom waged war against a foreign enemy to return harmony to the land.'[28]

More directly, there were strong indications that Canada deployed the politics of deflection to shift scrutiny away from its own record of conservation over fish stocks at home and on to the records of the Spanish and other foreign fleets. There is no disagreement about the effect of the crisis, namely that the Atlantic provinces have faced devastation because of the depletion of fish stocks. The collapse of the East Coast fisheries has brought with it not only an environmental crisis but social and economic collapse. Newfoundland especially has been hard hit, in that the end of the fisheries has meant the end of a way of life in the outports. Little, if any, alternative existed to replace this traditional livelihood. The disagreement centres on causation, about the question of who bears the brunt of the blame for the tragedy. The overwhelming view in Atlantic Canada generally, and in Newfoundland specifically, targets the foreigner as the major culprit. To be fair, Clyde Wells (the premier of Newfoundland) and other prominent East Coast politicians have been willing to acknowledge that Canada has 'sinned in the past' through defects in its own fishing management practices. The crucial difference between the responses by Canada and the foreigners was said to be that Canada had now recognized the seriousness of the problem and had taken action to rectify it. At the cost of putting 30,000 people out of work, Canada had introduced a moratorium on the fishing of northern cod in June 1992. In the face of this sort of internal action, designed to gradually (and painfully) bring the Grand Banks fisheries back to their sustainable levels, the Spanish fleet and other foreigners had continued to fish the 'nose' and 'tail.'

With such high stakes involved, Premier Wells went on the offensive in the early 1990s to try to mobilize support for a 'get-tough' approach on the fishing issue. As with the Meech Lake constitutional accord, this foray into foreign affairs revealed Wells's dogged determination. Highly sceptical about Canada's ability to negotiate a positive outcome via international conventions, Wells pressed for a legally binding treaty as a means to resolve the issue. In pursuing this first-best option, Wells did what he thought was necessary and right. His language included comparisons between the European claims that their fishing practices off the Grand Banks were legal and the assertions of Saddam Hussein justifying his invasion of Kuwait in August 1990.[29] Wells's fall-back solution was an initiative on the part of Canada to establish 'custodial management' of the areas just outside the Canadian Exclusive Economic Zone on the Grand Banks. Canada could not afford to wait long for a treaty. It had to take the lead in implementing strong precautionary management measures to keep fish stocks from becoming totally extinct.

This fall-back approach translated into vigorous support for unilateral action on the part of a broad coalition of political forces based in the Atlantic region. Impatient with the slow and frustrating pace of negotiating a settlement, this coalition (made up of representatives of such organizations as the Fisheries Council of Canada and the Fishermen, Food and Allied Workers (FFAW), the business and trade unions respectively) wanted decisive action to extend Canadian jurisdiction across the boundary of the continental shelf to include the 'nose' and 'tail.' The crisis was too desperate to be left to diplomacy and negotiators. What was required was an immediate, direct response to repel the threat of 'marauders' over-fishing off the Grand Banks. To press their point, the East Coast fishing industry mobilized through a number of ad hoc umbrella organizations; these included Sonar, or Save Our Northwest Atlantic Resources, and the Advisory Committee on Foreign Overfishing. Consistent with the national interest/security perspective, this coalition wanted Canada to show the flag and show it with a degree of firmness that would command respect and ensure compliance. In the words of Earle McCurdy, a leader of the FFAW in Newfoundland: 'This is a question of national will. We in Atlantic Canada expect to be protected from foreign invasion on the fishing grounds the same way that people on the Prairies would expect to be protected from foreign invasion on their farmlands.'[30]

The position of the environmental movement was very different, although there was some common ground. 'Green' groups, such as Greenpeace and the Natural Resource Defense Council, were adamant that the issue of environmental security, and the 'desecuritization' of the East Coast fishing communities, must be taken seriously. This stance allowed some coincidence of interest with the Canadian fishing industry. On strategy, the environmentalists agreed that voluntary measures were not enough to solve the crisis; what was required was a legally binding global agreement. On tactics, many of the 'green' groups were practitioners of the direct action techniques thought necessary by the Canadian fishing industry. Some radical (or extremely dark) 'greens' had moved ahead of the fishing industry, in confronting the foreign fishing fleets on the high seas. Paul Watson of the Sea Shepherd Conservation Society, the best-known advocate of these direct tactics, had engaged in a guerrilla campaign of this nature, attempting to force vessels to lift their nets and return home.[31]

This coincidence of interest did not mean a commonality of interest, however. Notwithstanding their overlap of perspective, the environmental movement maintained a fundamental critique of the Canadian position on the fish crisis. In terms of the causation of the crisis, the 'greens' rebuked Canada with respect to its own record on over-fishing and the pursuit of the agenda of sustainable development. The moratorium on northern cod, for example, was seen as a cynical attempt to redirect the spotlight of attention away from Canada's own culpability. This view was based largely on the argument that the fisheries crisis in the north-west Atlantic had only come about since 1977, when Canada extended in de facto fashion its jurisdiction to 200 miles off the coast. It was reinforced by the wealth of supporting evidence that Canada's own fisheries management system had been lax, allowing a great many exemptions and loopholes. The Cashin Report on the fishing industry, when released in November 1993, for instance, had directed a good deal of attention on to Canada's own 'destructive' fishing practices, such as highgrading (discarding and dumping of immature fish and non-target species).

In terms of solutions, the environmental movement took issue with the build-up of momentum to externalize the fish issue. Greenpeace, for example, pointed the finger at the contribution of the deep-sea fishing fleets (including Spain's) to the crisis. To point the finger at only the deep-sea fleet, however, was regarded as hypocritical in that it overlooked the contribution of the coastal fleet. Greenpeace, because of this attitude, refused to take sides in the fish dispute. To do so would play into the penchant to see nation states as the solution instead of the problem in dealing with this type of crisis. As one representative of Greenpeace stated, 'fisheries conservation has been held hostage to squabbling over national sovereignty versus international responsibility.'[32] Greenpeace Canada fisheries campaigners contested the view that Canada was the 'white knight' of the high seas.[33]

Greenpeace's own preference was to address the larger issues attached to the fishing crisis, especially those relating to the link between environmental security and broader issues such as consumerism, technology, democracy and militarism. In staking out this position, Greenpeace's concern was not with national sovereignty and territorial integrity but rather with environmentalism as a fundamental value designed for the common good in societal relations. As Greenpeace put it bluntly during the Rio Conference, 'the challenges of the contemporary system require moving from a military-centred notion of security to a new focus on resolving the problems threatening the earth's major ecosystems and human health and welfare. This means challenging the global sovereignty based on market needs and building a new global sovereignty with institutions responsible for assuring environmentally sound and socially equitable development. This new sovereignty should be rooted in empowered communities...

expressed globally in international institutions with the strength and legitimacy to hold their members accountable.'[34]

Rounding out this critique, Canada's use of force (albeit at a low level) in handling the episode was condemned as a resort to coercive diplomacy. In keeping with Daniel Deudney's basic attack on the whole notion of 'environmental security,' the fish issue was viewed by the 'greens' as being addressed not as part of a new security agenda but as part of the traditional security agenda.[35] Through the application of a geopolitical logic, environmental issues had become militarized. Instead of concentrating on trying to work out peaceful solutions in this sphere, force was deployed to demonstrate national mastery over issues that were really uncontrollable by individual countries. Rather than seeking to deal with 'threats' to the earth's resources, Canada had chosen to seek enemies. As one environmental campaigner expressed the 'green' view of the episode: 'Gunboat diplomacy is the end of the line for countries that fail to recognize that ecologically and socially sustainable development is a precondition for survival on this planet.'[36]

## Bureaucratic Politics

To give primacy to bureaucratic politics suggests the existence of an ongoing 'turf battle' between different elements within the Canadian state.[37] This perspective had some resonance in the case of the 'fish war' episode. In a variety of ways, the fish episode provides a textbook issue of intragovernmental tension at the federal level. On one side, the Department of Fisheries and Oceans was determined to lever the dispute—via 'any sort of high-profile victory'[38]—into an enhanced position for itself. In doing so, it was quite ready to 'poach' on the traditional turf of the Department of Foreign Affairs and International Trade. Moreover, in the person of Brian Tobin, Fisheries and Oceans possessed a minister well able to operationalize this approach. Indeed, Brian Tobin almost single-handedly was able to raise the fish issue to the apex of the national—and international—agenda. On the other side, the fish dispute provided a keen test of DFAIT's ability to retain its grip on Canadian diplomacy. Viewing itself as the authentic guardian not only of Canada's long-term national interest but of the traditional habits of Canadian statecraft, DFAIT needed to perform a delicate balancing act on the fish issue. As with the other intra- and inter-governmental challenges it had faced in the past, DFAIT worked hard to ensure that it rather than Fisheries and Oceans had the 'lead' position on the fish issue. At the same time, through a familiar process of adaptation, it sought to make good use of Fisheries and Oceans' aggressive diplomatic style to bring about a resolution to the fish dispute. DFAIT's 'quiet' diplomacy was thus meshed—somewhat awkwardly—with Fisheries and Oceans' 'get tough' approach.

The fisheries issue presented both a challenge and an opportunity to Tobin. Taking over the Fisheries and Oceans ministerial portfolio after the election of the Chrétien government in the fall of 1993, Tobin quickly discovered that he no longer could employ the variety of domestic policy instruments available to his predecessors in that position. The stark realities of Canada's fiscal condition imposed formidable constraints—in the sense, for instance, that money as income replacement could no longer be allocated to the East Coast fishing industry to cushion its decline. John Crosbie, when fisheries minister in the Mulroney government, had moved to deliver a relatively generous package in the form of a two-year $900-million Northern Cod Adjustment and Recovery Program, but this pay-out terminated after May 1994.[39] Nor, in a political/policy atmosphere dominated by cutbacks in transfer payments (as announced in Finance Minister Paul Martin's February 1994 budget) and the various rounds of cutbacks in Unemployment Insurance, could the East Coast fishing population rely on other forms of compensation to continue in the place of this income replacement package.

The opportunities that existed for Tobin emerged from his strong political position within the Chrétien Liberal government, his charismatic personality, and the client base attached to the ministry under his authority. One key component of Tobin's political strength in the Liberal government emanated from his reputation—gained mainly from his former membership in the so-called 'Rat Pack' of Liberal opposition critics—as a party loyalist during the years in opposition (1984–93). Another source of influence derived from his position as the political minister for Newfoundland, a position enormously enhanced by his ability to effectively deliver parliamentary seats to Chrétien in the 1993 election. Although the Liberals secured an overwhelming victory in this election, with wide-ranging regional support, the initial spark for the triumph was set off in the first key results in Newfoundland. Tightly wrapped up with these strengths was Tobin's image as a feisty champion of regional causes in general and Newfoundland causes in particular.

In taking on his ministerial responsibilities, Tobin displayed a political maturity without a loss of his street-smart and charismatic edge. To the surprise of many observers, Tobin moved quickly to broaden his hitherto abrasive image, as a good critic in the hurly-burly of a political scrum or debate but limited in his ability to generate constructive solutions.[40] Tobin's rhetoric incorporated the language of environmentalism as a lever to ratchet up the case for 'doing something' about the fishing issue. This 'green' ingredient allowed Tobin to frame the fish issue as one of vital import for 'humanity' rather than just for his own political constituency. Tobin was able to maximize media coverage by talking with conviction, opining that only tough measures on the Grand Banks would prevent this once rich fishing area from becoming a marine desert. The enormity of this problem could only be understood with this theme in mind: 'This is an ecological disaster. It is also a societal calamity. What do you do if your life, your family and your community are all linked to the fishery, but there are no fish? No fish today and maybe no fish ever again, unless the little that remains is protected.'[41]

Tobin was acutely aware of the need to acknowledge—and transcend—Canada's own poor record of fisheries management. In tandem with the call for action against the foreign fishing fleets operating outside of Canada's territorial waters, Tobin emphasized that Canada had already taken similar tough action on the home front to atone for its own culpability. Because of this reversal, Canada should be viewed as a committed, not a convenient, country on the fish issue: 'We have held up our own sins and publicly declared ourselves guilty of overfishing. We have apologized to the planet and we've changed our ways.'[42]

In terms of the reputation of the Fisheries and Oceans department, Tobin tried to turn weakness into strength. The image of the department had long been that of a strong-willed component—but somewhat of a loose cannon—within the federal government. This assessment had been engendered by Fisheries and Oceans' past record on fisheries conservation management. Given the mandate to gather information about the decline of fish stocks and to control over-fishing, Fisheries and Oceans was widely deemed to have fumbled both tasks. As shown by the outlook of the environmental movement, the fish crisis was widely considered to be a made-in-Canada problem. Despite Fisheries and Oceans' concentration of in-house technical expertise, the ministry had done a poor job of counting fish. Furthermore, Fisheries and Oceans gave the impression of having contributed to the depletion of stocks by poor monitoring of over-catching and under-reporting, and by granting exemptions to the East Coast fishing industry within Canada's own waters. Up until the moratorium on northern cod was put in place, neither precise, effective rules and regulations nor effective monitoring had been established where Canada's vessels exclusively fished. Even after the implementation of the moratorium, critics pointed to the presence of gaps that allowed this control mechanism to be skirted and other species (besides northern cod) to be over-caught.

Tobin cultivated the department's loose-cannon reputation to considerable advantage in the fish crisis. In keeping with his own image as an outsider, Tobin created political/policy space by playing up the 'rogue' qualities of Fisheries and Oceans. By promoting aggressive action against foreign over-fishing,[43] he could reinforce his personal popularity within his domestic constituency, while also differentiating his 'get tough' mode of operation from the traditional 'softly, softly' diplomatic approach favoured by DFAIT.[44]

Tobin's desire to challenge DFAIT for the 'lead' role on the international over-fishing issue was prompted in large part by the experience of John Crosbie as Fisheries and Oceans minister in the Mulroney government. As the Conservatives' political minister from Newfoundland, Crosbie had also been fixated by the issue of foreign over-fishing off Newfoundland. Akin to Tobin, Crosbie was a master in the use of colourful political rhetoric. He also possessed sharp elbows in political scrimmages. As intense political partisans, Crosbie and Tobin had often tangled in their parliamentary performances. Both politicians were motivated by a concern to outdo each other (and to be seen to be doing so) in terms of their willingness to go to bat for the East Coast fishing industry.

Crosbie's big chance to make his mark on the fish issue had come with the 1992 Rio Conference. In the build-up to the summit Crosbie had been given the green light to embark on a public information campaign on the question of over-fishing in the north-west Atlantic; a red light nevertheless remained in place concerning direct unilateral action against foreign vessels. This red light reflected the concerns of EAITC that any 'get tough' approach would be counter-productive to a settlement of the fish issue. Maintaining its faith in negotiation and coalition-building as the standard operating procedures of Canadian diplomacy, EAITC rejected unilateralism and the resort to coercion. Barbara McDougall laid out her department's attachment to these fixed ideas and principles in a March 1992 radio interview: 'we abide by our international commitments.... I don't believe in gun boat diplomacy.... We believe in multilat-eralism. We work with our allies.'[45]

These concerns described the limits of the Canadian diplomatic effort on the fish issue during Crosbie's watch. Canada was instrumental in getting the ques-tion of over-fishing on the high seas on to the agenda of the Rio Conference in June 1992. The most significant breakthrough came with the positive response given to Canada's call for a UN conference to deal specifically with high seas over-fishing. Out of this initiative, the UN procedural mechanisms began to tick. Two meetings were convened in 1993, an organizational session and a substan-tive working session. After a subsequent preparatory meeting, the high seas con-ference was convened in August 1994.

Throughout this campaign, Crosbie's activity was channelled through the familiar avenues of Canadian statecraft. In form, the approach had an institu-tional, rules-oriented bias. The Canadian objective remained that of creating a binding set of obligations through a global regime, which would allow both enforcement and arbitration. In style, Canada concentrated on coalition-building with like-minded countries, with special reference to a small group of coastal countries consisting of Iceland, New Zealand, Argentina and Chile, to which Norway and Peru were later added. This core group co-sponsored the so-called Santiago Resolution. Maintaining this associational vigour, Crosbie convened a forum, openly labelled the 'Like-Minded States Meeting' from 21 to 24 January 1993 in St. John's, Newfoundland, to work through a draft convention.

While Canada gained a great deal from this multilateral-directed activity on a procedural basis, with respect to results there was a palpable lack of success. To some extent this circumscription was a function of the internal weaknesses of the like-minded coalition. This group of coastal states shared an interest in the promotion of tighter regulations over straddling stocks of fish, but there were marked differences between the individual countries. The conflict between Norway and Iceland over fishing rights in the Barents Sea 'Loophole' stood out here. There were also a number of conflicting loyalties among the members of the coalition, as witnessed by New Zealand's straddling between its membership in the like-minded group and its shared interests with the group of South Pacific states that were pushing for a non-binding document on high seas fishing.

On top of these internal weaknesses was the problem Canada and its allies had in manufacturing support from other influential actors. Because the US was reluctant to accept global management, in the shape of a regime for highly migratory species, it joined with a number of other countries in a foot-dragging exercise on an international agreement. The so-called distant water fishing nations, including Japan, South Korea, Russia and China, were also opposed to the construction of a regime, opting instead for a non-binding resolution and much weaker obligations. The EU initially registered some flexibility, but under enormous Spanish counter-pressure it had shifted back to an uncompromising position of resistance by April 1994. Backing away from a serious attitude towards negotiation, the EU took an obstructionist approach, with the objective of having the conference run its course without conclusion. By August 1994 this defensive strategy had worked so well that concerns grew among the like-minded coalition that time would run out before the conference could finalize its work. A concerted diplomatic essay was required just to win an extension, whereby the UN allowed the high seas conference to carry on with its work into 1995.

With this experience in mind, Tobin was determined to keep the pressure up for action in both the 'international' and 'domestic' games. He did this through the pursuance of a dualistic 'game plan,' which raised the ante with respect to both Canadian statecraft and foreign countries. In the domestic game, Tobin focussed on unilateral legislative measures. Consistent with the AWPPA precedent, pride of place was given to the incremental use of the Coastal Fisheries Protection Act against foreign vessels. Although this type of action was scrupulous in avoiding the claim of Canadian sovereignty over 'straddling stocks,' it accorded stewardship for Canada over particular species of fish in waters that it conceded did not legally belong to it. In May 1994 parliament passed amendments to this legislation to allow greater (domestic) legitimacy for enforcement actions outside the 200-mile zone. The immediate targets of this move were the 'reflagged' or 'stateless' vessels—those flying flags of convenience or no flag at all. Room was left, nonetheless, to allow future action against other categories of fishing vessels, such as those from Spain and Portugal, an amendment that was carried forward in March 1995 immediately prior to the break-out of the 'fish war' with Spain. In the international game, Tobin used a new international agreement negotiated under the auspices of the Food and Agriculture Organization (FAO) to revoke the registration of 'stateless' vessels found to be fishing in contravention of international compliance measures on the high seas. The agreement put stricter burdens on flag states and created an international list of offending vessels.

Both the domestic and internationally oriented measures were enthusiastically endorsed by the political and economic coalition in Atlantic Canada campaigning for tougher action on the fish issue. Premier Wells termed the Coastal Fisheries Protection legislation 'an act of international leadership,' in that it demonstrated that 'Canada will no longer tolerate the wanton destruction of a world food resource' in the waters contiguous to its shores.[46]

Tobin, encouraged by this positive reception, stated that this escalation was necessary and right: 'These reflagged vessels are nothing less than modern-day pirates. It's obvious that if you are going to act, you have to be prepared to be...where lawless vessels are operating, you have to be prepared to stop...that fishing activity, and that is the determination Canada has.... It's an act of conservation; nobody could call it an act of war. We're not out to declare war, we're out to declare enough is enough when it comes to the declaration of cod stocks by nations that operate outside of any civilized norms.'[47]

Upping the ante still further, Canada moved to operationalize these tools. On the basis of the FAO agreement, Canada initiated an elaborate tracking operation to find out the true identities of 'reflagged' or 'stateless' vessels, and to get countries such as Panama and Honduras to deflag them.[48] More dramatically, Tobin moved to implement the measures provided in the Coastal Fisheries Protection Act. The first sign of this intention was the direct action taken against the *Kristina Logos* in April 1994. In doing this, Tobin used the unique circumstances of this case to his advantage. Although flying a Panamanian flag when boarded by Canadian authorities, this vessel had previously been registered in Canada. Therefore, a claim could be made that Canada still possessed jurisdiction over it.

Tobin's intrusion into the international dimension of the fishing issue imparted a contradictory dynamic into Canadian statecraft. The contrast between the operational style ingrained in DFAIT and the new directions favoured by Tobin could hardly be more divaricated. DFAIT's approach to the fish dispute was conducted with a minimum of fanfare, in the form of a low-key or quiet diplomacy. Building on its habit of advancing by way of co-operation and dialogue, DFAIT was determined to retain Canada's reputation as a responsible and influential player. It placed considerable store on Canada working in a steadfast fashion through the complex processes of international fishing diplomacy. In plain opposition, Tobin elected to employ a provocative 'exhortatory' style of statecraft. In lieu of a patient reliance on low-key, behind-the-scenes activity, Tobin and his department employed loud and often abrasive tactics designed to draw attention to the issue at hand. Above all, Tobin wanted to place drama at the centre of the stage.

In the course of this bureaucratic struggle, neither Tobin nor DFAIT did much to hide their contempt for each other. For Tobin, professional diplomacy had failed by not delivering the goods. DFAIT's low-key style constituted not a pragmatic attitude to getting results but a misguided overemphasis on staying the course procedurally. Rather than promoting dialogue, Canada had to deliver a clear and forceful message that it was willing to act to protect its national interest and international values. What was required was not patience but a sense of urgency. In Tobin's words: 'Canada is acting purely because it is driven to act. We have conducted diplomacy down to the last few pounds of fish. We either continue to talk about it, or we try to save those last few pounds and use them as a basis for restoring the stocks.'[49]

For DFAIT, Tobin's campaign was disruptive. By shifting the onus from multilateralism and bilateralism to unilateralism, Tobin was making waves with little appreciation about how this 'get tough' approach could impart harm to Canada. At one level, this approach was at odds with Canada's image as a good international citizen. At another level, the approach opened up the danger of tangible forms of retaliation being taken against Canada.[50]

This combination in Canada's high seas diplomacy, however, cannot be said to have worked exclusively at cross-purposes; there was a complementary dynamic as well. Canada could deal with Spain and the other countries covered by the Northwest Atlantic Fisheries Organization (the fourteen-nation group with responsibility over international waters in the region, including the 'nose' and 'tail' off the Grand Banks) in both a soft and a hard fashion. Precisely because they were so contradictory, the methods used by DFAIT and Tobin acted to reinforce each other's effectiveness in pushing for a tighter regulatory regime. At the risk of cliché, DFAIT and Tobin can be termed the nice cop and the tough cop of Canadian fish statecraft. Tobin's missionary zeal provided a flip side to the skills contained in DFAIT. While they never worked in tandem, the practical advantages derived from this two-sided mix should not be discounted.

The central thrust of Canadian diplomacy in the early 1990s had been directed to winning a bilateral agreement with the EU, whereby the EU would not only agree to abide by NAFO quotas but would also ensure through a self-monitoring system that the catch from its fleet did not exceed these quotas. Accordingly, a deal hinged on a trade-off between regulation and quotas. Progress towards a bilateral agreement along these lines had been initialled in December 1992. The actual signing of the agreement, though, had been delayed as both parties reassessed their positions. On the EU side, the complexities of internal community politics made a cautious posture inevitable. On the Canadian side, some considerable pressure was exerted on the new Liberal government by the East Coast fishing industry not to sign so as to keep Canadian options open for tougher control measures.

The sense of frustration imparted by the slow pace of the NAFO negotiations was magnified by the failure to secure a comprehensive international moratorium to allow fish stocks to rebuild. Despite the appearance of a Canadian triumph in securing a moratorium of this nature in February 1994,[51] it was short-sighted to claim complete victory. The agreement that transpired was not an omnibus one, in that it left out a number of species; nor, in the absence of any effective mechanism to monitor and/or induce compliance, did it work well in operation. Individual countries continued to set aside those NAFO rules that they did not like. They also continued to fish in the regulatory area beyond the 200-mile limit of the exclusive EEZ.

The specific issue that finally triggered unilateral action on the part of

Canada centred on what Tobin was later to call the 'unloved' turbot (or in EU parlance, the Greenland halibut). Unloved the turbot may have been, but at least historically that species had been Canada's own. This was no longer the case. Due to a number of scientific factors, the turbot had left their traditional location in Canadian waters and headed for deeper, warmer waters outside the 200-mile Canadian fishing zone. Acting within the framework of NAFO, Canada thought it had won an agreement, in September 1994, to stop a situation in which 'the rules of the Wild West' governed 'the tossed East Coast waters.'[52] NAFO agreed to continue a moratorium on six of the most depleted stocks— including cod—on the 10 percent of the Grand Banks that was in international waters. Moreover, it extended the rules to set a reduced quota for turbot stock for the next year. Again, however, this 'victory for conservation' proved to be an illusion. The difficulty came in getting the EU to abide by these measures. When the precise quota was allocated by NAFO in early 1995, a special committee allocated Canada a 60 percent share of the 27,000 tonne quota for turbot outside the Canadian 200-mile zone, with a 12.6 percent share to the EU. Complaining that their apportionment of the stock was unfairly small, the EU chose to ignore this ruling and grant itself a higher quota.

This defection provided the spark that set off the 'fish war' with Spain. On 3 March 1995, by Order in Council, Canada amended the Coastal Fisheries Protection Act's regulations, to have Spanish and Portuguese ships covered by the list of foreign vessels eligible to be boarded and seized for over-fishing off the Grand Banks. On 6 March, Tobin made it clear that Canada would take tough direct action if the EU did not adhere to NAFO rules. On 9 March, the incident involving the chase and arrest of the *Estai* took place. After a short pause, the process of escalation continued. On 26 March, Canadian patrol vessels cut the nets of another Spanish ship, the *Pescamero Uno*.

These actions shared a high-risk orientation. By having a (repeated) go at the Spanish fleet on the high seas, Canada's actions invited open condemnation on the basis that they comprised a deviation from the principles of international law. Critics of Canada's unilateral behaviour focussed on the collateral reputational damage done to Canada. No longer could Canada be seen as the 'responsible deputy' but—in the words of the EU's fisheries commissioner—as a state that acted 'as the lawmaker, the sheriff, and the judge.'[53] The impact of this kind of self-serving judgment from biased participants in the conflict was reinforced by the fact that the critical tone was echoed by more dispassionate observers. As one respected Canadian law professor stated: 'This is knee-jerk nationalism. It's unfortunate that a country like Canada that needs international law and has a reputation for respecting international law takes matters in its own hands like this.'[54]

The danger from the point of view of the Canadian national interest, as recognized by DFAIT, was not simply a symbolic one. By extending its authority beyond the internationally recognized 200-mile limit, Canada sent a signal of acceptance of unilateralism to other countries. This was particularly true of the big powers, which were instinctively tempted to move in this direction anyway. Canada might win short-term success on the fish issue, but this success had to be weighed against the longer-term negative implications. By departing from the high road on fish, Canada might weaken its ability to refer cases of maritime dispute with the US to the jurisdiction of the International Court in The Hague. The Canadian action might also strengthen the claims of the US on extraterritoriality. There was, too, the danger of a contagion effect, where Canada's performance would have a demonstration effect on the international community as a whole. Looking beyond the greats, the *Globe and Mail* warned of a future situation in which an 'outlaw nation...acting on intentions less honourable than conservation' acted as a pirate on the high seas and provided Canada's actions as a precedent.[55]

Another risk for Canada lay in the possibility of an extended escalation in the 'fish war.' Scenarios along these lines were raised by the 'sabre rattling' carried out by both sides in the Canada–Spain dispute. Prior to the conflict with Spain breaking out, the Canadian military had been asked to develop contingency plans for intercepting and boarding foreign trawlers beyond Canada's 200-mile limit. That is to say: 'We're asking defence to be prepared when the time comes to give the government options available to deal with overfishing.'[56] After the 'fish war' broke out, Spain sent one naval patrol boat to accompany the Spanish fishing fleet and announced its intention of sending another one. The possibility of a 'real' conflict breaking out, however, should not be exaggerated. The extent to which either Canada or Spain had the desire or the ability to flex their military muscle was severely limited by a blend of structural and logistical conditions.

Canada's Department of National Defence displayed little if any inclination to get involved in any naval action. DND was content to back up the effort by monitoring and surveillance work with what resources it possessed. These included military aircraft for surveillance (although for the most part aerial surveillance had been contracted out to the private sector), naval patrol ships (including HMCS *Terra Nova* of the improved Restigouche class of frigate) and even at least one submarine (of which Canada had three in active service). The Canadian enforcement measures did not include an explicit military component. Fisheries officers, backed up by armed RCMP officers, carried out the operation of boarding, arresting and detaining the *Estai*. The fisheries officers were from the patrol vessels *Cape Rogers* and *Leonard J. Cowley*. The RCMP officers were part of an emergency response team aboard the coastguard vessel *Sir Wilfred Grenfell*. These personnel did possess the legal authority to use coercive force. When the initial boarding of the *Estai* was thwarted by the Spanish crew—through a combination of tossing the Canadian boarding ladders back into the sea and cutting its own nets—the ensuing four-hour chase was brought to a halt only by four bursts of .50 calibre machine-gun fire shot across the bow of the Spanish ship.[57]

A longer-term risk for Canada was some form of political and/or economic retaliation. Canadian unilateralism on the fish question fed into the EU's appetite for the explicit application of linkage politics—as witnessed on several other resource issues, including beef exports. Countermeasures of this sort had direct material consequences for a wide number of Canadian producers, which became potential targets for European action. It also held indirect implications for Canadian statecraft in other arenas. One possible consequence was that the EU would act to terminate completely the UN High Seas Fisheries Conference. Another was that the EU would try to inflict hurt on Canada in a political/diplomatic way (for instance, by the exclusion of Canada from some forum or initiative). Although the EU said it wanted to 'avert a trade war,' warnings were also issued by the Europeans that if Canada seized one European vessel 'we will not stand still.'[58]

Amid all this drama, it needs to be reiterated that this 'get tough' behaviour formed only one side of Canada's approach in dealing with the fish dispute. Far from conceding the 'lead' position to the Department of Fisheries, DFAIT raised its own game in terms of dealing with the fish dispute. This statecraft made use of DFAIT's diffuse resources and points of access (including a special Fisheries Conservation Ambassador, Paul Lapointe, and the diplomatic personnel located in Brussels and the national capitals of the EU countries). In tone, DFAIT expressed its firm commitment to a negotiated settlement on the issue through multilateral/bilateral means. In substance, DFAIT mounted its own diplomatic offensive to achieve a deal with the EU. Pushing the dossier as it had never done before, effective charge of the Canada–EU negotiations was taken over by Gordon Smith, the recently appointed deputy minister of foreign affairs.[59]

By going on the offensive in this manner, DFAIT allowed Spain and the EU to negotiate without dealing directly with Tobin and the Department of Fisheries and Oceans. Moreover, without the close connection to a domestic constituency, DFAIT was in a position to bargain effectively. This meant, in effect, working out a compromise deal. DFAIT was prepared to relinquish some of Canada's fish quota, and to concede an allowance in the form of a transition measure whereby the EU would be allowed time to adjust to their reduced allocations. The bottom line was that Canada must receive in return a set of firm and effective enforcement mechanisms to be established under the auspices of NAFO. This quid pro quo appeared in two components of the formula eventually agreed: the first was the provision for having neutral observers on any and all fishing vessels fishing the 'nose' and 'tail' of the Grand Banks; the second created an additional enforcement regime through satellite tracking and home-port inspections under the scrutiny of independent monitors. This bilateral deal in turn opened the way for a breakthrough in the way of a comprehensive international agreement via a fish conservation regime. As ultimately settled on, at the July 1995 UN High Seas Fisheries Conference, the final convention was interpreted as providing Canada with the binding and enforceable instruments it had long sought.[60]

## AN ANOMALY OR A PROTOTYPE?

The 'fish war' episode may be seen as atypical in Canadian statecraft. By taking on Spain and the EU through a direct form of unilateral action, Canada deviated sharply from the diplomatic style it had cultivated over the entire span of the post-1945 period. Not only were Canada's national interests explicitly placed first, the case for a Canada-first approach was made (and justified) by its advocates in a plain and unapologetic way. As Brian Tobin said after the *Estai* episode, it is 'the mark of a patriot' to 'reach out in desperation at the 11th hour and try to save' the last of the fish stocks off the Grand Banks.[61]

This departure did much to complicate the expression of Canadian diplomacy. Many observers claimed that Canada's character had been stained and compromised by its behaviour during the fish crisis. Some went so far as to argue that the hypocrisy it displayed on this issue (preaching multilateralism and practising coercive 'self-help') would come to haunt Canada. The *Ottawa Citizen* asked poignantly whether, in the course of peacekeeping operations, Canada would be accused by rival parties 'of a double standard when we urge them to settle their differences without violence.'[62] Serious questions were raised about the splintering of Canadian diplomacy to reflect regional or local interests. Did Canadians join in a 'common purpose' or did Canada 'stand up' to Spain and the EU because of the enormous symbolic and instrumental importance of the fish issue to Newfoundland? If the latter, was Canadian diplomacy made a prisoner of domestic interests, with the interest of a declining resource industry put ahead of the material and diplomatic/political interests of Canadians, who could be hurt by EU countermeasures? Questions were also raised about the degree to which Tobin accurately 'spoke' for Canada when he insisted that 'tough action' was necessary and right; and whether this impression would have been changed if—through miscalculation or misadventure—lives had been lost in action on the high seas.

Tobin's actions also revealed the complexity of the discourse and practical application of 'environmental security.' Tobin buttressed the case for 'tough action' on the high seas enormously by reference to the global governance argument, that Canada was acting as a constructive internationalist to bring order where the search for co-operation had proved fruitless. Yet at the same time, the episode indicated the less than benign implications of framing an issue of resource depletion through this lens. The securitization of this type of resource question tended to concentrate attention on the activities of foreigners—or the 'other'—as the source of depletion or degradation. Furthermore, this process of securitization appeared at the same time to shift the focus towards rather than away from a link between resource depletion/degradation and conflict. Although Canada may have been high-minded, it risked being tagged a self-appointed 'conservation vigilante'—willing to justify violence for the purpose of the international good—on the fish issue.[63]

These arguments, nevertheless, should not be taken too far. If the 'fish war' indicated the potential for added complexity, it also indicated the potential for an increasingly rich and varied form of Canadian statecraft. Tobin's intrusion on the fish issue stretched the boundaries of Canadian diplomacy in a multifaceted and creative manner. Tobin—through his eloquence and theatrical flair—was able to stir the passions of Canadians, and attract attention in the mass media, in a way traditional Canadian diplomacy had not been able to do. This not only added lustre to Canadian diplomacy; in some ways it made it more credible. The juxtaposition of Canada's diplomatic expressions as tough cop and as nice cop allowed many of Canada's older habits of statecraft to be supplanted, refined and redirected. Rather than the habits of dialogue, co-operation and the centrality of institutions being marginalized or seen as irrelevant, they burst on to centre stage in the dénouement of the dispute.

This sense of creativity, in which disparate threads of Canadian statecraft were woven together in a complex pattern, highlights the paradox of Canadian statecraft at the end of the millennium. Notwithstanding all its pitfalls and risks, a positive quality underscores the Canadian performance in the fish episode. In terms of style, the static quality (or feeling of inertia) extant in some elements of Canadian diplomacy was absent in this drama. There was also a positive association with 'open'—media-friendly—diplomacy. In terms of substance, there was a sense that Canada had scored a victory in terms of the national interest and the international community.

This raised the question, in another form entirely, of whether the fish dispute was the exception that proved the rule. Canadian statecraft may have been advanced on the special, even unique, case of the fish issue. On the issues composing the twin pillars of post-1945 Canadian foreign policy, alternatively, a sense of retreat pervaded much of the discussion. To assess the accuracy of this feeling, it is imperative that we undertake a closer look at these twin pillars—peacekeeping and development aid—as they have evolved under changing conditions.

## NOTES

1   Andrew Cohen, 'Canada in the world: the return of the national interest,' *Behind the Headlines* 52, 4 (Toronto: Canadian Institute of International Affairs, 1995), 11.

2   Kevin Cox, 'Tobin moves on fish "pirates,"' *Globe and Mail*, 12 May 1994.

3   Robert Kaplan, 'The coming anarchy,' *Atlantic Monthly*, February 1994, 44–76.

4   Jessica Tuchman Mathews, 'Redefining security,' *Foreign Affairs* 68, 2 (Spring 1989), 162–77.

5   Richard H. Ullman, 'Redefining security,' *International Security* 8, 1 (Summer 1983), 133.

6   Thomas F. Homer-Dixon, 'On the threshold: environmental changes as causes of acute conflict,' *International Security* 16, 2 (Fall 1991), 76–116.

7   Terry Terriff, 'The "Earth Summit": are there any security implications?' *Arms Control: Contemporary Security Policy* 13, 2 (September 1992), 185.

8   Canada 21 Council, *Canada 21: Canada and Common Security in the Twenty-First Century* (Toronto: Centre for International Studies, University of Toronto, 1994), 10. Stein elaborated on this point in one of her appearances before the joint parliamentary committee on Canadian foreign policy: 'If we look very concretely at the security of our maritime population, and that affects Newfoundlanders very directly, security is threatened by the depletion of cod stocks. This is an environmental problem that has travelled across borders.' Testimony to the Special Joint Committee of the Senate and of the House of Commons, Reviewing Canadian Foreign Policy, *Minutes of Proceedings and Evidence*, 3 May 1994, 7:8. See also Thomas Homer-Dixon, 'Environmental and demographic threats to Canadian security,' *Canadian Foreign Policy* II, 2 (Fall 1994), especially 15–16.

9   Peter J. Stoett, 'Human rights, environmental security and foreign policy,' *Policy Options*, June 1994, 9.

10  Andrew Moravcsik, 'Integrating international and domestic theories of international bargaining,' in Peter B. Evans, Harold K. Jacobson and Robert D. Putnam, eds., *International Bargaining and Domestic Politics: Double-Edged Diplomacy* (Berkeley: University of California Press, 1993).

11  William Johnson, 'Canada is on the angels' side in high-seas battle over fish,' *Montreal Gazette*, 8 March 1995.

12  Cohen, 'Canada in the world: the return of the national interest,' 11.

13  Quoted in Huburt Bauch, 'Fish pirates back off, Tobin says,' *Montreal Gazette*, 8 March 1995.

14  *Toronto Sun*, 14 March 1995.

15  Bruce Russett, *Grasping the Democratic Peace: Principles for a Post-Cold War World* (Princeton, NJ: Princeton University Press, 1993), 119.

16  See, for example, William Johnson, 'Canada is on the angels' side.'

17  Michael Adams, quoted in Edward Greenspon, 'St. Brian among the turbot,' *Globe and Mail*, 18 March 1995.

18  Jim Meek, 'Canada, Spain take action on illegal fishing,' *Halifax Chronicle Herald*, 31 May 1986.

19  Robert Martin, 'Spain will stop boats in dispute over fish,' *Globe and Mail*, 31 May 1986.

20  David Vienneau, 'Get-tough Chrétien warns we won't back off,' *Toronto Star*, 11 March 1995.

21  Quoted in 'Canada is ready to act against foreign turbot ships,' *Montreal Gazette*, 6 March 1995.

22  See David Baldwin ed., *Neorealism and Neoliberalism: The Contemporary Debate* (New York: Columbia University Press, 1993).

23  See Barry Buzan, 'Canadian foreign policy and the exploitation of the seabed,' in Barbara Johnson and Mark Zacher, eds., *Canadian Foreign Policy and the Law of the Sea* (Vancouver: UBC Press, 1977).

24  Michael Tucker, *Canadian Foreign Policy: Contemporary Issues and Themes* (Toronto: McGraw-Hill Ryerson, 1980), 177–81.

25  J. Alan Beesley, 'The Law of the Sea Conference: factors behind Canada's stance,' *International Perspectives*, July/August 1972. Douglas Johnson has argued that 'perhaps the highest priority of all for Canada at UNCLOS III was the buttressing of legal claims to the Arctic Ocean,' in Clyde Sanger, *Ordering the Oceans* (Toronto: University of Toronto Press, 1987), 113. See also John Kirton and Don Munton, 'The Manhattan voyages and their aftermath,' in Franklyn Griffiths ed., *Politics of the Northwest Passage* (Montreal and Kingston: McGill–Queen's University Press, 1987).

26  CBC transcript, Jean Chrétien's speech in St. John's upon accepting petition from Fisherman's Crisis Alliance, 24 February 1994.

27  Bob Richardson, 'Gunboat cure best medicine for all our ills,' *Toronto Star*, 16 March 1995.

28  Lysiane Gagnon, 'The story of Canada's gunboat diplomacy is mighty fishy,' *Globe and Mail*, 18 March 1995. The hype given to the D-Day celebrations merely reinforced this more cynical interpretation, as did Brian Tobin's decision to don the cloak of Captain Canada not only against the Spanish but also in the cause of Canadian unity.

29  Quoted in Jacquie McNish, 'Angry Wells lashes out at EC countries,' *Globe and Mail*, 4 April 1992.

30  Quoted in Kevin Cox, 'Canada unable to stop foreign fishing of turbot,' *Globe and Mail*, 24 February 1995. Indeed, the East Coast fishing industry had moved to take direct action themselves. In 1992 a small flotilla of Newfoundland fishing boats had sailed outside the 200-mile zone to attempt to harass Spanish and Portuguese fishing vessels.

31  Paul Watson, *Ocean Warrior: My Battle to End the Illegal Slaughter on the High Seas* (Toronto: Key Porter, 1994).

32  Matthew Gianni, of Greenpeace International, quoted in David E. Pitt, 'Pact eluding fishing nations in talks on imperiled species,' *New York Times*, 5 April 1993. The passivity inherent in this neutral role attracted some scathing commentary in the Canadian media. See, for instance, Terence Corcoran, 'Where are the greens in the fish war?' *Globe and Mail*, 13 March 1995.

33  See '"Canada not without sin," Tobin admits,' *Toronto Star*, 15 March 1995.

34  Greenpeace International, *Beyond UNCED* (Amsterdam: May 1992), 25.

35  Daniel Deudney, 'The case against linking environmental degradation and national security,' *Millennium* 19, 3 (Winter 1990), 461–76; and 'Environment and security: muddled thinking,' *Bulletin of the Atomic Scientists*, April 1991.

36  Ms. Robin Round, MDB Campaign Co-ordinator, Sierra Club of Canada, testimony to House of Commons Standing Committee on Foreign Affairs and International Trade, *Minutes of Proceedings and Evidence*, 14 March 1995, 18:22.

37  See, for example, Elizabeth Riddell-Dixon, *Canada and the International Seabed: Domestic Determinants and External Constraints* (Montreal and Kingston: McGill–Queen's University Press, 1989).

38  'Gunboat diplomacy,' *Maclean's*, 20 March 1995, 10.

39  Giles Gherson, 'Not so much a program as a one-way ticket out of the fishing industry,' *Globe and Mail*, 13 January 1994.

40  This type of criticism may be seen in a *Globe and Mail* editorial, written after his appointment: 'As a Newfoundland MP and a former member of the Liberal Rat Pack, Brian Tobin has spent years railing against foreign overfishing on the Grand Banks. Now that he is Fisheries Minister in the new Liberal government, it is natural that he should want to do something about it. But Mr. Tobin must remember that he is more than an advocate for fishermen now. He is a representative of a nation with international duties and obligations.' 'Mr. Tobin's loose lips,' 13 January 1994.

41  Quoted in David E. Pitt, 'U.N. aides fear new cod wars as fish decline,' *New York Times*, 20 March 1994.

42  Quoted in Paul Koring, 'Brussels knocks Canada's practices,' *Globe and Mail*, 30 March 1995.

43  For a solid overview of this theme, see Ted L. McDorman, 'Canada's aggressive fisheries actions: will they improve the climate for international agreements,' *Canadian Foreign Policy* II, 3 (Winter 1994), 5–28.

44  Jeff Sallot, 'Get-tough policy doesn't entail apologies,' *Globe and Mail*, 20 September 1994.

45  Transcript, L'Agence France Presse, Ottawa, 17 March 1992.

46  Kevin Cox, 'Tobin moves.'

47  Paul Koring, 'Canada to block fish "pirates,"' *Globe and Mail*, 12 January 1994. In his earlier attacks on Crosbie for not going far enough to defend the interests of the East Coast fishing industry, Tobin had downplayed the possibility of armed conflict as a consequence of unilateral action on the part of Canada. Are 'nations so intent in pursuing a continuation of harvesting on the nose and tail on the Grand Banks,' he asked, 'that they would send over their navies to provide armed protection of their fleet to continue fishing. Is Spain preparing to declare war on Canada? I don't think so.' Quoted in Graham Fraser, 'Crosbie raises use of "big stick" on overfishing,' *Globe and Mail*, 4 April 1992.

48  Giles Gherson, 'Canada takes aim at rogue trawlers,' *Globe and Mail*, 14 April 1994.

49  Quoted in Clyde H. Farnsworth, 'Canada to seize boats fishing outside its zone,' *New York Times*, 22 May 1994.

50  'Gunboat diplomacy,' *Maclean's*, 20 March 1995, 10. Foreign Affairs diplomats were said to 'have looked with horror' on Tobin's attempts at 'gunboat diplomacy.' Ouellet said that he was 'not throwing in the towel yet. I am quite confident the diplomatic negotiations will succeed if all parties act in good faith and are willing to compromise.' Testimony to House of Commons Standing Committee on Foreign Affairs and International Trade, *Minutes of Proceedings and Evidence*, 14 March 1995, 18:65.

51  'International moratorium set on Grand Banks cod fishing,' *Toronto Star*, 18 February 1994.

52  Tobin, quoted in Kevin Cox, 'NAFO nations agree to cut catch of endangered fish,' *Globe and Mail*, 24 September 1994.

53  Emma Bonino, quoted in Paul Koring, 'EU threatens to suspend talks,' *Globe and Mail*, 28 March 1995.

54  Armand De Mestral, professor of international law at McGill University, quoted in Farnsworth, 'Canada to seize boats.' De Mestral was the co-author, with Sharon A. Williams, of *An Introduction to International Law: Chiefly as interpreted and applied to Canada* (Toronto: Butterworths, 1979).

55  'A dubious victory in the fish war,' *Globe and Mail*, 18 April 1995.

56  'Military asked for strategy on policing fishery,' *Globe and Mail*, 25 January 1995.

57  Jim Brown, 'Boarding a ship? Having a big machine-gun helps,' *Montreal Gazette*, 10 March 1995.

58  'Firepower for a war of words,' *Globe and Mail*, 9 March 1995. On the possible diplomatic repercussions arising out of Canada's actions, see 'Spain may have the last laugh in transatlantic trade push,' *Globe and Mail*, 22 May 1995.

59  See Jeff Sallot, 'Fish for a diplomatic solution,' *Globe and Mail*, 9 March 1995. Smith had extensive experience with Canadian–European issues, having previously served as the Canadian ambassador to both NATO and the EC/EU.

60  Clyde H. Farnsworth, 'North Atlantic fishing pact could become world model,' *New York Times*, 17 April 1995. See also Stephen Handelman, 'Tobin warns UN on fish law for Canada,' *Toronto Star*, 25 July 1995.

61  Quoted by Edison Stewart, 'Canadians seize Spanish trawler,' *Toronto Star*, 10 March 1995.

62  'Victory at sea,' *Ottawa Citizen*, 18 April 1995.

63  See John Darnton, '2 feuding nations with fish stories,' *New York Times*, 2 April 1995.

# TESTING THE LIMITS OF WILL: CANADA AND THE EVOLUTION OF PEACEKEEPING

Peacekeeping is more than an ordinary sphere of activity in Canadian foreign policy. Peacekeeping has been central to the definition of Canada's national identity, role and influence in the world. Peacekeeping remains a crucial element in—and symbol of—Canada's world-view. Uncomfortable with the settlement of disputes by military solutions, or coercive methods generally, peacekeeping has provided a staple tool for the application of constructive internationalism. Canada's sustained involvement, and record of performance, in terms of peacekeeping has been widely perceived to have given it an area of issue-specific comparative advantage. As Janice Stein told the Special Joint Committee on Canadian foreign policy: 'What can we do best?... It is international peacekeeping.'[1] In the international arena, Canada's skill and solid record of commitment to United Nations peacekeeping has provided Canada with a good deal of recognition. Domestically, the association of Canada with UN peacekeeping has proved enormously popular. Support for peacekeeping has become part of a national consensus. Sympathy with and appreciation for Canada taking part in peacekeeping missions has extended right through the Canadian public.

Despite these positive attributes, Canada's will to continue playing a prominent part in future peacekeeping operations has been severely tested by the post-Cold War experience. Canada's volunteerism and capabilities in this sphere of international activity were forged during a period when the boundaries of peacekeeping were clearly defined in terms of form, scope and intensity. In the post-Cold War world this is no longer the case, in that the terrain of peacekeeping has been split open to such an extent that these limitations no longer exist. Having entered the transitional era with a good deal of enthusiasm—if not euphoria—about the use of peacekeeping, Canada has found this extension of the conceptual/practical meaning of peacekeeping to be fatiguing. While the national consensus on peacekeeping cannot be said to have been shattered, this bedrock of support has been pounded to a noticeable extent.

## DEFAULT AND DESIGN

## The Development of Canada's Peacekeeping Role

Peacekeeping as Canada's forte in foreign policy came about largely by default, and not as the result of some grand design or strategy. The activity built up in an incremental and ad hoc fashion.[2] Canada's participation in the UN Military Observer Group India–Pakistan in 1949 on Jammu and Kashmir occurred only because a Canadian mediator had failed in an attempt to bring about an agreement between India and Pakistan on the status of those territories. The UN Emergency Force (UNEF 1) in the Sinai—the mission that did so much to inextricably link Canada and peacekeeping in the eyes of both the Canadian public and the international community—was initiated in the classic reactive 'seat of the pants' fashion so favoured by Lester Pearson and the old External hands.[3] Moreover, the way the peacekeeping force evolved on the Sinai was very different from the original intent. As unrealistic as this scenario seems in hindsight, Pearson had initially hoped that the British and French forces undertaking the invasion of Egypt and the Suez Canal might be transformed into a UN police force. Only when this initial proposal was ruled out as a non-starter did the notion of a UN force made up of national contingents (including one from Canada) get advanced as an alternative.

Canada demonstrated a keen desire to pick its venues for activity in a prudent fashion. All of the major episodes of Canadian involvement in peacekeeping were accompanied by a good deal of internal debate within government circles about the risks of making a commitment. In part, this cautious attitude was induced by the backlash in Canada against the decision to take a leading part in the Sinai mission. The new habit was not easily cultivated. In marked contrast to the ample international kudos showered on Pearson, including the 1957 Nobel Peace Prize, the reception at home proved to be more muted. Notwithstanding the retrospective image of this episode as representing the defining expression of Canada's post-1945 foreign policy, the positive national consensus about the value of Canada's participation had still not jelled. Many political commentators saw Canada's role not as a positive move with respect to 'good international citizenship' but as an abandonment of its traditional responsibilities to follow Britain's lead. If the Sinai mission constituted the pivotal moment of transition, in the words of Hillmer and Granatstein, from 'Empire' to 'Umpire,'[4] cognizance of this transition was not immediately apparent. The impact of this episode was only evident as it was slowly (but thoroughly) digested, and became lodged in the bloodstream of the Canadian political culture and public imagination.

Prudence was encouraged also by Canadian concerns about being trapped in missions in which the political/military/financial costs could be appreciably raised. Once again, this caution had been instilled by Canada's experience in Middle East peacekeeping operations. Canadian members of the UN Truce

Supervision Organization (dating back to 1948 armistice agreements between Israel and its immediate Arab neighbours), as well as Canada's contingent to the Sinai emergency force, faced direct threats to their safety. Indeed, one member of this former team was killed (by fire from a Jordanian sniper) and another two seriously injured (by a mine explosion). With respect to the time span of these missions, Canada found it had little or no say about when and under what conditions an exit could be made. Despite its substantive expenditure in terms of reputation and resources on the Sinai mission, Canada was ultimately left in the position of having to take its contingent out on forty-eight hours' notice when President Nasser of Egypt announced that the UNEF was no longer wanted.

This sense of caution was reinforced still further by the unique characteristics of a number of other missions mooted for Canadian peacekeeping activity. The first of these was the 1960 ONUC operation initiated by UN Secretary-General Dag Hammarskjöld in the Congo (now Zaire). Despite the seriousness of the crisis, in the aftermath of Belgium's precipitous withdrawal from its colonial possession, the Diefenbaker government expressed little interest in taking part in ONUC. Only the growing pressure from the Canadian public pushed the government to change its mind. What's more, as the Canadian role in the operation evolved, this initial reluctance seemed to be the wiser course if risks were to be avoided. In a foretaste of the 'failed state' situations of the 1990s, Canadian forces found themselves trying to keep the peace under extremely arduous conditions, featuring a breakdown of central authority, civil war and a proliferation of rogue military elements.

A second case, which brought out the Canadian fear of entrapment to an even greater extent, was the issue of peacekeeping in Indo-China. Canada found itself placed in a position of being a virtual hostage to its reputation for international service in the domain of peacekeeping through its activity on this issue. Although reluctant to get involved in what was rightly seen as a delicate and extremely difficult task, the Canadian government saw itself as having little room to opt out of the request that it serve as a member on the International Control Commissions (ICCs) created to supervise the cease-fire in Indo-China. When a choice had to be made about active participation on this body, Canada's instinctive response was to say yes. The result was another frustrating and draining experience from which Canada could not extract itself for another two decades. Even after being freed from its first commitment to the Vietnam ICC in 1973, Canada found itself dragged back into taking part in a revised control and supervision structure. Only in the last few months prior to the final end of the Vietnam conflict did Canada take the decision to pull out from this form of engagement in peacekeeping.

A variation on this theme of entrapment came in the form of overstretch in Canada's military/financial contribution. The prime illustration of this sort of dilemma came in the Cyprus peacekeeping mission. As in the Congo and Indo-China cases, Canada displayed some marked reservations about getting involved in this mission. When asked to sign on to a Cyprus UN force, Pearson had made a conditional reply: Canada would be willing to take part if a time-limit for the operation was provided and if supplementary means to induce a settlement between the rival Greek and Turk communities on the island were also provided. However, when open hostilities broke out between Turkey and Greece in 1964, these conditions were (problematically) laid aside. Canada rushed through with a commitment to send a contingent as part of a multinational force—a commitment it retained for twenty-nine years through the ironically named United Nations Interim Force in Cyprus (UNFICYP).

## The Style and Purpose of Canadian Peacekeeping

Originated mainly by way of default, peacekeeping in Canadian foreign policy has taken on a distinctive design as it has evolved. While this design retained a number of flaws associated with its genesis, the context from which it started also allowed an appreciation of discipline and limitations. The approach taken with regard to peacekeeping fitted well with Canada's privileging of the value of international order over justice. As drawn out most fully through the experience of the UNEF operation, peacekeeping in the Cold War years was mainly directed towards defusing a crisis situation by placing a force between the belligerent parties. Peacekeeping activity was therefore designed as an instrument to stabilize interstate disputes, not as a form of intervention against one side or the other based on a value judgment about who was right and who was wrong in the conflict. The deployment of peacekeepers was grounded on the criterion of impartiality, with consent required from each of the parties directly involved in the conflict.

Canada was guided in the development of this operational framework by its adherence to the traditional concepts of sovereignty and non-intervention.[5] Almost exclusively, Canadian peacekeeping activity was oriented towards regional 'bushfires,' which had the potential of escalating into more widespread conflicts with superpower involvement. This priority stands out in Pearson's justification of Canada's participation in Indo-China: 'Just as local conflicts can become general war; so conditions of security and stability in any part of the world will serve the cause of peace everywhere.'[6] This targeting could be misdirected in some cases, as for example on the Congo, which featured intrastate conflict. Nonetheless, the consistent motivation behind this mode of engagement—as with the other peacekeeping missions—was constraint and not the furtherance of an ambitious type of humanitarian intervention premised on the protection of human rights. Through the 1950s, 1960s and 1970s, in counterfactual fashion, Canada refrained from entertaining either the doctrine or the practice of any justice-oriented activity along these lines.

In its orientation, this approach to peacekeeping was in tune with the overall thrust of Canadian foreign policy. This form of participation was not only in sync with Canada's reputational impulses but with Canada's primary diplomatic

→ used in Suez

skills as well. Canada's talent for mediation remained at the core of Canada's efforts in this sphere of activity. Through its contribution to UNEF, the Cyprus mission and the other peacekeeping missions, Canada demonstrated that it was prepared to act as a 'bridge' or 'buffer' in an issue-specific fashion. These mediatory skills, in turn, extended from diplomatic activity behind the scenes to on-the-ground activity. Canadian peacekeeping personnel revealed their capacity to act as mediators and 'helpful fixers' on an issue by issue basis. This on-the-ground activity encompassed a whole range of micro-level measures designed to help build trust between the belligerent parties.

On top of these varied forms of mediatory activity, Canadian peacekeeping encouraged the development of complementary expressions of entrepreneurial and technical diplomacy. Because peacekeeping emerged as the preserve not of Canada individually but of a larger collection of self-identified middle powers, the habit of dialogue and co-operation with a core group of contributors was abetted. Between 1948 and 1990, Canada took part in the highest number of peacekeeping operations on a comparative basis (17); close behind were Sweden (15), Ireland (15), Finland and Norway (12 each), Denmark, India and Italy (11 each).[7] This pattern inculcated the attitude of 'like-mindedness' between Canada and the other members of this core group of contributors. Building on the informal networking common among most of these countries through the post-1945 period, this attitude allowed co-operation in all of the stages of peacekeeping. This included the pre-consultation necessary for setting the mandate of individual missions. It also facilitated co-ordination once the missions were launched.

It needs to be reiterated here that this form of middle power co-operation did not stem from an idealistic rationale. The active and ongoing attachment to peacekeeping shared by these predominantly 'older' middle powers was tied to the goal of system maintenance; it was not driven by a desire for radical transformation of the international system. In a close examination of the middle power interest in participating in peacekeeping operations through the Cold War period, Laura Neack has concluded that self-interest, in the form of maintenance of the international status quo, prevailed over any motivation for community improvement centred on claims of justice. Through that lengthy time period, middle powers were found to have acted primarily because of 'an obligation to protect the international peace and to preserve international norms and values.'[8]

## Canada's Technical Expertise

Canada's establishment of its expertise on the technical side of peacekeeping in a similar vein owes as much to default as design. The original plan in the UNEF Sinai operation called for Canada to provide a 'muscular' component to the peacekeeper force. Only with President Nasser's objection to the deployment of a Canadian infantry battalion from the Queen's Own Rifles (with the claim that its name and badges were too closely identified with the British) did this assumption change. Making a virtue of necessity, Canada chose thereafter to concentrate much of its peacekeeping efforts on logistical matters. Canada augmented its contribution to UNEF with respect to surveillance/patrol work through its ability to supply transportation, administrative expertise, signals, equipment maintenance and communications equipment. This type of activity became the standard mode of operation in subsequent missions. Canada's contribution to ONUC, for example, consisted of signallers and logistical personnel. Canada's contribution to the 1988 UN Iran–Iraq Military Observer Group (UNIIMOG) was made up of observers and a signal and support unit. The exception was the Cyprus case, where a more 'muscular' presence was appropriate because of the close proximity of the belligerents. To maintain the peace between the Greek and Turkish communities, through the establishment of a buffer zone across the island, Canada's toughest troops were utilized. Canada at first committed a battalion of the Royal 22e Regiment. From then on, almost all of Canada's army units had extended service in Cyprus—including the paratroopers of the Airborne Regiment.[9]

Whether originally by default or subsequently by design, this concentration of effort allowed Canada to carve out for itself a distinctive area of comparative advantage in peacekeeping. Canada's ability to perform a varied range of tasks became a source of pride and widespread support. The ability of Canada's military to showcase its wealth of technical competence did much to offset the defence establishment's reluctance to get involved in peacekeeping activities. Jack Granatstein has correctly identified the missionary background of so many of the old External hands as an important ingredient in implanting Canada's diplomatic 'calling' for peacekeeping. Still, as Granatstein acknowledges, this zeal was not shared by the Canadian military.[10] Any conversion that took place within the Department of National Defence came about not from an intellectual reconfiguration but because of an appreciation of the practical benefits derived by the Canadian military from this type of activity. This process emerged in different ways: collectively, the multifaceted nature of peacekeeping allowed the Canadian military to signal to the international community, to the Canadian public and to itself, not only that its store of skills was needed, but that it could adequately deliver these skills. Individually, a substantive national contribution provided career advancement through the appointment of high-ranking Canadian military officers to prominent positions in UN peacekeeping operations. The classic illustration of this phenomenon, in the early stages of Canadian participation, remains the selection of General E.L.M. Burns to be the commander of First UNEF.

While a good deal of the legacy of reluctance persisted into the 1990s, in both declaratory and operational terms the defence establishment adapted to peacekeeping. In terms of policy, the 1964 White Paper elevated peacekeeping to the top of the list of Canadian defence priorities, largely on the rationale of technical competence. The White Paper stated that 'Canada is one of a small number of powers capable of and eligible for United Nations service, with a highly trained and diversified military establishment.'[11] The call for Canada to take part in the revised and reinvigorated peacemaking agenda of the 1990s rested on a similar foundation. In the words of the document *Canada Defence Policy 1992*: 'Canadians are justifiably proud of the contributions the Canadian Forces have made to international peacekeeping.... Our experience and competence in this field are second to none, and the international community will continue to call upon Canada to assist in the design and conduct of such missions.'[12]

In terms of performance, the ability of Canadian peacekeeping personnel to perform their duties in a sound and conscientious manner reinforced the notion that 'Canada was a peacekeeper not only because it wanted to be, but also because it could be.'[13] This delivery function was often carried out in a highly charged—or politically sensitive—atmosphere. On occasion, Canadian peacekeepers had to operate under conditions of some risk to their own physical safety. Still, throughout the span of the Cold War era, the image of Canadian technical competence stands out. Even when there was 'confusion and embarrassment' about Canada's continued participation in a mission, as occurred in connection with UNEF in 1967, this image remained in place. As Granatstein and Bercuson note, the enforced (and extremely hasty) withdrawal of Canadian peacekeeping personnel from their positions in Sinai 'forced improvisation on National Defence Headquarters.' Despite the logistical concerns, three days after Nasser's demand for withdrawal was made, 'all the Canadians, except for a small rearguard preparing the heavy equipment, had flown out of Egypt in eighteen flights...along with over 100,000 kilos of equipment. As a result, Canada was spared the casualties that fell upon [other] UNEF units when Israel sent its forces against the Arabs (at the beginning of the Six-Day War).'[14]

## Public, Political and Diplomatic Support for Canadian Peacekeeping

The multifaceted nature of Canada's activities made it easier for the Canadian public to identify with peacekeeping. The mediatory role, displayed both at the diplomatic and the front-line levels, found considerable resonance in élite and popular attitudes concerning the salience of brokerage and accommodation in domestic politics. Rather than being identified as an unwanted meddler, there was a credibility attached to being invited as part of peacekeeping operations sanctioned by the UN. Canada was commonly viewed as being engaged in what Pat Sewell has termed 'ameliorative diplomacy.'[15] This positive identification was accentuated by the disposition of most Canadian political activists to support multilateral collaboration, especially when that collaboration was with like-minded countries. Analogous to the image of Canada's diplomatic personnel operating skillfully in UN forums, the image of Canada's peacekeeping personnel was a constructive one based on their ability to effectively act as buffers, go-betweens and micro-conflict resolvers between belligerents. The high degree of entrepreneurial and technical competence displayed in the peacekeeping operations cemented this positive image. These efforts lent credibility to Canada as a country of constructive doers, not just persuasive talkers. These activities also reinforced the notion of Canada as a nation willing to get involved in international affairs, even in cases that involved considerable risk, because it had the self-confidence and material resources to do so.

Some other factors provided additional support to peacekeeping from a political perspective. Firstly, a national consensus on the merits of a sustained Canadian commitment to peacekeeping activity served as a valuable contraposition to the normal partisan bickering on political/policy issues. That this national consensus—on the intersection of the national interest and the international good to be found in peacekeeping—was able to take hold despite the deep divide over the Suez crisis merely increased its value. Secondly, peacekeeping provided an area of activity—and jurisdiction—for Ottawa free of the constraints imposed by the federal dimension in Canadian politics. Finally, peacekeeping allowed the projection of the image of Canada as a bilingual and bicultural country in a specialized form of policy delivery. The practical spin-offs from this linguistic/cultural duality, in advancing Canadian functional representation, was made evident by the need for bilingual personnel to serve in a number of the earlier peacekeeping missions, including the Congo and Vietnam as well as the Lebanon (in 1958 and again in 1978).

All of these domestically oriented motivations were augmented by the diplomatic goal of trying to achieve a balance between Canada's obligations to the Western alliance and its concern with differentiating itself from the US and the other big powers. Canada's active participation in peacekeeping, with its onus on regional firefighting and the maintenance of stability within the East–West balance of power, received general encouragement and support from its alliance partners. Indeed, in some peacekeeping operations Canada may be said to have taken on a proxy role as the Western alliance's representative. This role was most contentious in the Vietnam ICC mission, where (albeit in circumstances where peacekeeping *per se* was impossible) Canadian personnel placed their reputation for impartiality in jeopardy by serving as diplomatic couriers for the Americans. A more flattering face of this role appeared in the Cyprus issue. Stalled in an attempt to use NATO personnel directly as a peacekeeping force, Canada was instrumental in building a UN operation that in effect did NATO's work for it. The bottom line for this mission was to prevent an open conflict between Greece and Turkey, two NATO 'partners.'

As one participant/observer reflected on Canada's constructive record on peacekeeping: 'If we examine the operations we have to ask how Canada established this reputation. Was it because our population was benign? Was it because of the nature of our military forces? Was it because we had an extraordinary interest in world events? Was it because we were a middle power? I do not think there is a simple answer but we need to look at some of the operations individually. We were involved in Cyprus because we were a NATO power imposed between two NATO countries. We were involved, I would suggest, in the International Control Commission in the mid-50s because we were a middle power.'[16]

If confining and restricting in some ways, Canada's position in the Western alliance was certainly a key ingredient in enhancing Canada's peacekeeping performance. From a technical point of view, it may be argued that Canada was only able to take on the multifaceted tasks required of it in its peacekeeping involvement because of its broader commitment to NATO service. Only its position as a Cold War 'warrior,' Canada's leading academic expert on peacekeeping insists, allowed Canada to possess 'the types of military forces that were the most useful for peacekeeping.'[17] In elaborating on this point, in testimony before the joint parliamentary committee reviewing Canadian defence policy, Professor Granatstein declared: 'Canadians...forget that our expertise in peacekeeping has come not from the purity of our souls or our imagined quasi-neutrality, but because we were part of and parcel of the western alliance. We were prepared to fight war overseas and we had the air, sea and ground capacity to do so. Our soldiers trained to fight the Russians in central Europe and they were very good at their tasks. Their war-fighting military skills made them readily able to switch to peacekeeping where discipline was also very much in demand. Our peacekeeping efforts almost always supported western interests. Certainly this was true in the Middle East, the Congo, Cyprus, Vietnam and Bosnia too.'[18]

It may be judged that Canada successfully pulled off this delicate balancing act during the Cold War years. Canada undoubtedly improved its standing, and its leverage, within the NATO alliance because of its peacekeeping contribution. At the very least, Canada's substantive commitment to peacekeeping made it much harder for other members of the alliance to criticize Canada for 'free riding' with respect to its overall NATO contribution—especially when the NATO alliance as an organization gained some element of associational pay-off via Canada's identification with this sphere of activity. Canadian participation in international peacekeeping represented 'burden sharing' in an alternative manner, a representation buttressed by such Canadian initiatives as the one that emerged out of the 1964 White Paper to set aside a stand-by battalion for peacekeeping duties (although a bolder initiative for the creation of an 'intervention force' never came to fruition). More positively, peacekeeping worked in compensatory fashion to help purchase Canada a ticket (or pay its dues), permitting it to continue to sit at the table of decision-makers in the Western alliance.

In counterpoise, a sustained involvement with peacekeeping offered Canada considerable leeway to send a clear signal about the degree of autonomy it possessed *vis-à-vis* not only the NATO alliance generally but the US more specifically. This balancing activity highlighted Canada's position as an ally that was both loyal and independent-minded.[19] While not compromising specific forms of military/strategic co-operation with the US, peacekeeping distanced Canada from the US in a number of important and distinctive ways. Unlike the US, Canada could represent itself as being prepared to work consistently through the UN rather than through unilateral means (symbolized by the wearing of the UN blue helmet). Also unlike the US, Canada could represent itself as having the will and the ability to pass on its store of peacekeeping skills (to other countries with a shorter tradition of peacekeeping activity).

## BEYOND TRADITIONAL PEACEKEEPING

### Rethinking the Design

With the recent seismic shocks in the international system, a sharp (and often harsh) spotlight has shone on peacekeeping activities. In theory, the opportunities available for moving beyond the conceptual/practical limits hitherto imposed on peacekeeping stretched considerably with the collapse of the old 'frozen' structure of the Cold War architecture. Thinking about the form, scope and intensity of peacekeeping could be pushed well past the traditional definitions. The reactive, ad hoc quality affixed to the practice was overtaken by an activist spirit. While the transformational events of the late 1980s and early 1990s threw up protean challenges and exposed kaleidoscopic vulnerabilities, they also allowed room for an expansion in imagination and undertakings on a selected basis.

A crucial ingredient in enabling this activist spirit to come to the fore is the enhanced role of the United Nations as a catalyst and agent for change in the transition years. The secretary-general's report, *An Agenda for Peace*, provided the first attempt to take advantage of the changing conditions manifest at the end of the Cold War (including, *inter alia*, the push towards democracy in many regions of the world and the rising status of the UN as an institution) to lay out the tectonics of a fundamental reordering of the international system. *An Agenda for Peace* accented the fact that alternative sources of initiative and innovation were crucial for the establishment of a new world order. In pointing forward to this goal, the document stressed the need to establish conflict management as a priority; in doing so, peacekeeping was accorded greater prominence.

A fundamental question at the anterior of the intellectual and political agenda on the edge of the millennium relates to the principle of sovereignty. It was the generalized adherence to this principle by the international community that had done much to restrict the application of peacekeeping activity in the Cold War years. Interventions that infringed on state sovereignty were deemed to be out of bounds. In the transition years, these borders of acceptability became increasingly porous. The passage towards a new agenda was informed by the recognition that there was a need to rethink the limits of state sovereignty. This issue was pushed to the fore with the United Nations Security Council Resolution 688 of 5 April 1991, which sanctioned intervention to provide 'safe havens' for the protection of the Kurds in northern Iraq; and it was reinforced by the application of the doctrine of 'humanitarian intervention' and a more activist mode of peacekeeping in Cambodia, Somalia and the former Yugoslavia.

If the concept of state sovereignty came under serious stress, it was far from spent. The action with regard to Kurdish refugees and displaced people, which allowed UN member states to send humanitarian personnel inside Iraq's borders without the permission of the Baghdad government, served as a stimulus for other UN actions of an interventionist nature (especially in 'failed states'). Nonetheless, as the secretary-general pointed out: 'The foundation-stone [for international organization] is and must remain the State. Respect for its fundamental sovereignty and integrity are crucial to any common international progress.'[20]

The tensions between state sovereignty and global obligations severely complicated the building of any new world order. Developing countries were willing to compromise on the principle of sovereignty in specific situations. UN intervention in Somalia, most notably, received broad acceptance at the outset of the operation on the rationale that, since effective authority had ceased to exist, the issue was survival not sovereignty. An argument was also made that a UN intervention in Somalia demonstrated equity in terms of the organization's concern over the condition of Africa as compared with the condition of crisis in other continents (especially Europe, with direct reference to the case of the former Yugoslavia). Where the developing countries had strong reservations was in interpreting this type of operation as a precedent for more generalized forms of intervention.

## The Mulroney Government's Response

What is most compelling for the purposes of this volume is the way the Mulroney government seized the opportunity presented by this transition in thinking at the global level to embrace an altered approach in terms of the balance between state sovereignty and international obligations in Canadian foreign policy. In terms of declaratory policy, Mulroney made it known in his convocation address to Stanford University on 29 September 1991 that Canada was receptive to 're-thinking the limits of national sovereignty in a world where problems respect no borders.'[21] This theme had been rehearsed four days earlier by Barbara McDougall, the Canadian secretary of state for external affairs, in an address to the UN general assembly: 'We must not allow the principle of nonintervention to impede an effective international response....the concept of sovereignty must respect higher principles, including the need to preserve human life from wanton destruction.'[22]

In operative policy, the Mulroney government delivered on this message. In the former Yugoslavia and Somalia, the two cases widely held up as examples that a new world order was being defined, Canada carved out a leadership position for itself. Prime Minister Mulroney was the first world leader to promote the idea of sending a UN peacekeeping force to the former Yugoslavia. In the autumn of 1991, Canada took the lead in requesting a meeting of the UN

Security Council to discuss the Yugoslavian situation, lobbing hard at the same time for the council to take action. When, on 21 February 1992, the UN went ahead with the decision to send a peacekeeping force to Croatia, Canada quickly volunteered to be part of the mission. In March 1992, DND confirmed that it would contribute personnel to the amount of 1200 peacekeepers to the United Nations Protection Force (UNPROFOR) for an initial one-year period.[23] Likewise, Canada backed up its declaratory support for a UN humanitarian mission to Somalia. The Mulroney government promised a contribution of approximately 750 troops to the original United Nations Operation in Somalia (UNOSOM), authorized in April 1992. In practical terms, Canada acted on this commitment by sending an airborne parachute battalion to Somalia to supplement the multinational force taking part in the UN operation.[24]

To fully understand the behaviour of the Mulroney government in fashioning this innovative (and risky) approach, both an international-level and a domestic-level analysis must be attempted.

On the international front, the Mulroney government's declaratory and operational activism on peacekeeping fed into the post-1945 image of Canada as a good international citizen. By taking a lead role both in the definition of humane interventionism and in its practice in the former Yugoslavia (and to a somewhat lesser extent in Somalia), the Mulroney government reinforced Canada's standing as a committed nation at the forefront of internationalism. This preference for taking the high road on the issue of humanitarian intervention is best captured in a 24 May 1992 speech, which Mulroney delivered in Montreal to an audience that included UN Secretary-General Boutros Boutros-Ghali. In this speech Mulroney asserted that: 'The UN and its member states must be prepared to intervene earlier and stronger in the future to prevent such disasters.... The UN needs to review urgently the full range of options available to it to preserve international peace and security. And member states must find within themselves the political will to use all of the instruments the Charter provides.'[25]

The focus of the Canadian government on this component of the widening international agenda also contained a strong dose of pragmatism. As in the Cold War years, there was an element of compensation attached to this behaviour. Canada's activism on peacekeeping came in the midst of the February 1992 decision of the Mulroney government to completely withdraw its military contingent from Western Europe. Going out in front on peacekeeping, from this angle, may be considered one means of offsetting the negative political and diplomatic fallout among Canada's NATO partners due to this decision.[26] If Canada was prepared to punch well below its weight on its direct commitment to collective security, it could deflect any criticism by showing that it was pulling more than its weight on peacekeeping. That this activity included a full commitment to European security, through its peacekeeping contribution in the former Yugoslavia, provided Canada with a key tool for reaffirming its European credentials precisely when these credentials were being openly questioned.

This activism on peacekeeping also constituted an elaborate exercise in image-building. From a political perspective, Mulroney had a number of good reasons for wanting to identify himself with the vehicle of peacekeeping. First of all, this identification allowed Mulroney to distance himself on a specific issue from the US. In contrast to the image of the Canadian government as a passive follower on the Gulf War, a distinctive stamp could be put on the Canadian commitment to the principle and practice of 'humane interventionism.' To give just one illustration, in its part in developing the document *An Agenda for Peace*, Canada associated with the familiar like-minded countries. In January 1992, the CANZ (Australia, New Zealand and Canada) and the Nordics submitted a joint brief to the UN secretary-general. This brief focussed on the need both for forward-looking assessments about potential crisis situations and for the Security Council to make greater efforts to involve other UN member states in its deliberations.[27]

Secondly, Mulroney's attempt to identify himself personally with Canada's activist peacekeeping must be seen in conjunction with the added space for foreign policy decision making available to the prime minister. With the move of Joe Clark to the constitutional affairs portfolio, Mulroney and his advisers within the PMO eagerly seized the opportunity to tighten their grip over foreign policy making. This centralized control had an air of inevitability to it. The degree of overt politicization of the Canadian foreign policy decision-making process (as noted in chapter 1) had speeded up rapidly over the span of the Mulroney years. And Canadian foreign policy, like other areas of political/policy life, abhorred a vacuum.

As in the later 'fish war' episode, activist peacekeeping contained an element of the politics of deflection. No action on the part of the Mulroney government in the early 1990s can be discussed without reference to that government's declining political fortunes. If it was to regain some of its lost credibility, the government had to be seen to be embracing popular issues such as activist peacekeeping. This drive to offset domestic difficulties with high-profile external action provided the spin for the media coverage of these initiatives. As one *Globe and Mail* journalist, specializing in foreign policy issues, wrote in May 1992: 'Frustrated by the slow pace of constitutional reform and the failure of the economy to rebound as quickly as anticipated, Mr. Mulroney has turned away from domestic issues in his public remarks...to focus on global issues of peace and security.'[28]

In addition to this opportunistic impulse, Mulroney appears to have been motivated to some extent at least by a genuine frustration with the manner in which the peacekeeping dossier had been handled prior to his intervention in this sphere of activity. This attitude was, in common with Trudeau's earlier forays into foreign policy initiatives, a reflection of a profound level of frustration with the cautious attitude of the professional diplomats to new thinking and practice on international affairs. Mulroney's Stanford University address, which raised the theme of a rebalancing between international obligations and sovereignty to the level of public debate, was done over the expressed concerns of the foreign service professionals. More tangibly, Mulroney's initiatives on the former

Yugoslavia were launched against a deep-seated bureaucratic resistance.[29]

On the other side of the ledger, the Mulroney government had a number of legitimate concerns about the way Canada had traditionally performed its peace-keeping duties. By limiting peacekeeping in terms of its intensity, form and scope, these duties had taken on a static look. Once in place, Canadian peace-keepers had the ability to stabilize a crisis situation; but they had no ability to force or even speed up a resolution in the underlying dispute. The archetypal case of this sort was Canada's experience in Cyprus. At the end of 1993, when Canada at last withdrew its peacekeeping contingent from UNFICYP (the UN peacekeeping force in Cyprus), the mandate of this operation had not been changed over a period of twenty-nine years—nor had any timetable been imple-mented to conclude its mission.[30]

Finally, a number of personal factors, of the type Nossal has termed idiosyn-cratic, may be entered into the equation as influences on Mulroney's peacekeep-ing initiatives.[31] The first of these relates to Mulroney's family connections as a source of inspiration for his initiatives with respect to the former Yugoslavia. As Jeff Sallot mentions: 'Mulroney has taken a direct personal interest in the Yugoslavian situation partly because his wife...was born in Sarajevo.... The Mulroneys spent part of their honeymoon in Yugoslavia.'[32] Mulroney's willing-ness to push Canada into new international initiatives was also useful in the aftermath of the prime minister's failed bid to be chosen as UN secretary-gen-eral. Besides the psychological element (i.e. as a consolation to offset this failure, which prevented Mulroney's 'graceful exit' from Canadian politics),[33] a high profile on activist peacekeeping was a useful card to play to counter the impres-sion that he was a 'lame duck' leader.

## BETWEEN RISING EXPECTATIONS AND A SHAKY POPULAR WILL

Peacekeeping, as it took expression in the immediate post-Cold War era, went well beyond the classic definition. A greater concentration on activist peacekeep-ing tapped into a deep bedrock of support among Canadians for this type of activ-ity as a means of national self-definition. In no other area of Canadian foreign policy did a consensus take as firm a hold, not only among the political élite in Ottawa but among the mass public in the country as a whole. The irony, how-ever, was that, as soon as peacekeeping moved from being a sideshow to being at centre stage, many Canadians got skittish about its application. The behavioural habits required for peacekeeping when it was delivered in a limited manner no longer held up so well under conditions in which the elevated form, scope and intensity of peacekeeping required very different risks and costs. The process of adaptation to the shifting direction that peacekeeping took became a draining experience—an experience in which much of Canada's will became exhausted.

## The Changes in Post-Cold War Peacekeeping

A first indication of the magnitude of change brought about in the immediate post-Cold War era may be seen in the broadened scope of peacekeeping operations in which Canada played a part. Between 1988 and 1993, the UN Security Council created fourteen new peacekeeping operations, as many missions as had been established over the previous four decades. As Joseph Jockel summarizes: 'With one exception, Canada joined all these new missions, most notably in the former Yugoslavia, Somalia, and Cambodia.'[34] Moreover, Canada quickly made up for its absence in the one mission in which it did not originally join—the first United Nations Angola Verification Mission, UNAVEM I—by participating in its successor operation, UNAVEM II. Canada's record in terms of simply 'being there' on peacekeeping, therefore, remained impressive. Nor did Canada's expanded scope only come out in quantitative terms: Canada's geographic orientation also spread, as the site of peacekeeping operations enlarged from its familiar locations (with the heavy traditional emphasis on the Middle East region) towards multiple locations in Eastern Europe, Asia, Africa and the Americas.

A second major change is the expanded form of the peacekeeping operations. One element of traditional peacekeeping has remained in place, both in the Middle East (on the Golan Heights) and elsewhere (including Croatia). In these cases, as previously outlined, Canadian personnel have continued to be deployed in a limited manner, i.e. deployed only by agreement with the parties directly engaged with the conflict, predicated on the non-use of force except in self-defence and the maintenance of neutrality toward the adversaries. The bulk of the newer missions, though, have gone well beyond the limits of classic peacekeeping to encompass peace enforcement and peace building.

Peace enforcement operations are those missions sanctioned by the UN under Chapter VII of the Charter only as a last resort. These actions have been historically associated with UN 'police' action, whether in Korea or in the Gulf War. The only exceptional case, where a Charter VII action has been closely identified with peacekeeping *per se*, was the short-lived Congo episode. The evolution of the Somalia operation raised the issue, for Canada as well as for the UN, of how peace enforcement fitted into the peacekeeping tool kit in a more sustained and controversial fashion. Unlike ONUC, in which Canada's contribution consisted of signallers and logistical personnel, Canada's contribution to the UN operation in Somalia included a battalion of the airborne division and a Canadian naval vessel. Although Canadian troops were not directly involved in the military operations against the Somalia clan/militia leaders, the Canadian role did include the mandate to establish a secure environment in which civil peace could be restored and humanitarian relief operations carried out. This work included the curtailing of armed looting, the searching for and putting under surveillance of the armed militias, and the seizure of weapons. The concept/practice of peacekeeping activity as applied in the former Yugoslavia was prolonged even further. In an effort to achieve a long-term agreement, peace enforcement became part of a longer mission in the former Yugoslavia, through to the eventual signing of the Dayton agreement in December 1995. Bogged down in the attempt to support a (non-existent) cease-fire as a prelude to a separate political process, force came to be incorporated into an ongoing humanitarian role.

The resort to the concept of peace building indicated a heightened appreciation of the need to look beyond tools directed at ending a conflict to tools directed at implementing a strategy of reconstruction within a conflict-torn society. Often this type of work had a clear military component to it. Canada devoted a great deal of attention in the Cambodia and Angola missions, for example, to the hazardous task of clearing mines. Canada also focussed heavily on the process of civilianization of the military (with special reference to the Ukraine and other parts of Eastern Europe) as part of peace building. Over the longer haul, this work had a nation-building component in political, diplomatic, economic and social terms. The vast array of activities located in this domain include refugee relief, resettlement operations, emergency aid for economic reconstruction, the restoration of civil administrations, and the monitoring of elections to ensure they are free and fair.[35]

A third change was the emphasis on 'humanitarian intervention' in so many of these operations. This entailed a shift from the onus placed in classic peace-keeping activities, on the maintenance of order in the East–West context (through the prevention of escalation in regional conflicts), to an onus on justice. Whereas peacekeeping during the Cold War years focussed almost exclusively on a response to interstate tensions, peacekeeping as it evolved in the late 1980s and early 1990s ventured into the intrastate dimension. A variety of the new peacekeeping operations were prompted by precisely the kind of disputes that had been frozen by the Cold War, involving as they did long-suppressed rivalries and urges for self-determination.

This broadening-out process responded to the desire by Canadians for an approach to peacekeeping that was not stagnant in nature. A central thrust of the pressure from NGOs for a thorough review of Canadian foreign policy, in the later stages of the Mulroney government, was that Ottawa should be responsive to the 'virtually unanimous' backing for peacekeeping at the societal level.[36] This spark turned into a roaring flame under the Chrétien government. A sizeable number of presentations by individuals and groups alike at the National Forum, and before the joint parliamentary committee, opined on the need for Canada to go further to distend its lead role in this area of activity. Tariq Rauf, from the Canadian Centre for Global Security, called on Canada 'to complement its long-standing commitment to peacekeeping with a strategy that addresses the fault lines of conflict.'[37] Ernie Regehr, of Project Ploughshares, echoed the theme of Canadian comparative advantage and selectivity: 'Canada needs to have a very interventionist foreign policy. The resources Canada has to make available, however, need to be carefully focused in those areas in which we can have the most significant impact. The seat at the table today...comes through being willing to take the severe risks of entering with military forces into highly dangerous conflict situations, such as Somalia and the former Yugoslavia, to bring protection to the people of those regions.'[38]

## The Response of the Military

The opinion of the Canadian military establishment about these changes was more ambivalent. In the initial stages of the broadening-out process, the higher profile of Canadian activist peacekeeping was seen as providing some tangible dividends in organizational terms to the Canadian military. Specifically, the shift towards peace enforcement and peace building held out some promise from a budgetary perspective. Through the late 1980s and early 1990s, the Canadian military had to cope with a series of deep cuts. In the period 1991–92 to 1995–96 alone, the Canadian defence budget was slashed from $12.83 billion to $10.5 billion.[39] The magnitude of this budgetary pressure made it imperative that hard choices be made in terms of resources and functions, the impact of which had already come into play with respect to reductions in defence procurement (especially on big ticket items) and the withdrawal of Canadian forces from Western Europe.

Yet, if compelling difficult trade-offs, the extension of peacekeeping to peace enforcement and peace building offered a semblance of a lifeline to alleviate some of the societal pressure towards an accelerated 'peace dividend.' The bottom line was that, for the Canadian public, peacekeeping remained by far the most popular of the activities carried out by the Canadian military.[40] Indeed, as suggested by Granatstein, a strong case can be made that peacekeeping served as 'the sole military role that had any public support.'[41] This positive image provided the military establishment with a useful (although specialized) lever to pull in its essay to ward off further budgetary cuts. The argument that the shift towards 'humane interventionism' justified defence spending, with respect to the adequate deployment of peacekeepers and upgraded equipment, might not be the one that the Canadian military wanted to use; but, in the circumstances, it afforded as good a one as the military possessed.

The continued appointment of Canadian personnel to high-ranking positions within the UN peacekeeping apparatus helped as well to maintain the standing of the Canadian military. Canada buttressed its reputation as an experienced peacekeeper with an abundant supply of skilled personnel. In a country lacking many recent action heroes, Canadian peacekeepers took on a shine rarely seen in public life. Moving past the collective sense of congratulation (as witnessed either when peacekeepers as an entity won the 1988 Nobel Peace Prize, or by the erection of a monument in downtown Ottawa extolling the virtues of Canadian peacekeepers), individual Canadian peacekeepers became media personalities in their own right. An excellent illustration of this phenomenon of Canadian peacekeeper as luminary has of course been Major-General

Lewis MacKenzie. MacKenzie's status was such that he was given the privilege of being the lead-off witness before the special joint committee reviewing defence policy. The same phenomenon extends to Major-General Dallaire, the commander of the 1994 UNAMIR operation in Rwanda. This type of recognition was reinforced by the equally important (albeit behind-the-scenes) role given to a number of other Canadians peacekeepers. These individuals included Major-General Baril, who served as the chief military officer at UN headquarters, as well as a number of other Canadian experts made available to the UN, the EU, the CSCE and other bodies.

The downside for both the Canadian military and the Canadian NGOs with respect to the evolution of peacekeeping derives from the constraints on effectiveness in carrying out these operations. By extending this sphere of activity beyond classic peacekeeping, Canadian personnel on the ground were exposed to increased risks. To a considerable extent, these risks were inherent in the move to extend peacekeeping into a wider spectrum of cases, where peace simply did not exist. Instead of dealing with state-to-state conflict, where peacekeepers could adopt the stance of being impartial and non-threatening, in cases such as Somalia and the former Yugoslavia, Canadian personnel were in effect dealing with civil wars.

These problems were exacerbated by the difficulty of applying the UN mandate given to these peacekeeping operations in any coherent fashion. In concept, the definition of the peacekeeping mandate was often quite fluid or elastic, containing a mixture of functional elements. In the case of Bosnia-Herzegovina, the Security Council gave the UNPROFOR a highly complex and multifaceted assignment not amenable to any mode of standard operation. These tasks included protection for the delivery of humanitarian supplies, enforcement of the ban on military flights, the establishment of a small number of 'safe areas,' the authorization of certain measures to protect the civilian population, and the demand for a comprehensive cease-fire.[42] The role assigned to the Canadian peacekeeping personnel, as a consequence, was constantly in flux due to the ever-changing mandate and volatile and often uncontrollable conditions found on the ground. In the case of Somalia, the Security Council authorized a military force under Charter VII to use all necessary means to establish a secure environment for humanitarian relief operations. The US interpreted this mandate as a rationale for waging what amounted to a 'humanitarian war.'[43] When this strategy resulted in a loss of life for a number of its own military personnel, the US quickly exited from the operation. This erratic behaviour by the US left the other participants in an awkward position: trying to carry on with a reduced operation amid a legacy of hostility generated by the use of 'coercive methods.'[44]

In this intricate context, Canadian personnel were caught up as never before in peacekeeping within a culture of violence. The Canadian participants in the UNPROFOR faced casualties, a number of kidnappings and hostage-takings replete with a mock execution and the use of Canadian peacekeepers as human shields, and ongoing psychological trauma (including a number of cases of suicide) after they returned home. The Somalia case proved quite Conradian in the scale of horror, as the characterization of Canadian peacekeeping activity descended from an image of philanthropy to one of barbarism. Canada's initial contribution to the routine aspects of 'humanitarian intervention' in the operation received favourable treatment in the international media.[45] This positive image was subsequently battered by a host of unsavoury incidents involving poor training, racism and brutality among Canadian forces—incidents that were kept in the public eye as the so-called Somalia affair/inquiry dragged on.

These problems generated a two-sided public backlash. On one side, there were those Canadians who pushed for the establishment of a clearer game plan for post-Cold War peacekeeping operations. Much of the criticism from this idealist camp was directed towards the muddle and inefficiencies emanating from the UN. To some in this camp, the UN was an institution in danger of fumbling away its opportunity to implement the *Agenda for Peace* program through its own inadequacies. What was needed to restore a measure of faith was some way of overhauling the mechanism for implementing peacekeeping operations to allow integration and co-ordination.[46]

These idealist instincts surfaced in a reinvigorated fashion during the 1994 Rwandan crisis. The 'CNN' factor, so visible in the total array of humanitarian crises of the post-Cold War era, played a substantial part in getting Rwanda on the radar of public opinion. In doing so, fundamental questions were asked about why UN member states had become sensitized to the need to intervene in certain cases and not in others. As opposed to the overstretch associated with the UN actions in the former Yugoslavia and Somalia, accusations were made that the world body had not acted quickly or decisively enough on Rwanda. There was much evidence to support the thesis that the UN peacekeeping system had failed. In the aftermath of a horrendous tragedy, in which over a million people were killed and two million took flight, the UN secretary-general was 'unable to obtain the peacekeeping troops required from UN members to establish order.'[47]

On the other side, there were those participants/observers who believed that Canada had gone in over its head with respect to activist peacekeeping. A number of media commentators expressed strong concerns about the pitfalls of what they termed international 'meddling.'[48] From this standpoint, Canada's idealistic impulse was counter-productive from both an external and an internal point of view. First of all, it helped to fuel unrealistic expectations about the ability of the international community to deliver through the mechanism of the UN on promises entailing a massive, long-term commitment. As Richard Gwyn contended: 'Can...an international bureaucracy really manage the domestic affairs of distant societies? And if it becomes responsible for them, and then makes the same mistakes all governments make everywhere, will not its credibility, and thus its ability to act, gradually erode?'[49]

Secondly, this 'meddling' was perceived as having the potential for a problematic spillover effect; for this expression of Canadian behaviour was bound to induce closer scrutiny of Canada's own domestic record. As another Canadian journalist has said: 'It is...natural to insist that the UN stops any outbreaks of fighting. But UN involvement rapidly turns into interference when one's own country is subject to international criticism.'[50] Gwyn adds, on the same note: 'We've...forgotten that we ourselves don't at all like others trying to do good to us.'[51]

This realist interpretation was backed up by the scepticism proffered by some of the most experienced of the Canadian practitioners with respect to peacekeeping activity. Major-General MacKenzie, on his return from his assignment as commander of the Sarajevo sector of the UN forces, became an outspoken critic of the mission in the former Yugoslavia. Among the many targets of his scorn was the lack of a clear chain of command, the absence of logistical support, and the deficiencies in co-ordination between UN headquarters and the field operation. He also laid stress on the contradictions between the mission's mandate—to provide protection for humanitarian relief convoys—and the settlement of the conflict. Still another object of criticism was the inadequate military structure and equipment the Canadian personnel had to make do with in carrying out their multifaceted tasks. The rapid transition in functions left a capability gap. As MacKenzie testified, the mission to the former Yugoslavia replicated a familiar pattern: 'in the early days it was a relatively conventional peacekeeping mission and it grew into a relatively safe humanitarian relief mission. But the only thing for sure in the last three or four missions that the UN has got itself involved in is that they have turned nasty.'[52]

## THE RESILIENCE OF CONSENSUS IN THE CHRÉTIEN YEARS

### The Arguments for Canadian Involvement

The Chrétien Liberal government had as many good reasons as the Mulroney government to embrace activist peacekeeping. While the Liberals were in opposition, Chrétien personally endorsed the new thinking on questions of sovereignty.[53] Back in office, an extension of Canadian peacekeeping activities by the Liberals was driven by many of the same factors that had played a role in generating enthusiasm among the Mulroney Conservatives.

As in the past, this type of participation served as a means by which Canada could pay its dues (and be seen to be doing so) to both NATO and the UN. It must be mentioned here that Canada's contribution with respect to expenditures on international peacekeeping operations rose (from $10–12 million in 1991–92 to some $130 million in 1993–94) as its defence budget sunk.[54] Given the attendant risks involved in peacekeeping activities in the 1980s and 1990s, the Liberal government could argue with some justification that this form of international engagement provided adequate compensation for reductions in other areas of military spending. Far from paying the 'minimum premium' on its insurance policy with the Western alliance, Canada's 'burden sharing' via this type of participation represented a tough assignment. Foreign Secretary Ouellet, through 1994 and 1995, repeatedly differentiated Canada's solid contribution on the front lines with the performance of other countries—most notably the US—which chose for long periods of time to excuse themselves from peacekeeping duties. As Ouellet said in the major House of Commons debate on the subject of peacekeeping: 'Beyond [the] humanitarian effort, it is often pointed out that Canada's presence in Bosnia has served to demonstrate our continuing commitment to act with our NATO allies in the promotion of European security. It also demonstrates to the world that Canada is a nation that is prepared to carry out its international obligations under difficult circumstances, while others are merely willing to offer advice from the sidelines.'[55]

An active participation in peacekeeping also held some value for the Liberals from an image-building standpoint. Looking backwards, an identification with peacekeeping activity allowed the Chrétien government to don the mantle of Pearsonian internationalism and bask in some reflected glory from the 'golden age' of Canadian foreign policy. Prime Minister Chrétien constantly made this historical connection, by invoking this legacy when referring to Canada's peacekeeping contribution. Looking forward into the future, the promotion of peacekeeping on a global scale provided a concrete means by which the Chrétien government could affirm its determination that Canada remain a credible and vital force in international affairs. A signalling exercise along these lines was designed to offset the impression that Canada had drifted away from its sense of international commitment by closing itself off in North America. Because it wanted to use peacekeeping for domestic political purposes, as part of an ongoing exercise to try to differentiate itself from the US, the Chrétien government retained considerable incentive to demonstrate its claim not only to be a 'good,' but also a comprehensively engaged, 'international citizen.' Put another way, peacekeeping was offered as tangible proof that 'We are not a carbon copy of the Americans.'[56]

## The Arguments against Canadian Involvement

For all these attractions, however, the Chrétien government had an equally good number of reasons to be wary of locking itself into a long-term commitment to peacekeeping.[57] One obvious worry for the Chrétien government was whether Canada could afford an involvement in an activist form of peacekeeping at a time of fiscal constraint. As noted, the Canadian commitment (and comparative share) in terms of monetary expenditure on peacekeeping had shown a sizeable increase with the proliferation of missions in the early 1990s. Moreover, this increase in expenditure related to an expansion not only in scope but also of intensity. To do peacekeeping properly, on the basis of a widening mandate encompassing peace enforcement and peace building, meant channelling more adequate resources towards those activities. No longer could peacekeeping activity be accomplished exclusively with lightly armed force. A change of this magnitude contributed in another way to the debate over the clash of national priorities—between the push for a greater allocation to peacekeeping by way of both personnel and equipment and the pull back from this participation for budgetary reasons.[58]

Another concern related to the Canadian public's threshold for sacrifice. Because peacekeeping had for so long a period of time been a relatively static exercise, with its focus being limited to monitoring and surveillance, Canadians had become accustomed to an absence of physical danger in these operations. With the shift to an activist style of peacekeeping, the question rose concurrently of whether or not Canadians would be willing to accept casualties as part of the price for involvement. Not surprisingly, the view that this price was an excessive one grew because of the contradictions found in the practice of peacekeeping, contradictions associated with a lack of a clearly defined mandate in some of the operations and the growing impression of stalemate, in which there was little possibility of getting a clear result on the missions.

This negative appraisal—that the risks of being involved in peacekeeping had grown out of proportion to the benefits of participating—was especially evident in the Canadian public's attitude to the operation in Bosnia. While the Canadian public retained its faith about the merits of peacekeeping in general terms, specific support for the operation in the former Yugoslavia fell markedly through the first few months in which the Chrétien government held office. A January 1994 Angus Reid–Southam News survey of 1500 Canadians found that 57 percent of the respondents felt that, due to the nature of the risks involved, Canada should withdraw from making a contribution to the mission when its participation was due to end in April 1994. When asked about a Canadian commitment in the eventuality of a cease-fire and an end of fighting in Bosnia, though, 56 percent of the respondents said they favoured a renewal.[59]

From a diplomatic perspective, the Chrétien government entertained second thoughts about how well the Canadian contribution to peacekeeping translated into institutional leverage. The experience with the Bosnian mission indicated that this line of argument should no longer be oversold as a motivation for Canadian participation in this sphere of activity. The assumption had long been made that a solid commitment by Canada on peacekeeping 'raises Canada's profile and strengthens our position across a broad range of international diplomatic negotiations.'[60] Bill Graham, the Liberal chair of the House of Commons foreign affairs committee, on the basis of this commonly held view, contended in the March 1995 parliamentary debate that Canada's contribution to the Bosnia operation 'establishes a credibility in dealing with the United States that we must never forget.' Being there, Graham added, also helped Canada's relationship with Europe: 'When we consider issues of global security and foreign policy we must never divorce one issue from another. Does anyone in this House not doubt the fact that one of the reasons we have been so successful in dealing with the Europeans over the issues on the Grand Banks is precisely because we are in Yugoslavia and because we are a force in Europe. Our European friends cannot turn to us and say: "We can treat you the way we want to."'[61]

When put to the test, nevertheless, this presumed linkage between participation and influence was found to be lacking. Most egregiously, Canada found itself denied access to the 'Contact Group,' the forum established in April 1994 with a membership made up of Britain, France, Germany, the US and the Russian Federation, which became the main mechanism through which the international community sought a political solution to the Bosnian conflict. Although the Chrétien government took the position in public that it was quite content not to be involved in this forum, Canada's lack of representation was clearly an irritation, if not an open wound, to its pride. At the very least, its exclusion indicated that Canada was not getting the credit it deserved as a player making a substantial contribution in the way of peacekeeping activity on the ground. More tellingly, it raised concerns about whether the picture of Canada having a recognized status in peacekeeping was fully accurate. With UNPROFOR made up of thirty-eight national contingents, including eleven NATO countries, Canada faced increasing competition from a variety of other countries. As the majors became involved, they brought with them superior equipment and/or larger contingents of personnel, which were more appropriate for high-intensity forms of peacekeeping.[62]

Undercutting its stature further, Canada found that it possessed little say over the precise form the operation in the former Yugoslavia was to take. In putting peacekeeping personnel on the ground, Canada assumed that it would have to approve any extension of the mission's mandate towards a more 'muscular' approach. Initially, this issue hinged on the question of whether there would be an escalation through NATO air strikes against Serb-held positions. Notwithstanding repeated assurances that Canada would have a veto over this important decision,[63] the Chrétien government discovered that when push came to shove the safety of Canadian peacekeeping personnel on the ground came second to what was deemed to be in the interests of the big powers in the Western alliance (even if some of these powers—like the US—did not have forces on the ground themselves). This reality was made plain when, on the way to a NATO summit in January 1994, Chrétien was put in the embarrassing situation of having to explain the discrepancy between Canada's habit of caution (reinforced by a fear that any aggressive action against the Serbs would provoke retaliation towards Canadian peacekeepers) and the new, higher-intensity direction the mission was taking. With considerable discomfort and clumsiness, Canadian policymakers tried to distinguish between 'less time urgent' cases, where the unanimous consent of the NATO partners should be required, and those cases (involving immediate danger to peacekeepers) where 'the commander of UNPROFOR could call on the UN Secretary General to authorise an air strike to assist UN troops where they are under attack.'[64]

Later on, Canadian concerns about this type of 'mission creep' surfaced on other issues. The most important of these was the gap that emerged between Canada and its allies on what to do after the Serbs overran a number of the so-called UN 'safe havens.' Canada, consistent with its past behaviour, was reluctant to promise more than it thought it could deliver. Priority was placed on achieving a firm cease-fire rather than taking on new forms of 'muscular' action, which held out the prospect, at least in the short term, of prolonging, not curtailing, hostilities. When Britain and France moved out ahead with the creation of a NATO 'rapid reaction force,' Canada opted out of this proposal. Only with the eventual implementation of the US-led, NATO-run peace plan under the auspices of the Dayton agreement did Canada make any promise to contribute towards a 'muscular' form of peacekeeping activity. Even then, it needs to be added, this commitment was contingent on the premise that 'Canadian soldiers are absolutely needed.'[65]

## The Debate over Canadian Involvement in Bosnia

In this fluid atmosphere, the Liberal government was tempted to at least consider the option of withdrawing from the peacekeeping operation in the former Yugoslavia. With the safety of Canadian peacekeepers paramount in the government's frame of reference, the stance was adopted that, if the conflict on the ground escalated to all-out war, the sensible decision would be for Canada to exit. As the prime minister was prone to pronounce: 'There is a limit sometimes to being a Boy Scout.'[66] Still, to its credit, the Chrétien government refrained from the choice of taking precipitous action to withdraw, notwithstanding all of the temptations to move in that direction. While pulling back from the cutting edge of activist peacekeeping, both qualitatively (Canadian peacekeepers, for instance, were pulled back from the Srebrenica enclave in early 1994) and quantitatively (the Canadian contingent in the former Yugoslavia was repeatedly cut back, from a peak of approximately 3000 personnel in October 1992),[67] the government was not prepared to do anything that could be interpreted as a decisive U-turn. When controversy cropped up, as for example in January 1994 over the use of NATO air strikes, the government tried its best to deflect the issue of Canada's overall position with regard to peacekeeping by referring the question to a special parliamentary debate. This device of 'allowing parliament to decide,' a throw-back to the older Liberal repertoire of the Mackenzie King era, bought time for the Chrétien government. Indeed, this device was so successful from a political standpoint that similar exercises were repeated in March and October of 1995.

The willingness of the Chrétien government to stay the course was facilitated by the extent to which the positive national consensus on peacekeeping held up. True, the negative backlash against this sphere of activity (or, more precisely, the activity within the 'peacekeeping' operations in Somalia and Bosnia) found some political expression. The conduit for this sense of disquiet was mainly through the Reform Party. This latest wave of Western Canadian populism may, with a good deal of validity, be considered the legitimate voice of the doctrine of English-Canadian isolationism stretching back to the interwar years. As Kim Nossal details, in his insightful survey of dominant ideas in Canadian foreign policy, this strain of thought was underpinned by a suspicion both of alliances and of foreign—particularly European—entanglements. Neither the UN nor NATO were regarded as institutions that could be trusted to act efficiently or in Canadian interests. None of the groups involved in the actual fighting on the ground were seen to 'have clean hands,'[68] with 'atrocities occurring on all sides.'[69] From this isolationist orientation, any commitment to the peacekeeping force in Bosnia was a morass from which Canada could not free itself without a great deal of human cost. As one Reform MP poignantly put it in one of the several parliamentary debates accorded to the subject of peacekeeping: 'How many troops are we prepared as Canadians to bring home in body bags? We have to ask that question and we have to take this as a very serious part of our discussion.'[70]

Fears of a worst-case scenario along these lines were inflated further by the intense media coverage given to the predicament of the peacekeepers caught in the crossfire by rival forces in the former Yugoslavia and Somalia. This coverage contributed to a yo-yo play, where the perception of success and failure of peacekeeping bobbed up and down in a vigorous manner. The CNN effect did much to generate the popular call for involvement, to 'do something' about these crises, in the first place. Having built up the enthusiasm for intervention, however, the media also contributed to a drainage of this desire for involvement. As these operations became bogged down and their image of effectiveness devalued, the blanket coverage of the practice of peacekeeping in hazardous circumstances induced a 'cut and run' mentality.

Notwithstanding all these strains and stresses, the national consensus in support of peacekeeping remained intact. Isolationist feelings, although able to tap into a widespread current of situational discontent, did not sweep aside the structure of support for peacekeeping. The staying power of this national consensus hinged on a number of important factors. One necessary feature was the support for Canadian peacekeeping from within the ranks of the Liberal Party. Not only did the Liberals, collectively and individually, see themselves as the rightful heirs to the tradition of Pearsonian internationalism, they had the weight of numbers in parliament to make this voice of engagement heard over the voice of isolationism.

What is striking, though, is not this familiar expression of support for Canadian peacekeeping but, rather, how far this support had spread across partisan lines. The extent of this inter-partisan consensus stands out, especially, when the views of the Bloc Québécois are factored into the equation. Despite Lucien Bouchard's fundamental disagreement with the Chrétien government right across the spectrum of the political/policy agenda, on peacekeeping there was broad agreement about what the priorities should be. In his speech during the first of the special parliamentary debates on peacekeeping, on 25 January 1994, Bouchard sounded as Pearsonian (if not more so) as any of the Liberal speakers. Although the leader of the BQ acknowledged that peace missions had become 'a thorn in the flesh of our diplomacy and our foreign commitments,' these difficulties should not compel a retreat. As Bouchard stated forcefully: 'Canada's peace missions [proved], like CIDA, a great source of pride for Canadians and Quebecers. The disinterested and humanitarian nature of our international interventions was hailed again and again. And did not the architect of Canada's peacekeeping role win the Nobel prize? Indeed, more than anybody, Lester B. Pearson symbolizes this necessary assuming of a democratic country's moral obligations. That is an aspect we must bear in mind when deciding... whether we must stay in Bosnia-Herzegovina, or withdraw and then establish criteria to govern any future foreign intervention.... The easy thing would be to throw our hands up, pack our bags and leave but this is not the way Canada earned its well deserved reputation abroad as a steady peacemaker willing to walk the extra mile in the name of peace.'[71]

The liberal internationalist themes of commitment and responsibility were repeated, with an admittedly sharper twist, by the leader of the official opposition's address in the 29 March 1995 parliamentary debate. In an increasingly charged atmosphere, fuelled by the emotional build-up around both the impending referendum on Quebec sovereignty and the choice of whether or not to engage in more 'muscular' forms of peacekeeping as a solution in Bosnia, Bouchard dared the Chrétien government to restate the 'guiding principles' of Canada's policy regarding peacekeeping, rather than going back to an ad hoc, reactive mode of decision making. Still, for all of these 'questions and doubts,' the bottom line for the BQ leader was the need for a clear 'yes' on peacekeeping. 'So can we just decide to withdraw?' Bouchard rhetorically asked: 'Of course not. We know perfectly well we cannot. The government knew this. The government thought that by starting this debate, it would necessarily get the support of the opposition.'[72]

Nor did the Reform Party constitute a monolithic entity. The potent populist brew, stirring up the isolationist sentiments, was mixed with other ingredients within the political party. One element that provided a different flavour was made up of those Reform MPs who had some form of military experience. These individuals had their own concerns about Canada's peacekeeping activities. But instead of fundamental ambivalence in principle, this element preferred to focus on practical measures (reducing the 'fat' at DND headquarters, upgrading the equipment provided to Canadian personnel in the field) that would enable peacekeeping to be carried out more effectively.[73] These disparate voices gave a decidedly mixed note to the Reform message. In the January 1994 parliamentary debate on peacekeeping, the tenor of the Reform contribution to the proceedings was that a Canadian withdrawal should only be a 'last ditch thing.'[74] A working consensus only emerged with the escalation of the Bosnian conflict, and the attendant rise in the danger to the participants in the peacekeeping operations. By the second debate, on 29 March 1995, Reform fell into line behind the view that: 'Canada [should] tell the UN that we would like our commitment [in the former Yugoslavia] to come to an end. We will give it a three-month period of grace after which time we will effectively withdraw.'[75]

## RENEWING CANADIAN PEACEKEEPING

It would be misleading to imply that the contemporary Canadian performance on peacekeeping has entailed a straight one-way course, with a shift from an extremely (over-) ambitious activism in the late 1980s to a more modest (under-) performance by the mid-1990s. Under the weight of extended mandates, expectations, costs and risks, Canadian peacekeeping has unquestionably undergone some substantive modifications over recent years. Instead of proving to be a recipe for a lag in will, however, this series of tests has also encouraged a process of renewal and re-engagement in the character of Canadian peacekeeping. The lack of an apparent comfortable fit between the traditional notion of peacekeeping and the spectrum of activity placed under that rubric in the post-Cold War years did generate a good deal of discomfort. But this discomfort was translated by the Chrétien government less towards a comprehensive retrenchment than into momentum on how this sphere of activity could be reformed and Canada's comparative advantage within it redefined and reinvigorated.

The first thrust of this reform dynamic concentrated on the means of improving the 'firefighting' performance of peacekeeping activities. With the expansion in their size, tasks and contextual application, peacekeeping operations took on an ad hoc and unwieldy look. In Rwanda, first and foremost, the international peacekeeping effort was commonly perceived as being put into place too slowly and too late to be effective.[76] As applied to Somalia and the former Yugoslavia, as well, the practice of peacekeeping received widespread criticism for being overly reactive and ill-defined in terms of its mandate. Nonetheless, from a Canadian perspective, the lesson to be drawn from these varied experiences was not that faith in UN peace operations should be abandoned. Rather, the conclusion reached centred on the need for a reassessment of how the overall system of peacekeeping could be overhauled to make it more efficient.

This dimension of the reform agenda had a number of components. To help get the logistics of the peacekeeping operations in better order, Canada took the lead in pushing for the establishment of a twenty-four-hour UN peacekeeping 'situations' centre at UN headquarters in New York. To improve the training of peacekeepers, the Chrétien government provided the financial and infrastructural backing for the establishment of The Lester B. Pearson Canadian International Peacekeeping Training Centre at a former Canadian Forces base in Cornwallis

Park, Nova Scotia, in 1994. To allow a quicker and smoother launch of peace-keeping missions, through the provision of an upgraded rapid reaction capability, a detailed Canadian plan for a large-scale UN Standby Force was presented in an address by André Ouellet to the United Nations general assembly in September 1994.[77] Citing the 1994 genocide in Rwanda as the prime case of defective practices, this plan emphasized the urgency of intervening before serious deterioration took place in a targeted situation: 'The critical lesson...is that modest but timely measures can make a difference between a situation which is stable or contained and a humanitarian disaster which has spiralled out of control.'[78]

All of these components offered evidence of a concerted Canadian process of rethinking and relearning about peacekeeping. They also provided evidence of Canada's stored capacity for making a solid contribution in this sphere of activity through intellectual, entrepreneurial and technical leadership. Each component was driven by a perceived need to fix specific elements of the peacekeeping apparatus that were found wanting in practice. Having identified these flaws, through its varied set of experiences, Canada set out to study in depth what could be done to remedy these deficiencies. With respect to the peacekeeping college, the priority was on doing a more complete job than other countries with expertise in the area of training (notably, Austria and Sweden). On the UN Standby Force, Canada worked with other like-minded countries (particularly the Netherlands and Denmark) to come up with a viable proposal to prevent the spread of a conflict. Technically, the objective was to overcome the practical obstacles in the way of implementation of these ideas. Instead of an ambitious permanent peacekeeping force, with all the attendant problems of cost and co-ordination, Canada proposed an improved standby arrangement via the creation of a multinational 'vanguard force,' which could establish a UN presence before the deployment of a regular peacekeeping force. Canada, for its own part, reserved the right to review requests for the deployment of Canadian forces through this route, stating that any decision about a contribution would ultimately be based on Canadian capabilities and other national objectives existing at the time of the request. With regard to training, some considerable onus was placed on the necessity of broadening the scope of the armed forces' repertoire to allow the military 'to perform a wide variety of tasks to help resolve conflicts, as well as be prepared for combat.'[79]

Another dimension of Canada's reform effort was directed towards a back-to-basics approach. Stepping back from any association with high-intensity peace enforcement activities, with their low comfort level, Canada explicitly concentrated its efforts on the opposite end of the continuum of instruments available to deal with conflict situations. The first of these instruments was preventative diplomacy, intended to act as a means of warding off the outbreak of hostilities by treating the underlying problems and root causes of a potential crisis situation. This focus has meant, in practice, a heavy Canadian orientation towards improving the nature of early-warning devices to anticipate and manage conflicts; fact-finding missions and the use of the good offices of representatives from international/regional institutions; and a variety of confidence-building measures, including mutual inspections to build up trust. A second element along the low-key side of the continuum of activities is preventative peacekeeping, especially the deployment of peacekeeping personnel prior to the outbreak of a conflict, and the establishment of demilitarized zones and frontier observation posts. A third element deals with particular aspects of peacemaking utilized after a conflict has actually flared up. While remaining quite leery about some indirect means of exerting pressure on belligerents (i.e. sanctions and embargoes), Canada demonstrated a sustained faith in the capability of international negotiations to bring about dispute settlement. A final element on this list extends right across the entire array of peace-building activities: actions directed towards long-term nation building.

This back-to-basics approach corresponds well to Canada's sense of constructive internationalism. Rather than going into the unknown with peace enforcement and other forms of 'muscular' peacemaking activity, these lower-key tools were forged out of a solid track record of practical achievement. The application of preventative diplomacy by the CSCE/OSCE has been instrumental in heading off conflict in a number of contentious cases, including Kosovo in the former Yugoslavia, and Nagorno-Karabakh. Preventative peacekeeping has worked in a similar fashion in the former Yugoslavian republic of Macedonia. The more ambitious enterprises associated with peace building, as witnessed by the operations in Somalia, Cambodia and Angola, have been more uneven in their outcomes. Yet the cluster of difficulties encountered in these problem cases has to be balanced against the signs of comparative success found in the missions on Namibia and El Salvador.

The back-to-basics approach has had the additional diplomatic appeal of allowing Canada to specialize more precisely in its own areas of comparative advantage. No longer able to easily differentiate itself from other countries on the basis of a commitment to peacekeeping *per se*, Canada has sought to carve out specific forms of specialization where it could be a recognized leader. This targeting of more precise forms of activity played to Canada's traditional strengths in the way of confidence building via monitoring, supervision and verification. But it also played into Canada's push to internationalize specific areas of skill that have until recently been primarily domestic in orientation, including the supervision of elections, the establishment of a free and open media, the resettlement of refugees, the maintenance of law and order, and improved access to education, health care and clean water. There was an important military component to this thrust, in that a crucial component of this specialized approach has highlighted the expertise Canada possesses in the area of communications, logistics and transportation. What was different was the offloading of so many responsibilities on to non-military personnel. This spread in functional distribution included electoral experts, journalists, the RCMP, engineers, educators and health care workers, as well as a wide variety of NGOs.

The best practical illustration of this process of specialization is the Implementation Force deployed in Bosnia in the aftermath of the Dayton agreement. By opting to send no more than 1000 troops to enforce the peace settlement, Canada signalled its intent of contributing only the 'bare minimum' to the multinational contingent.[80] Yet the real measure of Canada's contribution in the postwar context has little to do with troop levels. Where Canada has sought to make an ongoing solid contribution has been in a number of key (if low-profile) tasks. As Canada's special co-ordinator for reconstruction of the former Yugoslavia stated: 'What I like to think we bring is a balanced approach, an early focus on the continuing humanitarian needs; then, in terms of reconstruction, a focus on the social sector. Canada has developed a niche here.'[81]

Still another thrust of Canada's reform approach has been the promotion of more effective delivery through the varied agents of peacekeeping. At a geographic level, Canada has shifted a good deal of its attention from UN peacekeeping to peacekeeping operationalized through regional organizations. Whether through the CSCE/OSCE or the OAS, Canada has channelled more of its peacekeeping activities directly through regional bodies. In other instances, such as in co-operative endeavours with the Organization of African Unity, Canada has tried to strengthen the development of regional peacekeeping indirectly through the supply of equipment and technical assistance. At a functional level, Canada has tried to come to terms with the growing civilian–military interface in peacekeeping. Because of the expansion of multi-mandated operations, this process of adaptation has been absolutely necessary to avoid duplication and contradictions (most notably, between military and humanitarian activities). The additional space accorded to the civilian element has also been crucial for lending credibility and legitimacy to the missions.

Canada's ability to go out in front in building up this interface must be acknowledged. From 1993 onward, a number of joint sessions have been held, under the auspices of the NGO Division of CIDA, intended to bring members of the Canadian armed forces and civilian experts together. To formalize this pattern of dialogue, a Peacebuilding Contact Group was established, composed of members of CIDA, DND and Foreign Affairs, together with a wide number of representatives of the NGO community. This work was carried forward also by a number of other bodies, namely the Parliamentary Centre on Foreign Affairs, the ICHRDD and the Pearson Peacekeeping Training Centre.[82] In practice, the ability of NGOs/societal groups to work together was demonstrated in the midst of the Rwandan crisis. To give just one illustration, as part of its mission DND made up to two flights a week available to move relief supplies from Canada to Central Africa.

This being said, the degree of this military–civilian co-operation should not be exaggerated. As shown by the Namibian case, the relationship between the military and the RCMP could fray over questions of turf and tactics. As witnessed through the peacekeeping operations in Somalia and the former

Yugoslavia, the Canadian armed forces and the humanitarian relief workers pursued their aims in parallel form as much as in tandem. From the point of view of the military, any shift in mandate that featured a high priority on escorting the delivery of relief supplies contributed to a rise in uncertainty and risk; for a concentration on these duties made it less likely that the military peacekeeping personnel could be seen in an impartial, non-political light by the belligerents. From the relief NGO point of view, alternatively, any move towards 'muscular' peacekeeping put them in the uncomfortable position of being a 'trip wire.'[83] As Henry Wiseman has written, the issue of co-operation centres not so much on the question of whether 'the Canadian forces are properly trained to perform the military functions of peacekeeping but on the question [of] whether there is adequate appreciation of the complexity of the new generation of peacekeeping, of the involvement of military personnel in the politics of negotiation, and the administrative coordination with civilian governmental and non-governmental personnel who are equally responsible to fulfil their share of a peacekeeping mandate.'[84]

## RETHINKING CANADIAN PEACEKEEPING

What stands out about the scholarly analysis of Canadian peacekeeping is its confined nature. The Canadian performance in this sphere of activity has not completely escaped serious examination. The emergence of a fundamental tension in contemporary Canadian peacekeeping has been commented on by the best-known academic experts and practitioners of this area of Canadian international activity.[85] In no other issue-area covered in this volume, however, is there such a discrepancy between the amount of public and élite interest concerning an activity and the lack of sapient scrutiny. The tenor of the extant critiques of the Canadian contribution have been almost uniformly instrumental in quality, with the emphasis on what may be called a 'devil in the details' appraisal. The focus has been almost exclusively on an assessment of how Canadian peacekeeping has broadened out, through the transitional stages of the post-Cold War period, from the established pattern of activity during the Cold War years. Special reference is paid to concrete issues, pertaining to where, when and how Canada should (or should not) be involved with peacekeeping operations—that is to say, to what the evolving face of Canadian peacekeeping should look like.

What for the most part has been missing in all of this review has been a perspective that challenges not just the practical application but the fundamental assumptions and institutional structure into which peacekeeping activity has been organized. Applying the framework developed by Robert Cox, the mainstream view of Canadian peacekeeping has remained rooted in a measurement of its success or failure as a problem-solving instrument rather than being subjected to a thorough critical evaluation.[86]

There are signs that this assessment pattern is changing. Consistent with the broadening out of peacekeeping on the ground, an astute observer such as Wiseman has called for a widened lens to be cast over the role of non-military personnel. While these alternative type of actors have become central players in the practice of peacekeeping, this role has been inadequately covered in the Canadian literature. In Wiseman's words: 'Insufficient attention and analysis is given to the growing number of civilian peacekeeping functions and personnel. Too little is known of the role of Canadian and international NGOs, such as the Red Cross, Red Crescent, CARE, Médecins sans frontières, or of national police forces and election officials.'[87]

More ambitiously still, Sandra Whitworth has raised a number of provocative theoretical/normative questions about the social structure of Canadian peacekeeping. Reviewing some recent books on the topic, Whitworth asserts that, although these works are 'thorough and often rigorous' in their analysis, 'they focus exclusively on a series of technical, policy-relevant questions which begin with the unproblematized assumption that peacekeeping is a "good" which needs to be pursued.' What is left out are a number of critical questions relating to: 'should the United Nations or member countries be involved in peacekeeping? who benefits from peacekeeping operations? who is excluded? what is the effect of peacekeeping missions on the people in those countries in which the missions are deployed?'[88]

These challenges to orthodox assumptions have yet to crest. A research program directed towards a critical rethinking about Canadian peacekeeping remains in its formative stage. This lag demonstrates, more than anything else, the tight grip of established attitudes towards peacekeeping in Canada. Notwithstanding the enormous challenges faced through the necessary evolution of Canadian peacekeeping, the national consensus about the essential worthiness of Canada playing a lead role in this sphere of activity has remained firm. To be sure, some of the lustre of this contribution has been rubbed off with the revelations concerning ethical/cultural deficiencies in Canadian participation in the Somali and Bosnian operations.[89] Still, even with these revealed flaws, peacekeeping serves as an ingrained source of pride and distinction for Canadians. The values of order and restraint, long assumed to be the core character of the Canadian personality, have continued to be indelibly linked to peacekeeping. Although increasingly worried about the image as well as the logic of peacekeeping, as applied in individual cases, the will to carry on with peacekeeping has persisted. Peacekeeping (warts and all) continues to feed into Canada's (and Canadians') positive attributes, attitudes and self-image.

The embedded hold of this national consensus on peacekeeping deserves considerable reflection on its own merits. When contrasted with the outlook on development issues, the other long-standing pillar of Canadian foreign policy, the preservation of this consensus is extraordinary. Canadian participation in peacekeeping may be increasingly modest—and even suspect—but the impression is not of a country in reversal and disengagement from its familiar habits.

The evolution of the Canadian perspective (and internal controversies) on development assistance issues is very different. Rather than being for the most part confined and restricted to technical or problem-solving issues, the debate about the direction of Canadian development policy and programs has been opened up to encompass an extensive array of critical issues and questions.

# NOTES

1   Testimony to the Special Joint Committee of the Senate and of the House of Commons, Reviewing Canadian Foreign Policy, *Minutes of Proceedings and Evidence*, 3 May 1994, 7:10.

2   For background, see J.L. Granatstein and David J. Bercuson, *War and Peacekeeping: From South Africa to the Gulf—Canada's Limited Wars* (Toronto: Key Porter, 1991).

3   *Ibid.*, ch. VII.

4   Norman Hillmer and J.L. Granatstein, *Empire To Umpire: Canada and the World to the 1990s* (Toronto: Copp Clark Longman, 1994).

5   Tom Keating and Nicholas Gammer, 'The "new look" in Canada's foreign policy,' *International Journal* XLVIII, 4 (Autumn 1993), 721–5.

6   Quoted in Granatstein and Bercuson, *War and Peacekeeping*, 202.

7   Karen A. Mingst, 'State participation in international and regional peacekeeping: a comparative analysis,' paper prepared for presentation at the annual meeting of the International Studies Association, San Diego, 17–20 April 1996.

8   Laura Neack, 'UN peace-keeping: in the interest of community or self?' *Journal of Peace Research* 32, 2 (1995), 181–96.

9   Granatstein and Bercuson, *War and Peacekeeping*, ch. VIII.

10   J.L. Granatstein, 'Peacekeeping: did Canada make a difference? And what difference did peacekeeping make to Canada?' in John English and Norman Hillmer, eds., *Making a Difference: Canada's Foreign Policy in a Changing World Order* (Toronto: Lester, 1992).

11   Canada, *White Paper on Defence*, March 1964, 15.

12   Canada, Minister of National Defence, *Canadian Defence Policy 1992* (Ottawa: April 1992), 32.

13   Geoffrey Hayes, 'Canada as a middle power,' in Andrew F. Cooper ed., *Niche Diplomacy: Middle Powers After the Cold War* (London: Macmillan, forthcoming), 107.

14   Granatstein and Bercuson, *War and Peacekeeping*, 199–200.

15   James Patrick Sewell, 'A world without Canada: would today's United Nations be the same,' in English and Hillmer, *Making a Difference*, 183–99.

16   Fred Mifflin, Parliamentary Secretary to the Minister of National Defence and Minister of Veterans' Affairs, House of Commons, *Debates*, 25 January 1994, 291.

17   Granatstein, 'Peacekeeping: did Canada make a difference?' 228–9.

18   Testimony to the Special Joint Committee of the Senate and of the House of Commons on Canada's Defence Policy, *Minutes of Proceedings and Evidence*, 19 April 1994, 2:10.

19  Granatstein, 'Peacekeeping: did Canada make a difference?'; Joseph T. Jockel, *Canada and International Peacekeeping* (Toronto: Canadian Institute of Strategic Studies, 1994).

20  Boutros Boutros-Ghali, *An Agenda for Peace: Preventative Diplomacy, Peacemaking and Peacekeeping* (New York: United Nations, 1992), 9.

21  Notes for an address by Prime Minister Brian Mulroney on the occasion of the centennial anniversary convocation, Stanford University, 29 September 1991, Office of the Prime Minister 1991.

22  Quoted in Keating and Gammer, 'The "new look,"' 725.

23  Lewis MacKenzie, *Peacekeeper: The Road to Sarajevo* (Vancouver: Douglas & McIntyre, 1993), 61.

24  Keating and Gammer, 'The "new look."'

25  Notes for an address by Prime Minister Brian Mulroney to the International Council of Young Leaders, Montreal, 24 May 1992, Office of the Prime Minister 1992, 4–5.

26  'NATO members gang up on Canada over pullout,' *Globe and Mail*, 9 April 1992.

27  David Cox, 'Canada and the United Nations: pursuing common security,' *Canadian Foreign Policy* II, 1 (Spring 1994), 63–78.

28  Jeff Sallot, 'PM taking foreign approach,' *Globe and Mail*, 26 May 1992.

29  *Ibid.*

30  This process of rethinking on peacekeeping was encouraged by the work of two parliamentary committees. In February 1993, the Standing Senate Committee on Foreign Affairs produced *Meeting New Challenges: Canada's Response to a New Generation of Peacekeeping* (Ottawa, 1993). In June 1993, the House of Commons Standing Committee on National Defence and Veterans' Affairs released *The Dilemmas of a Committed Peacekeeper: Canada and the Renewal of Peacekeeping* (Ottawa, 1993).

31  On the importance of personal factors in Canadian foreign policy, see Kim Richard Nossal, 'Personal diplomacy and rational behaviour: Trudeau's North–South initiative,' *Dalhousie Review* 62, 2 (Summer 1982), 278–91.

32  Sallot, 'PM taking foreign approach.'

33  'The diplomatic round in a new era and groping,' *New Yorker*, 16 December 1991, 93–4.

34  Joseph T. Jockel, *Canada and International Peacekeeping* (Toronto: Canadian Institute of Strategic Studies, 1994), 2.

35  On these definitional questions, see 'Seminar on Canada's agenda for international peace and security' (Ottawa: External Affairs and International Trade Canada, 1993).

36  See Mark Neufeld, 'Hegemony and foreign policy analysis: the case of Canada as middle power,' *Studies in Political Economy* 48 (Autumn 1995); *Transformation Moment: A Canadian Vision of Common Security*, The Report of the Citizens' Inquiry into Peace and Security, March 1992, 23.

37  Testimony to the Special Joint Committee of the Senate and of the House of Commons Reviewing Canadian Foreign Policy, *Minutes of Proceedings and Evidence*, 5 May 1994, 8:20.

38  *Ibid.*, 8:27.

39  Canada, Department of National Defence, *1994 Defence White Paper* (Ottawa: Minister of Supply and Services Canada, 1994). On these cuts, see Claire Turenne Sjolander,

'Cashing in on the "peace dividend": national defence in the post-Cold War world,' in Gene Swimmer ed., *How Ottawa Spends 1996–97: Life Under the Knife* (Ottawa: Carleton University Press, 1996), 253–82.

40  Pierre Martin and Michel Fortmann, 'Canadian public opinion and peacekeeping in a turbulent world,' *International Journal* L, 2 (Spring 1995), 370–400.

41  Testimony to the Special Joint Committee of the Senate and of the House of Commons, on Canada's Defence Policy, *Minutes of Proceedings and Evidence*, 19 April 1994, 2:9.

42  Alan James, 'Peacekeeping in the post-Cold War era,' *International Journal* L, 2 (Spring 1994), 255–6.

43  Keating and Gammer, 'The "new look,"' 737–8.

44  James, 'Peacekeeping,' 256–7.

45  See Robert M. Press, 'Canadian troops win Somali kudos,' *Christian Science Monitor*, 17 February 1993.

46  'It's time to bring peacekeeping up to date,' *Globe and Mail*, 19 March 1993.

47  Notes for an address by the Honourable Christine Stewart, Secretary of State (Latin America and Africa), before the Standing Committee on Foreign Affairs and International Trade, 95/23, 23 March 1995. In other cases, such as the Sudan, where there was little media attention, there was complete inaction.

48  See Michael Bliss, 'Let's not get carried away by zeal for intervention,' *Toronto Star*, 7 January 1993.

49  Richard Gwyn, 'Idealistic internationalism may just be meddling,' *Toronto Star*, 8 January 1993. See also Gwyn, 'Canadians are beginning to get pushy in foreign affairs,' *Toronto Star*, 20 January 1993.

50  Joe Sinasac, 'Helpful busybody,' *Kitchener-Waterloo Record*, 15 October 1992.

51  Gwyn, 'Idealistic internationalism.'

52  Testimony to the Special Joint Committee of the Senate and of the House of Commons on Canada's Defence Policy, *Minutes of Proceedings and Evidence*, 19 April 1994, 2:32.

53  Keating and Gammer, 'The "new look,"' 727.

54  Ouellet, House of Commons, *Debates*, 25 January 1994, 264. Notes for an address by the Honourable André Ouellet, Minister of Foreign Affairs, at the parliamentary debate on peacekeeping, 25 January 1994, 94/2, 3.

55  *Ibid.*, 266.

56  Quoted in Jeff Sallot, 'Canadians inclined to stay in Bosnia,' *Globe and Mail*, 21 December 1994.

57  For a review of some of these problems in a wider context, see S.J. Stedman, 'Alchemy for a new world order: overselling "preventative diplomacy,"' *Foreign Affairs* 74, 3 (Summer 1995), 14–20.

58  See, for example, Peter Gizewski and Geoffrey Pearson, 'The burgeoning cost of United Nations peacekeeping: who pays and who benefits?' *Aurora Papers* 21 (Ottawa: Canadian Centre for Global Security, 1993).

59    Doug Fischer, 'Poll indicates most want peacekeepers out of Bosnia,' *Ottawa Citizen*, 26 January 1994. Ouellet, in his speech during the special parliamentary debate on peacekeeping, emphasized the newness of this risk factor: 'In the past, it would seem that the amount of risk incurred by our soldiers was rarely a problem. This is no longer the case; the risk factor has become an essential element in our decision-making.' House of Commons, *Debates*, 25 January 1994, 264.

60    David Cox, testimony to Senate Sub-Committee on Security and National Defence, *Minutes of Proceedings and Evidence*, 9 June 1992, 6:6.

61    Bill Graham, House of Commons, *Debates*, 29 March 1995, 11240–41.

62    For a fuller discussion on this theme, see James S. Sutterlin, 'Military force in the service of peace,' *Aurora Papers* 18 (Ottawa: Canadian Centre for Global Security, 1993).

63    David Vienneau, 'Canada has veto over air strikes,' *Toronto Star*, 17 January 1994; Anne Swardson, 'Canada with troops in Bosnia, stands firm against airstrikes,' *Washington Post*, 14 January 1994.

64    Ouellet, House of Commons, *Debates*, 25 January 1994, 266.

65    'Chrétien hedges on pledge to join U.S. mission in Bosnia,' *Globe and Mail*, 20 October 1995.

66    Quoted in Tim Harper, 'Canadians tired of being pushed around in Bosnia, PM says,' *Toronto Star*, 5 January 1994.

67    Paul Koring, 'Dropping the peacekeeping torch,' *Globe and Mail*, 7 October 1995.

68    Jack Frazer, Sannich–Gulf Islands, House of Commons, *Debates*, 25 January 1994, 272.

69    Bob Mills, Red Deer, House of Commons, *Debates*, 25 January 1994, 274.

70    *Ibid.*

71    House of Commons, *Debates*, 25 January 1994, 268, 270.

72    House of Commons, *Debates*, 29 March 1995, 11229, 11230.

73    Jeff Sallot, 'Redrawing the lines of battle,' *Globe and Mail*, 8 October 1994.

74    Mills, House of Commons, *Debates*, 25 January 1994, 273.

75    Jack Frazer, House of Commons, *Debates*, 29 March 1995, 11233.

76    For a fuller discussion, see Bruce D. Jones, 'Intervention without borders: humanitarian intervention in Rwanda, 1990–94,' *Millennium* 24, 2 (Fall 1995), 225–48.

77    Notes for an address by the Honourable André Ouellet, Minister of Foreign Affairs, to the 49th GA of the UN, 29 September 1994, NY, NY, 94/55. Canada's initiative had emerged out of an international conference of governmental representatives and experts. Notes for an address by the Honourable André Ouellet, Minister of Foreign Affairs, at the international conference on Improving the UN's Rapid Reaction Capability, Montebello, Quebec, 8 April 1995, 95/24.

78    Government of Canada, *Towards a Rapid Reaction Capability for the United Nations* (Ottawa: September 1995), 5.

79    For a review of this proposal, see Bill Robinson, 'The new vanguard of peacekeeping?' *Ploughshares Monitor* XVI, 4 (December 1995), 13–14.

80   Jeff Sallot, '1,000-troop commitment "bare minimum" for allies,' *Globe and Mail*, 8 December 1995.

81   Michael Berry, quoted in Allan Thompson, 'New rules apply in Bosnia mission,' *Toronto Star*, 6 January 1996.

82   For a review of some of these activities, see Ernie Regehr, 'The challenge of peace-building,' *Ploughshares Monitor* XVI, 4 (December 1995), 2–8.

83   See, for example, the views of John Watson, executive director, CARE Canada, 'Peacekeeping troops often misused,' *Ottawa Citizen*, 20 January 1993. See also Adam Roberts, 'Humanitarian war: military intervention and human rights,' *International Affairs* 69, 3 (July 1993), 429–50.

84   Henry Wiseman, 'United Nations peacekeeping and Canadian policy: a reassessment,' *Canadian Foreign Policy* I, 3 (Fall 1993), 147.

85   See, for example, Lewis MacKenzie, 'Military realities of peacekeeping operations,' *RUSI Journal* 138, 1 (February 1993), 21–4.

86   Robert W. Cox, 'Social forces, states, and world orders,' in Robert Keohane ed., *Neorealism and Its Critics* (New York: Columbia University Press, 1986), 208.

87   Wiseman, 'United Nations peacekeeping,' 147.

88   Sandra Whitworth, 'Where is the politics in peacekeeping?' *International Journal* L, 2 (Spring 1995), 428.

89   Tu Thanh Ha, 'Army to probe conduct in Bosnia,' *Globe and Mail*, 18 July 1996.

# CHAPTER 6

# THE SCATTERING OF PURPOSE: CANADA AND DEVELOPMENT ASSISTANCE

A prime site of contest on Canadian foreign policy relates to its vision and sense of public purpose. The most appropriate test of these attributes is the manner in which Canada has provided development assistance within the North–South context. In a fashion analogous to peacekeeping activity, development assistance became elevated through the post-1945 years to the status of a Canadian 'vocation.'[1] As the second of the twin pillars in the traditional hierarchy of Canadian international activity, development assistance was built on the idea of a distinctive area of specialized interest and expertise through which Canada could differentiate itself from other countries. Development assistance buttressed Canada's claim to be a committed and constructive international citizen. The issue-specific activity also provided a source of pride and creativity for Canadian state officials, allowing them not only prestige but a useful arena for the cultivation of innovative practices. By the delivery of development assistance programs outwards toward the global community, Canada signalled a seriousness of intent concerning both its willingness to take on an ambitious set of international responsibilities and its desire to carve out a specific place for itself in policy terms.

Because of this sense of high public purpose, any sign of retreat on development assistance has met with discomfort and controversy. A long and vigorous debate has taken place over the extent to which Canada has lived up to its self-identified image as a practical 'helpful fixer' between North and South. Keith Spicer asked in 1966 whether Canada was indeed a Samaritan State.[2] To this measured voice of interrogation was added a chorus of louder, and quite discordant, criticism through the 1970s and 1980s. The evolution of the debate surrounding development assistance, therefore, has been conducted in a very different way from the analogous process in peacekeeping. While the debate on peacekeeping has been conducted in the main on a discrete plane, with a concentration of attention on a cluster of narrow technical issues, the debate over development assistance has continually burst out to embrace larger critical and normative concerns. This process has had the effect of scattering the debate—or more precisely, the set of debates. It may be hyperbole to say that the extended controversy over development assistance now lacks a clearly defined core issue; but it is axiomatic that the issues and questions under review within the rubric of development assistance have become extremely diffuse. Whereas the debate on peacekeeping has only recently taken on greater scope and intensity, the debate on development assistance has been fundamentally recast to cover some of the key issues of national and global governance in the post-Cold War era.

## ESTABLISHING A SENSE OF PUBLIC PURPOSE

### Development Assistance in the Pearson Era

To suggest that Canada was propelled towards a prominent role on development assistance largely because of a sense of public purpose should not be an excuse to engage in nostalgic mythology. The origins of Canada's role on development assistance do not lie exclusively in the instincts of compassion and generosity to others. At the same time, though, any analysis of Canada's contribution in this sphere of activity should not go to the opposite extreme of completely dismissing altruism as a determinant. In the same way as the influence of the 'missionary strain' can be privileged in the evolution of Canadian peacekeeping,[3] much of the zeal with which Canada first embraced development assistance can be attributed to the power of this impulse in Canadian public life. A close reading of Spicer's account of the origins of this policy leaves little doubt of the 'strong resonance' of this missionary tradition on the discourse/action of Canadian policymakers in the 'golden years' of Canadian diplomacy. Lester Pearson declared in a 1961 parliamentary debate on external affairs that 'we help these countries because it is a good thing for us to do, it is a good thing for the peace of the world and because the world is one.'[4] Relying on the rhetoric Lincoln used in the fight against slavery in the nineteenth century, Pearson warned that 'the world cannot exist half poverty-stricken and half an affluent society.' The full impact of this missionary zeal as an animating force behind Canadian policy on development assistance is exhibited by a speech made in the same year by Mitchell Sharp, the veteran Canadian public servant, in which he called for a 'return to the simple principles of Christian charity.' In Sharp's view: 'There is one good and sufficient reason for international aid and that is that there are less fortunate people in the world who need our help. If they are grateful for our help so much the better. If by reason of the aid they receive they become bigger customers for Canadian goods and services, better still. If our aid helps them to...set their feet firmly on the road to higher standards of living without resort to Communist dictatorship, the benefits to us are beyond measure. But the inspiration for what we do must be essentially humanitarian and unselfish. If it is not, if the primary purpose of our aid is to help ourselves, rather than others, we will probably receive in return what we deserve and a good deal less than we expect.'[5]

*emp.*

*Peace*

This sense of obligation as an essential ingredient in the public purpose driving Canadian development assistance policy must be placed in the larger policy context. The parallel between the rise of the domestic social-security safety net system and the emergence of an externally directed development assistance order has only recently begun to receive the attention it deserves by political scientists. Overlooked in the older literature, this theme of externalization has been recently taken up by Noël and Thérien. Exploring the connection between the two sets of programs from a comparative context, they conclude that, as an entity, development assistance policy represents an 'international projection of the income-redistribution mechanisms that characterise the organization of social relations in developed countries.'[6] With their corresponding emphasis on income transfers from the rich to the poor, the paths of international development assistance and domestic welfarism are viewed as being inextricably intertwined and symmetrical.

Honing in on the Canadian experience, the treatment of development assistance policy as a mirror image of domestic welfarism has much to recommend it. From an inside-out perspective, this route showcases the importance of the variable of national state building as featured after the Second World War. Only with the prosperity derived from the economic boom in the postwar years did Canada go through its expansionist phase with respect to the welfare state. What had hitherto consisted of a hodge-podge of disparate and localized programs gradually became transformed into a relatively coherent and stabilized system. Equally, this rise in capabilities provided much of the impetus for the shift in Canadian external aid from a relatively modest and ad hoc approach to a higher-profile enterprise on a more ambitious scale. Just as many of the most dramatic (and expensive) initiatives in terms of health, unemployment insurance and other areas of social policy peaked in the mid- to late 1960s, so did the outlay on development assistance. Between 1964 and 1967, spending on international development assistance rose by some 280 percent.[7]

From an outside-in perspective, this domestic analogy points to the salience of the variable of legitimacy as provided through an adherence to a set of international rules of the game. Postwar Canadian governments were motivated to extend the welfare system not only because of the possession of the surplus capabilities to do so, but also because these activities were in conformity with the central norms and principles of governance generally adhered to during those years. As the overarching system of 'embedded liberalism' implanted during the immediate post-1945 era guided the implementation of the welfare state at home, the basic principles and rules for an international aid regime took hold. Both of these systems were flexible: within a broad set of parameters, a considerable degree of leeway in national policies was accepted. While allowing diversity, though, the extent to which a common approach was developed by these guidelines should not be ignored. As Thérien argues convincingly: 'Aid is global in scope. It is an expression of objectives that are shaped by the Western states at least as much as it is the product of domestic values and preferences.'[8]

In terms of foreign policy objectives, development assistance held attractions similar to peacekeeping. Taking a lead role in selective aid programs offered Canada the prospect of achieving a balance between its obligations as a loyal ally and its desire to differentiate itself from the US and the other big powers. The impetus to harness Canada's sense of public purpose on development assistance to the Western alliance's struggle against Communism is apparent in two distinct ways. During the immediate post-1945 period, the bulk of Canadian foreign assistance went directly to NATO members—a recovery strategy dictated by the Canadian government's 'overriding interest in supporting collective defence in Europe and in response to demands for increased defence spending from allies.'[9] The shift towards directing assistance to the South only came with the victory of Mao and the formation of the People's Republic of China in 1949. Galvanized by these events, Canada participated at the meeting of Commonwealth ministers in Colombo, Ceylon (now Sri Lanka), in January 1950, which launched the Colombo Plan for Co-operative Economic Development in South and Southeast Asia. In explaining Canada's contribution to this initiative, Pearson brought the geopolitical rationale to the fore: '[I] t seemed to all of us at the conference that if the tide of totalitarian expansion should flow over this general area, not only will the new nations lose the national independence which they have secured so recently, but the forces of the free world will have been driven off all but a relatively small bit of the great Eurasian land mass.... If southeast Asia and south Asia are not to be conquered by communism, we of the free democratic world...must demonstrate that it is we...who stand for national liberation and economic and social progress.'[10]

Like donning the blue helmet of UN peacekeeping, development assistance allowed Canada to pay its dues to the Western alliance in a different fashion and so offset its image as a 'free rider.' As Spicer suggests in his concluding section, this type of alternative contribution could be seen over time to be a wasting asset: 'Planners might ask, for instance, whether in preventing some local tensions from threatening world peace Canada should not curtail aid in order to concentrate her small resources' on other activities.[11] Indeed, through the 1950s, Canada argued that it could not afford to stretch its contribution in terms of overseas aid because of the costs imposed by defence spending.[12] Still, at least in the Cold War years, a solid rebuttal to this line of thinking could be made: building up a distinct (and recognized) profile in development assistance helped enormously in Canada's efforts to demonstrate that it was willing to take on its share of the burden of responsibilities within the Western alliance. The linkage (and sense of compensation) between Canada's lighter role on defence and heavier role in development assistance became more explicit. As one of the key 'old' External hands, Escott Reid, wrote in 1970: 'Canada can do relatively little to assist in preventing war by maintaining armed forces. That game has become too expensive. If Canada were to double its present defence expenditures of 1.8 billion Canadian dollars a year, this would increase the total expenditures of the

NATO countries by $\frac{1}{2}$ percent. But if Canada were to increase its net expenditures on foreign aid to poor countries by 1.8 billion Canadian dollars a year, this would increase the total expenditures of the wealthy white countries on foreign aid to poor countries by 33 percent.'[13]

While buttressing the notion of alliance solidarity, the design of this development assistance policy also provided another way by which Canada could distance itself from the US. By channelling its efforts primarily through the Colombo Plan, Canada sent another signal about the extent to which its commitment to the international order differed from the US's. In terms of form, the Colombo Plan concentrated on the narrower tools of technical aid and training rather than on mega-projects (although this contradistinction was reduced after 1958 when the US entered the Colombo Plan). In terms of intensity, the Colombo Plan was palpably low-key, with an emphasis on an unthreatening, non-combative style as opposed to the heavy dose of 'carrot and stick' contained in US diplomacy. In terms of scope, the Colombo Plan option meshed well with the Canadian concern with 'discipline' and 'limits.' Canada's delivery of development assistance, as opposed to the global reach observable in American behaviour, was intended to be tightly restricted with respect to its geographic application. John Holmes in the early 1960s cautioned against any overextension in this policy, which would diminish the impact of Canadian aid: 'We have fixed our attention on specific Commonwealth countries and thereby made some impression on their economies.... If we must choose, there is good reason for choosing areas to which we have a prior commitment for political and historical reasons.'[14]

'Being there' provided a good deal of additional incentive for Canadian activity in this specialized area. In the Pearsonian era, Canada enjoyed the cozy atmosphere of 'clubmanship' that the Colombo Plan encouraged through its quasi-multilateral form. The appeal of being recognized as a player of note on the international stage in this specialized area, as in peacekeeping activity, was not just for appearance's sake: Canada's contribution on development assistance was designed to gain fuller access to the important sites of decision making. An element of reciprocity was built into this approach. While the developing countries expected to be treated as 'equals' within the confines of the Colombo Plan,[15] Canada expected to be treated as an 'equal' with the other major donor countries across the entire spectrum of international economic/financial institutions governing the aid regime.

The same sort of expectation of a reputational return influenced the broadening out of Canada's development assistance strategy in the 1960s and 1970s. Through an extension of its aid commitment, Canada helped win not only increased prestige but influence in the core group of specialized institutions at the heart of the post-1945 order. Initially, the target of this attention was the International Bank for Reconstruction and Development (the World Bank)—or more precisely the committees of donors ('consortia' and 'consultative groups') established by this body to co-ordinate aid to specific regions—as well as the OECD. Helped by the extensive experience (and credibility) it had gained through its work in the Colombo Plan, Canada was included with the major donors in all three of the consortia set up by the IBRD in the mid-1960s for India, Pakistan and the Indus Basin. From 1960 on, Canada was an active participant in the OECD, which, via its Development Assistance Committee and its Annual Aid Review, served as the main instrument for harmonizing aid policies among donors.[16] By 1970, Canada had become an active contributor to the United Nations Development Program (UNDP) and the set of regional banks.

Nor did these concerns with access and influence disappear with the transition from Pearson to Trudeau. Trudeau's more explicit emphasis on Canada's national self-interest did provide a doctrine that rationalized some degree of backsliding in terms of liberal internationalism. Indeed, as noted in Chapter 2, it was during the Trudeau years that Canada's image for abiding by the rules of the post-1945 order suffered a number of corrosive dents. While Trudeau's rhetoric was impressive, in the empathy it articulated concerning the South's call for a 'New International Order,' the actions of his government did not live up to these words. Trudeau inserted a considerable amount of sizzle to the debates about equity and redistribution in the context of North–South relations, but the policy content was uneven in adopting any of the 'hard,' trade-related options. As Gerald Helleiner has summarized this record: 'Canadian tariffs are, on average, over twice as high on products of developing country origin as they are on others.... The Canadian preferential tariffs for manufactured products from developing countries, among the last to be introduced to the OECD, are severely limited in their impact...by exceptions, eligibility rules and safeguard clauses; their positive effect does not begin to make up the losses imposed by the discrimination against developing countries.'[17]

Nevertheless, Trudeau's caution on those sensitive questions relating to adjustment in the domestic economy did not translate into a diminution of development assistance as an instrument of Canadian foreign policy. On the contrary, it was during the Trudeau years that the notion of some clear linkage between Canada's standing in the world and its role as an aid contributor became firmly established. Acceptance as a member of the inner circle of Western industrialized countries was perceived as being contingent on a substantive commitment in this sphere of activity. Credibility as an exemplar—or 'mentor'— to countries outside this inner circle rested on the ability to perform this commitment in a way that was acceptable to the international community at large and to the countries of the South in particular.[18] As plainly recognized by the Trudeau government, 'the existence of [an official development assistance] programme is a minimal requisite for playing in the North–South game.'[19]

This status-oriented motivation coexisted with an impetus towards reputational/career enhancement on an individual and collective basis. Looking back at the formative stages of Canada's development assistance policies, what is striking is the extent to which it was the key figures of the Canadian foreign policy élite who dominated the discourse and activity in this issue-area. This tight grip from the centre, to some degree, can be explained simply· by the fact that there were few other actors in this phase of Canadian foreign policy to whom responsibility could be delegated. Until the mid-1960s, the bureaucrats involved with the development assistance dossier only consisted of a 'corporal's guard.'[20] The few voluntary groups with an active interest in development issues, such as the Canadian University Service Overseas, were in a nascent stage of operation. The time and energy that Lester Pearson, Escott Reid and A.F.W. Plumptre, to name just three from this old guard, devoted to development assistance issues was also perfectly consistent with their missionary determination to try 'to set a good example' for responsible and constructive public purpose.[21]

Whatever the precise cause, the effect of this closed approach was not only to help put Canada on the diplomatic map but to propel this cohort of 'old hands' into an extended series of high-profile positions relating to international development. Pearson's last major contribution to international affairs was to chair the 1969 Pearson Commission on International Development.[22] Reid served as the director, South Asia and Middle East Department of the IBRD before becoming the principal of Glendon College. Plumptre acted as Canadian executive director at the International Monetary Fund. The qualities of skill and reputation, developed in these individuals through their long and pre-eminent careers as Canadian public servants, continued to play well in this specialized dimension on the international stage.

## The Trudeau Years and the Formation of CIDA

The Trudeau years marked an acceleration in the dynamic of change, already building some momentum in the latter stages of the Pearson era, with respect to the administration of Canadian development assistance. The appointment of Maurice Strong in 1966 to head up DEA's External Aid Office—transformed into the Canadian International Development Agency (CIDA) in 1968—epitomized the intrusion of a new breed of 'ins' and 'outers' into what had been the preserve of a small, cozy, tight-knit group of decision-makers. Strong's appointment as president of this new body proved to be the turning-point in his own long and distinguished career, from private entrepreneurship (as president of Power Corporation) to international civil servant (launched when he was head-hunted by the UN to become the secretary-general of the 1972 UN Conference on the Human Environment). As an activist, outsider, head of CIDA, Strong embarked on a distinctive path of institution building (and personal opportunity), which his successors tried hard to emulate. This successor cohort included Paul Gérin-Lajoie, an ex-cabinet minister from Quebec, Margaret Catley-Carlson and Marcel Massé. This pattern was, in turn, extended to the International Development Research Centre

(IDRC), the body established to be in effect CIDA's research arm. Ivan Head, as Trudeau's principal foreign policy adviser, provided much of the inspiration and clout to launch this complementary enterprise (ultimately extending his hands-on role to become president of the Centre).[23]

The new cohort of development assistance administrators shared many of the personal values belonging to the 'old' External hands. A sense of obligation and volunteerism drove both groups not only towards public service within Canada but towards attempts to try to make a difference without. With respect to policy, they shared much of the same faith in the benefits obtained from the promotion of technical assistance, education and training. The dynamic of change coincided with some basic elements of continuity. As witnessed by the language contained in the 1970 Foreign Policy for Canadians—'developing' countries instead of 'underdeveloped,' 'development assistance' instead of 'aid'—declaratory policy leaped ahead quickly under the Trudeau government; operational policy, meanwhile, lagged more cautiously behind. Only in the mid-1970s, amid all of the international economics shocks, could a more substantive break with orthodoxy be discerned, with a redirected focus on alternative solutions via a basic needs approach, an integrated rural development program and other strategies that put the onus more directly on helping the global poor. This sense of continuity was bolstered further by the fact that the members of this new cohort shared the concern of the 'old hands' about the need to enhance Canada's reputation and standing in the world on a segmented basis. As much as in the Pearson era, development assistance in the Trudeau years was considered to be an activity in which Canada had a distinct national comparative advantage.

The initial changes hinged as much on degree as on substance. The style favoured by the new cohort sharply diverged from the established mode of operation. The 'old hands' instinctively leaned towards a modest and understated approach to aid. The preference of Strong, Head and the rest of the ascendant group of administrators in the Trudeau years was for the assertion of a more ostentatious and adventuresome approach. Casting off the geographic limits and disciplines, the new cohort diversified the scope of Canada's development assistance. While retaining a concentration on sub-Saharan Africa and south Asia,[24] the Trudeau government rejigged the composition of recipient countries in a number of ways. Most notably, the profile of Canada's bilateral assistance was directed away from its narrow focus on English-speaking/Commonwealth countries (where from the outset of the Colombo Plan the bulk of Canadian aid had been channelled). One prime target, in the early phase of this diversification exercise, was the francophone countries of West Africa. In keeping with Canada's growing interest in 'concentrated bilateralism,' the framework subsequently expanded to encompass the cluster of so-called newly industrializing states.

Functionally, a fundamental priority of the Trudeau government was to raise Canada's presence in multilateral institutions. In particular, the Trudeau government sought to ensure that Canada belonged to the assemblage of multilateral development banks that had been created. As such, Canada's broadening out in representational terms was largely a function of institutional proliferation at the international level. As Culpeper and Clark summarize this process of evolution: 'Among middle powers, Canada has always been the foremost advocate for and supporter of the multilateral development banks (MDBs). Canada was a leading participant at the Bretton Woods Conference which led to the creation of the World Bank.... Canada supported the formation of the World Bank's International Development Agency (IDA) in 1960, was a founding member of the Asian Development Bank in 1965, the Caribbean Development Bank in 1970 and the African Development Fund (a concessional window for non-African donor countries) in 1972—a year in which it also joined the Inter-American Development Bank. By 1982, when the African Development Bank admitted non-African members, Canada was the only country represented by its own national at the Executive Boards of all the MDBs.'[25]

Driving this ambition, both in its geographic and functional dimension, was the discomfort of the new cohort of administrators with the image of Canada as a junior partner in the international assistance hierarchy. They wanted Canada to be accorded recognition and status as a country of the first tier in this sphere of activity. An element of compensation continued to be attached to this aspiration. By taking on a highly visible role in international development assistance, Canada could offset its relatively low contribution in some other domains (especially on military spending). More positively, this search for an elevated status on an issue-selective basis came as part of the Trudeau government's bid to project Canada in a hybrid fashion; namely, while retaining many of the instincts and characteristics associated with the 'like-minded' countries, Canada was also to be regarded as a country that belonged to the exclusive club of major industrial countries.

Another important feature distinguishing the new cohort of development assistance administrators from the 'old guard' of foreign policy makers centred on their very different preferences on organizational technique. Foreign aid had been the quintessential 'seat of the pants' operation in the 1950s and early 1960s, its distinguishing feature being the talent for improvisation identified with Pearsonian diplomacy. This loose and informal approach had its strengths, in that it allowed some considerable amount of flexibility in both routine and emergency (disaster relief etc.) activity. From the point of view of the new cohort, however, it was hopelessly outdated. What was required was the infusion of more 'professional and sophisticated' techniques.[26] Under the influence of this technocracy-minded group of administrators, CIDA soon became a working model for the application of the system of rational management—replete with cost–benefit analyses, priority setting, and complex planning and evaluation exercises.

A vital component of this organizational reform was the process of client building. With their bred in the bone confidence that they represented the national interest, the old guard perceived little need to open up the foreign-policy-making process to alternative voices and sources of influence. Canadian business and the Canadian voluntary sector were kept very much at arm's length. This state-centred approach had some value in terms of its simplicity; a clubby mentality could quite easily be maintained within this sort of closed atmosphere. This advantage, however, was counterbalanced by losses with respect to political legitimacy and technical efficiency.

Gradually, a two-track strategy for integrating state and societal concerns into development assistance policymaking was substituted for this traditional approach. The first of these tracks was intended to bring the voluntary sector into the operation of development assistance. This opening up cannot be divorced from the NGOs' own efforts. The spirit of the 1960s brought with it a rapid increase in NGO mobilization, much of it focussed on development issues. Canadian NGOs are estimated to have shot up from approximately 20 in 1963 to over 120 in 1972.[27] The Miles for Millions marches, in which Canadians walked in exchange for donations to help with development projects, proved to be a particularly valuable vehicle for generating interest in NGO work in this area.[28] Equally important, though, was CIDA's willingness to respond to these societal pressures in a creative, if still somewhat restricted, fashion—despite the fact that many of these NGOs were part of a radical 'counter-consensus' acting in 'serious opposition to many components of the present consensus which underlies Canadian foreign policy.'[29] By 1968, an NGO program had been set up within CIDA via the organization's Special Program Branch. The Institutional Cooperation program allocated funds to NGOs on a matching grants basis with donations raised by the NGOs themselves. Some additional projects were also funded through a system of block funding in grant form. A formative 'partnership' between CIDA and NGOs had been established.

The second component of this integrative process attached commercial interests directly to development assistance policy. By 1971, a rudimentary industrial co-operation program had been initiated, with the intention of increasing the involvement of Canadian firms in the South through the tools of investment, joint ventures and the transfer of technology.[30] This strategy was constantly upgraded thereafter. A full-scale Industrial Co-operation Division of CIDA was established in September 1978, followed by the creation of a Business Co-operation Branch in 1984 to guide an expansion of CIDA's connections with Canadian firms. This comprehensive approach was supplemented by a number of sector-specific programs. As part of its mandate to be a 'window' on the world of international energy, for example, the Petro-Canada International Assistance Corporation provided a segmented 'aid' instrument directed towards developing oil and gas production in the South.

Throughout this ongoing pattern of evolution, CIDA was able to form a distinctive corporate culture and capacity within government. In terms of its organizational ethos, the extension of the long-standing commitment to 'good work' stands out. Even when under critical review, CIDA received applause for the 'high sense of mission found in most employees and managers concerning their work.'[31] In terms of its organizational capacity, CIDA composed an aberration in the Ottawa administrative matrix. It was neither a department nor a crown corporation. Instead of having a hierarchy topped by a deputy minister or assistant/associate deputy ministers, CIDA was directed by a president and vice-presidents. Unlike other agencies, CIDA did not have a board of directors. Without a minister exclusively to call its own (except for a brief spell during the time of the Clark government in 1979), CIDA was wont to describe itself as a 'policy taker' rather than a 'policy maker.'[32] Yet this anomalous position provided CIDA with certain advantages in its ability to carve out an extensive degree of autonomy. Helped by its continued sense of purpose, the personnel and financial resources it had in hand, and the strong personality and bureaucratic/political clout of the majority of its presidents, CIDA was able to find and retain considerable space in which to operate independently on international development assistance through to the 1980s.

## DEBATING THE PURPOSE

The heavy amount of criticism to which Canadian development assistance became subjected in the 1970s and 1980s relates in large part to the combination of impulses behind this policy agenda. Grant Reuber spelled out this theme of 'mixed motivation' early on: 'Foreign aid is motivated by a combination of moral and philanthropic impulses together with a desire to promote the economic and political interests of Canadian citizens.'[33] Kim Nossal reprised, and updated, this mode of analysis at the end of the 1980s with a shift in the frame of reference away from both the beneficiaries of Canadian development assistance in the South and 'Canadian citizens' generally to the interests of the Canadian state and its officials more specifically.[34] Precisely because of the projection of these multiple aims, Canada's approach in this issue-area could be attacked from several directions at once. What represented a source of strength from one point of view was critiqued for undermining the credibility and effectiveness of policy delivery from another.

That so much of the debate was directed towards the question of 'dominance' among these contending motivations confirms the extent of coexistence between them. As Reuber notes, these divergent motivations do not necessarily conflict to the point 'where they are mutually exclusive.'[35] So long as there was expansion of the development assistance allocation, analysts could afford to bicker about who (under the influence of what impulse) was getting the bigger piece of that allocation (and why). Until the first cutbacks (inflicted in 1978) deepened over time, the internal debate over development assistance remained largely associated with the 'problem' of Canada trying to 'be everywhere and doing everything'—not with the far more contentious issue of making difficult choices under conditions of 'understretch.' Through the 1970s and even into the early 1980s, a consensus still prevailed that all of the contending motivations could be taken seriously, even if they were not treated equally or fully addressed. From the 1980s on, the need for adjustment (with trade-offs between the different motivations) changed the nature of the debate.

## The Philanthropic Motivation

Consistent with the altruistic impulse, one major motivation remained that of philanthropy towards the disadvantaged in the South. In declaratory terms, this type of motivation was clearly expressed in the 1987 report of the House of Commons Standing Committee on External Affairs and International Trade, *For Whose Benefit?*[36] Chaired by William Winegard, a Conservative MP (and former president of Guelph University), this committee had conducted an exhaustive review of the goals and instruments of Canadian development assistance. While recapitulating the view that a combination of humanitarian, economic and political motivations animated the Canadian approach in this sphere of activity, the Winegard report opted for specificity over diffuseness. With a directness unusual in parliamentary reports, the committee stated that: 'the primary purpose of ODA is to help the poorest countries and people. ODA must strengthen the human and institutional capacity of developing countries to solve their own problems in harmony with the natural environment.'[37]

Notwithstanding this expression of clarity, the 'counter-consensus' negatively evaluated the performance of the Canadian government in meeting this objective. The conceptual underpinning of Canadian development assistance was critiqued on the basis that its goal was not long-term redistributive reform but short-term system maintenance. Globally, instead of encouraging the promotion of a 'new international economic order,' the operational aim was perceived to be that of propping up the status quo with little or 'any absolute narrowing of the...poverty gap.'[38] This judgment took into account a number of factors stretching well beyond the parameters of development assistance policy *per se*. One of these factors was the permeation of a well-established protectionist structure within Canada's own economy, restricting the entry of goods from the South. Another was the response of Canadian governments towards any form of initiative intended to substantially reform the structure of the international economic system. Rather than moving out in front on measures such as the implementation of a Common Fund for the stabilization of prices for primary commodities, Canada chose to maintain a cautious, safety-first attitude.[39]

In terms of its impact on individual countries within the South, the application of Canadian development assistance met with a similar form of repudiation from the 'counter-consensus.' As Brian Tomlinson stated in his introduction to a 1991 edited collection: 'From the standpoint of the poor, the development strategies of the last three decades have failed dramatically.'[40] Instead of addressing the problem of poverty within the larger population, this 'counter-consensus' interpreted the effect of this instrument as stabilization of the position of the national élite. What was required if poverty was to be alleviated in the South was a bottom-up model, empowering the poor themselves to be agents of structural change. Development, from this assessment, could not be defined just as a system of redistribution or 'catch-up' within the international political economy between North and South; development had to be conceptualized as a comprehensive process that addressed 'those social, economic, cultural, and political needs [embedded within] unjust structures of society' and 'ultimately contribute to the restructuring of social, economic, and political relationships.'[41]

The degree to which the Canadian government lived up to its own declaratory goals was critically assessed as well. The test of commitment was held to be the achievement of the internationally agreed (from 1970) performance target of aid as 0.7 percent of Gross National Product (GNP). A ritual of official adherence to this target was retained into the 1990s, but the gap between formalism and practice remained large. Repetitively, Canadian governments made positive indications about moving up to this standard. In terms of actual performance, though, the contribution fell short. While sometimes edging up to the standard (reaching 0.5 percent in 1984 and 1988), Canada never achieved this target.[42]

## The Foreign Policy Motivation

Consistent with the foreign policy impulse, another strong motivation for the promotion of international development assistance continued to be the heightened profile this activity lent to Canada. Due to its lack of precise articulation as a basis for action, this motivation has been hard to grasp precisely until recently. Canadian declaratory language frequently intoned the mantra of 'increasing stability and peace' through the device of development assistance.[43] How Canada actually intended to maximize its national interest through development assistance was purposely left vague. This vagueness reflected more than Canadian modesty. To sell the Canadian public on the notions of development assistance as a tool to win 'goodwill,' 'a voice' or 'institutional access' was a difficult task. An appreciation of the benefits derived from this form of diplomatic engagement in reputational terms was restricted almost exclusively to the official foreign policy makers. Lavergne, in taking a closer look at Canadian development assistance from this angle, perceptively notes that the 'prestige' factor is of some considerable import since it accrues disproportionately 'to the "foreign policy elite" responsible for designing a donor's aid policy.'[44]

The thin distribution of Canada's development assistance reinforces the salience of the prestige factor. As Nossal spells out this spread: 'in 1986... Canadian development assistance was distributed to 119 states, numerous regional development banks, international organizations, and Canadian and foreign NGOs. It might be suggested that such a global reach is motivated by the returns in prestige brought by such discrete contributions, no matter how small...[with] the beneficiaries of such "returns"...primarily state officials.'[45] One can add that this 'prestige' factor has operated in a double-edged manner: while allowing enhanced status, it can also contribute to image problems relating to an 'ugly' or 'imperious' Canada.[46]

Two subsidiary points need to raised about Canadian diplomacy on development assistance. The first relates to the absence of an explicit foreign policy motivation in this sphere of activity. Canada's targeting of francophone Africa in the early Trudeau years is a case in point. The aims of this expression of Canadian development assistance were both direct and transparent: strategically, this geographic targeting was intended to send out a clear signal that Canada was a bilingual and bicultural country. If straightforward, however, the incorporation of this message into Canadian foreign policy was also a contentious one; for the strategy was played out against the backdrop of escalating competition between the federal government and Quebec on the international stage, which was so prominent on the political/policy scene in the late 1960s and early 1970s. The result was a close identification between the allocation of development assistance and the bitter rows between Ottawa and Quebec City. Rather than being helpful in the retention of a measured diplomatic image, Canadian development assistance was cast as a controversial (and erratic) political football thrown to where it was needed in the ongoing constitutional struggle. The fact that so much of this struggle involved symbolic gestures simply reinforced the impression of extravagance and insubstantiality, with development assistance being utilized as part of an elaborate image-building exercise rather than as an instrumental device directed towards the achievement of real benefits for the South.

The second point centres on the question of whether Canadian development assistance has become so thinned out in terms of geographical distribution that its presence in some countries has become little more than a skeleton. Thérien, in his detailed examination of recent trends in Canadian development assistance, dissects this problem in a variety of aspects. Although fully cognizant of the 'time-honoured tradition' behind this thinning process, Thérien highlights the difficulty of 'maximizing the effectiveness of Canada's program' under these conditions.[47] Despite a professed interest in 'concentrated bilateralism,' not only is Canada rarely at the top of the donors' list on a country-specific basis (the only consistent exception being Guyana), but in regional terms Canada has held back from making a concerted effort to establish 'a true zone of influence in which it could wield decisive power over the development policy goals of the countries it provides with aid.' What is more, this problem of diffusion goes well beyond being one of whether or not Canada can play an influential role in shaping the policies of recipient countries. As Thérien notes, the pattern of the disbursement of Canadian development assistance is such that this thin dispersion may pose over time an obstacle to effective co-ordination between Canada and other donors.[48]

## The Economic Motivation

Consistent with the economic impulse, the other significant motivation for the promotion of international development assistance was the boost this activity gave to Canadian export trade. Commercial priorities, directed towards facilitating the countries of the South to become better customers for Canadian goods and services, existed below the surface through the Pearson years. A combination of the Trudeau government's desire to pursue the 'national interest' through more tangible means, persistent pressure from the Canadian Export Association and other business groups,[49] and the onset of tough economic times allowed this economic motivation to come into full view by the late 1970s. Although debate persists in the literature about the extent to which business considerations have become Canada's 'primary' interest in development assistance,[50] there is little doubt that (in accordance with the organizational changes noted above) these economic concerns have become fully integrated into CIDA's policymaking process. The clearest manifestation of this integrative dynamic has been CIDA's attachment to the concept of tied aid, by which development assistance is linked to the supply of a certain proportion of Canadian products.

This mixing of international development assistance and domestic economic interests has remained a source of considerable stress and controversy. For a variety of commentators, this mixture is taken to be a recipe for inefficiency. Mainstream economists, in Canada as elsewhere, have long been critical of foreign aid in principle. As Reuber commented in 1970: 'Foreign aid almost certainly makes Canada worse off rather than better off economically, in the long run and in the short.'[51] The move towards an institutionalized form of 'tied aid' was, for these economists, even worse. These practices 'compromised' the development criteria on which aid had traditionally rested, substituting in their place a complex system of subsidization.[52] An examination conducted by the Export Development Corporation in the early 1980s concluded that the benefits of this system were 'by no means clear' in producing a positive spin-off in terms of job creation.[53] Development economists with more radical leanings took up the same theme from a different slant: 'The tying of aid to procurement in the donor country reduces its direct value to the recipient, raises administrative costs, and slows disbursements. Worse still, it biases techniques in favour of imported inputs and technologies, distorts overall priorities and makes it extremely difficult to employ aid for direct poverty-alleviating projects, particularly in rural areas.'[54]

To this range of intellectual criticism have been added the voices of complaint of both populist and technical/practitioner hues. In the Trudeau years, most of the vitriol with which populist elements had attacked development assistance was generated by the issue of whom this aid was targeted towards. Critics on the extreme right-wing fringe of Canadian politics placed the projects directed towards Tanzania (whose leader, Julius Nyerere, enjoyed a close relationship with Trudeau) in an especially negative light. But this brand of extremist critic also reserved some harsh words for the way development assistance was given out. Fromm and Hull, for example, pointed to the way the Canadian taxpayer had 'to dole out money' for Canadian firms bidding on development assistance contracts.[55]

More technically sophisticated and experienced analysts who examined the evolution of the practices of Canadian development assistance also found evidence that waste and mismanagement had become built into the tying of aid. After scrutinizing Canadian aid policies, programs and performance, through an in-depth assessment of case-studies from Tanzania, Bangladesh, Haiti and Senegal, researchers with the North–South Institute subjected the defects in this system to particular critical attention. In the field, these researchers proffered detailed snapshots of how tied aid had proved to be deficient. The best-known of these illustrative examples was the case of the Tanzanian bakery—the 'grossly overpriced' equipment for this project being supplied without competitive tender and without due consideration to local conditions.[56] At headquarters in Ottawa, they contended that this system created a built-in bias towards certain types of programs: 'What often transpires as a result of these policies governing procurement is that the recipient countries request Canadian assistance for infrastructure and food aid knowing that this is what Canada is prepared to finance. It should not be surprising that the government then interprets these requests as being reflective of the recipients' needs.'[57]

The system of tied aid had the additional effect of tilting the balance between the multilateral and bilateral dimension in Canadian development assistance. Through its evolutionary process, the proportion of Canadian development assistance allocated via multilateral agencies has dropped noticeably (from 40 percent in the late 1970s to 32.2 percent in 1988–89).[58] To be sure, this shift meshed with an efficiency perspective, in that the effectiveness of using multilateral institutions (including the regional banks) as delivery mechanisms has become a matter of growing doubt. The motivation behind this tilt, however, appears to have had more to do with national control than international efficiency. Bilateral mechanisms offered a greater degree of influence at the national level over the process of delivery. The fact that Canadian firms had a mediocre record in getting contracts for multilateral projects reinforced this shift.

## REASSESSING THE PURPOSE

### Changes to Development Assistance during the Mulroney Years

Two issues must be addressed to get a handle on why the international development agenda was recalibrated through the 1980s. The first issue relates to what has been termed 'aid fatigue.' In Canada, this question is associated with a decline in governmental capacity, having to do with a host of problems surrounding 'overload,' the national deficit, and declining financial and institutional capabilities. Bluntly put, the resources the Canadian government was prepared to allocate to development assistance were no longer up to the tasks anticipated for the future. An atmosphere of having to work with less, begun in the late 1970s with the budgetary reductions introduced by the Trudeau government, hung heavy during the Mulroney years. The fact that the threats were worse than the actual bite of reduction—at least prior to the 23.3 percent cuts (or about $1.8 billion) imposed in the April 1989 budget—offered little in the way of compensation.[59] A reformist attitude—that development had to be done differently—began to grow.

Private activity did much to fill some of the vacuum left by government. This substitution was particularly evident in terms of famine relief, as witnessed most notably during the Ethiopian crisis of 1984 and 1985. Galvanized by television images of the catastrophe, the Canadian public responded *en masse*. While established NGOs, such as Inter Pares, Oxfam Canada, Care Canada and the Canadian University Services Overseas, played an important role, one of the distinctive features of this campaign was the high degree of mobilization of ad hoc groupings, such as the Ethiopian Airlift and the Ethiopian Famine Relief Fund. Another was the scope of this type of activity, which ranged from high-profile campaigns by popular performers to create a 'Northern Lights' trust fund to widespread grass roots endeavours. These public campaigns, in turn, prompted the Canadian government to do more in terms of its own efforts. Less than a year after the government had rejected a proposal for a massive relief operation as being unnecessary, a special fund for Africa was initiated, and an emergency co-ordinator of African relief was appointed. As Joe Clark admitted, 'Governments, particularly democratic governments, are affected by public priorities.'[60]

The second issue in the changing agenda for international development is the question of structural adjustment. In the aid-recipient countries, this issue is causally linked with the serious structural decline in economic conditions through the 1970s and 1980s, prompted by the devastating combination of oil shocks, inflation and soaring interest rates, intensifying global economic competition, neo-mercantilism and the 'new' protectionism in the North, and the debt crisis. The main effect was to spawn a variation of the double movement in discourse/action: strong forces located in international financial institutions pushed for a release of the creativity in market forces, and a counter-mobilization wanted to pull back towards a renewal of civil society. The first movement pointed towards an ambitious (and often extremely onerous) process of restructuring, to encourage investment, competition and access to markets. As part of the drive to implement this strategy, external leverage was applied to the macroeconomic policies of the individual countries. The second movement pointed towards a process of decentralization, with an emphasis on equity and self-help. The primary policy focus was on strengthening institutions, democratic development and dealing with the problems of poverty.

In some ways, the Mulroney government bought heavily into the idea of structural adjustment. Without the personal exposure to North–South issues (except in a narrowly defined business context) that Pearson and Trudeau possessed, Prime Minister Mulroney looked at development assistance through a very different lens—when he looked at this sphere of activity at all. In the absence of sustained leadership at the apex of the political system, the main process of rethinking on development assistance took place at the bureaucratic level. The reappointment in September 1989 of Marcel Massé as the president of CIDA was the most visible sign of this process. As the Canadian representative at the IMF, Massé had been identified with a number of specific structural adjustment programs (including the program for Guyana, on which Canada had taken the lead). In declaratory terms, Massé stressed the relevance of structural adjustment to Canadian development assistance. In an address he made shortly after taking up his new position, Massé asserted: 'CIDA has taken the leap of faith and plunged into the unchartered seas of structural adjustment.... Structural adjustment figures among the priorities for Canadian development assistance.'[61]

It would be misleading to say that the Mulroney government neglected the decentralization and civil society component of the emergent policy agenda. If interested in placing a greater onus on competition, the Mulroney government also allowed space for both CIDA and Canadian NGOs to explore new ideas on what has come to be called global governance issues. As traced concisely by Allison Van Rooy in a recent monograph,[62] these issues marched forward in prominence through the Mulroney years. Signposting the flow of this intellectual current were the official reports produced during this time. A major thrust of the Commons Standing Committee's report *For Whose Benefit?* was the advocacy of a switch from the traditional large-scale capital/infrastructural bias of developmental assistance over to programs designed to create human resource development; and from short-term project building to the building of long-term relationships.[63] The government's reply, through the 1987 *Sharing Our Future* document, concurred with this basic shift in orientation, offering support for a people-directed approach.[64] By 1991, CIDA had officially embraced the principle of 'sustainable development,' a concept revised by the end of the Conservatives' term of office to include 'sustainable human development.'[65]

In the course of this journey of adaptation, a different sort of partnership was forged between CIDA and the development NGO community. Guided by a desire to decentralize responsibility over development assistance, more operational authority was accorded to societal actors. In part, this move could be construed as making a virtue of necessity. As Massé most clearly recognized, many of the new limits on government were imposed because the resources available in the past were no longer there. To adjust, government had to reduce the scope of its ambition, especially 'as an implementer of programs,' and be content to 'play a more strategic role,' one that tackles complex issues by 'enlisting and drawing on other forces in a society.' Thus, the role of the state will shift from being a 'doer' to being a coordinator, a persuader, and a builder of consensus, in...drawing up the broad lines of policy and bringing together alliances who have the ability to get things done.'[66]

This type of offloading had some ideological flavour to it, in the sense that an approach along these lines was perfectly consistent with an expansive move towards privatization advocated by the neo-conservative political ideas. A shift in this direction also could be justified on practical grounds: by moving responsibility downwards, many of the problems identified as being endemic in development assistance policies and programs (a top-heavy management structure, a concentration of personnel at headquarters, a lack of accountability, a complex management style) could be dealt with. Concomitantly, government could attempt to tap into the technical expertise and transnational networks already established by a good many NGOs. As Monique Landry, the Conservative minister for international development, stated, international non-governmental organizations 'tend to be at their best in the areas where bureaucracies of all kinds—national governments, international organizations, and multinational corporations too, for that matter— are at their worst: in breaking new ground by coming to grips with neglected and sensitive social issues.... International citizens par excellence. Like no one else, they combine a grassroots reach with a global span.'[67]

More cynically, one can see this move towards decentralization as part of a wider governmental strategy to 'buy support' (or at least 'buy peace') from NGOs in a period of considerable state–societal tension. If prepared to dive into the deep unknown on issues extending from free trade to constitutional change, the Mulroney government showed that it favoured backing off from some other risky endeavours. The backlash of the 'grey lobby' on indexation (with the cries that the Conservatives were breaking a 'sacred trust') provides just one illustration of this instinct for caution in the domestic social policy domain.[68]

All of this being said, the Conservative government showed a willingness to put some considerable amount of money where its mouth was. Funding was increasingly channelled through NGOs, not just for famine relief (the high-water mark of this form of partnership was reached in 1985 with the establishment of a 3:1 matching formula for funding) but more comprehensively. While difficult to pin down with complete accuracy, it is clear that the Conservatives showed some extensive generosity—if not in the absolute amount given to development assistance, then at least in the relative amount it apportioned directly through NGOs. By one set of calculations, done by the Canadian Council for International Co-operation: 'Funding to NGOs increased steadily throughout the 1980s and 1990s, reaching a peak in 1992/93, when Canadian NGOs received a total of $310 million for their international programs from CIDA.'[69]

## The Ongoing Debates

### The Relationship between Government and NGOs

Despite (or because of) these efforts, the debates over development policies and programs proliferated rather than dissipated. One of the major sources of controversy proved to be the fragile basis of the government–NGO relationship itself.

While many development NGOs were ready and willing to use the space (and monies) offered them by government, there remained a deep-seated wariness about the embrace of government. In part this attitude stems from frustrations about the actual mechanisms of consultation, and the true nature of the 'partnership.' This type of dilemma reflected both ongoing suspicions about being managed (or co-opted) by government and practical concerns about impediments to their activities.

There were also concerns about the fickleness of governmental activity on development assistance. At one level, there were constant concerns about political/partisan interference on a tactical basis.[70] At another level, broader strategic concerns continued to intrude. Not long after the Conservatives moved in 1988 and 1989 to implement some of the proposals taken from *For Whose Benefit?* and *Sharing Our Future* with respect to the decentralization of program delivery, a reversal took place. The reform process entailed in shaking up the managerial structure of CIDA—and especially the move to put more people in the field— proved to be both expensive in terms of administration costs and not as efficient as it was hoped. Acting on these different concerns, a strategic management review was struck.[71] This supplementary review tried to revise the form of partnership between CIDA and NGOs, privileging selected principal NGOs as 'stakeholders' with a considerable range to design and execute programs themselves. The plus for the NGOs included in this chosen category was that the space accorded them to operate would expand still further; CIDA, on the basis of these recommendations, would limit its direct management over projects, concentrating its attention on policy. The drawback was that these changes opened up the possibility of new forms of internal competition (intensified by the fact that the smaller NGOs would lose their direct link to CIDA). The emphasis was on tactical innovation, not on strategic co-ordination and priority making.[72]

The fragile nature of the government–NGO relationship was intensified by the polarized composition of the development NGO community. On one side, there existed a small group of NGOs that had taken on a professional and transnational form; these groups included Care Canada and Oxfam Canada. On the other side, there existed the bulk of the development NGO community. As detailed in the 1988 study for the North–South Institute by Brodhead, Herbert-Copley and Lambert, *Bridges of Hope*, this latter group remained small and financially weak: 36 percent had budgets of less than $250,000, and fully 60 percent had budgets less than $1 million. The NGO community had grown rapidly but consisted mostly of small non-religious organizations (72 percent were secular, but there was a great deal of inter-church activity and coalition work), with tiny staffs dependent on a volunteer base.[73] A second study, done in 1991 by Ian Smillie for the Canadian Council for International Co-operation (CCIC), confirmed many of these earlier findings. Smillie reported: 'On a per capita basis, Canada has 4.4 times more NGOs than Britain, and yet all Canadian NGOs combined raise less money from the public than Oxfam UK and Save the Children Fund alone.'[74] Significantly, the government was found to have made up the shortfall, creating an 'imbalance between public and governmental support for the voluntary sector [that] is striking, and is far higher than in most other OECD member countries.'[75]

This image of fragility was compounded further by the mounting presence of a number of other features. One of these was the whiff of organizational uncertainty around many of the development NGOs. Some organizations, most notably the World University Services of Canada in the early 1990s, were forced to go through an extensive process of reorganization in terms of their management and operations, aimed at insuring their long-term survival. Other organizations, such as Oxfam Quebec, had serious problems stemming from the financial management practices of some of their officials. Still others, such as Care Canada on Somalia, faced media criticism of their work in delivering aid in specific situations—criticisms that often downplayed the difficult conditions in which these operations were performed or the countless lives saved.

Another element that should not be overlooked is the diversity of cultures and modes of operation within the development NGO community.[76] An organization like World Vision Canada, with its massive fund-raising/direct mail campaigns featuring graphic descriptions of poverty and human misery, had a very distinctive (and visible) way of operating. A variety of other groups also had distinctive profiles and styles, including the Canadian Council of Churches, the Catholic Organization For Development and Peace, the Mennonite Central Committee, the YMCA, the Salvation Army, Lutheran World Relief and Match International (a women's organization committed to working with sister organizations in the South for a feminist vision of development). This diversity added immensely to the variety of NGO activity, with an attendant range of expertise and use of media. This same diversity, nonetheless, made joint appeals and co-ordination quite difficult.

### The Targets of Canadian Development Assistance

A second source of controversy was the direction of dispersal of development assistance. With the budget cuts, in the 1980s especially, came a pronounced choice about the hierarchy of the countries to receive Canadian development assistance. Downgraded were the poorest countries; upgraded by the same measure were the NICs. On efficiency grounds alone, given the Canadian pattern of distribution, some move towards a concentration of targeting could be justified.[77] By spreading this activity so thinly—between approximately 140 countries—some dilution in impact had inevitably taken place. What could be objected to in the choice was the lack of equity and balance. By giving preferential treatment to the group of countries with rapidly expanding markets, the Canadian government belied the language contained in *For Whose Benefit?* and *Sharing Our Future*, which emphasized the need to address the problems of the poorest people of the world together with the goal of stimulating international trade and Canada's own economic prospects.

By the accentuated commercialization of development assistance, moreover, the fragility of the development NGOs' own relationship with CIDA was underscored. This relationship had never been an exclusive one, in that the Canadian business community had built up their own extensive set of ties with CIDA. This parallel partnership between the private sector and CIDA had been facilitated by the expansion of CIDA–INC, the Industrial Cooperation Program, and by the establishment of a CIDA liaison committee. At the sectoral level, a number of specialized partnerships had also been cemented. Appearing before a parliamentary committee in 1992, for example, the Association of Consulting Engineers enthused about the satisfactory way in which the Industrial Cooperation Program was going and its ability to take advantage of a new development fund that would allow the private sector to plan, design and deliver activities on its own.[78] The NGO community also faced pressure from business interests to make a commitment to new types of partnerships, by which an integrated Canadian group (with a consortia made up of Canadian NGOs, consultants and manufacturers) would design and deliver projects.

The geographic bias of the new targeting approach was quite evident. By the latter stages of the Conservatives' reign, parts of Sub-Saharan Africa faced increasing neglect. The impact of the cuts to development assistance imposed in 1992–93 were felt most heavily in East Africa.[79] Indeed, when Prime Minister Campbell addressed the UN General Assembly, many African delegates walked out in protest. By way of contrast, Asia became the focal point for a number of upgraded initiatives.[80] The CIDA Regional Program was an especially important vehicle for using aid programs as a tool for achieving an improved presence in the markets of those middle-income countries of interest to Canadian firms.

This geographic distribution was made still more complicated, after the political convulsions of the late 1980s, by the claims of the former Communist countries for funding with respect to their economic transition. These new types of demands were instrumental in pushing the Conservative government towards making clearer (and tougher) choices between recipients. To keep up with the new demands in East Africa was hard enough, given the added pressure on various components of the development assistance budget brought about by the Somali crisis. At the same time, though, Canadian officials were under intense political pressure to win a heightened Canadian presence in Central and Eastern Europe. This differential treatment became a standard feature of Canadian policy. While deep cuts were again imposed on official development assistance in 1993–94, for example, a number of new programs directed towards the reconstruction of the CEE/former Soviet Union came on stream.[81]

### The Struggle between CIDA and DFAIT

A third source of controversy stemmed from the question of which bureaucratic entity was to be in command over Canadian development assistance. The two contenders in this long-running grudge match were CIDA and DEA/EAITC/DFAIT.

The description given by Nossal to this pair of rivals, as an 'ill-matched team of horses,' remained perfectly apt.[82] The only difference was the way in which these contenders were bound together. The institutional confidence of CIDA had expanded enormously in the late 1980s and 1990s with respect to interdepartmental politics.[83] Breaking free from its traditional role as an 'executing' agency, CIDA had become a policymaking instrument with enhanced status and an extensive domain of interests.[84] Its championing of the cause of 'global governance,' in particular, had allowed CIDA to expand its space and capacity in decision making beyond the traditional development assistance dossier, to encompass a wider spectrum of issues including the environment, women in development, structural adjustment, and human rights and democratic governance.

Some of these organizational ambitions were held in check by the erosion in some aspects of CIDA's institutional autonomy *vis-à-vis* External/Foreign Affairs. Firstly, ministerial oversight of CIDA in the Mulroney years had been given to the minister of external relations (Monique Vézina from 1984 to 1986, and Monique Landry thereafter). Secondly, an increasing amount of CIDA's budget was administered for it by External/Foreign Affairs.[85] Thirdly, External/Foreign Affairs doggedly tried to maintain its position as the driver of the team.

These bureaucratic tensions bubbled to the surface on repeated occasions throughout the 1980s. Massé openly resisted the move on the part of External/Foreign Affairs to exercise supervision over CIDA, pushing instead for the agency to be treated as a major player alongside External/Foreign Affairs. Jocelyne Bourgon, Massé's successor as president of CIDA, continued to do the same thing. As she argued before a parliamentary committee: 'We are operating within a context which is normally defined by the foreign policy. Aid policy is a subset....we should make sure that we have the maximum possible impact with the instruments we have....there is interdependence and linkages between instruments that are not in the hands of CIDA, whether it is trade, defence, investment or banking. Maybe it's about time we start focusing on the interdependence of policy instruments and agencies.... It would be my hope that CIDA, in the grouping of departments and agencies, could become the undisputed leader and the centre of expertise when it comes to the developing countries and the development tools and instruments.'[86]

### The Controversy over Conditionality

A fourth source of controversy has emerged over the question of conditionality on development assistance. As alluded to in an earlier discussion, the human rights NGOs regarded the application of this linkage concept with some ambivalence. On the one hand, they could rejoice at the higher visibility that Prime Minister Mulroney gave to human rights concerns and their relationship to development assistance through the Commonwealth (the October 1991 Harare Commonwealth Heads of Government Meeting) and La Francophonie (the November 1991 Chaillot summit). On the other hand, they had considerable reservations about the use of conditionality in either a blunt and punitive or a subjective and ad hoc manner. Nor, it was argued by these societal groups, could strict guidelines be drawn up when human rights were so multidimensional (including individual and collective rights, social-cultural, political and democratic rights); different from case to case; and so difficult to assess by means of charts or report cards. What the human rights NGOs wanted was consistency, where conditionality would not be treated as 'a card to be played or held back as an advantage in a wider game.'[87]

Scepticism about the appropriateness of conditionality ran even deeper among the development NGOs. One of the recommendations of *Sharing Our Future* was that Canadian aid should be curtailed when there was evidence of 'systematic, gross and continuous' violations of human rights. No firm consensus existed, however, among development NGOs about what kind of response should be made by Canada when a developing country was perceived to be guilty of serious human rights violations. Some groups were sympathetic to tough action on an official, bilateral basis, so long as these actions did not penalize civil society in those countries. Indeed, the argument was frequently made that if Canada did cut off development assistance through official channels, then NGOs should be used to identify how that assistance could be rechannelled so that the government, as opposed to the people, would be punished. Other groups were completely wary of conditionality. One argument that hung over this entire debate was that the concept of conditionality could be used as an excuse to reduce the overall development assistance budget. Reductions in the flow of aid to a targeted country would, from this perspective, not release funds to other recipients but be deployed as a means to reduce the aggregate level of aid. Another argument was that conditionality between human rights and aid fed into the agenda of structural adjustment. Opening the door to conditionality on a national basis, some development NGOs contended, would provide added momentum to the international strategy of tying aid to a country's acceptance of an IMF-imposed structural adjustment program.

At the very least, development NGOs wanted transparency. Any decision on conditionality, accordingly, should be made only after an extensive consultative review with societal groups. The question of linkage between human rights and development was too sensitive to be left to government alone. As one NGO representative said: 'we believe that Cabinet should not be the only body to determine which countries respect human rights and which do not. The whole matter becomes too political. We think the issue is much broader, and that as part of its human rights policy, the Canadian government should have broader instruments at its disposal.'[88] Tim Brodhead, speaking for the Canadian Council on International Cooperation, echoed this sentiment: 'there has to be a forum where we can have this debate. Otherwise, it happens in the corridors, it happens in Cabinet, and nobody knows precisely what the criteria are or why this country was included, another one excluded.'[89]

## RENEWING THE SENSE OF PURPOSE IN THE CHRÉTIEN YEARS?

One of the key foreign policy aims of the Chrétien Liberals was to try to distance themselves from the Mulroney government on development assistance. This exercise centred, in large part, on an attempt to recover some of the original sense of purpose associated with this sphere of activity. The main gesture towards this sentiment was the promise in the February 1995 governmental statement on foreign policy, *Canada in the World*, that 25 percent of the ODA budget would be targeted towards 'basic human needs.' Under this definition was included primary health care, basic education, family planning and reproductive health care, nutrition, water and sanitation, and shelter.[90] Such an approach built on to the agenda of social and environmental sustainability, as applied through Women In Development and a variety of other programs pursued by CIDA for over a decade. Qualitatively, what was different was the shift in emphasis to an expanded 'human-centred' or 'people-centred' form of activity.[91] Moving beyond the confines of 'human resource development' and 'poverty alleviation,' the focus was directed towards a comprehensive strategy of social development. Quantitatively, what was different was the size of the budgetary commitment contained in this promise. Having lagged behind on basic human needs, a financial contribution on this scale allowed Canada an opportunity to catch up in the way of creative programs. As O'Neil and Clark noted in a chapter in the 1992–93 *Canada Among Nations*: 'One important way of targeting the poorest is through support for the social sector, specifically primary health care and basic education (especially if this support is even more specifically targeted at women, who make up the majority of the world's poor).... [The UNDP's Development Report 1991] argues convincingly that most donor countries have neglected the social sectors.... Canada's performance is worse than most. In 1989 only 20 percent of Canada's ODA budget went to the health and education sectors. An even more critical aspect was that only 25 percent of this aid went to primary health care, basic education and water and sanitation. Thus only 5 percent of Canada's ODA reaches these sectors which specifically concern the poorest. Clearly there is room for restructuring and redirecting Canada's aid budget.'[92]

Concurrently, as 'basic human needs' and social development were given pride of place, the Liberals worked hard to alter the tone of discourse/action affecting a number of the other controversies that had dominated the Mulroney years. The Liberal government's fulfillment of its Red Book promise to organize a National Forum on Canada's International Relations, together with establishment of the Special Joint Committee Reviewing Canadian Foreign Policy, were particularly valuable devices for giving the impression of 'openness' in the way of foreign policy making. Whatever goodwill the Conservatives had derived from the application of the CIDA–development NGOs 'partnership' schemes had been thoroughly dissipated by the time of their defeat in the autumn of 1993. The successive cuts inflicted on the development assistance budget by the

Conservatives were bad enough. The 'stealth' with which the selective cuts, beginning with the 10 percent cut imposed by the December 1992 economic statement, were implemented—punctuated by the infighting between DFAIT and CIDA, and a good deal of delay in announcing the full list of cuts on a country by country basis—eroded the state–societal relationship still further.[93] One foreign policy columnist described the decision-making process utilized by the Conservatives as 'a review of aid policy that has been both clandestine and timid. It proceeds by surreptitious memos and secret meetings, leaving only tittle-tattle and rumour as clues to its progress.... Hence the leaks. CIDA people and NGOs, outraged by the [proposed cuts and a policy of concentration], moved to stop the process by exposing the process.'[94] Having failed in their attempt to make their voices heard during this stage of Conservative government, the development NGOs welcomed the opportunity to participate in the extensive 'dialogue' and 'consultation' allowed under the Liberal review process. A good many of the 277 NGOs submitting briefs to the joint committee came from development NGOs. A significant number of individuals associated with the NGO development community also participated at the National Forum on Canada's International Relations, held in Ottawa on 21 and 22 March 1994.

The Liberals also attempted to alter the focus of the policy debates about structural adjustment and conditionality. On structural adjustment, the main concern of the Liberals was to soften the texture of the debate. Any structural adjustment programs initiated by the World Bank or the IMF, Liberal ministers constantly intoned, should be extremely sensitive in their design and implementation to mitigate the social costs of the reform process. The specific conditions of each country should be taken into account, with due consideration given to the protection of social programs and to investment in human development directed towards the most vulnerable groups in society. This theme of contextual awareness is especially strong in the declaratory statements of Christine Stewart, the secretary of state for Africa and Latin America: 'The structural adjustment programs are necessary in many countries in the world, but I think [they] were put in place...with a very narrow vision that did not contemplate or include the very negative socio-economic repercussions that we saw.'[95]

On conditionality, the Chrétien government has made a concerted effort to redirect attention away from the larger debates about linkage to human rights and good governance that dominated political debate in the Mulroney years. Trying to find some form of lowest common denominator, the Liberals concentrated instead on locating specific policy components by which Canada could find both international favour and domestic popularity. This search for specialized areas of interest was reflected, for example, in Canada's initiative on an aid–arms spending linkage. Entrepreneurially, Canada devoted some considerable time and resources to mobilizing a coalition on the basis of the idea that there should be a foreign aid reduction imposed on those regimes that spent above a certain percentage of GNP on military expenditure. Facing a negative reception from the major powers—a group of countries that accounted for the bulk of international arms sales—Canada concentrated on building a new coalition of the 'like-minded,' including Japan, the Nordics, Australia and New Zealand.[96] Technically, at the same time as they acknowledged all of the difficulties attached to the establishment of 'hard and fast' guidelines, Canadian officials attempted to work out some more precise rules about how this type of conditionality could be operationalized. In the words of Louise Fréchette, whose own bureaucratic experience covered the United Nations, financial institutions and defence: 'Whether we can…have an actual numerical criterion [on the] military expenditure side, [by which] no country should spend more than x on defence, or the proportion of defence to social sector expenditures should be such—that is more difficult to define. But it is certainly something we, Canada, have been pressing in the World Bank. In particular, we think we should be looking at how to factor in these issues of military expenditure more directly.'[97]

As another element of this image-building exercise, the Chrétien government used development assistance to help remake its reputation as an effective manager of public policy. In terms of foreign policy, the Liberals tried to blend development policy and programs more comprehensively into its overall foreign policy agenda. Recasting the 'mixed motivations' theme in a fundamentally altered fashion, development assistance was referred to in *Canada in the World* as a 'vital instrument of Canadian foreign policy.' From this point of reference, the intrinsic merits of development assistance became subordinated to its contribution towards the larger goals of an 'integrated' foreign policy based on the three core objectives: namely, the manner in which 'it promotes prosperity and employment, protects global security and projects Canadian values and culture.'[98]

In terms of administrative behaviour, development assistance constituted a dossier in which the Chrétien government had a great incentive to demonstrate its talent for operational efficiency. The Liberals faced many of the same cross-cutting pressures confronted by the Mulroney and Campbell governments. One dilemma was the need to show that better development assistance could be delivered with fewer resources. Notwithstanding the Liberal Red Book's affirmation of 'Canada's will to help the world's poor,'[99] the Liberal government had little inclination (or, arguably, capacity) to throw more money at the problem. On the contrary, Paul Martin's February 1994 budget imposed a cut of another 15 percent to Canada's ODA. A second ongoing dilemma centred on the choice of recipients. The *Canada in the World* document revealed the extent of the studied ambiguity that continued to inform the debate about how many countries should be eligible for aid. While professing to favour a concentration on 'a limited number of countries,' the Liberal government provided ample space to deviate from this approach by confirming its commitment to offer 'programs in other countries through low-cost, administratively-simple delivery mechanisms.'[100] A third dilemma was the struggle to incorporate commercial objectives into a renewed system of development assistance. A core commitment to 'basic human needs' did not mean that the Liberals were prepared to jettison aid as an economic tool. Indeed, in some ways the Liberals were more forthright about their desire to mesh commercial goals with development assistance policies and programs. For one thing, *Canada in the World* emphasized the importance of an engagement by Canada in providing 'infrastructure services' for the South, a strategy that played directly into many of Canada's strengths in the provision of technical services. Akin to the debate over structural adjustment, nonetheless, an attempt was made to cushion this proposal with caveats to the effect that this activity should be undertaken only when both 'environmentally sound' and in accordance with the interests of 'poorer groups and capacity-building.'[101] As well, the recommendations of *Canada in the World* marked a decided shift in orientation towards the utilization of the 'private sector' and local entrepreneurs in the South as agents of development.

Integral to this process of renewal was a higher degree of control imposed on the work of the development NGOs within Canada. The blunt end of this control mechanism was a retreat from a variety of activities hitherto regarded as being in the mainstream of the development NGO–government partnership. One of the activities so affected was promotion of the work by international NGOs (INGOs). As part of the 1994 Martin budget, those groups without a Canadian base were excluded from funding through CIDA's Partnership Programs. Among the hardest hit of these INGOs was the International Planned Parenthood Federation, which lost its annual grant of approximately $8 million. Consistent with the 'basic human needs' approach, financial support for family planning and population education programs in poor countries would continue, but this support would be routed through multilateral and bilateral channels.[102] Similarly, CIDA's Public Participation Program and Youth Initiatives Program, together with the funding for separate educational programs about international development, were eliminated. As one NGO representative complained: 'We keep hearing from the government that we are being linked internationally in so many ways. Yet at the same time they are cutting one of the avenues for Canadians to understand these international links.'[103]

The sharp end of this control mechanism consisted of a number of steps intended to rationalize the administration of Canada's development assistance policies and programs. Part and parcel with the design of an 'integrated' foreign policy (in the drawing up of which CIDA had little input), some elements of DFAIT's supervisory powers over CIDA were tightened. All of CIDA's major policy and program decisions (with their funding requirements) had to be approved by DFAIT, with overall responsibility for CIDA firmly positioned in the hands of the minister of foreign affairs. DFAIT's own capacity to act as a 'lead' agency over global governance, furthermore, was given a boost by the creation of the Bureau for Global Issues as part of a new branch on Global Issues and Culture. The trade-off for CIDA was that its own operational responsibilities with respect to the implementation of this design were extended. Control over assistance operations to Central/Eastern Europe and the FSU were handed back from

DFAIT to CIDA.[104] Control over the commercially oriented development assistance programs (with particular reference to those under the mandate of CIDA-INC) was also retained by CIDA—despite calls by many participants and observers for a hiving off of these functions to DFAIT.[105]

The onus on CIDA was to embrace the agenda of managerial efficiency. CIDA attempted to tailor its approach towards this new shape in a variety of ways. Premised on the notion of heightened expectations about accountability at a time of reduced financial resources, CIDA moved to implement a 'results-based' mode of operation.[106] To begin with, CIDA worked to establish a system whereby the activities of NGOs would be evaluated on a formal set of 'measurement of results' criteria. Further, CIDA moved to adjust its basic partnership programs with Canadian development NGOs. In a new set of guidelines, CIDA reduced the autonomy of NGOs and other members of the voluntary sector to set their own priorities for activity as partners; CIDA itself was to identify exclusive areas of supported activity for this sector. As the vice-president of CIDA's Partnership Branch explained: 'We have to ensure that the majority of resources go toward the development objectives that the Canadian taxpayer feels he or she is paying for.'[107]

The response of the NGOs (or the larger voluntary sector) to this process of reform reflected the deepening divide within the development community.[108] One element among the development NGOs balked at any efforts to forge a closer relationship with government. This group included many of the smaller NGOs, which in any case were increasingly excluded from access to CIDA programs. Others were among the advocacy groups and/or grass roots organizations that had value-driven objections to a tighter and more directed partnership with the Canadian government. As a representative from one small agency, involved in development projects within Central America, bluntly declared through the media: 'Being beholden to CIDA is [not] the way to go.'[109]

From the perspective of these actors, the tenets of the post-World War II aid regime no longer seemed relevant. Instead of attempts at forging a renewed partnership, through the shoals of the controversies over structural adjustment, conditionality, global governance and long-term poverty reduction strategies, what was needed was a more or less complete break with the past. The primary concern here was the establishment of a different kind of common political project, based on an equitable relationship with civil society in the South. This shift would focus on themes such as capacity building with Southern NGOs, reciprocal obligations, mutual respect and shared learning. As a representative of Inter Pares stated: 'Partnership does not challenge existing relations or disparities...of power, resources or affluence. Partnership, based within disparity, can only work to maintain and increase the existing disparity and fundamental inequality between and among partners.'[110]

Another cross-section, made up primarily of the well-established NGOs, was willing to go some way along the path of a reform agenda based on managerial efficiency. This course of adaptation was conditioned in large part by the recognition by these NGOs of the need for a stable relationship (and core funding) with CIDA if they were to maintain their global networks and effective role in international development. In this process, this constituency had taken on the status of 'stakeholders' in the policymaking and delivery process. A certain nervousness remained, however, about perceptual distortions arising from this type of close working relationship. As Tim Brodhead, the executive director of the umbrella organization, the CCIC, had earlier warned: 'We are certainly stakeholders in CIDA, but we are not simply potential executing agencies for government programs. NGOs see themselves as having an autonomous mission, in some cases long predating the existence of CIDA. In most cases their programs and activities are based very fundamentally on their own sense of mission, a mandate given to them by their own boards and by their own support base within the Canadian community.'[111]

This constituency had embarked on a number of initiatives of their own to improve the professionalism of development NGOs. A start in this direction came with the publication of the 1991 CCIC document 'A Time to Build Up: New Forms of Cooperation between NGOs and CIDA,' which highlighted the need for an alternative relationship between NGOs and government. This new deal was premised on a quid pro quo between a long-term financial commitment by government and an NGO code of ethics, better training and structure of management and programs, and a standard for advertisement. A follow-up study looked more closely at this type of quid pro quo via an examination of a series of questions relating to the effectiveness, accountability and legitimacy of voluntary organizations in the development sphere; special attention was devoted to the means by which the retention of a distinctive character by these organizations could be balanced with the need for collaboration with government, and the way in which the organizations could be restructured to meet new challenges in a context of diminished resources. As the CCIC concluded: 'Questions of accountability are going to increase if 1/ relative cuts to ODA place more pressure on NGOs as service deliverers on behalf of official donors, and 2/ international NGOs and the UN are successful in convincing bilateral and multilateral aid programs to invest more in basic human needs programming. CIDA is not positioned and does not have the independent capacity to deliver this kind of programming itself. If the NGOs are expected to play a more prominent role, what kind of accountabilities will follow? A critical mechanism for promoting accountability and learning is evaluation. Unfortunately it tends to be used by official donors as a method of control. Yet if learning is to take place, the financial threat that seems to accompany failure must be removed.'[112]

## CONCLUSION

In general terms, this detailed examination of Canada's approach to development assistance may be seen to fit well with the overall theme of this volume. An appreciation of the ingrained habits of Canadian statecraft must inform any sustained discussion about this sphere of activity. Development assistance has proven to be an issue-area where Canada has been able to display many of its skills in international politics. By its ability to go through stages of self-criticism and renewal, Canada has been able to show its tremendous capacity for reflection and innovation. Canada has constantly caught new waves of ideas about international development, which it has tried to factor into its own policies and programs. Some of these notions can be critiqued as faddism or clever wordplay, but this intellectual agility has allowed Canada to keep up a sense of public purpose about international development even as the focal point changed from aid, to development assistance, to the multifaceted agenda of global governance and beyond. Domestically, the time and resources devoted to building a co-operative governmental–NGO relationship on the development agenda reinforced the impression of a country inculcated with the skills of consensual decision-making. The fact that this co-operative relationship was often marred by tensions, if revealing the limitations of 'partnership,' also demonstrated the room for mobilization and dissent that Canadian societal activists retained.

Reputationally, the development issue has proven to be both a plus and a minus for Canada. From the positive side, development assistance stands out as an activity that showcased Canada's capacity for 'good international citizenship.' As Thérien points out, at least up to the early 1990s, Canada's overall profile on development assistance, based on the criteria of volume as a percentage of GNP and multilateral aid as a proportion of aid, located Canada exactly between the G-7 countries and the 'like-minded' countries. A similar picture of Canada's international standing emerges with respect to the Canadian approach to structural adjustment.[113] From the negative side, Canada has been stigmatized as a country that has continually compromised its international sense of commitment by subordinating welfarism to a variety of other goals.

Whatever the flaws in its basic design, however, the mixed motivations shaping Canada's approach to development assistance have not been a completely negative asset. True, the foundations of this activity have begun to be shaken at the edges by the scattering of purpose. No longer is there the clear vision, or the unqualified support among opinion-leaders, that development assistance enjoyed in the past. Moreover, the dynamic of constant reconstruction has taken its toll on the core supporters of this sphere of activity. Still, if the sheer number of forces—international welfarism, commercial interests and diplomatic standing—behind Canadian development assistance have proven to be a curse in militating against policy and programmatic coherence, this same multiplicity of purpose may also serve as a blessing. With so many facets of Canada's unique blend of constructive internationalism at play, the complete dislodging of development assistance as a symbolic and instrumental pillar of Canadian foreign policy will prove difficult. Development assistance, in the near future as in the past, will continue to be reshaped and expanded, in form if not in expenditure.

# NOTES

1   Parliament of Canada, Special Joint Committee of the Senate and the House of Commons on Canada's International Relations, *Independence and Internationalism* (Ottawa: June 1986), 88.

2   Keith Spicer, *A Samaritan State? External Aid in Canada's Foreign Policy* (Toronto: University of Toronto Press, 1966).

3   J.L. Granatstein, 'Peacekeeping: did Canada make a difference? And what difference did peacekeeping make to Canada?' in John English and Norman Hillmer, eds., *Making a Difference: Canada's Foreign Policy in a Changing World Order* (Toronto: Lester, 1992), 223–4.

4   Quoted in Spicer, *A Samaritan State?*, 10.

5   Mitchell Sharp, 'Canada's stake in international programmes,' in *Dialogue 1961*. Quoted in *ibid.*, 6.

6   Alain Noël and Jean-Philippe Thérien, 'From domestic to international justice: the welfare state and foreign aid,' *International Organization* 49, 3 (Summer 1995), 523–54.

7   Robert Carty, 'Going for gain: foreign aid and CIDA,' in R. Swift and R. Clarke, eds., *Ties That Bind: Canada and the Third World* (Toronto: Alger Press, 1981), 149–213.

8   Jean-Philippe Thérien, 'Canadian aid: a comparative analysis,' in Cranford Pratt ed., *Canadian International Development Assistance Policies: An Appraisal*, 2nd edn. (Montreal and Kingston: McGill–Queen's University Press, 1994), 315.

9   Tom F. Keating, *Canada and World Order: The Multilateralist Tradition in Canadian Foreign Policy* (Toronto: McClelland and Stewart, 1993), 130.

10  Quoted in Keith Spicer, 'Clubmanship upstaged: Canada's twenty years in the Colombo Plan,' *International Journal* XXV, 1 (Winter 1969–70), 25. On 'embedded liberalism,' see John Gerard Ruggie, 'International regimes, transactions, and change: embedded liberalism in the post-war economic order,' in Stephen Krasner ed., *International Regimes* (Ithaca, NY: Cornell University Press, 1983).

11  Spicer, *A Samaritan State?*, 246–7.

12  Keating, *Canada and World Order*, 126.

13  Escott Reid, 'Canada and the struggle against world poverty,' *International Journal* XXV, 1 (Winter 1969–70), 145–6.

14  Quoted in Spicer, 'Clubmanship upstaged,' 25–6.

15  Spicer, *A Samaritan State?*, 71.

16  *Ibid.*, 72–3.

17  Gerald K. Helleiner, 'Canada, the developing countries and the international economy: what next?' Working Paper No. B.5, Department of Economics, University of Toronto, September 1984.

18  On this 'mentor' role, see Michael Tucker, *Canadian Foreign Policy: Contemporary Issues and Themes* (Toronto: McGraw-Hill Ryerson, 1980), 234–6.

19  Carty, 'Going for gain,' quoted in Kim Richard Nossal, *The Politics of Canadian Foreign Policy* (Scarborough: Prentice Hall, 1989), 51.

20  Spicer, 'Clubmanship upstaged,' 31.

21  James Eayrs, 'Sunny side up,' *Weekend Magazine*, 17 December 1977, 4.

22  *Partners in Development* (New York: Praeger, 1969), 400.

23  J.L. Granatstein and Robert Bothwell, *Pirouette: Pierre Trudeau and Canadian Foreign Policy* (Toronto: University of Toronto Press, 1990), 286–7.

24  Jean-Philippe Thérien, 'Canadian aid: a comparative analysis,' in Cranford Pratt ed., *Canadian International Development Assistance Policies: An Appraisal*, 2nd edn. (Montreal and Kingston: McGill–Queen's University Press, 1994), 323–5.

25  Roy Culpeper and Andrew Clark, *High Stakes and Low Incomes: Canada and the Development Banks* (Ottawa: North–South Institute, 1994), 1.

26  Spicer, *A Samaritan State?*, 24.

27  Réal P. Lavergne, 'Determinants of Canadian aid policy: prepared for the Western middle powers and Global Poverty Project,' subproject on Aid Policy, Ottawa, 27 April 1987, 14.

28  *Ibid.*, 41.

29  Cranford Pratt, 'Dominant class theory and Canadian foreign policy: the case of the counter-consensus,' *International Journal* XXXIX, 1 (Winter 1983–4), 100.

30  Lavergne, 'Determinants, 42–4.'

31  SECOR group, Strategic Management Review Working Document (Study for the Canadian International Development Agency, October 1991). Quoted in Laura Macdonald, 'Unequal partnerships: the politics of Canada's relations with the Third World,' *Studies in Political Economy* 47 (Summer 1995), 125.

32  Philip Rawkins, 'An institutional analysis of CIDA,' in Cranford Pratt ed., *Canadian International Development Assistance Policies: An Appraisal*, 2nd edn. (Montreal and Kingston: McGill–Queen's University Press, 1994), 162.

33  Grant L. Reuber, 'The trade-offs among the objectives of Canadian foreign aid,' *International Journal* XXV, 1 (Winter 1969–70), 129.

34  Kim Richard Nossal, 'Mixed motives revisited: Canada's interests in development assistance,' *Canadian Journal of Political Science* 21, 1 (March 1988), 36.

35  Reuber, 'The trade-offs,' 129.

36  House of Commons, Standing Committee on External Affairs and International Trade, *For Whose Benefit?*, 1987.

37  *Ibid.*, 12.

38  G.K. Helleiner, 'The development business: next steps,' *International Journal* XXV, 1 (Winter 1969–70), 160.

39  Cranford Pratt, 'Canada: an eroding and limited internationalism,' in Pratt, *Internationalism Under Strain: The North–South Policies of Canada, the Netherlands, Norway, and Sweden* (Toronto: University of Toronto Press, 1989).

40  Brian Tomlinson, 'Development in the 1990s: critical reflections on Canada's economic relations with the Third World,' in Jamie Swift and Brian Tomlinson, eds., *Conflicts of Interest: Canada and the Third World* (Toronto: Between the Lines, 1991), 28.

41  *Ibid.*, 34. An early sign that CIDA felt the sting of these criticisms came with the publication of *Strategy for International Development Cooperation 1975–1980* (Ottawa: Information Canada, 1975).

42  Thérien, 'Canadian aid,' 319–20.

43  House of Commons, *For Whose Benefit?*, 7.

44  Lavergne, 'Determinants,' 4.

45  Nossal, 'Mixed motives revisited,' 52.

46  This image problem has been demonstrated not only on 'tours' of recipient countries by high-ranking Canadian officials, but in the day-to-day work of aid workers in the field.

47  Thérien, 'Canadian aid,' 323.

48  *Ibid.*, 325. From a partisan political perspective, Lucien Bouchard (when leader of the BQ) stated that a sovereign Quebec would concentrate its efforts on Africa: 'We should focus our aid to be more efficient in what we do. We are really spread thin all over the world with the dilution we have when we spread $2 billion over more than 100 countries and 1000 programs.' Quoted in Edward Greenspon, 'Canada can't sway China on rights, PM says,' *Globe and Mail*, 19 March 1994.

49  *Strengthening Canada Abroad* (or the 'Hatch Report'), the report of the Export Promotion Review Committee (Ottawa: Department of Industry, Trade and Commerce, 1979), powerfully represented these views. The main focal point for criticism of this report was CIDA's 'overly philanthropic giveaway approach to aid,' 11.

50  This contrast emerges in the interpretations offered by Pratt and Lavergne. See Lavergne, 'Determinants,' 25–6. It also provides the major point of difference between Carty and Smith and Nossal.

51  Reuber, 'The trade-offs,' 130.

52  *Ibid.*, 132.

53  A. Raynauld, J.M. Dufour and D. Racette, *Government Assistance in Export Financing* (Ottawa: Economic Council of Canada, 1983), 53, 60. Cited in David W. Gillies, 'Commerce over conscience? Export promotion in Canada's international development programme,' *International Journal* XLIV, 1 (Winter 1988–9), 119.

54  Helleiner, 'Canada, the developing countries and the international economy,' 5.

55  Paul Fromm and James P. Hull, *Down The Drain?: A critical re-examination of Canadian foreign aid* (Toronto: Griffin House, 1981), 9.

56  Roger Young, *Canadian Development Assistance to Tanzania* (Ottawa: North–South Institute, 1983), 5–11. See also Granatstein and Bothwell, *Pirouette*, 289.

57  Young, *Canadian Development Assistance to Tanzania*, 9.

58  Thérien, 'Canadian aid,' 320.

59  'The nervous nineties: uncertainties cloud decade for the third world,' *Review '89 Outlook '90* (Ottawa: North–South Institute, 1990).

60  Quoted in Andrew F. Cooper, Richard A. Higgott and Kim Richard Nossal, *Relocating Middle Powers: Australia and Canada in a Changing World Order* (Vancouver: University of British Columbia Press, 1993), 23.

61  Marcel Massé, 'Adjustment in perspective,' address to an international colloquium on Structural Adjustment and Social Realities in Africa, at the Institute for International Development and Cooperation, University of Ottawa, 17 November 1989, 4. Quoted in Robert E. Clarke, 'Overseas development assistance: the neo-conservative challenge,' in Maureen Appel Molot and Fen Osler Hampson, eds., *Canada Among Nations 1989: The Challenge of Choice* (Ottawa: Carleton University Press, 1990), 203. For a critical assessment of structural adjustment see, for example, Brian Murphy, 'The dice are loaded,' *Canadian Forum* LXIX (November 1990), 794.

62  Allison Van Rooy, *A Partial Promise? Canadian Support to Social Development in the South* (Ottawa: North–South Institute, 1995).

63  *Ibid.*, 4.

64  CIDA, *Sharing Our Future: Canadian International Development Assistance* (Hull: Supply and Services, 1987).

65  Van Rooy, *A Partial Promise?*, 5.

66  Marcel Massé, 'The future role and organization of government,' address to the Advanced Management Program, Canadian Centre For Management Development, Ottawa, 19 April 1991.

67  Notes for remarks by the Honourable Monique Landry, Minister for External Relations and International Development, to a forum of INGOs, 31 October 1991.

68  See, for example, David Bercuson, J.L. Granatstein and W.R. Young, *Sacred Trust: Brian Mulroney and the Conservative Party in Power* (Toronto: Doubleday, 1986).

69  CCIC, 'The role of the voluntary sector in Canadian ODA,' Draft For Discussion, October 1995, 12.

70  See Martin Rudner, 'Trade cum aid in Canada's official development assistance strategy,' in Brian W. Tomlin and Maureen Appel Molot, eds., *Canada Among Nations 1986: Talking Trade* (Toronto: James Lorimer, 1987); 'Canada's official development assistance strategy: process, goals and priorities,' *Canadian Journal of Development Studies* XII, 1 (1991), 9–38.

71  Cranford Pratt, 'Humane internationalism and Canadian development assistance policies,' in Pratt ed., *Canadian International Development Assistance Policies: An Appraisal*, 2nd edn. (Montreal and Kingston: McGill–Queen's University Press, 1994), 354–5.

72  *Ibid.*

73  Tim Brodhead, Brent Herbert-Copley and Anne-Marie Lambert, *Bridges of Hope? Canadian Voluntary Agenices and the Third World* (Ottawa: North–South Institute, 1988).

74  Ian Smillie, 'A time to build up: new forms of cooperation between NGOs and CIDA,' a study commissioned by the Canadian Council for International Co-operation, Ottawa, December 1991.

75  *Ibid.*, 7.

76  Jean-Philippe Thérien, 'Non-governmental organizations and international development assistance,' *Canadian Journal of Development Studies* XII, 2 (1991), 263–80.

77  The 1993 auditor general's report stated, for example, that 'CIDA's bilateral programs need to concentrate more on those countries and activities where there is the greatest potential.' *Report of the Auditor General of Canada to the House of Commons* (Ottawa: Supply and Services, 1993), 303.

78 Testimony to the House of Commons Standing Committee on External Affairs and International Trade, Sub-Committee on Development and Human Rights, *Minutes of Proceedings and Evidence*, 17 February 1992, 11:30.

79 See Michael Valpy, 'The aid that Canada will not be giving,' 'Figuring out how not to help the poor,' *Globe and Mail*, 4 and 5 February 1993; Jeff Sallot, 'The changing face of foreign aid,' *Globe and Mail*, 13 February 1993.

80 Martin Rudner, 'Canadian development assistance to Asia,' *Programs, Objectives and Future Foreign Policy Directions* 1, 3 (Fall 1993), 67–95.

81 See, for example, testimony to the House of Commons Standing Committee on Foreign Affairs and International Trade, *Minutes of Proceedings and Evidence*, 23 February 1995, 17:10.

82 Kim Richard Nossal, *The Politics of Canadian Foreign Policy* (Scarborough: Prentice Hall, 1989), 287.

83 Cranford Pratt, 'Canada's development assistance: some lessons from the latest review,' *International Journal* XLIX, 1 (Winter 1993–4), 109–11; Rawkins, 'An institutional analysis,' 173–82.

84 *Ibid.*, 111.

85 See testimony to the House of Commons Standing Committee on External Affairs and International Trade, Sub-Committee on Development and Human Rights, *Minutes of Proceedings and Evidence*, 27 May 1993, 42:20.

86 *Ibid.*, 27 May 1993, 42:18.

87 Testimony of Thérèse Bouchard, Assistant Executive Director, Peace and Development, to *ibid.*, 26 November 1992, 29:18.

88 Mme. Bouchard, testimony to *ibid.*, 9 December 1991, 9:15.

89 *Ibid.*, 17 February 1992, 11:46.

90 Canada, DFAIT, *Canada in the World: Government Statement* (Canada: Canada Communications Group, 1995), 40, 42.

91 Van Rooy, *A Partial Promise?*, 6.

92 Fen Osler Hampson and Christopher Maule, eds., *Canada Among Nations 1992-93: A New World Order?* (Ottawa: Carleton University Press, 1992), 225.

93 Betty Plewes, 'Preparing for the 21st century: why Canada needs a foreign policy review,' *Canadian Foreign Policy* I, 1 (Spring 1993), 107.

94 John Hay, 'Canadians should have a say in reshaping aid policy,' *Ottawa Citizen*, 7 February 1993.

95 Testimony to the House of Commons Standing Committee on Foreign Affairs and International Trade, *Minutes of Proceedings and Evidence*, 16 March 1994, 5:10.

96 Dave Todd, 'Ottawa eyes linking aid to foreign defence cost,' *Toronto Star*, 27 October 1994.

97 Louise Fréchette, testimony to the House of Commons Standing Committee on Foreign Affairs and International Trade, *Minutes of Proceedings and Evidence*, 22 February 1995, 16:61.

98 Canada, DFAIT, *Canada in the World*, 47.

99  *Creating Opportunity: The Liberal Plan for Canada* (Ottawa: Liberal Party of Canada, 1993), 108.

100  Canada, DFAIT, *Canada in the World*, 45.

101  *Ibid.*, 42.

102  Paul Knox, 'Canada chops aid-agency grant,' *Globe and Mail*, 4 April 1995.

103  Debbie Culbertson, Resource Co-ordinator, Ten Days for World Development. Quoted in *ibid.*

104  See Jeanne Kirk Laux, 'From South to East? Financing the transition in Central and Eastern Europe,' in Maureen Appel Molot and Harald von Riekhoff, eds., *Canada Among Nations 1994: A Part of the Peace* (Ottawa: Carleton University Press, 1994).

105  See, for example, Cranford Pratt, 'To ensure CIDA's humanitarian focus,' *Globe and Mail*, 28 October 1994.

106  See Canada, DFAIT, *Canada in the World*, 40, 42.

107  Quoted in Paul Knox and John Stackhouse, 'Aid agencies compelled to dance to Ottawa's tune,' *Globe and Mail*, 8 November 1995.

108  See, for example, North–South Institute, 'From friction to a fresh start: CIDA, the NGOs and foreign policy,' *Briefing paper 1994* - B37.

109  David Morley, Executive Director, Pueblito Canada, quoted in Paul Knox and John Stackhouse, 'Aid agencies compelled to dance to Ottawa's tune,' *Globe and Mail*, 8 November 1995.

110  Brian Murphy, 'Towards the 21st century: reflections on the future of the Canadian NGOs,' Ottawa, October 1993, 9–10. Quoted in Laura Macdonald, 'Unequal partnerships: the politics of Canada's relations with the Third World,' *Studies in Political Economy* 47 (Summer 1995), 134–5.

111  Testimony to the House of Commons Standing Committee on External Affairs and International Trade, Sub-Committee on Development and Human Rights, *Minutes of Proceedings and Evidence*, 17 February 1992, 11:23.

112  CCIC, 'The role of the voluntary sector in Canadian ODA,' Draft for Discussion, October 1995, 13.

113  Thérien, 'Canadian aid,' 329–30.

# THE SEARCH FOR NEIGHBOURHOOD: CANADA'S PLACE IN THE WORLD

Canada is often said to be a regional power without a region. More accurately, Canada may be portrayed as a country without a clearly defined and comfortable neighbourhood to call its own. By the logic of geographical setting, Canada belongs firmly in North America. Canada's contiguity to the United States, in a continental domain, is highly salient to Canada's place in the world. The growth of a high degree of historical, political, economic and societal interaction lends credence to the view of North America as Canada's 'natural' region.[1] As a growing body of literature reminds us, however, it is important to distinguish between 'regionalism as description and regionalism as prescription.'[2] Canada's perception of regionalism remains highly 'politically contested.'[3] Any notion of being isolated with the United States in a narrowly defined neighbourhood, within North America, brings out much of Canada's fundamental ambivalence about where it fits or 'sits' in the global arena. Through its complex web of interdependence on a bilateral basis, Canada has enjoyed many benefits because of its close proximity to the United States. Yet serious reservations remain about the value Canada ought to place on this pattern of continental engagement. Canada fears entrapment with, as much as estrangement from, the US.

Canadian foreign policy, in all of its manifestations, reflects this dual set of contradictory impulses. On the one hand, Canada has been repeatedly drawn to the light of the power at the centre of the international system. This impulse has featured a search for a tighter form of connection with the US. On the other hand, the sense of vulnerability brought on by fears of being located in too close a relationship with its immediate neighbour has stimulated in Canada an interest in pursuing a strategy of diversification. This impulse has featured a search for alternative neighbourhoods, through a process of regional relocation away from the US and towards other spaces of activity.

# THE PUSH OF CONTINENTAL ENGAGEMENT

The question of Canada's spatial place in the world has long been a central theme in Canadian foreign policy. Throughout the immediate post-1945 era, though, an explicit expression of regionalism was avoided. When asked where Canada best fitted into the international system, the dominant answer was through the multi-lateral arena. In institutional terms, Canada identified most keenly with global (UN) or cross-regional (Commonwealth, La Francophonie, NATO) organizations. What feeling of regional consciousness had been instilled into Canadian policy-makers was more likely expressed through sentiments about the 'Atlantic Community,' sentiments not 'easily or unproblematically translated into concrete schemes for regional cooperation.'[4] From a middle power perspective, any form of 'excessive' regionalism presented a negative and debilitating challenge to Canada's traditional mode of statecraft. Such an approach had the potential of cutting into Canada's comparative advantage in several ways. To begin with, regionalization might compromise Canada's range of choice with respect to functional behaviour. Specifically, an enhanced regional orientation might diminish Canada's role as a 'go-between' or 'mediator' on the global stage. Secondly, a shift in this direction might close off some elements of Canada's pattern of associational behaviour. Most of the 'like-minded' actors that Canada tended to work with in its coalition and confidence-building activities remained those countries not firmly attached to a single regional home, but rather those which straddled regions.

Historically, Canada tried to manage Canadian–US relations in two very different ways. As rehearsed previously, one tactic was to avoid direct head-on conflicts with the US by routing controversial issues through multilateral channels. This choice had obvious attractions for Canada. By attempting to deal with the US through the multilateral framework, Canada tried to lessen the salience of the disparate power relationship between the two countries. Canada could work with other countries, in an issue-specific fashion, to try to temper the US's behaviour and tie it more firmly into a constraining set of international rules of the game. The other tactic was to build on the multifaceted processes of interaction—featuring the myriad of 'networks,' 'flows' and 'complexes'—that went along with the world's largest undefended border, the largest bilateral trading relationship, and the dense pattern of interaction with respect to markets and people. The key aim here was to win concessions from the US by playing up the concept of a 'special relationship' between the two countries. Exemptions were consistently sought from American actions on the premise that Canada offered the US access to its domestic market and a secure supply of natural resources.[5]

The intensity of this push–pull dynamic—between engagement with and diversification from the US—has been accentuated through the 1970s, 1980s and 1990s. Under conditions of mounting uncertainty, the pressure on Canada to gear its efforts towards the establishment of more structured means of dealing with the Canada–US relationship increased. The 'special relationship' had been pursued in the 1950s and 1960s through ad hoc quiet diplomacy. Resort to particularistic forms of institutional machinery was made in some select instances where deemed to be necessary or advantageous, as in the case of the North American Air/Aerospace Defence Command and the International Joint Commission.[6] Structures of this type, nonetheless, were comparatively rare. What stands out about the Canada–US relationship in the earlier era is the informality with which it was conducted. Initiatives towards a formal trade treaty, as in the case of the 1947–8 free trade negotiations, were ultimately rejected.[7] The sectoral deals that were embraced, such as the Defence Sharing Production Act and the Auto Pact, were those requiring little in the way of administrative machinery.

Formality only came with the attempt by Canada to resuscitate the 'special' nature of the relationship after all the convolutions of the 1970s and early 1980s, i.e. the 'Nixon shocks,' the ebbing of the 'imperial presidency' and the emergence of Congress as an ascendant force in foreign policy making, as well as the 'divergent nationalisms' of North America.[8] As early as 1982 there were signs that the Trudeau government wanted to stabilize the Canada–US relationship. This new approach was predicated on the assumption that the complexity of the relationship had to be met head-on. A background document on the discussion paper *Canadian Trade Policy for the 1980s* indicated the centrality of the United States in Canadian foreign policy: 'The task of managing the Canadian–US trade relationship is fundamental to Canada's well-being and to other trading partners.'[9]

A formalized system of public diplomacy emerged as a key element in this new strategy. In terms of goals, Canadian public diplomacy was intended to provide greater coherence to the bilateral management function. To a large extent this approach had an image-building, public relations purpose of 'explaining Canadian political, economic and cultural realities...and defending Canadian economic policies and practices to influential US circles.'[10] As Allan Gotlieb, in his capacity as Canadian ambassador to the US, elaborated in a speech in April 1984 at the Brookings Institution: 'It is essential for us to bring our message to the principal actors on a particular issue, wherever they may be.'[11] But public diplomacy was also intended to act as a feedback system for Canadian policy-making, 'factoring into domestic calculations international, particularly US considerations.'[12] In other words, this mode of statecraft was to serve as a two-way channel for the flow of information, from Canadian to American decision-makers and back again.

Public diplomacy promised to fulfill a number of domestically oriented purposes. From a bureaucratic perspective, a formalized system of public diplomacy provided the reformers with a strong means of critiquing what they considered the long-standing deficiencies of Canadian foreign policy making. As an element of a 'centrally managed, comprehensive and strategic' approach,[13] it stood in direct contrast to the 'flying by the seat of our pants' approach characteristic of Canadian diplomacy in the past. Public diplomacy thus was linked to the development and implementation of a 'coherent Canadian approach' in pursuing Canada's interests *vis-à-vis* the United States.

The assertive nature of public diplomacy also contrasted with the 'quiet diplomacy' favoured by the External 'old hands.' As Gotlieb said in his Brookings speech: 'We need not get too excited about the phenomenon of public disagreement.'[14] At a 1982 seminar, Gotlieb added: 'There is nothing wrong with letting our problems hang out.... It is good for the public to understand the differences.... Canada and the US are not always on parallel paths.'[15] This decisive break with the past served two essential purposes. Externally, it could be argued that, by bringing disagreements with the US out into the open, Canadian diplomacy could be made more effective.[16] Domestically, it was evident to policymakers that such a departure would have appeal to the vocal segment of Canadian public opinion that had expressed criticism about quiet diplomacy for being overly cautious and passive.

In terms of means, Canadian public diplomacy represented an attempt to influence or 'work' the American political system in a full and ongoing manner. In doing so, it shifted the emphasis away from the executive/bureaucratic élite towards monitoring and gaining access to Congress and interest groups. As Gotlieb put it: 'Canadian diplomacy can never again go by the book which says you must deal only with the foreign ministry or, by extension, the administration. To do so would ignore the constitutional and political realities of the US.'[17] This approach relied on the use of a wide variety of insiders whose function was to gain information about specific issues, to develop strategies on how best to get Canada's point of view across to American decision-makers, and to facilitate access to those decision-makers. These experts included lawyers, media consultants, pollsters, public relations specialists and private lobbyists. It was an ongoing process for, as Gotlieb quickly realized, building on a well-known American adage, 'In the Congress of the US, it's never over until it's over. And when it's over, it's still not over. Nothing is over definitively.'[18]

Canada has continued to engage in structured forms of lobbying within the American political system. Still, this form of management technique became overshadowed by the immediate change of focus under the Mulroney government. In terms of style, a shift took place in the early part of the Mulroney years from a Washington-centred diplomacy towards a diplomacy centred on the prime minister and his immediate advisers in the PMO. This shift was exemplified by the March 1985 'Shamrock' Summit between Reagan and Mulroney in Quebec City, where the spotlight of attention was directed almost exclusively at the rapport and relationship forged between the two leaders. As Richard Gwyn commented: 'Direct calls between Ottawa and the White House now represent the principal north–south link.'[19]

In substance, the tilt that took place was from a public relations/lobbying campaign to the initiative on a comprehensive free trade deal. Rather than trying to respond tactically to American protectionism, by applying pressure when necessary on a case-by-case basis, the Mulroney government wanted to establish a general framework through which trade issues could be dealt with on a more regularized basis. As in the past, this desire to come to a new sort of regional accommodation stemmed in large part from the search by Canada, as the smaller state in the bilateral relationship, for special concessions from the US. As Hurrell suggests, a strategy along these lines is based on some calculation of the trade-offs involved: 'Although prompted by actual or potential vulnerability, such a strategy offers the small state the possibility of material benefit.'[20]

The willingness of the Mulroney government to make these trade-offs was increased by a number of other factors. From a systemic perspective, the capacity of the multilateralist order to hold the US's protectionist impulses in check had been seriously called into question. Both the volume and intensity of trade disputes had grown rapidly, as witnessed by the controversies in the mid-1980s over softwood lumber, steel, pork, autos and other products. From a domestic-level perspective, some considerable import must be accorded to the idea of policy reform. The attraction of the FTA for Canada lay first and foremost in the promise it held of obtaining security of access while reducing the threat of contingency protectionism through anti-dumping and countervailing duty actions.[21] Doern and Tomlin hone in on this main goal in their account of the FTA negotiations, stating that 'the free trade initiative was seen in Canada primarily as a means to secure market access and deal with the problem of American protectionism.'[22] But, as Winham notes, behind this primary reason lay the expectation that the deal would facilitate as well 'the ordered adjustment towards a more competitive Canadian economy.'[23] By placing competitiveness squarely on the agenda, the advocates of market liberalization contended, Canadian business would be encouraged to move in a new direction that would allow them to take on more efficient production methods and economies of scale. At the same time, it was hoped that the old habits by which producers focussed narrowly on the domestic market and sought help from government would be broken once and for all. This theme stands out in the intellectual underpinning of the move towards FTA. As the Macdonald Commission emphasized: 'Increased competition from the world in general, and the United States in particular, would work powerfully to induce Canadians to allocate our human, capital and natural resources in ways that would improve the country's productivity.'[24]

## THE PULL OF DIVERSIFICATION

The problems associated with privileging continentalism as Canada's pre-eminent relationship have always stemmed from its exclusivity. If continentalism succeeded in crowding out Canada's other connections, common thinking has had it, Canada's room for manoeuvrability in the international arena would become more restricted. A narrower North American focus has continually raised the spectre of a return to the isolationist thinking of the 1920s and 1930s in a new guise—a move towards the formation of a 'North American fortress,' from the grasp of which it is difficult to escape. Moreover, as has been commented upon as well, this retreat from internationalism has the potential of limiting the effectiveness of Canada's own bilateral diplomacy. Given Canada's asymmetrical position with regard to the US, the seclusion of Canada in a more confined neighbourhood may well reduce, rather than enhance, its zone of comfort.

## The European Community

These fears of entrapment have provided the impetus behind Canada's pull towards diversification in its relationships, as encapsulated by the Third Option. During the Trudeau era, the primary target in this search for some form of regional 'counterweight' to the United States was the European Community. In terms of potential as a neighbourhood where Canada had a comfortable fit, looking at the EC made some sense from both an inside-out and outside-in perspective. Because of its close historical connection with Britain and France, and its traditional pattern of immigration, Canada had a clear identification with the countries of Western Europe in terms of heritage, culture, social attributes, etc. Because of the perceived threat from the Soviet Union and its allies, Canada maintained a commonality of interest on geo-security matters as well.

What is striking about Canada's diversification strategy is its multidimensional character. Diplomatically, the targeting of Western Europe meshed together older and newer impulses. Looking backwards, this strategy tapped into the Canadian tradition of identifying itself as a valuable bridge between the US and Europe within the 'Atlantic Community.' Looking forwards, the rekindling of some form of 'special' relationship with Western Europe had value as an instrument to offset the change in the nature of American leadership. From a general standpoint, the 'Nixon shocks' revealed the extent to which Canada was to be exposed to new vulnerabilities in the evolving international political economy. More specifically, Henry Kissinger's 'Year of Europe' initiative (1973) showed the degree to which Canada's Atlanticist conception of security had been overtaken by a more explicitly national-self-interest construct.[25] As a writer for the *Manchester Guardian Weekly* put it at the time: 'Canada is groping for a special relationship with the Community, perhaps less for economic reasons than as a durable reminder that she is an Atlantic power in her own right, not to be bracketed with the United States.'[26]

Politically, the Trudeau government had a strong incentive to develop stronger European ties, as a means to enhance the image of Canada as a bilingual and bicultural country and, at the same time, to rein in the Quebec government's own international ambitions. Although the diplomatic struggles between Ottawa and Quebec City within the context of the international francophone community have received most of the attention, the centre stage of these struggles remained Western Europe. Using cultural diplomacy on a concerted basis, a host of Canadian artists and exhibits toured not only France but Belgium and Switzerland in the late 1960s and early 1970s. In the forefront of this effort were the exhibitions 'Canada: Art d'aujourd'hui,' which opened at the Musée National d'Art Moderne in Paris in January 1968; 'Réalités canadiennes,' a portable exhibition that had its première in the French capital at the same time; and 'Canada Trajectoires 73,' an exhibition that opened at the Musée d'Art Moderne de la Ville de Paris in the summer of 1973. All of these exhibitions were put on with considerable flair, utilizing with pronounced effect sophisticated new devices such as video.

In its attempt to outdo Quebec's own diplomatic drive, Ottawa had some considerable advantages. It could mobilize substantially more financial and personnel resources. A Canadian cultural centre was opened in Paris at great cost in 1970. The cultural events themselves were often glittering and lavish affairs, and one gets the impression that there were few other nations in the world that would or could make this type of effort. In this undertaking the federal government could draw on a number of cultural institutions for support, including the National Museum, the National Arts Centre, the CBC, the NFB, the Canada Council and the Art Bank.[27]

Economically, a European 'counterweight' offered the prospect of a strategic way to balance Canada's commercial ties with the US. This desire for balance had been behind Prime Minister Diefenbaker's brief flirtation with the notion of diverting up to 15 percent of Canadian imports from the US to imports from Britain. It was also behind the interest of a host of Canadian politicians—especially among the nationalist wing of the Liberal Party—in forging some form of 'associate' status with the nascent European Community in the late 1950s and early 1960s.[28]

This strategy of diversification on the part of Canada should not be equated with regionalism *per se*. The signing of a Framework Agreement on Commercial and Economic Cooperation in July 1976 did constitute a significant step towards institutionalization of the Canada–EC relationship. Little evidence can be found, however, of a sustained feeling of 'regional awareness or regional consciousness' between Canada and the EC.[29] Canada and the EC could build on the foundations of their common social, cultural and political character, together with the added degree of economic complementarity.[30] There was no sense, though, that they belonged in the same regional constellation. Instead of being readily and rapidly translated into a wide number of specific programs of co-operation, the contractual link withered away through mutual neglect.

In comparison with the dense set of 'networks,' 'flows' and 'complexes' found in the Canada–US relationship, the non-state connections between Canada and the EC remained sparse. The Canadian business community as a totality showed little concerted interest in Europe throughout the 1960s and early 1970s. Rather than taking the time to lay the groundwork (through research, language skills and personal connections) to gain access into the EC market, Canadian producers preferred to concentrate on the North American market.[31] As the Senate Committee on Canadian Relations with the European Community noted in 1973,[32] the 'natural propensity for the closer and more accessible American market' remained firmly embedded. The lack of an ongoing governmental instrument to provide psychological support and material incentives reinforced the inclination of Canadian business to avoid focussing on the European market. Although the political/geographic arm of External Affairs with responsibility for Western Europe was extremely enthusiastic about the 'counterweight' idea, the economic-oriented bureaucracy remained sceptical and proved unwilling to mobilize either its own administrative machinery or its clientele behind the concept.

By the early 1980s, Canadian business had for the most part written off the European market as either 'a closed shop' or one that was so difficult to crack that it was not worth the effort. Indeed, when the EC delegation to Canada hosted a seminar in 1984 to highlight the attractions of Europe for Canadian firms, the head of the delegation was stunned by the poor attendance.[33] While this lack of interest may be attributed in part to recession, and to the psychology of Euro-pessimism during that time, it also reflected the process of marginalization rather than consolidation in terms of the two-way trade between Canada and the EC. Europe's share of Canadian exports fell steadily throughout the existence of the EC, from 29 percent in 1960 to just over 7 percent in 1993.[34]

This problematic blend of heightened expectations on the part of the government and diminished performance on the part of firms severely complicated the Canadian response to the EC's 1992 initiative. As part of the Challenge 1992 initiative, an integrated EAITC had produced a number of sectoral studies on the opportunities and challenges open to Canadian business in Europe.[35] The federal government had also set up a number of interdepartmental working groups to explore in detail the impact of EC trade policies in particular sectors. Yet this adaptive behaviour could not disguise the fact that an enormous imbalance remained between the behaviour of Canadian firms as directed towards the US and as directed towards Europe.

Some corporate decisions were influenced by the necessity of responding to the 1992 initiative (and fears of a 'Fortress Europe'), as witnessed by the fact that a number of prominent Canadian companies moved to gain a secure 'presence' in the single market. Northern Telecom moved to expand its share of the EC telecommunications equipment market by locating in every one of the EC countries. McCain Foods, Bombardier and Labatt, to name just a few, tried to enhance their competitiveness within the region. Investment flows picked up.[36] Yet few of the central dynamics of regionalization were visible. Few strategic alliances have been created between Canadian and European concerns.[37] Nor has there appeared to be a growth of intra-firm trade or (with few exceptions) an expanding list of mergers and acquisitions. Nor have Canadian business groups moved to develop an extensive lobbying capacity in Brussels and other major political/commercial centres of Western Europe in a bid to gain knowledge (if not influence) with respect to the EC decision-making process. The logic of this kind of involvement rested on the need to come to terms with both the expanding web of EC directives (on technical standards, government procurement, rules of origin, treatment of services, etc.) and the ongoing evolution of the EC in the 1990s towards and beyond the EU.[38]

It may be added, in passing, that this sparseness in terms of 'networks' has not been compensated for by an extension of contacts at the sub-national level. During the 1980s, there were some signs that the transnational regionalism so strongly established in North America (Quebec and New England, Cascadia, and Ontario and the Great Lakes states) might be extended to Western Europe. The move by Ontario to associate itself with the so-called 'four motors of Europe' attracted particular attention by opening the possibility of co-operation with respect to technology and advanced education. Although lacking any formal organization, building linkages with the most advanced regions of Germany (Baden-Württemberg), Italy (Lombardy), Spain (Catalonia) and France (Rhone-Alpes) was seen by many participants and observers as being in the forefront of a move towards an innovative form of micro-regionalism.[39] By the late 1980s and early 1990s, hopes of this sort had withered away due to a combination of self-absorption on the part of the Europeans and declining capabilities on the part of the Canadian provinces.

What solid rationale the contractual link had was based on the extent to which there was a complementarity between the economies of Canada and the EC. For all of its economic deficiencies, Canada had the good fortune of being a 'have' country with respect to resource wealth. Western Europe, by way of contrast, had long suffered from being a 'have not' region on this criteria. This discrepancy became more pronounced with the resource crises of the 1970s. From the European standpoint, the wave of commodity shocks pointed out the advantages of closer ties with Canada as a 'storehouse' of raw materials in the Northern Hemisphere. In particular, the EC had considerable interest in securing cheap and reliable energy supplies, most notably uranium. From the Canadian standpoint, there was a recognition that the resources card provided the type of leverage required to bring about a contractual arrangement with the EC. As Trudeau stated: 'We are telling the Europeans bilaterally and as a community: you may think you are going to be able to take all our raw materials out, but you aren't.... We are defining our policies and if you [the Europeans] want to get in there, you'd better embark on this process of negotiations.'[40]

Built on resources, the institutional manifestation of the Canada–EC relationship has floundered on resources. What appeared to be the greatest strength of the link in the 1970s has proved to be its most disruptive element in the 1980s and 1990s. Even as the wider agenda has been transformed, the dialogue (and disputes) between Canada and the EC has become increasingly concentrated on issues surrounding energy supplies, lumber and newsprint, fur, beer and wine, and a variety of agricultural products, as well as the fisheries.

A wide array of systemic and domestic-related factors helped bring about this reversal. Notwithstanding the brief phase where Canada and the EC had some coincidence of interest based on international resource scarcity, the lack of an ongoing mutuality of interest soon came to the fore. If resource dependency/vulnerability dominated the bilateral agenda during the immediate period surrounding the signing of the contractual agreement, conflict over regulatory mechanisms and market share dominated thereafter. The Europeans complained bitterly about the controls Canada imposed on the access to and supply of raw materials given to outsiders. These difficulties began with Canada's controls on the export of uranium in the 1970s (which touched Europeans' sensitivities that they were considered potentially 'irresponsible' in their use of this material),[41] and intensified in waves—first with the introduction of the NEP and tighter controls of investment through FIRA, and later on with the restrictions on the European fishing fleet. Canada complained about many facets associated with the outward expression of Europe's resource politics and policy. Whereas most of the resource-centred irritants found in the Canada–EC relationship during the 1970s were related to questions of access into the European 'home' market, by the 1980s and 1990s these irritants had become internationalized in the sense that Canada faced serious competition from Europe in third markets, and in North America itself. The EU, as a consequence, became treated not only as a rival rather than as a complementary trade partner, but as a trade rival that often bent the 'rules of the game' (through export subsidies on agricultural products, unfair fishing practices, etc.) to meet its own needs and interests.

The vigour with which conflicts were fought was accentuated by the way they transcended the economic to move into the social and environmental dimensions. The fishing dispute represented only the latest (and sharpest) example of this spillover effect. The beef hormone issue provides another illustration of the same phenomenon, with the Europeans claiming that their prohibitions imposed in the early 1980s on Canadian meat treated with growth hormones were necessary on health grounds, and Canadian cattle producers claiming that these restrictions provided an example of how environmental standards could be manipulated for protectionist purposes. Likewise the more recent example of the EC ban on shipments of 'green' lumber: the ban could be justified by Brussels on the grounds that it protected their forests from disease, while it was criticized by Canadian exporters as a non-tariff trade barrier aimed at a business worth approximately $700 million in BC alone.

With the removal of the key element on which the contractual arrangement was grounded, the inability of the EC to provide balance with respect to the Canada–US relationship was exposed for all to see. During the Mulroney years, the Europeans were under no illusions about Canada's position as a 'bridge' between the US and the EC. As one EC commissioner declared in early 1985, after Canada joined with the Americans in pressing for the commencement of another round of multilateral trade negotiations: 'Canada is on the same wavelength as the United States. The result is that in multilateral relations, Canada will be on the side of the United States.'[42]

This impression of a widening imbalance was compounded by style as well as substance. Diplomatic contact between Canada and the EC fell off appreciably during the Mulroney period. Few trips were made by Canadian ministers to the

EC, and those that took place were usually tacked on to some other (NATO, La Francophonie, G7) form of business.[43] Secretary of State Joe Clark did not attend the annual EC–Canada ministerial meeting in Brussels for three years running, between 1986 and 1988. Senior officials from Canada and the EC did continue to meet twice a year to discuss issues of bilateral and mutual concern. This form of regularized bureaucratic contact did not, however, compensate for the loss of interest at the political level.

During its second mandate, with the introduction of the FTA behind it, the Mulroney government made a number of symbolic gestures of reconciliation towards the EC. The most interesting of these overtures was the signing of an EC–Canada Transatlantic Declaration in November 1990.[44] Still, despite the worthy sentiments expressed in this document concerning common values and goals and the establishment of some formal consultative mechanism to co-ordinate policy, the political and policy gulf between Canada and the EC/EU has remained wide. On some high-profile issues, the hopes of forging a close relationship with the EC/EU have been dashed by a figurative, if not (as in the case of the fishing dispute) a literal, bang. More commonly, though, a closer Canada–European relationship has continued to be pursued, albeit in an atmosphere of unfulfilled expectations.

## Asia-Pacific

The other geographic area receiving some attention as a target in the strategy of diversification was the Asia-Pacific region. This constituted a looser form of neighbourhood than Western Europe. There is no community in the Pacific from an inside-out sense; that is to say, historically there is little or no evidence of the development of a regional consciousness based on linguistic, religious, cultural, political or ideological cohesiveness.[45] Nor have outside-in factors provided the same impetus for formal regional integration and institutions as found in Western Europe. The clear perception of an external threat, or 'other,' which provided much of the momentum towards the launch of the integrative project in Europe, has been traditionally lacking in the Asia-Pacific.

The Canadian approach to the Asia-Pacific relationship (or more precisely, relationships) has been shaped by these regional differences. In the absence of a well-defined neighbourhood, Canada has directed its focus towards the Asia-Pacific in a cautious manner. Canada has remained wary of any form of structured regionalism in this geographical area, which involved a variety of sensitive questions about who belonged or did not belong. Despite a profound concern about the risks of 'excessive regionalism' in the Asia-Pacific context, however, Canada remained determined to be included in any talks concerning the prospect of an emerging regional grouping. This approach may, in part, be explained in reputational terms, by Canada's self-identification as a 'good international citizen' and institutional joiner. More important, however, Canada's interest may be explained in both a medium- and long-term tactical way. The acquisition of a regional option provided Canada with added manoeuvrability, while its exclusion from this institution-building exercise would have left it potentially vulnerable if, in the future, the initiative moved from the goal of open economic co-operation to the creation of a regional economic bloc (with the attendant discriminatory trading practices). The hope was not that Canadian involvement could, in itself, prevent the rise of an Asia-centred economic bloc in response to the growth of European and North American blocs; rather, it was hoped that a Canadian (along with the American) presence might serve to dampen fears in east Asia about the rise of blocs elsewhere in the international political economy.

Consequently, Canada campaigned hard in the early stages of the APEC initiative to ensure that it was not excluded. This was done in two ways. First, Ottawa engaged in some tough lobbying at the senior ministerial level, targeting Japanese support in particular. Second, it engaged in an exercise of image building to convince regional states, especially ASEAN, of Canada's bona fide regional status. A key element of this effort was the announcement in May 1989 of the 'Pacific 2000' initiative, a set of proposals designed to further Canada's linkages with the region; to raise Canada's profile in the Asia-Pacific; and to overcome the common Asian perception that 'Canada is an unimportant part of North America.' As Joe Clark, the secretary of state for external affairs, put it, the Pacific 2000 initiative was designed to 'dispel the myth that we are content to put all our eggs in the North American basket.'[46]

While it wanted to be a player, Canada's enthusiasm for the content of APEC remained restrained. Canada had serious reservations about any suggestion of creating a Pacific OECD-like organization. Canada was also initially opposed to the idea that APEC should have decision-making powers. Its strong preference was for a body that was consultative only. As John Crosbie, the minister of international trade, argued to the OECD ministerial meeting in May 1989: 'Canada supports initiatives toward the creation of arrangements to enable the countries of the Pacific to consult on economic matters affecting the area.... Consultation among Pacific countries could provide the basis for greater co-operation on regional economic concerns and for common approaches to adjustment.'[47]

Canada's role in APEC has, in many ways, remained ambivalent. In the economic arena, Canada's preference has remained what Douglas Ross in the 1980s termed 'ad hoc bilateralism.'[48] Rather than interacting with the countries of the Asia-Pacific region as a group, Canada has continued to deal with these countries primarily on a bilateral, and issue-by-issue, basis. For example, it was significant that, during his trip to Hong Kong and Japan in May 1991, Prime Minister Brian Mulroney focussed on specific issues of mutual concern—such as refugees, immigration, trade and investment—and did not seek to use the trip to advance the wider agenda of regional co-operation.

Unlike the diversification strategy directed towards Western Europe as part of the Third Option, the main thrust of Canada's engagement with the Asia-Pacific area has not been exclusively (or even predominantly) state-led. A marked feature of Canada's co-operative endeavour towards the Asia-Pacific has, instead, been it's bottom up or private sector approach.'[49] Members of the Canadian business and academic communities, as well as state officials, actively participated in the array of informal bodies, most notably the Pacific Trade and Development Conference (PAFTAD), the Pacific Economic Cooperation Conference (PECC) and the Pacific Basin Economic Committee (PBEC), on which the main networks and linkages among Asia-Pacific opinion-leaders were built. After the launching of APEC, a representative from Canadian business (the president of the Canadian Chamber of Commerce) has taken part in the more focussed activity of the Pacific Business Forum, a private-sector government advisory group. Included among the proposals put forward by this latter body have been the calls for APEC-country 'ombudsmen' to deal with trade disputes among members and the establishment of a permanent Business Council.[50]

This onus on the private sector fits well with Canada's preference for framing its relationships with the Asia-Pacific on economic criteria. Whereas Canadian scholars have maintained an active interest in European affairs from the perspectives of the nation state, sub-national entities and the institutional make-up of the EC/EU, the recent academic literature (as well as the activity on the ground) on the Asia-Pacific has concentrated on examining the area from the perspective of the forces of production. Paul Evans has, for example, argued that East Asia should be seen as 'the outer boundaries of an integrated production zone, producing goods through a regional division of labour primarily for export across the Pacific and to Europe.'[51]

However accurate a portrayal, this type of framework may well work against easing Canada's ambivalence towards a grand design of regional co-operation. On economic criteria alone, the argument for Canada pursuing the APEC option as a central ingredient of Canadian foreign policy is rather flimsy. Indeed, it may be counter-productive in raising suspicions that Canada—like other non-Asian countries—is merely trying to 'hitch a ride' with the expanding Asian economies.[52] By placing the emphasis for regional co-operation on an exclusively economic grounding, the rationale for Canada (or, for that matter, North America) belonging to APEC as opposed to the EC/EU is diminished. This point is reinforced, of course, by the dynamic towards a form of European–Asian institutionalized dialogue. By looking at Canada's relationship with the individual Asian APEC countries through an economic lens, the focus turns on the many weaknesses as well as the strengths in the Canadian position. There has of course been an increased flow of people, products and services between Canada and the Asia-Pacific over the last decade. Canada's trade with the Asia-Pacific has surpassed its trade with Europe since 1983, and is now almost 50 percent greater. Ten of Canada's twenty-five top trading partners are Asia-Pacific countries. The area has also become an increasingly important (and diversified) source of foreign direct investment and immigrants. Yet for all its apparent promise, this relationship has to be put into the wider context. As a recent DFAIT Policy Staff paper has pointed out: 'Despite the greater importance of Asia to Canada's merchandise trade, Canada remains a marginal trading partner for Asian Countries. Canada, for example, accounted for only 2 percent of South Korea's exports and imports in 1993.'[53]

These structural limitations contribute to the impression that Canada is not only still different from the Asian countries but that it remains the unimportant part of (or junior partner in) North America. As part of a concerted learning process, Canada has worked hard to alter the stereotyped images of itself. Economically, considerable effort has been made to try to dispel Canada's image as a producer of logs and rocks. Ottawa's prestige has been lent to the marketing of Canadian technology (Candus, Stols, communications technology and equipment, engineering expertise) on a project/contract basis. New consulates have been opened in commercial hubs of the region (Shanghai and Osaka, for instance).

Diplomatically, as noted in Chapter 2, Canada has recently tried harder to differentiate itself from the US. Canada has attempted especially to maintain an equidistant approach with respect to the disputes between the US and Japan. On specific issues, Canadian ministers with responsibility over international trade have expressed disapproval of American methods. Pat Carney, when she served as trade minister in the Mulroney government, expressed Canadian disapproval of American 'excesses' on one of the many sensitive issues (semi-conductors) in US–Japan trade negotiations: 'I want to say very bluntly that Canada is not engaged in Japan-bashing, publicly or privately.'[54]

In the same vein, the Canadian government has been willing to put a more positive interpretation on Japan's changing role in the world. Among other things, Mulroney's May 1991 trip to Japan constituted an important signalling exercise with regard to Canada's backing for Japan's accession to a permanent seat on the Security Council of the UN and an enhanced role in terms of international organizations.[55] This type of support has remained a focal point of the Chrétien government's approach. Indeed, by including Japan in a number of coalitions of the 'like-minded' (such as the one on the creation of a standing peacekeeping force), the Liberals have attempted to widen the focus on Japan from institutional reform to policy content.

Neither these economic nor diplomatic efforts have been unqualified successes. Notwithstanding the Canadian bid to sell itself to Asia as a technologically rich country, much of the trade with those countries has remained resource oriented. Most significantly, only a small proportion of Canadian exports to Japan involves the export of end-products. As H. Edward English detailed at the beginning of the 1990s: 'On the export side, trade is still dominated by natural resources in raw and processed forms, reflecting Canada's diverse natural endowments. Among the top six categories of exports to Japan...all four major resource sectors—mining, agriculture, forestry, and fisheries—are represented.'[56]

Moreover, the confines of the parameters with respect to the diplomatic initiatives Canada could pursue in the region were brought home by the fate of the initiative on a North Pacific Co-operative Security Dialogue. Joe Clark outlined this initiative in three speeches delivered in Victoria, BC, Tokyo and Jakarta in July 1990. The essence of Clark's plan was a call for a 'process' of confidence building in the North Pacific area through the establishment of a regional multi-lateral dialogue. Ottawa was careful to assert that this notion of a regional dia-logue was not simply the adaptation of the CSCE structure to the North Pacific region. Nonetheless, this initiative was commonly viewed by other players in the region as little more than an inappropriate attempt to transpose the European model into the Asian context. For example, in a speech to an academic confer-ence on the United States, Japan and Canada in October 1990, the Japanese ambassador to Canada sought to put some distance between his government and the Canadian proposal, arguing that the conditions in the Asia-Pacific region were so different from those in Europe that a multilateral dialogue would 'become more realistic once a favourable atmosphere has been created and major issues have been resolved through bilateral dialogue.'[57]

With the limits of its ambition clearly delineated, Canada has concentrated attention in its regional approach to the Asia-Pacific on creating the habit of dia-logue as a basis for future co-operation. From the time of the November 1993 Seattle Summit, to which Jean Chrétien made his first international trip as prime minister, Canada has continued to play a constructive role as the APEC agenda has evolved in an incremental fashion. Transparency and consensus building have been promoted through the meetings of the APEC summits in Bogor, Indonesia (November 1994) and Osaka, Japan (November 1995); the meeting of APEC finance ministers; the work agendas on trade and investment issues; and the 'Eminent Persons' task force report. With respect to the security dialogue, Canada has tried to demonstrate its comparative advantage in low-key initiatives focussed on regional confidence-building measures. The first track of this approach, through the interstate diplomatic route, has been directed towards the ASEAN Regional Forum. The second, non-governmental track has involved a sustained enterprise to 'build informational bases and to promote more sophisticated understanding of national attitudes and perceptions regard-ing security issues.'[58] Both tracks have concentrated on issue-specific forms of mediatory activity, as seen for example on Canada's effort to support the imple-mentation of a maritime dispute settlement in the South China Sea.

## The Hemisphere of the Americas

### *Avoiding the Hemisphere*

Having looked in a backward fashion at the Canadian strategy for diversification, it is necessary to look more closely at how this option has played out in the late 1980s and 1990s. In moving to do so, the theme of the relationship between Canada's familiar habits (protecting the international order) and new directions (the search for regional space) will be examined through a fuller look at the Canadian relationship with the Hemisphere of the Americas. Although in many ways building on the traditional debate about the scope of engagement, this case has some distinctive elements about it. In part, this distinctiveness stems from its dramatic quality. With little in the way of exaggeration, it is accurate to say that Canada has 'discovered' the Americas in the 1990s.[59]

Canada's difficulty in coming to terms with its 'immediate' neighbourhood has been a function of both self-image and structural location in the international economy. While Canada is clearly a North American country, it was far from emotionally connected to Latin America (if not the Caribbean). Contacts were neither broad nor deep. Involving very different histories, political systems and perceptions of national interest, these relations were 'modest and episodic.'[60] Rather than perceiving itself as a country of the Americas, Canada's position in the hemisphere was subordinated to its identification initially as an 'Atlantic' and later as a 'Pacific' (or even 'Arctic') country.

At the governmental level, Canada's long-standing wariness about building closer relations with the Americas was reinforced by two other, intertwining factors. The first of these related to a general fear of 'excessive regionalism' focussed specifically at the hemisphere. Any such concentration was perceived as being detrimental to Canada's overall diplomatic manoeuvrability, in that it would lock Canada into a region dominated by the 'core' actor—the United States. Hemispheric association was, therefore, to be avoided. In any case, up until the late 1980s, the needs of the 'periphery' countries in Latin America were seen as being very different from Canada's. While some specific forms of economic collaboration were mooted, any more ambitious push towards economic integration was widely perceived as being 'unnatural.'[61]

Moreover, several of the Latin American countries were viewed as 'middle power' competitors. This rivalry was particularly evident during the period of creation of the UN institutions immediately after the war. As suggested earlier, a good deal of the enthusiasm Canada had for functionalism was related to status seeking: by moving to take greater responsibilities on the international stage, the place of Canada could not only be differentiated from the 'greats' but also from the 'minor' actors. This type of functional approach, however, was contested by the Latin American countries. During the 1944 Dumbarton Oaks conference, for instance, the Latin American group of countries opposed tying eligibility for representation on the UN Security Council to a commitment to provide forces for UN services.[62] For their part, the Latin American countries favoured 'regional' rather than 'functional' representation—a formula that (at least according to Canada) would provide benefits to 'middle powers' such as Brazil, Argentina and Mexico.

As with the Asia-Pacific, there existed neither an inside-out nor an outside-in impetus for Canada to identify with the Americas.[63] In terms of climate, language and cultural/sporting links, there were few traits that tied Canada and Latin

America together. In many ways, the only real similarity with respect to political/psychological attitudes was an ingrained desire to differentiate themselves from the US. This point of commonality—because of their shared proximity to the US—especially bound Canada and Mexico together. Historically, the priority of the governments in both Mexico City and Ottawa was to restrain the overweening influence of the US. Thus, up until the 1980s, Washington's attempts to forge a North American common market were always viewed as a means by which the US could extract additional benefits by playing the two other countries off against each other. For example, Ronald Reagan's call for a North American 'accord' in late 1979 was treated not as an opportunity but as a threat.[64] In their foreign policy, Canada and Mexico made similar efforts to shift the United States away from aggressive unilateralism and towards the maintenance of the international order. Both countries sought to highlight issues on which they differed from the United States—most notably on the embargo against Cuba and on the Reagan administration's policy towards Central America in the 1980s. Both countries sought to temper American behaviour and channel it towards multilateral forums. Lopez Portillo and Pierre Trudeau participated in a joint effort to promote a North–South dialogue at Cancun in 1981. Nonetheless, despite this episodic coincidence of interests, the two countries were not closely connected via a sustained mutuality of interest in foreign policy.

Nor was there any external threat that helped implant in Canada the idea of a hemispheric region. In David Haglund's words, the security dimension has long been a crucial 'missing link' in Canadian foreign policy towards Latin America.[65] Throughout the Cold War era, the Canadian government's overriding security concern, reflected in the White Papers of 1971 and 1987, was over the impact of a central nuclear exchange between the United States and the Soviet Union, a fear that drove much of its policy towards NATO and the European region. This deep involvement reinforced the marginality of a hemispheric connection. Canada and the Americas did not constitute a 'security complex,' defined 'as a group of states whose primary security concerns link together sufficiently closely that their national securities cannot realistically be considered apart from one another.'[66] The question to 'what extent the Organization of American States should be strengthened or maintained' was therefore left to the US and the Latin Americans to decide. Notwithstanding its (well-deserved) reputation as the quintessential joiner of organizations, Canada stayed out of the OAS until November 1989. At odds with its habit of mediation, Canada expressed little interest in taking on the putative role of go-between on a hemispheric basis as a 'professional occupation.' The trouble with any heightened involvement with the Americas remained, as always, the concern that, rather than opening up diplomatic room for Canada, this type of involvement would restrict its space. Instead of being able to take on a leadership role, Canada would inevitably become identified as part of a 'North American bloc in the OAS.'[67] As such, it was best to leave this option unexploited.

## Discovering the Hemisphere

In analysing why Canada has recently 'discovered' the Hemisphere of the Americas, both domestic and international factors must be considered. From a domestic point of view, it is tempting to see this regional voyage of discovery as part of a more general shift under the Mulroney Conservative government to restrict or limit the contours of Canadian foreign policy. Certainly, some careful academics have expressed concern that the bilateral/regional orientation of Canadian foreign policy in the 1980s and 1990s—symbolized by the negotiation of the Canada–US Free Trade Agreement and the North American Free Trade Agreement—has had the effect of retrenching Canadian foreign policy. Kim Nossal, for example, states that 'the pull of geography' and 'the weight of trade that has become more heavily American and less transatlantic,' along with 'the impact of changes in patterns of immigration, and the rapid diminution of the Soviet threat,' have 'played a role in the decline of the Atlantic idea.'[68]

Yet, in economic terms, a regional strategy was well down the list of priorities for the Mulroney government. Canada was at the outset a 'reluctant' participant in the NAFTA project.[69] Having signed its own deal with its dominant trading partner, Canada was initially sceptical about the value of entering into negotiations that would extend this type of arrangement to other countries. Moreover, from a domestic political point of view, the Mulroney government had little interest in stirring up renewed controversy through a process of extended debate or reflection about Canada's changing regional identity or consciousness. When situated against the background of the bitter constitutional debates and its growing unpopularity, the Mulroney government had little to gain from the campaign to sell NAFTA to Canadians. Opponents of the Canada–United States trade agreement were given another chance to rally against the perceived costs of trade liberalization,[70] a campaign in which the Conservative government could be criticized for the potential loss of jobs due to structural adjustment; for the flight of Canadian firms to low-wage areas; and for signing an agreement with a country widely considered to tolerate low environmental standards and human rights abuses.

Such a safety-first approach was challenged initially not by any change in Canadian attitudes but by external pressures. A crucial factor was the change in Mexican economic strategy. Mexico was hit hard by the shocks of the 1980s: tumbling oil prices, rising debt, dramatic devaluations, and the failure of import substitution industrialization and statist intervention. The government of Carlos Salinas de Goratari was galvanized to embrace a vigorous and outward-looking program of reform. At the same time, the United States was also changing its thinking: American policymakers became increasingly attracted to the idea of moving from bilateral trade deals to regional economic integration. At first, policymakers in Washington were attracted to bilateral and regional options because they appeared to offer useful demonstration effects for others in the international trading system. In particular, it was believed that flirting with bilateral or regional free trade areas would show Europe and Japan that alternatives to the multilateralism under GATT were possible.[71] However, as the Uruguay Round bogged down, the regional approach was increasingly regarded not as a fall-back option but as a preferred first option, gaining credibility and legitimacy on its own merit.

The result of these shifts in Mexican and American thinking was a renewed effort at creating a North American economic arrangement. But the NAFTA initiative posed a serious dilemma for Canadian policymakers. Any extension of the Canada–US trade agreement jeopardized Canada's privileged status in terms of the institutionalization of its 'special relationship' with the United States. Indeed, NAFTA raised the spectre that Canada would no longer be special, in the sense that it would join Mexico as a spoke to the American hub, as Richard Lipsey and Ronald J. Wonnacott have characterized it.[72] This scenario held a number of problematic consequences for Canada, in that Canadian exporters would be at a disadvantage relative to American exporters in terms of access to the Mexican market and relative to US producers in terms of access to duty-free Mexican inputs. On top of this, it was argued that Canada would be placed at a disadvantage in terms of attracting foreign direct investment. Finally, if NAFTA eventually moved to serve as a prototype for a more comprehensive set of pan-American agreements, the number of those spokes would be expanded, opening the way for the US to utilize an explicit divide-and-conquer strategy.[73]

The intellectual advocates of NAFTA argued that the status quo was not a viable option for Canada. Economically, they pointed to the broader trends of 'silent' market integration in North America, necessitating further changes in the institutional and legal barriers to trade and capital movements. This silent process was being played out through the activities of those Canadian firms that were actively responding to the larger dynamics relating to the internationalization of production and/or the establishment of maquiladoras in Mexico. Historically, Canadian commercial ties with Mexico (as with other parts of Latin America) had a strong resources component. By the late 1980s, however, a different pattern was emerging—a pattern marked by open investment and strategic alliances in the manufacturing and high-technology sectors (primarily automobiles, auto parts and telecommunications).[74]

These advocates of NAFTA also argued that, diplomatically, Canada had little choice but to be a player in NAFTA. Regionalization created more of an imbalance in bargaining strength than did the bilateral option. Nonetheless, the protection of Canadian interests seemed to be better achieved by taking part in the expanded negotiations rather than by remaining on the sidelines. 'Being there' was deemed essential for Canadian interests, particularly if the government in Ottawa was to make its influence felt. As one Canadian official put it: 'If Canada is not at the table, it cannot make its views known—the absent party is always wrong.'[75]

Put together, these international and domestic factors proved difficult to resist. While continuing to exhibit an ambiguity towards 'excessive regionalism,' Canada did not want to be excluded in any talks concerning the prospect of an emerging regional grouping. Forced to make a choice, the government in Ottawa decided in instrumental fashion that 'going along' with NAFTA was tactically preferable to being excluded from a bilateral Mexican–American free trade deal.[76]

If the Mulroney government joined the NAFTA process because it felt there were few other alternatives, it also did so (initially at least) without enthusiasm. Ottawa adopted a cautious approach. In its declarations, the Canadian government stressed that it intended to use the NAFTA negotiations to strengthen its bilateral trade agreement with the United States, particularly the dispute-settlement mechanisms; in reality, however, the Canadian approach concentrated on 'damage containment.' Far from going on the offensive to extract new benefits, Canada had to fight hard just to avoid giving away any existing benefits through NAFTA that it had obtained during the bilateral free trade negotiations. As an editorial in the *Globe and Mail* stated: 'Ottawa's, and Canada's, commitment to the [NAFTA] negotiation has never been wholehearted and has always been defensive.'[77]

The Canadian government's emphasis was on trying to maintain the basic structure of the Canada–United States agreement, especially in such sensitive areas as culture, agricultural marketing boards, and environment and health standards. However, Ottawa did press for modifications in areas where the Canada–United States agreement itself needed clarification. For example, Canada wanted a clearer definition of the rules of origin regarding the production in North America of Asian automobiles. A particularly narrow interpretation of rules of origin as applied to Hondas manufactured in Alliston, Ontario, led in the fall of 1991 to Canadian allegations of unfair harassment concerning these products at the US border. Likewise, from the outset Canada paid special attention to the possible extension of NAFTA to the Western hemisphere as a whole. It took a distinctly minimalist line on the issue of additional members, pressing for a 'special accession' clause, which would fix the minimum concessions that other countries would be required to give before being allowed to join.[78]

It may be added here that this ambivalent attitude extended from government to the Canadian business community. A number of individual firms (including McCains, Magna and Northern Telecom) demonstrated an early enthusiasm for a trade deal with Mexico, as a means both to better source components and to access the Mexican market. While maintaining its focus on rationalization and market expansion, however, the wider Canadian business community was content to play a low-key role in the negotiations. There was no pro-NAFTA committee to replicate the performance of the Canadian Alliance for Trade and Job Opportunities during the Canada–US free trade negotiations. Moreover, the Business Council on National Issues (BCNI), the peak organization of Canadian business, did not display either the cohesion or the degree of mobilization on NAFTA that it had on the FTA. Unsure about the impact of NAFTA on either the protectionist debate in the US or the level of competition from Mexican goods in the US, the BCNI went along with NAFTA but did not engage in an active (and expensive) public relations campaign behind the extension of the Canada–US bilateral trade deal.

### 'Enmeshment' with the Americas

In economic terms, the impact of NAFTA may be interpreted as confirming many of the positive scenarios laid out by its proponents. As Lipsey and others have suggested, NAFTA consolidated many of the gains of the FTA: ensuring that Mexico did not get better treatment than Canada and preserving many of the exemptions won in the FTA. In several areas, most notably with respect to improving the vague set of rules in terms of content requirements for North American auto and parts manufacturers, NAFTA also tightened up the provisions of the FTA. At the same time, NAFTA broadened the coverage of the FTA in a variety of areas—intellectual property and the liberalization of cross-border land transportation, for instance.

NAFTA introduced new elements of uncertainty, as well as clarity, into Canada's trading approach. Many of the rules established in the context either of the FTA or the GATT faced a process of reshaping via NAFTA. Far from consistently introducing elements of relief or redress from American pressure, therefore, NAFTA brought with it additional sources of stress in the search for a stable trading regime.[79]

A number of sectors, or segmented issue-areas, could be examined to explore the pros and the cons of the economic impact of NAFTA. Agriculture stands out as a case-study that illustrates both sides of this dynamic. In some areas, agriculture demonstrates the attraction of NAFTA for Canada. From an export perspective, Canada's efforts meshed with its push to seek clarification of the FTA, or to extend the provisions of the FTA into areas where it was deemed to be deficient. The most obvious illustration of this point was the push by Canada to extend NAFTA to cover US export subsidies in third-country markets. This type of program, encompassing the Export Enhancement Program, had hit Canadian sales in a variety of countries, including Mexico itself. More specifically, Canada could eye the potential benefits in gaining easier access to the Mexican market in livestock, grain and other products. From an import perspective, however, it was the sensitivity of agriculture as a domestic issue that stood out in the context of NAFTA. Although in principle many of the main sources of this sensitivity were tempered by the NAFTA outcome, in practice the US raised the level of volatility associated with NAFTA by targeting specific programs maintained under the FTA. Most significantly, American pressure built up to close what were considered the loopholes in the agricultural relationship derived from the Canadian structure of supply management.

This ingrained Canadian ambivalence about the deepening of regional trade ties was undoubtedly reinforced by volatility in other areas of the economic relationship; one needs only to think of the turbulence, sense of crisis and fears (especially concerning competitive devaluations) produced by the Mexican financial shocks—notwithstanding the existence of a shock absorber in the form of an arrangement by the NAFTA countries to assist Mexico in steadying its currency.[80]

Still, far from reinforcing the distance between Canada and the Americas,

NAFTA has opened up space for Canada to operate in. Breaking out of the defensive shell with which it entered NAFTA, Canada has gone on the offensive in encouraging the broadening of the project. Since the implementation of NAFTA, the Canadian approach has undergone a fundamental transformation. If some of the language used to describe this process of transformation is exaggerated in form ('vocation as a nation of the Americas,' as Michael Hart has put it),[81] Canada has embraced the region in an increasingly multifaceted fashion.

This widening engagement, as noted by the earlier reference to Canada's entry into the Organization of American States (OAS), was started by the Mulroney government. Although not accompanied by a public discourse on options, the reversal of the long Canadian tradition of remaining outside the OAS was just one component of a much wider strategical reassessment of Canada's approach to Latin America. Based on a document prepared by Louise Fréchette, the assistant deputy minister for Latin America and former ambassador to Argentina, and Richard Gorham, who had served as Canada's observer to the OAS, this revised strategy called for an extension of dialogue, linkages and co-operation along a broad continuum in order to advance Canada's credentials as 'a nation of the Americas.'[82]

As part of this shift, the Mulroney government began to co-operate more closely with many of its former 'rivals' among Latin America's 'middle powers.' On Haiti, the Mulroney government worked closely with the special representative of the secretary-general, Dante Caputo (the former foreign minister of Argentina), and with the 'Friends of the Secretary-General' group to identify concrete proposals for consideration by the Security Council with respect to sanctions. Another case of this type of cross-cutting co-operation, via a more formalized coalition, was the Cairns group in agricultural trade (in which a wide number of Latin American countries, including Argentina, Chile and Brazil, were represented). Another was the high seas fishing issue, in which Canada forged a co-operative relationship with the Permanent Commission for the South Pacific (a group to which Colombia, Ecuador, Peru and Chile belonged).

Nonetheless, it was only with the election of the Chrétien government in the fall of 1993 that Canada's determination to show that it was not only 'in' but 'of' the region was more fully expressed. In some ways, admittedly, this signal demonstrated the continuity between the governments—a continuity found in the Liberal government's volte-face on renegotiating NAFTA and in the attention the Liberals gave to pushing forward with initiatives on Haiti and high seas fishing. What is most striking about the Liberal government's approach, nevertheless, has been its willingness to go out ahead of its NAFTA partners in extending the membership of the group. Whereas the Clinton administration grew more muted in its enthusiasm for the broadening of NAFTA—as seen most vividly in the lead-up to the December 1994 Miami Summit of the Americas—the Chrétien government not only warmly embraced the accession of Chile as the 'fourth amigo' but followed through with a high-profile 'Team Canada' mission to the major countries in the region in early 1995 and with the ongoing negotiations towards an interim bilateral trade deal with Chile.

To a considerable extent, this determination by the Chrétien government to go on the offensive and establish its own set of hemispheric links in strategic fashion is tied up with the ascendancy within the Liberal Party of what may be termed the economic rationalists. The two leading examples of this tendency have been Paul Martin, the present finance minister, and Roy MacLaren, until recently the trade minister. When the Liberals were in opposition, these two individuals were the lone voices within the party calling for an expanded economic engagement with the region. Martin, as early as mid-1992, was asking publicly whether Canada 'intended to participate in the free trade negotiations with Chile.'[83] By way of contrast, the main representatives of the economic nationalist wing of the Liberal Party, who had long expressed a greater degree of ambivalence about NAFTA (most significantly, Lloyd Axworthy), were confined for the first two years of the Chrétien government to domestic-oriented portfolios.[84]

From this perspective, the initial approach taken by the Chrétien government may be seen as primarily economically motivated. Martin and MacLaren have long and close ties to the Montreal and Toronto commercial élites respectively, and as such may be taken to be not only guides but conduits *vis-à-vis* the growing attraction within the Canadian business community for Latin America. This attraction parallels the Mexican experience. For some companies, especially in the mining industry, the attraction is bound up with the search for abundant and more cheaply extracted raw materials. For other companies, as witnessed by the strong presence in the Chrétien 'Team Canada' mission of representatives from engineering and communications companies, the attraction is found in the lure of strategic alliances and enhanced market access.

If taking advantage of the newly available opportunities in Latin America was an important incentive, broader motivations also played a part in the enmeshment strategy. From a foreign policy as well as an economic perspective, this approach was entirely consistent with the desire of the Liberals throughout the post-1945 era to diversify trade away from the US.[85] Although overshadowed by the push for a contractual agreement with Western Europe, and doomed to a relatively brief existence, some interest in the Americas was expressed as a result of the Third Option strategy. One of the six booklets published in 1970 as part of the Canadian foreign policy review focussed on Latin America. Moreover, a number of tours of the region by Canadian ministers were carried out as part of this exercise. The first of these was a wide-ranging visit by Mitchell Sharp, then secretary of state for external affairs, in 1968. Trudeau himself visited Mexico, Venezuela and Cuba in 1976.

As in the Third Option, the recent initiatives of the Chrétien government in the hemisphere have been aimed at countering the perception of vulnerability arising from Canada's proximity to the US. By engaging with a wider number of partners through NAFTA and other regional activities, the Liberals hope to dilute the power of the US.[86] As Prime Minister Chrétien stated in the context of the entry of Chile into NAFTA: 'To sleep with an elephant is dangerous, now we will be three to watch the elephant.' 'After Chile,' Chrétien added, 'others will fall into line.'[87]

Extending the scope of hemispheric economic regionalism, in other words, was seen by the Liberals as preferable to a deepening North American connection. Indeed, this strategy allowed for some semblance of balance between the economic rationalists and the nationalists within the party. Both tendencies, prior to the Liberals coming to office, could join in a condemnation of the Conservatives' approach for its lack of 'forethought and vision.' As co-chairs of the party's 'Western Hemisphere Consultative Group,' Axworthy and MacLaren could join in producing a manifesto calling for Canada to become 'Part of the Americas.' This manifesto called for a 'liberalized trade policy' and resistance to 'the narrowing of trade relations,' together with a diversification of Canada's 'diplomatic and trade relations in the hemisphere.'[88]

## Testing the New Relationship

In coming to terms with the Hemisphere of the Americas, Canada may be seen to have moved a long way in a short time. Canada's ability to jettison much of its traditional reluctance about a regional approach in what was considered the US's 'backyard,' and its willingness to move towards a flexible and multifaceted approach to engagement in the Americas, demonstrates much about the maturity of Canadian diplomacy in the 1990s. Unquestionably, some of the residue of Canada's ambivalent legacy still exists. Both the deepening of NAFTA and the widening of the notion of regionalism in the Americas remain messy and full of irritants. What is clear from an examination of Canada's broadening out of its hemispheric ties, though, is Canada's more instrumental assessment of the world and its own position in it.[89]

This positive assessment of Canadian strategy should not be taken to suggest the absence of any serious tests for this approach in the future. The push towards solidifying Canada's relations with the Americas remains a delicate exercise. It is one thing to recognize the economic and diplomatic potential in a closer enmeshment in the hemisphere; it is another thing to capitalize on that potential. As the Third Option strategy demonstrated in the 1970s, the key to diversification is a solid and consistent follow-through to reveal the benefits of this approach.

At the domestic level, the most sensitive test may lie in meshing NGOs or societal forces with the governmental approach. So long as the governmental approach focussed on Mexico and NAFTA, it was highly contested. As alluded to above, the dominant expression of this accentuated involvement by activist societal interests was a defensive reaction to NAFTA. Social activists, made up of representatives from labour unions, women's groups, church organizations and anti-poverty organizations, fought hard during the negotiations to display their vehement opposition to the agreement. Whereas advocates of free trade concentrated primarily on arguments centred on economic efficiency, the opponents disputed not only the economic benefits to be derived from this market-oriented approach but contended that, even if some benefits did emerge from this approach, they would come at a very high social and cultural price.

This is not to say that the response by Canadian social activists should be cast in an exclusively inward or parochial framework. As noted, many Canadian NGOs have also expanded their links and 'communication networks' with their counterparts in the United States and Mexico (for example, through the operation of the Common Frontiers project on Human Rights and Economic Integration). At the same time, though, this focus accentuated the 'differences' rather than 'similarities' between Canada and its 'immediate neighbourhood.'[90]

These 'differences' emerge most clearly on the question of human rights. In particular, the Chrétien government has come under intense pressure from Canadian NGOs for its 'pragmatic' handling of the Chiapas episode. Although it may be noted that Christine Stewart, the secretary of state for Latin America and Africa, did publicly criticize the Mexican government, the Canadian government as a whole played down the episode. Both Trade Minister MacLaren and Prime Minister Chrétien himself, in visits to Mexico City, gave the impression that not only was there no connection between NAFTA and the revolt but that the Mexican government had done a good deal to accommodate the rebels through a cease-fire, the appointment of a negotiator and an amnesty.[91] By way of contrast, after conducting immediate investigations, both the Inter-Church Committee and a commission headed by Assembly of First Nations chief Ovide Mercredi were critical of the Mexican government's handling of the revolt. Mercredi went so far as to urge the Canadian government to 'lean on' Mexico to deal seriously with indigenous issues.[92]

If problematic, these types of tensions also reinforce the impetus towards widening Canada's notion of what Canada's region of the Americas is. So long as it is narrowly defined, these tensions will be fed by every sign of injustice in Mexican politics. By alternatively defining the region in a more comprehensive fashion, Canada could tap into the image of the Americas' democratizing and 'opening up' in a comprehensive fashion within the international order. The Chilean minister responsible for negotiating accession into NAFTA underscored these 'similarities' by stating: 'We deeply are rooted in democratic values and we care about labour rights, environmental standards and sustainable development.'[93]

This pattern and psychology are evident in the emergent Canadian relationship with the hemisphere on the strategic agenda. Specific Canadian initiatives on hemispheric security have concentrated on the development of the doctrine of co-operative, comprehensive and common security, looked upon with some favour by countries such as Argentina and Chile, if not by Mexico. Canada built on its experiences on segmented issues, such as the Haitian sea blockade and coalition building in the high seas fishing case, to play an important role in convening a meeting on confidence and security building in Buenos Aires in March 1994.

Generally speaking, Canada has concentrated its efforts on selected activities, such as the development of a regional register of conventional arms transfers and military expenditures, and support for conflict prevention and resolution mechanisms.[94] In all likelihood, this approach will be extended with Lloyd Axworthy as foreign minister. One of his moves was to signal Canada's willingness to contribute to (and pay for) an expanded OAS peacekeeping force in Haiti.

Significantly, a wide number of Canadian NGOs have moved in parallel fashion to the government's approach. This pattern is featured in the relationship that the Canadian government has forged with the International Centre on Human Rights and Democratic Development (ICHRDD). On a wide range of issues, the ICHRDD has differed markedly with official policy. Indeed, on a number of particularly sensitive issues, the ICHRDD launched public campaigns to either embarrass or undercut the government's position; one case of this type was the ICHRDD's campaign to explore the human rights implications of NAFTA. On the other hand, as part of a wider movement towards 'progressive internationalism' exhibited in the region, the activities of this organization have been complementary to the governmental approach. Most notably, the ICHRDD's work was supportive of the pursuit of wider Canadian foreign policy interests at the 1993 Vienna conference with respect to bringing human rights of women into the mainstream human rights mechanism, the adoption of the declaration on violence against women, and the appointment of a special rapporteur on violence against women with a broad investigative and reporting mandate. This process had an important regional dimension. At an early meeting in San José, Costa Rica, for example, a women's NGO conference took place on a hemispheric basis to co-ordinate efforts and develop strategies to ensure the integration of a gender perspective into existing human rights mechanisms.

At the external level, Canada continues to fear being isolated in one trade bloc. Canada's preference has remained a non-discriminatory regionalism that allows it to hedge its bets. To gain this leeway, the Chrétien government has consistently emphasized that hemispheric regionalism is a means to a more all-encompassing system of open trade; it is not an end in itself. Canada has promoted not only the expansion of NAFTA within the Americas but a NAFTA-plus arrangement via expansion to other regions. As Roy MacLaren has suggested, the 'NAFTA accession clause does not limit membership to the Americas.'[95] Given its cross-cutting membership, the most likely possibility of a connection of this sort would appear to be with APEC. The Chrétien government, however, has also suggested the idea of a NAFTA–European Union free trade agreement. On top of all this, a scenario has also been put forward concerning an 'eventual convergence' between NAFTA, the EU and APEC to avoid 'the inherently exclusionary nature' of regional blocs.[96]

Canada's hopes for success along these lines remain hinged on a careful use of statecraft. From this standpoint it is significant that the Chrétien government has continued to pursue its aims by applying many of the quintessential features of Canadian middle power diplomacy. Canada has not only worked hard to multilateralize its relationship with the US through NAFTA and other institutional arrangements, but it has cast itself in the role of a bridge or mediator between regions for similar purposes. As in the past, then, this approach has been based not just on principle but on calculation of national interest. As MacLaren stated in another speech: 'there is more than one way to harness an elephant.... This strategy of building an architecture of overlapping circles of free trade not only strengthens the world economic system, it strengthens our critical relationship with the United States.'[97]

## CLOSE, BUT NOT TOO CLOSE

Canada, in many ways, remains entangled in a narrow and intense form of continentalism. By any measure of underlying economic conditions, the United States connection has been tightened, not loosened, over the past decade. Canada, far from becoming a global trading nation, exists as a country that for the most part trades solely with the US. Since the implementation of the FTA, for example, it has been estimated that trade between Canada and the US has risen by approximately 75 percent, as opposed to a 10 percent increase with the rest of the world.[98] Given these structural conditions, there is a solid rationale for a fixation by policymakers on the management of the 'main game' of Canada–US relations. By the immediate calculations of economic logic, all else in Canadian foreign policy may be perceived to be embellishment.[99]

From a political as opposed to a commercial perspective, however, Canada's lack of 'counterweights' in terms of trading partners continues to be a problem. Canada's location with the US in North America, while encouraging extensive forms of co-operation, also raises fears about domination. If Canada has a clear imperative to reap as much benefit as it can from its closeness to the US, Canada as in the past does not want to succumb to the 'stifling bilateral embrace' and close itself off in North America.[100]

Regionalism, therefore, has still not entered Canadian foreign policy as a goal in itself. Instead, regionalism has been mobilized as a problem-solving instrument designed to help mitigate fears of entrapment. These forms of interaction are not intended to speed up but to work against having to make a clear choice about which international space Canada belongs to. Canada has shed much of its ambiguity about the regional option directed at the Hemisphere of the Americas, as opposed to Western Europe and the Asia-Pacific. The 'mental map' of Canada's neighbourhood, however, is still drawn as widely as possible by state officials, allowing some balance (albeit not complete reconciliation) between the impulses of continental engagement and diversification. Most of the older Canadian diplomatic habits have remained intact, further mitigating the development of any form of exclusive relationship.[101] Canada will in many ways move to become a country more firmly located 'in' and 'of' the Americas—but not necessarily 'only' in North America. The embedded hold of the international order in Canadian foreign policy has been loosened by the pressure to seek comfort in a more precise geographical neighbourhood. Inevitably, this means that the Canada–US relationship will be privileged. But the bounds of Canada's global definition have not been broken completely.

## NOTES

1   See Robert O. Keohane and Joseph S. Nye, *Power and Interdependence: World Politics in Transition* (Boston: Little, Brown, 1977).

2   Andrew Hurrell, 'Explaining the resurgence of regionalism in world politics,' *Review of International Studies* 21, 4 (October 1995), 334.

3   *Ibid.*

4   *Ibid.*

5   For a good analysis of this theme, see Michael K. Hawes, 'Canada–U.S. relations in the Mulroney era: how special the relationship?' in Brian W. Tomlin and Maureen Appel Molot, eds., *Canada Among Nations 1988: The Tory Record* (Toronto: James Lorimer, 1989), 189–208.

6   *Ibid.*, 191.

7   See Robert Cuff and J.L. Granatstein, 'The Rise and fall of Canadian–American free trade, 1947–8,' *Canadian Historical Review* LVIII, 4 (December 1977); Michael Hart, 'Almost but not quite: the 1947–8 bilateral Canada–U.S. relations,' *American Journal of Canadian Studies* 19, 1 (Spring 1989), 25–58.

8   Stephen Clarkson, *Canada and the Reagan Challenge* (Toronto: James Lorimer, 1985), 17.

9   External Affairs Canada, *A Review of Canadian Trade Policy: A Background Document to Canadian Trade Policy for the 1980s* (Ottawa: Minister of Supply and Services, 1983), 213.

10  *Ibid.*

11  Allan E. Gotlieb, 'Managing Canadian–US interdependence,' in Edward R. Fried and Philip H. Trezise, eds., *US–Canadian Economic Relations: Next Steps?* (Washington, DC: The Brookings Institution, 1984), 133.

12  External Affairs Canada, *Canadian Trade Policy for the 1980s*, 213. For a fuller discussion, see Andrew F. Cooper, 'Playing by new rules: Allan Gotlieb, public diplomacy, and the management of Canada–US relations,' *Fletcher Forum of World Affairs* 14, 1 (Winter 1990), 93–110.

13  Gotlieb, 'Managing,' 134.

14  *Ibid.*

15  Hyman Solomon, 'Old-style diplomacy no longer rules,' *Financial Post*, 21 August 1982.

16  See, for example, 'With friends like these,' *Globe and Mail*, 21 November 1982.

17  Allan E. Gotlieb, 'How to smooth diplomatic rough spots,' *Financial Post*, 3 July 1982.

18  Quoted in David Shribman, 'Mr. Ambassador: Canada's top envoy cuts wide swath,' *Wall Street Journal*, 29 July 1985, 1.

19 Richard Gwyn, *The 49th Paradox: Canada in North America* (Toronto: McClelland and Stewart, 1985), 265. These management techniques were tightened still further when Derek Burney, Mulroney's chief of staff, succeeded Gotlieb as Canadian ambassador to the US in February 1989.

20 Hurrell, 'Explaining,' 343.

21 Gilbert R. Winham, 'NAFTA and the trade policy revolution of the 1980s: a Canadian perspective,' *International Journal* XLIX, 3 (Summer 1994), 479.

22 G. Bruce Doern and Brian W. Tomlin, *Faith and Fear: The Free Trade Story* (Toronto: Stoddart, 1991), 285.

23 Winham, 'NAFTA.'

24 Macdonald Commission, *Report*, 11, 201. Quoted in *ibid.*, 482.

25 For an excellent analysis of these notions, see Kim Richard Nossal, 'A European nation? The life and times of Atlanticism in Canada,' in John English and Norman Hillmer, eds., *Making a Difference: Canada's Foreign Policy in a Changing World Order* (Toronto: Lester, 1992).

26 Hella Pick, 'Hired hands across the ocean,' *Guardian*, 5 November 1973.

27 See Andrew F. Cooper ed., *Canadian Culture: International Dimensions* (Toronto: Canadian Institute of International Affairs, 1985); and 'Roots and directions: functional and geographical aspects of Canadian cultural diplomacy,' in Association for Canadian Studies, *Culture, Development and Regional Policy* (Montreal: Canadian Issues IX, 1988), 17–32.

28 See, for example, 'Kierans sure Canada could be Associate in Common Market,' *Globe and Mail*, 25 November 1961; 'Canada could join ECM as Associate: NDP leader,' *Globe and Mail*, 24 November 1961.

29 Hurrell, 'Explaining,' 332.

30 *Ibid.*, 333.

31 See, for example, 'Trade link with U.S. "inevitable,"' *Montreal Star*, 18 August 1962.

32 *Report of the Standing Senate Committee on Foreign Affairs*, July 1973.

33 'Representative urges more trade with EEC,' *Globe and Mail*, 19 January 1984.

34 Stephen Wilson, 'Changing partners: trends in Canada's regional economic relations,' *DFAIT Policy Staff Paper*, 2/95, March 1995, 9–10.

35 External Affairs and International Trade, *1992: Implications of A Single European Market*, (Ottawa: 1989–90).

36 See Robert Wolfe, 'Hope and fear in the Atlantic: the "new transatlantic marketplace" and the fate of the WTO,' paper presented at the annual meeting of the Canadian Political Science Association, Brock University, June 1996.

37 N.G. Papadopolous, *Canada and the European Community: An Uncomfortable Partnership?* (Montreal: Institute for Research on Public Policy, 1986).

38 Gordon Pitts, *Storming the Fortress: How Canadian Business Can Conquer Europe in 1992* (Toronto: Harper Collins, 1990), 161–7; Hyman Solomon, 'Canadians should be lobbying in Europe,' *Financial Post*, 17 April 1989.

39   Andrew Cohen, 'Ontario developing its foreign relations,' *Financial Post*, 18 June 1990. On this theme more generally, see Brian Hocking, *Localizing Foreign Policy: Non-Central Governments and Multilayered Diplomacy* (New York: St. Martin's Press, 1993).

40   Leo Ryan, 'Resources are Trudeau's lever for trade agreement with EEC,' *Globe and Mail*, 26 October 1974.

41   See, for example, 'The Missing Link,' *Financial Times* (Toronto), 10 April 1977.

42   Willy de Clercq, quoted in Jeffrey Simpson, 'A steady corrosion,' *Globe and Mail*, 27 April 1985. See also Brian Milner, 'Europeans worry Canada is drifting into the U.S. orbit,' *Globe and Mail*, 3 December 1984.

43   See, for example, Gordon Pitts, *Storming the Fortress*, 144–5.

44   Evan Potter, 'Canadian foreign policy-making and the European Community—Canada Transatlantic Declaration: leadership or followership,' EAITC, *Policy Planning Staff Paper*, 92/6.

45   See L. Krause, 'The Pacific economy in an interdependent world: a new institution for the Pacific Basin,' in J. Crawford and G. Scow, eds., *Pacific Economic Cooperation: Suggestions for Action* (Kuala Lumpur: Heinemann Asia, 1981).

46   Canada, EAITC, Canadian Foreign Policy Series, 89/14, quoted in Andrew F. Cooper, Richard A. Higgott and Kim Richard Nossal, *Relocating Middle Powers: Australia and Canada in a Changing World Order* (Vancouver: University of British Columbia Press, 1993), 106.

47   Canada, EAITC, Canadian Foreign Policy Series, 89/20, quoted in *ibid.*, 106.

48   Douglas A. Ross, 'Canadian foreign policy and the Pacific Rim: from national security anxiety to creative economic cooperation,' in F. Quei Quo ed., *Politics of the Pacific Rim: Perspectives on the 1980's* (Burnaby, BC: Simon Fraser University Publications, 1982), 28. On the suggestion that Canada formalize this approach through a Canada–Japan free trade deal, see Wendy Dobson ed., 'Canadian–Japanese economic relations in a triangular perspective,' *C.D. Howe Institute Observation* 30 (Montreal: C.D. Howe Institute, 1987), 17.

49   L.T. Woods, 'The business of Canada's Pacific relations,' *Canadian Journal of Administrative Sciences* 4 (1987), 418.

50   Neville Nankivell, 'Business gives APEC leaders advice,' *Financial Post*, 6 July 1995; 'A "road-map" for APEC leaders,' *Financial Post*, 27 July 1995; 'Business forum hopes APEC ombudsmen will head off disputes,' *Financial Post*, 29 August 1995; 'Practical advice from business on freer Asia-Pacific trade,' *Financial Post*, 23 September 1995.

51   Paul M. Evans, 'The emergence of Eastern Asia and its implications for Canada,' *International Journal* XLVII, 3 (Summer 1992), 508. This theme has also been at the centre of more ambitious conceptual work. See, for example, Mitchell Bernard and John Ravenhill, 'Beyond product cycles and flying geese: regionalism, hierarchy and the industrialization of East Asia,' *World Politics* 47, 2 (January 1995), 171–209.

52   On this point, see Richard Higgott, 'APEC—a sceptical view,' in Andrew Mack and John Ravenhill, eds., *Pacific Cooperation: Building Economic and Security Regimes in the Asia-Pacific Region* (St. Leonards, NSW: Allen & Unwin, 1994), 91.

53   Wilson, 'Changing partners,' 9–10.

[54] House of Commons Standing Committee on External Affairs and International Trade, *Minutes of Proceedings and Evidence*, 9 April 1987, 23:19. Japanese scholars have questioned, however, the accuracy of this differentiation exercise. Pointing back to the well-known case where Canada applied unilateral restrictions of its own—the episode in 1982 when Canada stalled the customs clearance of Japanese autos at Vancouver harbour for several months—Sato Hideo suggested that this was an example of Canada 'riding on the coattails of the US.' 'Canadian–Japanese economic relations: a Japanese perspective,' in John Schultz and Kimitada Miwa, eds., *Canada and Japan In The Twentieth Century* (Toronto: Oxford University Press, 1991), 173.

[55] See Jeffrey Simpson, 'One gaffe aside, Mr. Mulroney carried an important message to Japan,' *Globe and Mail*, 4 June 1991.

[56] *Tomorrow the Pacific* (Montreal: C.D. Howe Institute, 1991), 65. A major way Canada has been able to break into the markets of the NIEs remains through international development assistance—as seen particularly in the associational pattern with respect to China and Indonesia.

[57] Canada, Secretary of State for External Affairs, Statement 90/40. Quoted in Andrew F. Cooper, Richard A. Higgott and Kim Richard Nossal, *Relocating Middle Powers: Australia and Canada in a Changing World Order* (Vancouver: University of British Columbia Press, 1993), 155.

[58] Quoted in *ibid.*, 155.

[59] For a comprehensive examination of this theme, see James Rochlin, *Discovering the Americas: The Evolution of Canadian Foreign Policy Towards Latin America* (Vancouver: University of British Columbia Press, 1994).

[60] J.L. Granatstein and Robert Bothwell, *Pirouette: Pierre Trudeau and Canadian Foreign Policy* (Toronto: University of Toronto Press, 1990), 269. For a discussion of the economic linkages between the two countries, see Maxwell A. Cameron, Lorraine Eden and Maureen Appel Molot, 'North American free trade: co-operation and conflict in Canada–Mexico relations,' in Fen Osler Hampson and Christopher J. Maule, eds., *Canada Among Nations 1992–93: A New World Order* (Ottawa: Carleton University Press, 1992), 175–9.

[61] John W. Holmes, *The Better Part of Valour: Essays on Canadian Diplomacy* (Toronto: McClelland and Stewart, 1970), 236.

[62] John W. Holmes, *The Shaping of Peace: Canada and the Search for World Order*, vol. 1 (Toronto: University of Toronto Press, 1979), 236, 367.

[63] Iver B. Neumann, 'A region-building approach to Northern Europe,' *Review of International Studies* 20, 1 (1994), 53–74.

[64] Robert Lindsey, 'Reagan, entering presidency race, calls for North American "accord,"' *New York Times*, 14 November 1979; Alan Richman, '2 nations are cool to Reagan plan,' *New York Times*, 15 November 1979.

[65] David G. Haglund, 'The missing link: Canada's security interests and the Central American crisis,' *International Journal* XLII, 4 (Autumn 1987), 790.

[66] Barry Buzan, *People, States and Fear: An Agenda for International Security Studies in the Post-Cold War Era* (Hemel Hempstead: Harvester, 1991), 218.

[67] Holmes, *The Better Part of Valour*, 237.

68   Kim Richard Nossal, 'A European nation? The life and times of Atlanticism in Canada,' in John English and Norman Hillmer, *Making a Difference: Canada's Foreign Policy in a Changing World Order* (Toronto: Lester, 1992), 96. See also Laura Neack, 'UN peace-keeping: in the interest of community or self?' *Journal of Peace Research* 32, 2 (1995), 181–96.

69   Al Berry, Leonard Waverman and Ann Weston, 'Canada and the Enterprise for the Americas initiative: a case of reluctant regionalism,' *Business Economics* 15 (April 1992).

70   See Sylvia B. Bashevkin, *True Patriot Love: The Politics of Canadian Nationalism* (Toronto: Oxford University Press, 1991).

71   Michael Hart, *A North American Free Trade Agreement: The Strategic Implications for Canada* (Ottawa: Centre for Trade Policy, 1990).

72   Richard Lipsey, 'Canada at the U.S.–Mexico trade dance: wallflower or partner?' *C.D. Howe Institute Commentary* 20 (Toronto: C.D. Howe Institute, 1990); Ronald J. Wonnacott, 'U.S. hub-and-spoke bilaterals and the multilateral trading system,' *C.D. Howe Institute Commentary* 23 (Toronto: C.D. Howe Institute, 1990).

73   Richard G. Lipsey, Daniel Schwanen and Ronald J. Wonnacott, 'The NAFTA; What's In, What's Out, What's Next,' *Policy Study* 21 (Toronto: C.D. Howe Institute, July 1994).

74   Lorraine Eden and Maureen Appel Molot, 'The view from the spokes: Canada and Mexico face the U.S.,' in Stephen J. Randall, H. Konrad and S. Silverman, eds., *The Challenge of North American Integration* (Calgary: University of Calgary Press, 1993); Lorraine Eden and Maureen Appel Molot, 'From silent integration to strategic alliance: the political economy of North American free trade,' *Occasional Paper No. 17* (Ottawa: Centre for Trade Policy and Law, 1991).

75   Sylvia Ostry, 'The NAFTA: its international economic background,' in Stephen J. Randall et al., eds., *North America Without Borders? Integrating Canada, the United States and Mexico* (Calgary: University of Calgary Press, 1992), 28. See also Peter Morici, 'NAFTA, the GATT, and U.S. relations with major trading partners,' in Robert G. Cushing et al., eds., *North America, New Zealand and the World Trade Regime* (Austin, TX: Lyndon B. Johnson School of Public Affairs/Clark Center For Australian Studies, 1993).

76   Stephen J. Randall, 'Canada, the United States and Mexico: the development of tri-lateralism,' *Frontera Norte* 3 (julio–diciembre 1991), 121–36.

77   'Trying to avoid a Mexican standoff,' *Globe and Mail*, 20 July 1992.

78   Clyde Graham, 'Canada resists US move to re-open free-trade pact to admit Latin America,' *Ottawa Citizen*, 8 May 1992.

79   Peter Morici, 'NAFTA, the GATT, and U.S. relations with major trading partners,' in Robert G. Cushing et al., eds., *North America, New Zealand and the World Trade Regime* (Austin, TX: Lyndon B. Johnson School of Public Affairs/Clark Center for Australian Studies, 1993), 76.

80   Drew Fagan, 'Peso crisis has roots in NAFTA,' *Globe and Mail*, 31 December 1994. See also Maxwell Cameron, 'NAFTA and economic security: lessons from the financial crisis in Mexico,' paper presented at the International Studies Association, San Diego, 16–21 April 1996.

81     Michael Hart, 'Canada discovers its vocation as a nation of the Americas,' in Fen Osler Hampson and Christopher J. Maule, eds., *Canada Among Nations 1990–91: After the Cold War* (Ottawa: Carleton University Press, 1991), 83–107.

82     Edgar J. Dosman, 'Canada and Latin America: the new look,' *International Journal* XLVIII, 3 (Summer 1992), 536.

83     See Carol Goar, 'Free trade: will we miss the next boat?' *Toronto Star*, 23 May 1992.

84     For Axworthy's views, see his 'Canadian foreign policy: a Liberal Party perspective,' *Canadian Foreign Policy* I, 1 (Winter 1992), 7–15.

85     Gordon Mace and Gérard Hervouet, 'Canada's third options: a complete failure?' *Canadian Public Policy* 15, 4 (December 1989), 387–404.

86     The Liberal 'Red Book' had stated: 'If a Western Hemisphere free trade bloc evolves, Canada must play an active independent role in defining that bloc instead of merely reacting.... Canada should be working with other countries to minimize dominance by the strongest.' Quoted in Alan S. Alexandroff, 'Global economic change: fashioning our own way,' in Maureen Appel Molot and Harald von Riekhoff, eds., *Canada Among Nations 1994: A Part of the Peace* (Ottawa: Carleton University Press, 1994). See also David Crane, 'Letting others into Nafta may dilute American power,' *Toronto Star*, 16 July 1994. For a critique of this approach, see James Laxer, 'We need straight talk on Mexico, not another amigo,' *Toronto Star*, 2 April 1995.

87     Julian Beltrame, 'Chile's NAFTA entry protection from U.S. "elephant," Chrétien says,' *Ottawa Citizen*, 12 December 1994; Drew Fagan, 'Chile viewed as NAFTA trail blazer,' *Globe and Mail*, 21 January 1995.

88     'Part of the Americas: a Liberal policy for Canada in the Western Hemisphere, co-chairs, the Western Hemisphere Consultative Group,' 29 November 1991.

89     As one state official, who later became Canada's chief negotiator with Chile, stated: 'We have to harness the [trade negotiating] process in a way that does the most possible...for our own economic interest. That means we have to be at the forefront, creative, and leading the debate rather than trying to drag it back. [In particular] we should be creative in terms of the kinds of coalition-building we do internationally... From a trade policy perspective we have much more in common with people in Chile than we do with a lot of people in Brussels and a fair number of people in Washington.' Keith Christie, Director, Economic and Trade Policy Division, DFAIT, testimony to the Special Joint Committee of the Senate and of the House of Commons, Reviewing Canadian Foreign Policy, *Minutes of Proceedings and Evidence*, 21 June 1994, 46:30.

90     For a critical analysis, see Laura Macdonald, 'A mixed blessing: the NGO boom in Latin America,' *NACLA Report on the Americas* 28, 5 (March–April 1995), 30–35.

91     Chrétien accentuated the difference between Canada and Mexico by stating: 'They have a democracy that is not our type of democracy in many ways.' Quoted in Shawn McCarthy, 'PM places trade ahead of rights in Mexico agenda,' *Toronto Star*, 26 March 1994.

92     Quoted in Allan Thompson, 'Ottawa urged to study role of NAFTA in Mexico revolt,' *Toronto Star*, 18 January 1994.

93     Rick Haliechuk, 'NAFTA talks start with Chile,' *Toronto Star*, 8 June 1995.

94  *Government Response to the Recommendations of the Special Joint Parliamentary Committee Reviewing Canadian Foreign Policy* (Ottawa: Government of Canada, 7 February 1995).

95  Notes for an address by the Hon. Roy MacLaren, Minister for International Trade, to the Americas Society, 94/26, New York, 31 May 1994.

96  'Canada's trade policy for the 21st century: the walls of Jericho fall down,' notes for an address by the Hon. Roy MacLaren, Minister for International Trade, to the Centre for International Studies and the Centre for International Business, University of Toronto, 95/2, Toronto, 18 January 1995.

97  *Ibid.*

98  Helen Sinclair, 'Beyond the Third Option: trade policy in the 1990s,' the John W. Holmes Memorial Lecture Series, Glendon College, York University, North York, 1995.

99  Denis Stairs goes so far as to say: 'there is only one imperative in Canadian foreign policy. That imperative is the maintenance of a politically amicable, and hence economically effective, working relationship with the United States.' 'Canada in the new international environment,' notes for presentation to Inaugural Meeting of the Canadian Consortium on Asia Pacific Security (CANCAPS), York University, North York, 3–4 December 1993.

100  Leigh Sarty, 'Sunset Boulevard revisited? Canadian internationalism after the Cold War,' *International Journal* XLVIII, 4 (Autumn 1993), 759. As Lester Pearson had expressed this fear: 'In one form or another, for Canada, there was always security in numbers. We did not want to be alone with our close friend and neighbour.' John A. Monroe and Alex I. Inglis, eds., *Mike, the Memoirs of the Right Honourable Lester B. Pearson, Vol. 2: 1948–1957* (Toronto: University of Toronto Press, 1973), 32–3.

101  For example, Canada has given sympathetic treatment to other forms of sub-regionalism. William A. Dymond and C. William Robinson, 'Mercosur: a southern partner for NAFTA,' *Policy Options*, November 1995, 3–7. On this theme more generally, see William Wallace, *Regional Integration: The West European Experience* (Washington, DC: The Brookings Institution, 1994), especially ch. 5.

# THE ONGOING PATTERN OF CANADIAN FOREIGN POLICY

The pattern of Canadian foreign policy must be re-evaluated in light of the changing context of international politics. No longer hemmed in by the rigid contours of the Cold War, many of the fundamental aspects of Canada's foreign policy have opened up. Conventional wisdoms, relating to what Canada can and should be doing in the world, and how and where it should be doing it, are no longer accepted without contestation. A good deal about Canadian foreign policy is up for grabs.

Canada no longer need only sit back and absorb ideas imposed on it by others. Canada will have to continue to be reactive and responsive to the shift in the general sweep of thinking regarding globalization, security, and the interaction of domestic and international politics. Still, with the transformed conditions of the post-Cold War world, Canada has an opportunity to be more than simply an idea-taker, with little or no room to influence the intellectual/policy agenda. Across the spectrum of the new thinking on security, peacekeeping/peacemaking and multifaceted regionalism, the latitude for Canada to present ideas within the international system has grown as the boundaries of discourse and action have been stretched beyond their former limits.

In large part, the space for Canada to take on a variety of different forms of policy initiative in the post-Cold War world comes as a reflection on the inability of other actors to do so. What stands out in almost all of the issues under review in this volume has been the absence of solid and attractive ideas emanating from the top of the global hierarchy. Hampered by its own internal political difficulties, centred on budgetary concerns, executive/legislative gridlock and the quick electoral cycle, the US has not been able to translate its position as the one remaining superpower into a coherent vision. Although the cultural climate of the post-Cold War world has affirmed many of the values associated with the American experience, the US has offered an inconsistent form of intellectual leadership. When crises build up, the instinct has been to resort to muscle, not skill. When this approach has been found wanting, the instinctive response of US policymakers has been to jettison the attempt to act as an international 'cop' and withdraw into an inward-looking shell. Nor have the ascendant 'civilian' powers moved to fill the vacuum. Preoccupied with their own processes of domestic and regional-level adjustment, neither Japan, Germany nor the EC/EU have demonstrated much in the way of sustained interest in providing a framework of constructive engagement. The overall effect has been that, on the new agenda for the UN and other important issues, the 'great powers don't get involved in innovation very often.'[1]

The established set of qualities possessed by Canada facilitate its ability to take on these types of tasks. By dint of its much-used tool kit of skills and reputational attributes, Canada is well placed to take advantage of the premium the new world order has placed on diplomatic flexibility and speed. As Susan Strange has noted: 'states today have to be alert, adaptable to external change, quick to note what other states are up to.'[2] This point is particularly relevant when put into the context of the emphasis international governance has accorded to learning. Canada's ability to acquire new information about its environment, and to accept and run with new concepts, provides it with an advantage in dealing with complex issues.

There are of course some fundamental limits placed on the application of Canada's intellectual capabilities. From a systemic level of analysis, Canada has continued to be wedded to a supporting role in international affairs. In keeping with its middle power tradition, the desire to stabilize the world order lies at the heart of Canada's statecraft. While leery of being labelled a 'camp follower' to the US, Canada retains a 'commitment to orderliness and security in interstate relations and to the facilitation of orderly change in the world system' in pursuit of 'an environment within which [its] own interests and those of [its] populations could be pursued.'[3] While this emphasis on system maintenance allows Canada adequate space to take on an issue-specific leadership role (focussing especially on the promotion of the rule of law, universal norms and institutional structures), it is not conducive to the pursuit of transformational ideas involving some major element of radical reform.

From a country level of analysis, Canada's statecraft continues to be shaped by its distinctive national style. In contrast to some other countries traditionally categorized as middle powers (Australia and Sweden come readily to mind), Canada has been reluctant to go out in front through a campaign to target and sell big ideas in a single-minded fashion. Canada's forte has been what may be depicted as context-sensitive or 'just in time' ideas—ideas that are designed to launch (or kick-start) a new institution, break procedural deadlocks, or advance an established agenda in a new or different direction. Canada does not operate on the assumption that these ideas in themselves 'can make a difference' but that they will 'get the ball rolling' in problem resolution.[4]

In the move from ideas to action, the range of activity available to Canada on the international stage is also impressive. In light of the transformation in international politics, Canada has both greater room for manoeuvre and a greater margin of safety. Military threats are of less concern in the post-Cold War world. Multilateralism has become more refined and pervasive. These tendencies play into Canada's source of strength and away from its weaknesses. It is one thing, however, for Canada to have abundant opportunities to contribute above its traditional weight; it is quite another for Canadian foreign policy to seize these assembled opportunities in a whole-hearted fashion, with a requisite amount of vision, confidence and will.

Canada fell into some problematic habits during the Trudeau and Mulroney years—habits that had the effect of distorting in some appreciable ways Canada's diplomatic performance. One of these problematic habits concerned the uneven expectations surrounding the delivery of foreign policy. For all its flaws and restrictions, Canadians knew what to expect from the application of Canadian foreign policy during the Pearson era. Functionalism, as the core organizing principle of post-1945 Canadian foreign policy, imposed a number of self-imposed 'limits' and 'disciplines.' It legitimized the targeting of diplomatic attention towards spheres where Canada had plentiful resources and strengths. It avoided the dangers of 'overstretch' where there was a growing discrepancy between commitment and capability.

The Trudeau and Mulroney governments, by way of contrast, turned in an inconsistent performance on foreign policy. In coming into office, both of these governments advocated a modest (arguably, an overly modest) approach to foreign policy. Resistance was offered to the notion of Canada playing the role of mediator or go-between in international politics. Preference instead was given to instrumentality, or 'getting on with the job' of projecting Canadian interests in a more concrete fashion. Over time, however, the approach of these two governments became less measured. Notwithstanding their initial concern with rationality and practicality, the foreign policy approach of both the Trudeau and Mulroney governments took on an increasingly impulsive and scattered look. On top of the concern with self-interest was superimposed a tendency towards international grandstanding.

Personal diplomacy, at the prime ministerial level, took on a greater import during these years. While taking a hands-off approach on the day-to-day management of foreign policy, both Trudeau and Mulroney showed themselves willing to intrude forcefully on particular questions. These initiatives did have an upside, as witnessed by their ability to cut through accepted policies and programs. Trudeau may be said to have been ahead of his time on some of the proposals contained in the Peace Crusade. Mulroney has to be given some considerable kudos for making a break with accepted thinking and practices about the evolution of Eastern Europe. Nonetheless, this positive side was overshadowed by the logistical and image problems surrounding the erratic (and even arrogant) nature of this type of initiative-mongering.

This inconsistent performance reflected an undue concern with status seeking in the international arena. The search for status, of course, had animated much of the outward-looking expression of Pearsonian diplomacy. The difference was that the established tenet of functionalism kept this search within strict confines, by underscoring the rationale that Canada define its priorities and calculate how its resources could be applied most effectively. The Trudeau and Mulroney governments made the mistake of forgetting John Holmes's dictum that 'status is okay, provided you don't inhale.'[5] Canada's reputation for team playing became distorted in this process. Instead of being most readily associated, as in the past, with the cultivation of loose, ad hoc coalitions composed of 'like-minded' countries, Canada became identified almost exclusively with its partners in the G-7.[6] Much of the store of Canada's diplomatic skills became dissipated with the increase of range and domain in international activity. A great deal of the self-imposed discipline and many of the limits of functionalism disappeared.

Another problematic set of habits was the more explicit politicization of Canadian foreign policy. The Trudeau and Mulroney governments have to be given credit for the way the process of Canadian foreign policy making was opened up to encompass non-governmental actors in a way never envisaged in the Peason era. Yet this process of societal mobilization and validation remained an uneven one. The influence of Canadian society was not felt in the same fashion, and with the same degree of magnitude, right across the policy agenda. The impact of non-state actors was felt most readily and substantially in the economic and social spheres of activity, contributing further to the impression of unevenness. The erosion of the governmental monopoly over the security agenda only came with the unleashing of new thinking and action amidst the trauma over the breakdown of bipolarity.

The intrusion of domestic actors cut into foreign policy making with a very different level of intensity as well. As found in the areas of the environment, human rights and development assistance, non-state actors in general, and non-governmental organizations in particular, were able to move out in front of government in some areas of international activity. The impact of these groups, nevertheless, has remained amorphous. In the economic arena, this heightened form of internal pressure has been exerted in a more concentrated way. Canada's reputation as a good international citizen, correspondingly, has become more double-edged (or double-faced). Canada's virtues became more closely identified with the actions of Canadians (or more precisely, subgroups of Canadians) than with Canada as a national entity. Canada's vices as a selective defector or 'chisler,' alternatively, were linked with the Canadian government's 'self-help' measures.

Finally, the pattern of change in internal governance was not unidirectional. The process of 'opening up' was counteracted by other features that had the opposite effect. These features included the consolidation of the powers of the political bureaucracy (particularly through the PMO and the other central agencies); the expanded use of political appointments to senior advisory positions and high-profile diplomatic postings; and the creation of an influential (or fast-track) cohort of ins and outers in the foreign policy bureaucracy. If not designed for the purpose of outright closure, these instruments had the effect of offsetting those political pressures exerted from the outside.

Another set of problematic habits formed as a result of the breakdown of Canada's traditional 'special relationship' with the US. Although the tools utilized to create and maintain this associational arrangement had been the subject of a great deal of criticism from many who were apart from the mainstream mode of thinking and practice in Canadian foreign policy, it is fair to say that Canada derived some considerable benefits from this arrangement in the way of market access and exemptions. In tandem with the first option of multilateralism, it provided a relatively soft cushion on which Canada could find comfort. In looking for a substitute, the Trudeau government failed completely in its bid to find an 'optimal balance' between its North American trade and its trade with the rest of the world. Not only did the Trudeau government do a poor job of exploiting 'the advantages to be derived from [Canada's] unique situation relative to the United States,'[7] it did not persist in the pursuit of a coherent and consistent strategy of diversification. For its part, the approach initiated by the Mulroney government failed not only from the perspective of its critics ('cozying up') but on its own terms as well. The attempt to revive the 'special relationship' through institutionalized means proved to be a non-starter. As Michael Hawes has aptly put it, around the time of the signing of the FTA: 'At the most basic level, the relationship has become more civil, more cooperative and more extensive. At a somewhat more sophisticated level, the relationship has found its way to the very core of Canadian political and economic life.... However, even with the most liberal interpretation of 'specialness' the Mulroney government has failed in its bid to re-establish a relationship with the United States based on exemptionalism and on a mutual (albeit implicit) agreement to accord one another special status.'[8]

Aware of these difficulties, the Chrétien government signalled from the outset an intention to put its own stamp on the foreign policy agenda. This goal has been wrapped up in an extensive process of rebalancing. Taking up the theme of a return to core principles, the Chrétien government has played up its desire to go back to a strong identification with the established doctrine of Canadian foreign policy. The fundamental tenets of Pearsonian internationalism have returned—in declaratory terms at least—as the guiding framework, with special attention given to strengthening the international order generally and a focus on defined areas of Canadian comparative advantage (peacekeeping/peacemaking, new forms of security and humanitarian intervention) in particular.

This return to the familiar has been intertwined with a strong emphasis in operational terms on an economy of action. Faced with the exigencies of Canada's vulnerable position within the international political economy, the Chrétien government has placed great store on government effectively integrating foreign policy within a wider strategy of policy adjustment. Any notion of Canada acting as a 'global boy scout' has been subordinated to an instrumental, results-oriented concern with the national interest and the 'main game' of economic competitiveness.

This rebalancing approach has been played out in a number of ways. While not entirely precluding mediatory efforts, these endeavours have been directed in a concentrated manner, where Canada's central regional, institutional and functional concerns are reinforced rather than diluted. A consistent theme has been a return to basics, with the eschewing of any grand design (as featured in attempts to achieve a bargain between haves and have-nots). Ambitious forms of personal diplomacy, with their overtures of 'rescues, crusades, and moral interventions,'[9] have been downplayed. The benefits of Canada's extensive range of expertise have been played up. No longer does there seem to be any self-consciousness about Canada working on some of the margins of the international agenda—on the assumption that these margins often provide some tangible type of value-added benefits. To make a difference means staying the course, not necessarily through a display of 'heroic action' but by the deployment of a wide array of often 'routine' activities associated with forms of technical leadership.

The rebalancing approach has also been applied to finding the middle ground between closeness to and diversification away from the US. Issue-specific irritants have continued to mar the Canada–US relationship. The Chrétien government, however, has avoided trying to solve these problems by dramatic lurches towards either economic nationalism or the relocation of a 'special relationship' that no longer exists. Nowhere is the low-key (or 'compact economy model') style of Prime Minister Chrétien more evident than in his approach to the US. Rather than going in a sharp new direction, Chrétien has tried to build on many of the older habits in the Canada–US relationship, i.e. quiet diplomacy, and the use of institutional mechanisms and multiple contacts to temper US actions.

Chrétien's adaptation to the forces of continental integration has been complemented by the effort to utilize the regional option in an innovative fashion. Through NAFTA and the OAS, Canada has moved to embrace the American hemisphere in a multidimensional manner. Canada is deeply engaged with Chile in the enterprise of extending NAFTA to new partners. Canada has also attempted to widen the mandate of the OAS to allow it to become a more effective force for regional stability and collective, value-based action. What remains entrenched is a fear of 'excessive' regionalism, in which Canada is isolated within the Hemisphere of the Americas. The older Atlanticist frame of reference has been reduced, but it has not been rendered completely irrelevant. The Asia-Pacific connection has remained primarily market driven; Canada, nonetheless, has tried to expand the scope of co-operative action as part of the widening security agenda.

In overall terms, the Chrétien government may be said to have moved to integrate Canada's unique geographic position more closely into foreign policy, and especially foreign trade policy. At the same time, though, the rebalancing approach does not sacrifice functionalism to spatial concerns. International recognition and standing, the Chrétien government has reiterated, should hinge not just on geographical location but on commitment and performance. Any suggestion of reform of the UN Security Council along geographic lines was described as 'not very helpful to us.' Canada retained the firm belief that 'the membership of the Security Council should not exclusively be a question of geography, but should be more questions of political implications and dedications to the cause.'[10]

Notwithstanding its ability to avoid some of the most obvious deficiencies of the Trudeau and Mulroney foreign policies, the Chrétien government faces a number of obstacles in the pursuit of this rebalancing project. The constitutional imbroglio, with the ongoing debate about a redistribution of federal powers and the continuing need to resolve the question of special status for Quebec, has presented the Chrétien government with one conundrum. Any sign of a loss of capability on the part of Ottawa, through a reduction in peacekeeping and/or international institutional participation, certainly works against the image of a strong and internationally committed Canada. Although the question of whether moves by the federal government towards international retrenchment actually provides the sovereignty movement in Quebec with added political leverage is a moot one, the way this question has played out acts to distort the debate over Canadian foreign policy. All choices, particularly in the run-up to the October 1995 referendum, were held against the sensitive light of the constitutional/national unity question—not necessarily the most helpful light for making decisions.

Another conundrum is the question of declining resources. This question cuts into the foreign policy debate in several ways. The logic of a 'compact economy model' of foreign policy, on the face of it, implies a scaled-down statecraft, where Canada's limited resources would be marshalled towards particular purposes in sync with a strategy of rational adaptation and modernization. Indeed, a model of this type, where activity is no longer spread thinly across a wide number of areas, has become a prime determinant shaping the articulate expression of Canadian foreign policy. As Janice Stein has warned, in the security domain: 'Canada cannot be everywhere and do everything. If it attempts to do so, it risks dissipating its resources and slipping into mediocrity. Canada must define its priorities, identify areas of comparative advantage, develop "niche" policies, and focus its resources so that Canada contributes distinctively across the broad spectrum of common security.'[11] The National Forum, in the same vein, stated: 'The government cannot legitimately do everything. Nor should it try.'[12]

Any move to cut back the scope of Canadian diplomatic activity, however, is highly sensitive on a number of criteria. The first of these relates to the nature of Canada's constructive engagement: how are Canada's niches to be selected? If based primarily on the rationale of increasing Canada's global competitiveness or market share, Canada's internationalist image will be substantially damaged. As it is, many critics (especially those within the 'counter-consensus' tradition) contend that the Liberals have used the logic of this rational model as an excuse for a retreat from various forms of global commitment. Instead of visualizing the problem as one of overstretch, these critical observers perceive the problem to be understretch, where foreign policy is dominated by an economic-centred political agenda based on the pragmatic calculation of costs and benefits.[13]

A second area of sensitivity centres on Canada's institutional profile. Much of the character of Canada's statecraft has hinged on Canada participating in a wide variety of international forums. Canada's insider status within the most exclusive economic forums (the OECD and the Quadrilaterals, as well as the G-7) has brought with it tangible benefits in terms of agenda setting. Against a background of increased debate about the capacity of international institutions and internal debate concerning the need to look to other sources 'for more creative and less expensive solutions to enduring and new problems,' it may be that Canada will have to pick and choose more carefully the clubs that it wants (and is able) to join.[14]

This issue of institutional membership relates, concomitantly, to the nature of Canada's coalitional diplomacy. Canada's choice of partners has to a large extent reflected its hybrid standing as both a member of the G-7 and a self-identified middle power. Canada's position in the G-7 allows it to be heard on a wide variety of issues. The upside of this role is the visibility it gives to Canada as 'an international actor of consequence.'[15] The downside is that it reinforces the tendency to diffuseness—thus further complicating the process towards the development of areas of comparative advantage, or niche selection, in Canadian foreign policy. Foreign Minister Lloyd Axworthy, in a presentation to the House of Commons Standing Committee on Foreign Affairs and International Trade on 16 April 1996, stated that 'by dint' of its membership in the G-7 club Canada has assumed international 'obligations.' In wanting to be 'in the loop,' Canada has had the tendency to get involved in some issues (terrorism and drugs come to mind) in which other countries have greater interests and expertise. In other cases (such as the trial balloon on the so-called Tobin tax), considerable effort was expended on proposals on which it was found impossible to build a domestic consensus—never mind the mobilization of support among Canada's G-7 partners. To complicate things still further, Canada's G-7 status gives rise to a misleading impression internationally (not to mention some unwarranted frustration domestically) when Canada is excluded from other groupings of major powers, as witnessed by the experience of the Contact Group on the former Yugoslavia.[16]

An attractive alternative mode of statecraft continues to be a focus on 'entrepreneurial' leadership through groupings of 'like-minded' countries. The assembly of coalitions of the willing and able stands out as the *idée fixe* of Canadian diplomacy, allowing some degree of compensation for Canada's lack of structural power and facilitating practical solutions to problems to be put forward in conjunction with other countries. From one angle this approach is a cautious, reactive one. As André Ouellet stated: 'As a medium-sized country, it is obvious that we will not call the shots. We have to be humble enough to realize this. But in cooperation with others we could influence a lot of decisions.'[17]

From another angle the approach contains a more ambitious, activist dimension. This latter tendency, with its positive appreciation of the ability of this type of coalition to drive the international agenda forward at least on a segmented basis, was expressed by Lloyd Axworthy when he was still human resources minister: 'There are similar countries who have similar interests. We should get together...as a grouping, as a coalition, to try to move the agenda on some of these issues of structural employment...and try to redefine the UN mandate in terms of these security issues as far as individuals are concerned.'[18]

In terms of composition, the core element of this associational activity historically has been the middle power countries with which Canada has long identified. More recently, the coalitions have become more mixed. Many of the developing countries previously identified with the G-77 have shown themselves to be increasingly willing to engage in cross-cutting forms of coalitional activity with advanced industrialized countries, where there is a common interest in managing shared challenges. Yet amid this greater variation in choice, Canada needs to pick its spots for focussed joint activity most carefully. If the opportunities for 'like-minded' partners has been expanded, so have the risks of involvement. The 'like-mindedness' of such a wide constellation of countries differs from issue to issue. So does their comparative ability to deliver results in the short or longer term.

On some issues, it may be added, Canada's hybrid status works in a complementary fashion in select problem-solving exercises. A case in point is the recent campaign against the US Congress's Helms–Burton action on Cuba. Canada's efforts to mobilize concerted resistance to this legislation have been helped by its place within NAFTA and its ability to wrap itself in the G-7 mantle as well. By initiating an appeal through NAFTA, in close tandem with Mexico (and backed up by the OAS membership), Canada has demonstrated its ability to update its traditional method of rules-oriented diplomacy. By its willingness to join forces with the European countries, Canada could help apply added leverage. The two components might not form a successful blocking coalition in the short term (as evident by the results of the 1996 Lyon G-7 meeting). Still, this two-pronged activity represents, from a Canadian perspective, a potent mix of right and might over the longer haul.

A third area of sensitivity lies in the bureaucratic dynamics involved in foreign policy making. From an administrative point of view, the initial thrust of the Chrétien government's rebalancing approach was towards some resolution of the long-standing tensions between DFAIT and its rivals. The Chrétien government, as part of the first wave of an ongoing review, provided DFAIT with a number of new tools to enhance its strategic position. In conformity with the view that the diplomats were making a 'come-back,'[19] the first organizational moves undertaken by the Liberals suggested an interest in providing DFAIT with an increased ability with respect to the overall management of foreign policy. One sign of this trend was the delegation of authority over the National Forum to DFAIT's policy staff. Another was the expansion of DFAIT's capacity over emerging 'global issues,' including an increasing amount of control over the activities of CIDA.[20]

On top of these organizational changes came the infusion of energy with the appointment of Axworthy as foreign affairs minister. André Ouellet had remained a distracted minister throughout his stint in office. Preoccupied by events leading up to the Quebec referendum and by his responsibilities as Ottawa's point man in the campaign, Ouellet's initiatives tended to be directed almost exclusively to the twin objects of bolstering the federal government's prestige and applying foreign policy as another kind of glue to hold the country together. Axworthy's personality and style are very different. Primed to take on this position by his time as the Liberals' foreign policy critic, and with a hands-on (even hyperactive) bent, Axworthy has the ambition and expertise to effectively handle the foreign policy dossier. His reputation as a social reformer serves a vital function in sending a message that the Chrétien government seeks to find an acceptable equilibrium between the imperatives of trade and its responsibilities relating to social justice issues. Nor does Axworthy have to contend with Roy MacLaren, his old rival for the intellectual heart and soul of the Liberal Party. Having done much of the running to operationalize the view that foreign policy was primarily about foreign trade policy (and market shares), MacLaren has gone off to his reward as High Commissioner to the United Kingdom. The personnel changes at the apex of the DFAIT bureaucracy are compatible with this move at the ministerial level. Gordon Smith, the deputy minister of foreign affairs, has had a long connection with policy initiatives, dating back to Trudeau's review of the late 1960s.[21]

So long as Axworthy is foreign minister, he will do his best to make sure that Canada continues to be listened to in the world. His style will be more akin to what has been expected of Canadian foreign ministers, in the sense that he will try to act as a catalyst on a number of specific issues. Axworthy has quickly tried to demonstrate his willingness to go out ahead of the international consensus in this fashion (for example, on sanctions against Nigeria in the wake of the execution of Ken Saro-Wiwa and eight other human rights activists in November 1995). At the same time, Axworthy has signalled his adjustment to the realities of regionalism directed at Canada's immediate neighbourhood. Most dramatically, Axworthy moved to take Canada into the OAS peacekeeping force in Haiti (even when Canada had to take on the burden of financing this involvement itself). More routinely, he has built on the substantive Canadian efforts already taken in this region to build alternative forms of security links. Many of the issues have continued to be low key (for example, the banning of land-mines in the hemisphere), but the list of these issues has become quite extensive.

As Axworthy attempts assertively to be heard as the official voice of Canadian foreign policy, Canada will speak with a growing number of voices on international issues. Canadian foreign policy making has become (and will remain) a far more messy process than that encapsulated in the Pearson era. Multiple pressures will continue to be applied to government to 'do something' (or 'stop something') on issues that in the past were regarded as being well beyond the range of Canadian foreign policy. Moreover, these pressures will be applied increasingly by the manipulation of a wide array of emotional buttons and by the sophisticated use of media communications; the episode of the Canada–Spain 'fish war' bears witness to the impact of these forces. Cases of 'instant diplomacy' will become more commonplace and difficult to cope with. The interests and voices aiming to trigger immediate and direct action to rectify particular local/issue-specific grievances want a very different form of action from the classic expression of Canadian statecraft; as such, they represent a different kind of test for Canada's reputational qualities and diplomatic skills.

This tendency towards fragmentation among foreign policy voices is accentuated by the difficulties of providing a coherent framework for Canadian policy-making. Notwithstanding the persistent concern with establishing an effective form of strategic management over foreign policy, fragmentation has become the norm. Ministerial responsibility has not only been divided between a foreign minister and a minister of international trade, but also between a number of geographically and functionally focussed secretaries of state. If overshadowed by the tension between DFAIT and CIDA, a host of internal differences exists within the foreign policy bureaucracy itself. Notwithstanding the integrative dynamic of the 1980s, the stance of DFAIT's officials remains dependent on which part of the Pearson Building they sit in. The issue-specific interests of the International Organizations Bureau personnel differs considerably from the concerns of the geographic desk officers. The Trade and Economic ("E") Policy Branch, in turn, has had its own distinct perspective and priorities. So ingrained are these differences that a new wave of administrative reform is underway that concentrates on methods of streamlining and merger in order to break down these in-house differences. For one thing, a new executive committee is being created, with a small group of assistant deputy ministers having oversight but not line management responsibilities. For another thing, the number of bureaus and divisions is being reduced to cut down on the large number of 'interests' (political, economic, issue-specific and geographic). The overall design has been directed towards the integration of policy and the delivery of programs.

As DFAIT continues to go through this process of administrative change, the look of Canadian foreign policy making is being transformed in a number of other ways as well. An important ingredient here has been the intrusion of macroeconomic concerns into policymaking in a persistent and comprehensive fashion. As part of the attempt to put Canada's fiscal house in order, the stamp of Paul Martin's Ministry of Finance and the other departmental advocates of fiscal constraint has been felt in the Ministry of Foreign Affairs. To the dismay of the 'counter-consensus' critics, a bottom-line mentality has taken hold in foreign policy with a strong grip. Policies and programs—including the accepted 'pillars' of post-1945 Canadian foreign policy—are increasingly judged on their tangible return and/or their capability to be used as effective vehicles of delivery.

These conditions contribute to the building of a greater sense of coexistence between official and unofficial voices on the making of Canadian foreign policy. An exclusively top-down, Ottawa-centric strategy is no longer viable. As Senator MacEachen pronounced during the recent foreign policy review, there is 'more to foreign policy than the federal government. There are provinces; there is the private sector. A whole civil society is involved in the foreign policy. If Canada is to succeed, it must involve these sectors more.'[22] For over two decades, these multiple voices have been increasingly released through a number of larger forces, including the decline of institutional capacity, globalization and the culture of participation. The key question still to be resolved is the precise nature of this coexistence. The implementation of the promises for 'democratization' contained in the Liberal Red Book, and the 'open' and expansionist framework of the National Forum and the Special Joint Committee, have been fraught with problems over co-option, representation, accountability and translation into policy. When the perception took hold that this process had not come up to the (elevated) expectations, the National Forum veered towards becoming a standard advisory board.

The momentum towards an established pattern of coexistence between government and non-state actors will take shape in a less ambitious and more issue-specific mode. Axworthy has begun to talk of Canada's role in the world as a 'facilitator.' This type of activity may at the outset be largely externally driven, as a result of the way that Canada has become *inter alia* enmeshed in a network of collaborative arrangements or regimes.[23] Nonetheless, a 'facilitator' role has profound implications for the evolution of a partnership between government and non-state actors. This facilitative approach has surfaced in the multifaceted statecraft targeted towards gaining an enhanced market share and a competitive advantage in emerging markets. Driven by the imperatives of the international economy, this dynamic contains elements of what Susan Strange identifies as a 'triangular diplomacy,' in which government–firm and firm–firm diplomacy intertwines with traditional governmental diplomacy.[24] The facilitator role as applied across the continuum of the expanded security and social agendas has lagged behind the joint enterprises found in the economic agenda (notwithstanding the integration of NGO representatives in the Canadian delegations to major international conferences and the development of innovative forms of security dialogue), because the services of government have an immediacy (and profitability) on the economic agenda that are absent in other spheres of activity. The pursuit of foreign contracts bears this out, in that it remains an advantage to have the national government on side to clear away legal and/or operational impediments. There is good reason to believe, however, that the non-economic agendas are catching up in this process. As government seeks to signal its changing priorities and circumstances, for example by an offloading of specific responsibilities in development assistance and peacekeeping/peace building, this process will inevitably speed up.

The success of these joint activities will depend, as ever, on an appreciation of the trade-offs involved. For government, the main trade-off is between its ability to tap into the resources and credibility of non-state actors via an accelerated shift towards depoliticization, on the one hand, and a diffusion or layering of responsibility, on the other. For non-state actors, the trade-offs are essentially about the benefits of some form of privileged status (with a say as well as a voice) versus the imposition of disciplines and limits on activity through a co-operative structure. The relationship between civil society and the foreign policy bureaucracy will continue to be a paradoxical one. As government and non-state actors rub up against each other, the differences between them will be more noticeable. These differences are grounded on a number of factors. There are numerous organizational impediments to co-operation. Many NGOs, akin to firms, are simply not consortia, partnership or co-ordination minded; their identity, as individual entities, 'depends on autonomy and independence.'[25] The very different sets of internalized values also have to be considered. Whereas, for instance, the government's emphasis is on norm and standard building, the emphasis of societal activists is on enforcement on human rights, the environment and other issues. Notwithstanding all of this antagonism, however, the government's search for areas of comparative advantage will have some influence in helping nudge NGOs to carve out their own specific geographic/functional niches on which to concentrate attention. These selective niches will in turn reinforce the government's own activities, in the areas of election monitoring, population and refugee resettlement, the delivery of emergency relief, etc.

The make-up of Canadian foreign policy on the edge of the millennium ultimately confirms the impression of ambiguity. In response to the passage of the Cold War and the transition to an uncertain future, Canada and Canadians have begun to embark on a process of rethinking about how to accommodate change while hanging on to many of the accepted ideas and practices of the past. Many of the traditional habits of Canadian statecraft have been clung to, albeit in a looser guise. Skill and reputation remain as core ingredients, providing definition to Canadian activity on the international stage. Yet these ingredients are not sufficient to guide analysis. In a myriad ways, Canadian foreign policy is in a transitional stage in the late 1990s. The demands are greater, with respect to both the pace and multitude of stimuli and the raised economic and political stakes. The foreign policy agenda is increasingly crowded, with a widened concept of security and a closer intersection between domestic and international issues. Capacity, at the same time, has been altered through pluralization, globalization and the requirement for legitimization. Alteration in form and function, however, does not mean a reduction in importance. The twenty-first century is unlikely to belong to Canada. But Canada's brand of diplomacy, combining a unique blend of creativity and a sense of constraint, remains central to the evolution of the new architecture of the global system. Although it is easy to be dismissive of Canada's solid but unspectacular contribution, in the sense of labelling Canada as having 'a passion for bronze...the ability to put in the middling performance apparently appropriate to a middle-sized power,' it must also be acknowledged that Canada has been reluctant to recognize success even when it 'does something rather well.'[26] The exogenous and endogenous challenges in the way of maintaining this record of constructive engagement are formidable. In a world where bargaining and negotiation have become more pervasive, and where institutions and coalitions increasingly matter, however, so have the opportunities expanded for Canada to perform well on the world stage.

# NOTES

[1]   Lloyd Axworthy, testimony to the House of Commons Standing Committee on Human Resources Development, *Minutes of Proceedings and Evidence*, 5 April 1995, 73:27.

[2]   Susan Strange, 'States, firms and diplomacy,' *International Affairs* 68, 1 (January 1992), 10.

[3]   Robert Cox, 'Middlepowermanship, Japan, and the future world order,' *International Journal* XLIV, 3 (Autumn 1989), 824.

[4]   André Ouellet, testimony to the House of Commons Standing Committee on Foreign Affairs and International Trade, *Minutes of Proceedings and Evidence*, 14 March 1995, 18:65. The continuing capacity of Canada to generate these ideas opens up a very different debate. See Janice Gross Stein, 'Ideas, even good ideas, are not enough: changing Canada's foreign and defence policies,' *International Journal* L, 1 (Winter 1994–5), 40–70.

[5]   John Holmes, 'The new agenda,' in John Holmes and John Kirton, eds., *Canada and the New Internationalism* (Toronto: Centre for International Studies, University of Toronto/Canadian Institute of International Affairs, 1988), 19.

[6]   See Arthur Andrew, *The Rise and Fall of a Middle Power* (Toronto: James Lorimer, 1993).

[7]   Helen Sinclair, 'Beyond the Third Option: trade policy in the 1990s,' the John W. Holmes Memorial Lecture Series, Glendon College, York University, North York, 1995, 36.

[8]   Michael K. Hawes, 'Canada–U.S. relations in the Mulroney era: how special the relationship?' in Brian W. Tomlin and Maureen Appel Molot, eds., *Canada Among Nations 1988: The Tory Record* (Toronto: James Lorimer, 1989), 206.

[9]   John W. Holmes, 'Most safely in the middle,' *International Journal* XXXIX, 2 (Spring 1984), 102.

[10]   Interview with André Ouellet, National CBC Morning News, 30 September 1994, by Henry Champ.

[11]   Janice Gross Stein, 'Canada 21: a moment and a model,' *Canadian Foreign Policy* II, 1 (Spring 1994), 11.

[12]   National Forum on Canada's International Relations, March 1994. Quoted in Andrew Cohen, 'Canada in the world: the return of the national interest,' *Behind the Headlines* 52, 4 (Toronto: Canadian Institute of International Affairs, 1995), 5.

[13]   'So long Dudley Do-right: Canadian foreign policy reflects self-interests of the '90s,' *Montreal Gazette*, 12 February 1995; Gordon Barthos, 'Radical foreign policy banks on trade Liberals' pro-business agenda, stands tradition on its head,' *Toronto Star*, 8 February 1995.

14   Evan H. Potter, 'Canada and the reform of international organizations: visions for the future,' *Canadian Foreign Policy* III, 2 (Fall 1995), 83–102.

15   Fen Osler Hampson and Maureen Appel Molot, 'Being heard and the role of leadership,' in Hampson and Molot, eds., *Canada Among Nations 1996: Big Enough to be Heard* (Ottawa: Carleton University Press, 1996), 4.

16   An argument can be made that the real measure of Canada's contribution is not made on the basis of these or other symbolic criteria. Where Canada appears to have the best chance of making a difference is in the number of key (if lower profile) tasks including logistical support, election reform and media training. More to the point, the question of 'being at the table' becomes intertwined with bureaucratic politics. It is not coincidental that it has been DND that has been most vocal in its displeasure about Canada being left out. David Collenette told the Commons that this exclusion represented 'a shame and a disgrace... We, Canada, have a right to be part of the strategy that designs the peace process.' 'More input on Bosnia,' *Globe and Mail* editorial, 2 December 1994. See also Andrew F. Cooper, 'In search of niches: saying "yes" and saying "no" in Canada's international relations,' *Canadian Foreign Policy* III, 3 (Winter 1995), 1–13.

17   André Ouellet, testimony to the House of Commons Standing Committee on Foreign Affairs and International Trade, *Minutes of Proceedings and Evidence*, 16 February 1994, 1:34.

18   Lloyd Axworthy, testimony to the House of Commons Standing Committee on Human Resources Development, *Minutes of Proceedings and Evidence*, 5 April 1994, 73:27.

19   Andrew Cohen, 'The diplomats make a come-back,' *Globe and Mail*, 19 November 1994.

20   See Cranford Pratt, 'Development assistance and Canadian foreign policy: where we now are,' *Canadian Foreign Policy* II, 3 (Winter 1994), 77–85.

21   Jeff Sallot, 'Mr. Smith goes to Foreign Affairs,' *Globe and Mail*, 5 August 1994.

22   Proceeding of the Standing Senate Committee on Foreign Affairs, *Minutes of Proceedings and Evidence*, 13 December 1994, 9:21.

23   On this general theme, see Mark Zacher, 'The decaying pillars of the Westphalian Temple: implications for international order and governance,' in James N. Rosenau and Ernst-Otto Czempiel, *Governance Without Governments: Order and Change in World Politics* (Cambridge: Cambridge University Press, 1992). See also Andrew F. Cooper, 'Questions of sovereignty: Canada and the widening international agenda,' *Behind the Headlines* 50, 3 (Toronto: Canadian Institute of International Affairs, 1993), 1–16.

24   Susan Strange and John Stopford, *Rival States, Rival Firms: Competition for World Market Shares* (Cambridge: Cambridge University Press, 1991).

25   Alison Van Rooy, North–South Institute, testimony to the Special Joint Committee of the Senate and of the House of Commons, Reviewing Canadian Foreign Policy, *Minutes of Proceedings and Evidence*, 26 July 1994, 48:9.

26   'Born to lose, Survey Canada,' *Economist*, 29 June 1991, 14–15.

# I N D E X

120; constructive internationalism, 21, 82, 101, 183-85; countertrade 96; deal-making 67, 94; diplomacy, 35, 40; development assistance 226-27, 234, 236; domestic priorities, 2, 287; fishing crisis, 158-59; La Francophonie 48; free trade, 17, 20, 57, 99-100, 120, 250-51, 256, 264; Green Paper, 61; human rights, 122-23, 126, 134, 232, 235; Iron Ore Company of Canada, 96; Japan, 260; NAFTA, 264, 266; OAS, 268; peacekeeping, 184-85, 188, 192; personal diplomacy, 283-84; middle power, 20; politicization of foreign policy, 50, 52-54, 185; 'Shamrock' summit, , 250; 'special' relationship with US, 285; 'two track' path, 99-100; UN, 56, 133

Multilateral development banks, 218

multilateralism, 1, 18, 22, 67fn, 74, 81, 83, 87-88, 90, 100, 146, 160, 163, 166-67, 214, 225, 273, 283; Bretton Woods financial institutions, 82, 88, 217-18, 236; multilateral trade, 57, 76, 80, 91-92, 97-100, 251

Nagorno-Karabakh, 201

Namibia, 201-2

Nasser, Gamal, 175, 177, 179

National Energy Program (NEP), 16, 46, 89, 256

National Forum on Canada's International Relations, 62-64, 188, 234-35, 287, 289, 292

Native Council of Canada, 60

Natural Resources Defense Council, 128, 155

Neak, Laura, 4, 177

Neufeld, Mark, 25

New England Coalition for Efficiency and the Environment, 128

New International Economic Order (NIEO), 85, 215, 221

new world order, 3

New Zealand, 21, 49, 90, 185, 236

*New York Times*, 39

Newfoundland, 142, 146, 150-52, 154, 158-60, 167, 169fn

Newly Industrializing Countries (NICs), 89, 230

Nigeria, 290

'Nixon shocks,' 89, 249

Noël, Alain, 212

non-governmental organizations (NGOs): budget cuts, 234-35, 237-39; Circumpolar summit, 132; conditionality, 232-33; democratization, 62-64 ; development assistance, 219, 222, 226-30; environment 59, 60; expansion of peacekeeping, 188, 201-4; human rights, 63, 123, 232-33, 271; indige-

nous rights, 127-28, 132; international conferences, 59-61; mobilization, 55-56, 59-62, 188, 240, 284,293; NAFTA, 270-71; partnership, 229, 233-35, 237-40, 292; representative ability, 63-64; security debate, 132-33; technical skills, 61, 133, 228; transnational nature, 5-6, 81, 228; 'track two' diplomacy, 131, 261

Nordic countries, 185, 236

North American Aerospace/Air Defence Command (NORAD), 73, 133, 249

North American Free Trade Agreement (NAFTA), 28, 125, 264-72, 286, 289

North Atlantic Treaty Organization (NATO), 39-40, 74, 113, 147, 149, 172fn, 180, 195, 257; air strikes, 195, 196, 196; Canadian-American relationship, 13, 73; Canadian role in, 20, 55, 56, 114-16, 119, 126-27, 129, 132, 180-81, 184, 192-93, 197, 212-14, 248; expansion of, 117

North Korea, nuclear weapon program in, 114

North Pacific Co-operative Security Dialogue, 131, 261

North-South Institute, 67fn, 68fn, 91, 225, 229

North-South relations, 14, 210, 215, 221-22, 226, 237, 241fn; Trudeau initiative, 40, 215, 263, 286

Northern Cod Adjustment and Recovery Program, 158

Northern Telecom, 57, 123, 254, 266

Northwest Atlantic Fisheries Organization (NAFO), 153, 163-64, 166

Norway, 21, 49, 160, 177

Nossal, Kim Richard, 8, 186, 197, 220, 222, 232, 243fn, 264

Nye, Joseph S., 'complex interdependence,' 18

Nyerere, Julius, 224

October Crisis, 129

Oka crisis, 128-29

offsets, 93-95

O'Neil, Maureen, 67fn, 234

Ontario, economic profile, 91, 94, 255

Organization for Economic Co-operation and Development (OECD), formerly the Organization for European Economic Co-operation (OEEC), 12, 37, 49, 77, 83, 215, 258, 288

Organization for Security and Co-operation in Europe (OSCE), formerly the Conference on Security and Co-operation in Europe (CSCE), 117-18, 131, 190, 201, 202, 261

Organization of African Unity, 202

United Nations (UN), 11, 19, 39-40, 56, 74, 86, 133, 161, 173-74, 179, 182-85, 189-192, 195, 197, 199-200, 204, 236, 262, 287, 289; Canada's involvement, 37, 39, 49, 53, 248, 260, 268; Korea, 38; Suez, 39

United Nations Angola Verification Mission (UNAVEM), 187-88, 201

United Nations Assistance Mission in Rwanda (UNAMIR), 190-91, 199

United Nations Atomic Energy Commission, 40

United Nations Commission on Human Rights (UNCHR), 128, 135, 141fn

United Nations Conference on Environment and Development (UNCED),53-54, 59-61, 157, 160, 166; parallel NGO conference, 59

United Nations Conference on the Human Environment, 46, 53, 59, 134, 216

United Nations Decade of Women's Conference, 54, 68fn

United Nations Development Program (UNDP), 215, 234

United Nations Emergency Force (UNEF), 39-40, 174, 176-79

United Nations High Commissioner for Refugees (UNHCR), 5, 53

United Nations High Seas Fisheries Conference, 166, 268

United Nations Interim Force in Cyprus (UNFI-CYP), 175-78, 180-81, 186

United Nations International Children's Emergency Fund (UNICEF), 53

United Nations International Conference on Population and Development, 61

United Nations Iran-Iraq Military Observer Group (UNIlMOG), 178

United Nations Military Observer Group India-Pakistan, 174

United Nations Operation in the Congo (ONUC), 175-77, 179, 181, 187

United Nations Operation in Somalia (UNO-SOM), 184, 187, 189-91, 197, 199, 201-2, 204

United Nations Protection Force, in the former Yugoslavia (UNPROFOR), 184, 187-99, 201, 203-4

United Nations Relief and Rehabilitation Administration (UNRRA), 53

United Nations World Conference on Human Rights, 61, 125, 272

United Nations World Summit for Children, 134

United States: agricultural policies, 78, 267; Canada's 'special relationship' with, 77, 89, 97, 101, 247-48, 251, 253, 256, 262-63, 273, 280fn, 285-86; Canadian defence/military relationship, 13, 113, 180, 193, 213; European relations, 77-78, 195, 252; financial institutions, 78; fish conflict, 149, 161, 165; former Yugoslavia, 195-96; Gulf conflict, 11, 12; international leadership, 4, 73, 81, 101, 214, 252, 281; Korean War, 38; Suez, 39; trade relations with Canada, 45, 77, 87, 98, 100, 248-50, 252, 260, 264-66, 269, 286; unilateralism, 81-82, 90, 152-53, 182, 190, 263

University of Ottawa, Human Rights Centre, 61

van Rooy, Allison, 227
Venezuela, 269
Vézina, Monique, 232
Victoria College, University of Toronto, 72
Vietnam, 42; bombing of North, 14

Warley, T.K., 78
Watson, Paul, 155
Webb, Michael, 88
Whalley, John, 100
Whelan, Eugene, 45-46
Whitworth, Sandra, 24, 204
Wells, Clyde, 154-55, 161
Wilgress, Dana, 76
Winegard, William, 221
Winham, Gilbert, 68fn, 251
Wiseman, Henry, 203-4
Wolfe, Robert, 10
Women and Environmental Education and Development, 60
Women's rights, 54, 60, 124-25, 234, 272
Wonnacott, Ronald J., 265
Wood, Bernard, 91
World Bank (International Bank for Reconstruction and Development), 37, 78, 83, 214-15, 235-36
World Food Conference , 46, 59
World Trade Organization (WTO), 81, 83
World University Services of Canada, 230
World Vision Canada, 230
Worthington, Peter, 147
Wrong, Hume, 84

Yugoslavia, the former, 4, 183-88, 190-91, 194-97, 199, 201, 203; see also United Nations Protection Force, in the former Yugoslavia

Zacher, Mark, 88, 90-91